THE LAST SHAH OF IRAN

FATAL COUNTDOWN OF
A GREAT MAN BETRAYED BY THE FREE WORLD
A GREAT COUNTRY WHOSE FAULT WAS SUCCESS

WORKS BY HOUCHANG NAHAVANDI

In Farsee

Published before the Revolution:
History of economic thought
Economic developpement matters
The European Common Market
Etc...

———

Last days, End of reign, death of the Shah, Khetab, 2004
آخرین روزما، پایان سلطنت و درگذشت شاه

In French

Iran, deux rêves brisés (*Iran: two broken dreams*),
Albin Michel

Le dossier noir de l'intégrisme islamique (*The Black Dossier of Islamic Fundamentalism*), Nouvelles Editions Debresse)

Le voile déchiré de l'islamisme (*The Torn Veil of Islamism*),
Première Ligne

Shah Abbas, empereur de Perse (*Shah Abbas, Emperor of Persia*),
Perrin - with Yves Bomati - which received a French
Academy award in 1999

Révolution iranienne, vérité et mensonge (*The Iranian Revolution, Truth and Lies*), L'Âge d'Homme, 2000

Carnet secrets, chute et mort du Shah (*Secret reports, fall and death of the Shah*), Editions Osmondes, 2004

HOUCHANG NAHAVANDI

THE LAST SHAH OF IRAN

Fatal Countdown of
A Great Patriot betrayed by the Free World
A Great Country whose Fault was Success

Aquilion Ltd.
The Nova Building
Herschel street
Slough, Berkshire
SL1 1XS United Kingdom

First published in french in France by Éditions Osmonde 2004:
Carnets secrets, chute et mort du Shah (ISBN 2 951036020)
English translation Copyright © A. S. Reed 2005 (asreed@lastings.co.uk)

This edition, revised an enlarged, published by Aquilion Ltd 2005

Copyright © Houshang Nahavandi 2005

ISBN 1-904997-03-1
10 9 8 7 6 5 4 3 2 1
Set in Times New Roman

Printed and bound in Spain by Itxaropeña

The right of Houchang Nahavandi to be identified as the author, and A. S.
Reed to be identified as the translator of this work has been asserted by
them in accordance with the Copyright, Designs and Patents Act, 1988.

All these peoples were great, because they had great prejudices. They no longer have them. Are they still nations? Nothing more than incoherent crowds!

*   *

*

For having succeeded in all his endeavors, Hercules was punished. Troy also, being too fortunate, had to perish. In pondering this vision which the tragedians shared, one can't help but think that the so-called free world, blessed by fortune, will inevitably share the fate of Ilium, since the jealousy of the gods lives on after their disappearance.

E. M. CIORAN

Aknowledgement and Sources

For the most part, this enquiry is based on my personal recollection of events and on the notes I made, following the long conversations I had with the last Shah of Iran, before his final departure from Iran, but mainly during his exile; first in Mexico, and then in the course of two journeys to Cairo.

It owes much, also, to the memories and testimony of those, who – always with courtesy, and sometimes with great patience - were good enough to take part in it. I know how painful recalling this evidence must have been for many of them.

My thanks go, first, to two people, whose contributions were of outstanding importance – Ardeshir Zahedi and Amir-Aslan Afshar.

Ambassador Amir Aslan Afshar, the last Grand Master of Protocol to the Imperial Court, and Mohammad Reza Pahlavi's closest confidant and ally, for the final eighteen months of his reign, at the beginning of his exile and during the last days of his life. The dozens of pages of notes, which he so kindly drafted for me, our many telephone-conversations and the seven-hour interview – all about this book - which we had at Nice, on 12th February 2001, and the details he sent me after the publication of the first, French edition, have been my benchmark.

Ambassador Ardeshir Zahedi, the Sovereign's ex-son-in-law - formerly ambassador to London, and to Washington, and Minister of Foreign Affairs – who had an insider's view of the life of Mohammad Reza Pahlavi, and of Iran's diplomacy and internal politics, over several decades. After reading the first edition, he did me the honour of imparting his observations to me at length, and of allowing me to consult, and quote from, some of his notes about the events I relate.

My sincere thanks are due also to *Mr. Chodja-ol-Dine Chafa*, the Shah's Cultural Councillor, to *Professor Abbas Safavian*, the Sovereign's personal physician, to the former Ministers, *Hadi Hedayati* and *Kazem Vadii*, to the former ambassadors, *Hossein Montazem*, and *Assadollah Fahimi*, to the Rectors, *Parviz Amouzegar*, and *Ahmad Ghoreyshi*, to *Prince Ali Patrick Pahlavi*, to *Mrs Elahe Ghotbi*, to *Colonel Aghilipour*, Iranian military attaché in Paris when Rouhollah Khomeyni was a guest at Neauphle-le-Château, to *Dr Darioush Shirvani*, observer of, and participant in, some of the significant episodes of the last months of the reign, to *Professor Abolghassem Banihashemi*, to *Messrs. Mohammad Reza Taghizadeh* and *Djavad M. Ershadi*, to *Senator Ali Rezai*, to *Colonel Amine Elahi*, to the former Deputy, *Nasser Olyai Shirazi*, to *Mr Iradj Mobasher*, Chamberlain to the Imperial Court, to a former Secretary of State for Agriculture, Hossein Sepehri, to the journalist, *Mohammad Reza Shahid* and, last but not least, the former commander of the special forces, all of whom provided useful statements and details.

*   *
*

My kind thanks to *Pierre F. de Villemarest*, for encouraging me to carry out this enquiry and for giving me access to the Centre Européen d'Information (CEI) and special thanks to *Jean-Michel Pedrazzani*, the Shahbanou's biographer, for his advice and information, as well as to *Professor Pierre Gervais* for his counsel and support.

I owe immense gratitude equally to numerous officers of the armed forces, especially those of the Imperial Guard, who, although they were rendered impotent by the political power, witnessed the life of the Shah and the national tragedy, at first hand, and provided me with statements, which were always sincere and often moving. I am permitted to cite, most notably, in this context, *Brigadier General Manoutchehr Beyglari, Brigadier General Houshang Firouzbakhch* and *Colonels Kiourmars Djahanbini, Yazdan Nevissi* and *Cyrus Khiltash*, but there were very many others …

I must also acknowledge several other people, now dead, who sent me witness-statements and other precious information. These were:

Amir Khosrow Afshar, former amabassador to London, Paris and Bonn, and Minister for Foreign Affairs in the Cabinets of Sharif Emami and Azhari. Over the years, I often exchanged views and analyses, with him, concerning the events related here. His knowledge and lucidity have been of constant service to me.

Ambassador Djamchid Gharib.

Manoutchehr Sanei, Chamberlain to the Imperial Court, who was present at several of the important episodes described in my enquiry.

Mohammad Ali Ghotbi, the Shahbanou Farah's uncle.

Francois Charles-Roux, Ambassadeur de France.

The books, especially of historical research or of detailed reports, which have helped me to complete this work, are as follows.

Chronology of the Fifty-Year Reign of the Pahlavi Dynasty (5 vols) new edition, published at Paris.

Biographies of Mohammad Reza Pahlavi – especially *The Man Who Wanted to be Cyrus*, by count Bertrand de Castelbajac (Albatros 1987)
The Shah-in-Shah, in Farsee, by Siavash Bashiri (Parang, Paris 1990)
The Shah of Iran, a chronological anthology, 1998
And, of course, *A Reply to History* (Albin Michel, 1979) written by the Shah himself.

Some works about the Shahbanou: *Farah, Empress of Iran*, by Jean-Michel Pedrazzani (Publimonde 1977), *The Real Farah*, by Vincent Meylan (Pygmalion, 2000).

A book of *Interviews with Prince Reza*, the eldest of the imperial couple's children, by Christian Mallard and Alain Rodier (Plon, 1987)
The researches of William Shawcross – *The Shah: Exile and Death of a Troublemaker* (Stock 1988) – of Pierre Salinger, *Hostages* (Buchet/Chastel, 1981) – and of Michael Laden and William Lewis, *Debacle* (Albin Michel, 1981) were all profitably consulted.

Finally, the memoirs of Count Alexandre de Marenches, *Inside the Princes' Secret* (published in France, Stock, 1986) was of great interest, as much for its detail as for the notes of the ambassador, Anthony Parsons, the recollections of the ambassador, William Sullivan and the accounts of the Huyser-mission.

Many thanks to my publisher, William D. Wolf, for his enthusiasm and courteous consideration.

Brussels 25th January 2005

Preface

The attacks of 11th September 2001, in the United States, have made western opinion aware of the danger arising from Islamism: that perversion, by a violent, extremist, radical minority, of a great religion, which is thus used as an excuse for xenophobia, murder and crime in general – an excuse for what has been called "absolute evil".

This movement began many years ago, at the end of the nineteenth century, but it would have remained at the periphery, sustained, sometimes only as a folk-tradition, by small groups, if certain interests or powers, alien to Islam, had not found it of service for attaining objectives, which had, and have, nothing whatever to do with that religion. We need hardly cite, in support of this, how certain British interests and agencies exploited the Muslim Brotherhoods, in order to counter the rise of Arab nationalism, immediately after the First World War, nor how Nazi Germany used them, similarly, against the Allies, both before, and during, the second War.

Nevertheless, it was not until the latter 1970's that radical Islamism stepped fully out of the shadows – not that its leading thinkers had ever tried to disguise either its ideology or its methods. In the West, however, many people preferred not to see or understand these matters, when powerful interests perceived, yet again, an advantage in making use of this movement; and, although some brave spirits arose here and there to denounce the deception, their voices were quickly muffled by the clamour of intellectual conformity to the single point of view that it was not politically-correct to criticise people who – quite wrongly, I believe - proclaimed themselves to be the revolutionaries of a great religion.

However, it was then, in 1978, was it not, that the influences, which succeeded in committing the hideous atrocity of 11th September, were launched, or re-launched, by the Islamic Revolution in Iran, whose figurehead – one Rouhollah Khomenyi – had been so well protected and pampered, as a guest, at Neauphle-le-Château? The seizure of power in Iran, by this person – as neatly put together, in a few weeks, by the global propaganda-machine – was a masterpiece of disinformation, which will remain a case-study. The coup was then hailed as a miraculous event, a "return to authenticity" and a victory for democracy and human rights!

For reasons, and by means of mechanisms, which have been clearly analysed and demonstrated since then, Washington and, consequently, London and Paris, promoted the rise to power of Islamic Radicalism, partly in order to apply a supposedly desirable and viable zone-of-containment to a section of the frontiers of Communism, and partly through hatred of the last Shah, Mohammad Reza Pahlavi, and fear of the ambitions of Iran, which they thought excessive and quite intolerable. Moreover, this hatred continued to show itself, after the Shah departed from the political scene, and even when he lay at death's door.

What we are witnessing now is the boomerang-effect of this policy, just as many clear-sighted commentators foresaw and predicted, only to be ignored. In order to achieve a short-term objective, a monster was created – then several more – and then these monsters got out of control: Afghan Fundamentalism, the FIS in Algeria, Egyptian terrorists, the Kosovo Liberation Army – to mention only the most well known... and have not the reformist forces, in such Muslim countries as Egypt, Morocco and Tunisia, which sincerely desired to combat violent radicalism - because it threatened civil order and social progress – have they not been criticised, and even attacked, in the name of a biased and partial concept of democracy and human rights? Damn this selective indignation!

The massacre carried out, on 11th September, by people belonging vaguely to Islamism (no doubt is permitted, it seems, about the guilt of other influences, even if responsibility might be traced to them) immediately reminded me of another atrocity, perpetrated on 19th August 1978, at Abadan, capital of the Iranian petroleum-industry. The "revolutionaries", supported at that time by a quasi-unanimous chorus of admiration and approbation across the western world, set fire to "The Rex", one of that great city's cinemas. It was on a Thursday afternoon – the beginning of the weekend, that is – during a special film-show for children and young adults, accompanied, for the most part, by their mothers. All the exits had been carefully blocked, so that no-one should escape: 477 people died there, by burning or asphyxia.

Some months later, after the triumph of the revolution, this terrible crime was completely vindicated and glorified, by the Teheran-regime, as a Fundamentalist-Revolutionary act, and the rest of the world was silent.

Thus, the Islamists inaugurated the revolutionary technique of mass-assassination, whose object is to terrorise, destabilise, subvert and destroy. The thousands of victims of 11th September were only the latest in a long series of crimes committed sporadically everywhere in the world, but, pre-eminently, in Muslim countries, where there was a will to resist - in Egypt, Algeria, the Lebanon and elsewhere, not forgetting the 300 000 victims of political oppression in Iran. The unhappy Afghans, noble and brave as they are, if one knows them well, have been, more than anyone, the victims and martyrs of Islamism: in this case, that of the monstrous Taliban-regime, which was installed, financed and protected by unprincipled interests.

In accordance with its methods and its crimes – with its record – Islamism may be located in the same rank as

Communism and Nazism. Khomeyni and Bin Laden, like Pol Pot or Mengistu Haile Mariam, are nothing but simulacra of Stalin and Hitler. Let us have the courage to say so directly.

This book, finished a few days after 11th September 2001, is not just one more commentary on the Islamic revolution in Iran – still less another biography of Mohammad Reza Pahlavi. It could have been called "Enquiry into the Birth [or even the construction] of Islamic Radicalism". Its aim is to describe, as minutely as possible, the underside, or hidden face, of events; to penetrate the secrets of people who played a role in them – their actions behind-the-scenes, their intrigues and their manipulations. To do this, I based my enquiry on my own recollections – my personal experience of these events – on my long conversations with the Shah and, especially, after his departure from Iran, on the numerous accounts, almost all unpublished, of people, most of whom were direct participants or observers of what happened.

Some of the witness-statements, which have contributed to this enquiry, reached me only by virtue of great courage and great concern for the accuracy of history.

Western leaders try nowadays to give the impression, to world opinion, that they wish to combat Islamic terrorism. Such an intention is nowhere more manifest than in the United States of America, where it exhibits itself in spectacular decisions, which her allies follow, sometimes with reservations.

The list of organisations – many of them tiny, although this by no means detracts from their terrible effectiveness – has been made public. They were known, therefore, but not spoken of.

Here and there – with a great deal more publicity in the USA (a country which suddenly realises it is no longer a place of safety) - occurs the discovery of arms-caches, plans of attack and assassination-plots. It would even seem that not all is being revealed to the public, out of concern – legitimate, perhaps – to avoid frightening people; but why was no action taken previously?

Many bank-accounts have been sealed, in order to dam the sources of terrorist-funds. Why was this not done sooner?

It would be legitimate to ask these questions and many others. Readers of this book will discover the process of the foetal development of events. Nothing arises suddenly. Prevention is much better than cure. The experience of the birth – or the construction – of Islamic Radicalism, over the last 25 years, which is the object of this enquiry, may thus be of use today.

The true answer to barbarism consists of a radical change of attitude; of a rending revision of the policies, which bear on this problem. If there was no promotion – and this word is no more than a euphemism, as the reader will discover, when reading this work from a particular angle – if there was no "promotion", I say, of the Islamic Revolution in Iran, it would have been possible to avoid many other shocks. If the Taliban had not been placed in control of Afghanistan, and help had been given to that country's patriotic, national resistance (a Muslim movement, indeed, but not a fundamentalist one) then the shadowy Bin Laden would never have installed his bases there.

At the present, if we do not support, from within the Muslim world, those who wish to reform, develop, progressively secularise the institutions and combat terrorism, it will do no good to make gestures or to deploy great forces. The monster will arise again quicker than may be imagined.

That, at any rate, is the hope, which I express; the interest, which this enquiry suddenly acquired, during its gestation long ago, and which has appeared in writing over the last eighteen months. Experience should always do the trick. It is a hard school, but some will not learn in any other.

12st October 1971

Solemn tribute to Cyrus the Great.

Two-thousand-five-hundredth anniversary of
the founding of the Empire.

Prologue

21st September 1971
The Shah and Shahbanou in academic dress: having offi-
cially opened the new Central Library of Teheran University,
the Royal Couple are proceeding to a further part of the
ceremony.
Left: Prime Minister Hoveyda
Right foreground: Houchang Nahavandi
(appointed Rector of the University, three months before)
Right background: (in military uniform) General Ali Neshat,
Commander of The Immortals.
(*Photo courtesy of Mrs. Seda Aghassian*)

Chapter I

"Rest in peace, Cyrus, for we keep watch!"

Persepolis, Shiraz, Teheran:
12th to 17th October 1971

On 12th October 1971, at 11 a.m., in warm autumn-sunshine, on an esplanade specially prepared for the occasion, the Shah of Iran, Light of the Aryans, Mohammad Reza Pahlavi, paid solemn tribute to Cyrus the Great, Founder of the Empire, at the latter's imposing Mausoleum. The ancient building had stood, almost intact, for twenty centuries. It was the two-thousand-five-hundredth anniversary of the founding of the Empire. Mohammad Reza Pahlavi was then 51, in perfect health and in full possession of his physical and intellectual powers. He was sure of himself and of the future of his country, whose development, over the past two decades, had been a dazzling example to the world. According to the eminent, French economist, André Piettre, Iran was a country of "growth without inflation", combining astounding productivity with social progress.

Lined up behind the Shah – according to a rigorous protocol – were Iran's leading, official figures, in all their ceremonial finery: the entire Imperial Family, the Prime Minister and his Government, the Presidents of both Chambers and the Supreme Court, the Rectors of the Universities, the Directors of public-sector companies... and also numerous, foreign dignitaries, including the heads of diplomatic missions accredited to the Sovereign's court.

Foreign attendees notwithstanding, the ceremony was authentically Iranian. It was televised live by the national channel, hundreds of journalists from all over the world had come to cover it, and it was a solemn and emotional moment for the Shah – there, in Passagardes, first capital of the Persian Empire.

Through this ceremony, and in his message, addressed symbolically to The Founder, Mohammad Reza Pahlavi wished to emphasise Iran's historical continuity, as a spiritual, even mystic, link, uniting his people over the millennia. He intended also to pay formal tribute to all those who had built Iran – especially to the great Kings, who were symbolic of them and whose gigantic portraits decorated the principal arteries of the Iranian capital. One of these was Agha Mohammad, founder of the Qadjar Dynasty, which the Pahlavi Dynasty had succeeded.

For Iranians, Cyrus is a legendary figure - so also Darius (522 – 486 b.c.) who was Cyrus' cousin and son-in-law, and who came to the throne after the brief reign of Cambyses (530 – 522 b.c.) – so also Shah Abbas (1587 – 1629 a.d.) To these three kings, the history and people of Iran, without any official decision on the matter, unanimously accorded the title of "the Great".

Cyrus was the man whom Mohammad Reza Pahlavi

admired most - Cyrus was descended, on his father's side, from the king of a small, Persian realm, and, on his mother's side, from Astyages, last king of the Medes and cousin of Croesus, who was King of Lydia - for it was Cyrus who had created the Persian Empire. This "liberator of peoples, most engaging hero of antiquity", as his recent biographer, Gérard Israel, called him, dreamed of founding a global empire. Alexander admired his desire to respect the traditions, cultures and identities of the countries he controlled, and, subsequently, tried to follow his example. After the conquest of Babylon, in a document preserved today at London, and known as "the Cyrus Scroll", Cyrus proclaimed the principles, which constitute history's first charter of human rights:

"I have granted to all men the freedom to worship their own gods and ordered that no man has the right to mistreat others on this account.
"I have ordered that no house may be destroyed nor inhabitant be despoiled ... I have guaranteed peace and tranquillity to all men ..."

Cyrus and his successors actually put this policy of tolerance and liberty into practice, so that the influence of their "pax persica" eventually pervaded most of the known world.

This is the same text, which, some years ago, many Iranian municipalities used to have inscribed and exhibited in their public squares.

This was the man, whom the Shah addressed in the very beautiful prose of a speech delivered in a touching, at times emotional, lyrical style.

The "Address to Cyrus" had been written by Chodja-

Ol-Dine Chafa, researcher, man-of-letters, historian and the Sovereign's cultural counsellor, after long discussion about its content. When he had finished it, the Shah asked for only minor changes to be made. Mohammad Reza Pahlavi was not a great orator, but, when he spoke without notes to formal or informal gatherings, his mastery of himself and his perfect elocution always allowed him to come through it creditably. If he had to read a text in public – which, over more than a decade, was nearly always prepared by the same counsellor – he used to read it through once, beforehand, and then read it out perfectly.

This was not the case with his "Address to Cyrus". Aware of its historical significance and publicity-value, he spent hours practising the text and discovering the intonations he liked.

He enunciated the speech faultlessly:
"Great King Cyrus, king of kings! I, the Shah-in-Shah of Iran, and my people salute you.
"At this moment, when Iran renews its ties with history, we bear witness here to the nation's gratitude to you, Immortal Hero of History, Founder of the oldest empire in the world, great liberator, worthy son of humanity.
"Cyrus, before the place of your eternal rest, we address to you this solemn speech: rest in peace; for we watch, and shall keep watch for ever, over your glorious heritage...!"

In Iran, ten million viewers watched the ceremony and noted the great emotion, with which the Shah brought his oration to a close.

At the end of the message, a 101-gun salute shook the blue skies above Passagardes, and a sumptuous, floral wreath was laid at the foot of the tomb of the Great King. This was the crowning moment.

That day, and this moment in particular, were certainly also the high-point of the reign of Mohammad Reza Pahlavi.

That year marked the thirtieth anniversary of his accession to the throne, following his father's abdication, in 1941. It was, furthermore, the tenth anniversary of the launching of the reforms, which had been dubbed "the white revolution", and thanks to which the country had accomplished a real leap-forward – agricultural reform, rapid industrialisation, infrastructural development and political equality for men and women.

Iran had also emerged as an international player, taking responsibility, after the withdrawal of the British, for the security of Persian Gulf region; and OPEC had just achieved its first, great success – in raising considerably the price of oil – an operation, in which the Shah, and King Faisal of Saudi Arabia, had played leading roles, and for which both were to pay dearly.

The crowning-moment at Passagardes was thus, in an imperceptible way, also the beginning of the end – the commencement of mistakes, which would be adroitly exploited – as the hours which followed would show.

At first, the celebration of the foundation of the empire, and the tribute to Cyrus, were supposed to be like the jubilee, in October 1967, marking the anniversary of the Shah's coronation – a purely national occasion. Then, it seemed like a good idea to bring in the world's orientalists and experts-on-Persia, to whom the country owed so much, for all their researches into its history and civilisation. Then, at the beginning of 1969, another scheme surfaced – to invite the Heads-of-State, Sovereigns or Presidents, of all the nations of the Earth – and the Shah was immediately sold on it. To him, Iran seemed quite entitled to receive them, and equal to the task, both financially and politically. Discreet soundings were taken in the chancelleries, and positive responses came through. The "Festival of Persepolis" was decided upon.

But how should these dozens of crowned heads, presidents and political figures be welcomed, and where were they going to stay? The Shah thought of accommodating all his guests at one or more of the hotels he was having built. The "Darius-the-Great" – an intercontinental hotel at Shiraz – had already been completed, and the "Cyrus-the-Great" – in Persepolitan style, a few hundred yards from the magnificent ruins – was well on the way. All that was necessary, the Sovereign said, was to get these ready; and why not, he went on, lodge a party of attendees in Shiraz' delightful, 18th/19th century palaces, or in some of the luxurious town-houses there?

The idea of creating accommodation under canvas – like the field-pavilions of yore, at one with the grandeur of the desert – entranced the Shahbanou in September 1970, and she converted the Shah to it. The security services were opposed to dispersing the distinguished guests. A large faction, at the Ministry of the Imperial Court, backed the scheme for a camp.

Years later, at Cairo – a few weeks before he died – Mohammad Reza Pahlavi told me of his conviction that this celebration, "evoking the glorious past of Iran, and the phenomenon of its historical continuity," had been an excellent idea.

"Iran," he continued, *"has remained itself, through the centuries: it never lost its identity, conquering at length, and assimilating, the conquerors – Alexander, the Arabs, the Mongols – and it is in remaining faithful to its identity, through remembering and celebrating its past, that it could, and should, continue its progress.*

"Besides, it will be by returning to its Iranian, national roots that our people will put an end to this so-called Islamic regime – a graft which will not take."

Nevertheless, he regretted the way the festivities turned out – the excessive reliance on the services of foreigners: *"we were led along that route,"* he said, *"we should not have let it happen."*

Once he had given his approval, it was his wont not bother with the details, and a steering-committee, chaired by the Shahbanou, took over the decision-making. She it was who acted as the actual head of construction, decorating, event-organising and lighting-design, and it was thus the Ministry of the Court, not the Government, which was responsible for the administration and execution of the work.

In private, Prime Minister Hoveyda, and the Finance Minister, Djamchid Amouzegar, voiced their criticisms and worried about the size of the sums involved. Ardeshir Zahedi – head of the Iranian Diplomatic Corps, at that time – whose initiative had made it possible to persuade the world's great-and-good to take part in the festival, was not at all happy with the way preparations were going. Indeed, he often expressed his reservations and did not hesitate to impart them to the Shah:

"In my view, it was a mistake," he commented later, *"I might*

*have been wrong, but I thought the influence of the Shahbanou
and of Alam, Minister of the Court, was too strong."*

In public, everyone accepted the situation. No incident
occurred. There were no hitches or problems.

In a year, the Jansen company, assisted by local technicians
and labourers, completed a colossal work. This was what the
international press would call "the Iranian version of *the Field
of the Cloth of Gold*"; a huge encampment of sixty-eight tents,
placed on an esplanade, into which the *Place de la Concorde*
would easily have fitted four-and-a-half times over, was ready
to receive the invited guests. These temporary shelters were
made of synthetic material, stretched over wooden frames and
based on concrete foundations. There was no incendiary risk -
the tents were fireproof. They were designed to resist winds of
more than 60 mph, and they were air-conditioned throughout.

The "village" was in the shape of a star. At the centre were
a pavilion of honour - over 38 yards in diameter – which was
to house the Sovereign's apartments, a dining-tent, nearly 75
yards by 26, and a reception-tent of the same dimensions. The
walls of the dining-tent were of purple velvet, while those of
the reception-tent were of a thick, blue material. It was whispered that the central pavilion had been inspired by the tent of
Alexander of Macedon. This surprised people and had a very
deleterious effect on public opinion, Persepolis having been
razed by this invading Greek, whom the common people still
refer to as "the devil"!

In the central tent, the Shah had at his disposal an office-
reception room, a bedroom and a wholly modern bathroom
with all the latest accessories. The furnishings were covered
with gold-leaf. A black, fitted carpet, with a motif in old gold,

spread between walls lined with yellow material, figured in blue. The walls of the reception-room in the Queen's apartments were blue: here, white-leather sofas rested upon an equally-white fitted-carpet. White too was the carpet in the Shahbanou's bedroom, where she had a modern bed, but with a canopy, whose blue-and-white diamond-pattern matched the curtains. Her bathroom, in pale rose, was hung with a brilliant, shimmering white material, featuring geometric shapes.

In the great dining-room, there was a high-table, at which the Shah and Shahbanou would be seated, with Kings and Heads of State. Around this, evenly spaced throughout the room, were twenty-or-so tables, with twelve places at each, to welcome the other guests. Paradoxically, Iranians were a small minority.

Fifty tents, in which the interiors were especially immaculate, were allocated to the most eminent guests. The Shahbanou's instructions had been categorical: each guest should feel that he was in a real palace, in which the décor would vary, from the truly classical to the completely modern.

No expense was spared: the House of *Baccarat* received an order for a dinner-service of several thousand pieces; a prestigious, Parisian couturier – the Shahbanou's dressmaker – made thirty town-dresses and as many evening-gowns for the ladies-of-honour, who would accompany the eminent guests during the three days. The sartorial elegance, of the male members of the escort-team, was entrusted to the House of *Lanvin*. The fire-works and fountains were provided by the House of *Ouiry*. The hairdressers, *Alexandre and Carita*, and the House of *Elizabeth Arden*, set up salons employing forty people – the latter having created for the occasion a range of products, called "Farah", to be offered to the guests. Haviland provided a coffee-service, which was to be used only once. All the linen was ordered from *Porthault*.

The cuisine was commissioned from *Maxim's*. Iranian cuisine is reputed to be among the finest in the world, but the only Iranian dish to be found on the menu was the caviar! Everything else was French. This was the only point on which the Shahbanou hesitated before deciding.

Even before this conglomeration was deployed, the damage it was doing became apparent, although the scale of the rumours could not be defined, and an attempt was made to impose secrecy, which only made things worse. Afterwards, when its lamps had been extinguished, no-one knew what to do with this luxurious, ornate camp. It could not be exhibited, because Iranians, having been excluded from it, were infuriated by it. It might profitably have been turned into a tourist-attraction – a Club Med for millionaires – but the risk of opening it for show was unthinkable. It also seemed unreasonable just to dismantle it; and so it became a forbidden city, which everyone could see from a distance, but which no-one was allowed to visit. The effect may be imagined. Even the revolutionaries did not venture to touch it. Some years later, its remains were transformed into a kind of museum of horrors, whose tour-commentary need not be described. Then it was closed – but, on the eve of the ceremony at Passagardes, that was still in the future.

The organisation of the guest-welcome, at the airport - which had been newly painted and re-fitted for the occasion - and the conveyance of the visitors to Persepolis, on the new motorway – built specially for the festival – was a complete success. The prominent foreigners were greeted, as they alighted from aircraft, by a half-brother of the Shah, or by Prime Minister

Hoveyda, in an official ceremony, featuring – for the Heads-of-State - national anthems and a military guard-of-honour, and less elaborate arrangements, according to their rank, for the rest. It had to be like a ballet, choreographed with the precision to cope with arrivals, which succeeded one another, sometimes at fifteen-minute intervals, and the Imperial Guard, who were in charge of it, executed it faultlessly.

Cars for the guests – Mercedes 280-SE's – air-conditioned, of aubergine hue - bought for the occasion (but sold, after the festival, at a profit to the public purse) swept along the broad highway, linking the airport with Shiraz, and into the flamboyant "town-of-roses" itself. Iran's visitors were thus able to see the beautiful museum of fine art – a single-storey building of the eighteenth-century – the monumental gateway to the bazaar and the Vakil Mosque – built by the good king, Karim Khan Zand – some of the University-buildings and the Eram Palace, before leaving Shiraz, by the Koran Gate – an ancient monument, whose earthenware and intricate decoration had been lovingly restored a few years previously. Coming out of the town, the guests were given a clear view of the emerging, modern Iran – the huge campus of the University's agricultural and veterinary-medical faculties (designed by the architect, Mohammad Reza Moghtader, and his associates) the factories and Shiraz' new satellite-suburbs …not "Potemkin-villages", but a reality, which the international press scarcely deigned to look at and see. Notice was taken only of the festival, and especially of its negative aspects.

The Shah and Shahbanou greeted the guests in the camp's ceremonial, open space. The ritual was unvarying. Tirelessly, the Sovereign repeated the same phrase, in English, French or Farsee, with a translation for anyone not conversant with these languages:

"On behalf of the Shahbanou and myself, I bid you welcome to Iran, on the occasion of our Empire's two-thousand-five-hundredth anniversary."

Handshakes, national anthems, guards of honour – it all took about a quarter-of-an-hour – and then the visitors were conducted to their tents.

The list of personalities attending was impressive. It was probably the biggest gathering of Heads-of-State in modern times and, incontestably, an enormous diplomatic coup for Iran and her sovereign, so that the Government was right to declare:

"During these unforgettable days, this august assembly will make Persepolis the centre-of-gravity of the world."

Actually making the trip in person were the Emperor of Ethiopia, Haile Selassie, the oldest Head-of-State on Earth, the Kings and Queens of Belgium, Denmark and Jordan, the Prince and Princess of Monaco, the Heir-to-the-Throne of Japan and his wife, the King of Morocco, King Olaf of Norway and the sovereigns of Thailand and Nepal. Queen Elizabeth of Great Britain was represented by her husband, Prince Philip, Duke of Edinburgh, and their daughter, Princess Anne. Queen Juliana of the Netherlands had sent her husband, Prince Bernhard. All the kings and princes of the Arabian Peninsula were there.

The number of Presidents and politicians of the first rank, whose power was less symbolic than that of most of the crowned heads, was even more important. There was President Podgorny of the USSR, Marshal Tito, the Presidents of Turkey (Sunay) Pakistan (Yahya Khan) Tunisia (Bourghiba) and Senegal (Leopold Sedar Senghor) ... and those of Poland, Italy, Austria, Switzerland, West Germany and India, and of several Socialist and African countries.

Two friends and allies of Iran were sorely missed. Richard Nixon was represented by his vice-president, Spiro Agnew, as had been agreed from the first; but the last-minute absence of the President of France, Georges Pompidou, who had accepted an invitation, precipitated a genuine diplomatic incident and a long freeze in Franco-Iranian relations.

Officially, the reason given was procedural. Georges Pompidou, it was said, wanted to be placed higher, at the dinner-table, than all the other French-speaking Heads-of-State – a quite unjustifiable request. In fact, in spite of the exceptional relations between the two countries, and the eminence of French companies in providing goods for the festival – which was a veritable shop-window for Gallic expertise in numerous areas – Georges Pompidou had given way to the germano-pratine lobby and the reaction of certain newspapers of the Left. On learning of the procedural pretext, is supposed to have said,
"For de Gaulle, we would undoubtedly have found an exceptional placing, which would have been his, but, for that man ... who does he think he is?"

Prime Minister Jacques Chaban-Delmas, whom the Sovereign knew and liked personally, had been designated to stand in for the French Head-of-State. The French ambassador expressed the wish that M and Mme Chaban might be lodged in the tent, which had been reserved for the President, but Iranian protocol could not allow this. Right up to the last minute, squabbles about precedence persisted, and no-one knew whether France would be represented at all, at Persepolis, or, if so, by whom.

At the last minute, the pleadings of Princess Ashraf, the Shah's twin-sister, and of Prime Minister Hoveyda, prevailed upon the Shah to authorise a change-of-protocol, whereby Jacques Chaban-Delmas and his wife might be accommodated in the presidential tent. In recognition of this, France then presented, to the Imperial Couple, a very beautiful painting, by Bernard Buffet – a gift, which the Shahbanou said she appreciated very much.

Besides the high officials, a number of celebrities also attended, such as Prince Juan Carlos, future King of Spain - who was representing General Franco – and Constantine, former King of Greece, whom the Shah didn't think much of – but whom, together with his wife, the Shahbanou liked. Then there was the Pretender to the Throne of Italy, a regular at the Iranian court, and Prince Aga Khan – who, like his forebears was of Persian descent and an Iranian passport-holder – Imelda Marcos, from the Philippines, and Prince Michael of Greece.

The 14th October would be the fullest day, the pivot of the festivities and the focus of media-attention, commencing, in the morning, with a historical march-past by the Army. The official rostrum, reserved for the prominenti (Heads-of-State - Sovereigns and Presidents - in the front row) was set up, at the foot of the monumental stairway to the gate of Persepolis' central palace, which had been built by Darius I (522 – 486 b.c.) the greatest, most powerful Emperor in Persian history. Persepolis, unrivalled in magnificence by any city in antiquity, was the reflection of his power and his conquests. The central palace had been a town in itself. Every day, its kitchens had fed more than fifteen thousand people. At its heart, the *Apadana*, the audience-hall of the King-of-Kings (or, rather, the *Shah-in-Shah* – his official title, in Farsee) was a square 82 yards on-aside and able to hold ten thousand guests. This great stairway led up to it, past bas-reliefs showing two processions – on the left, dignitaries and soldiers, and, on the right, the Chiefs, Kings and other representatives of the peoples of the Empire, of which the Shah-in-Shah was the suzerain.

The presence of so many of the world's figureheads, at the foot of this staircase, must have seemed, to Mohammad Reza Pahlavi, like a snapshot of history. Had they not come to pay tribute to Iran's renaissance, after so many decades of decline and humiliating subjection?

The rostrum was constructed facing the sun, in order to facilitate the work of the photographers of the press and television. The ladies were provided with the shelter of parasols, but the grand spectacle, which all Iran, with joy and pride – and millions of foreign viewers too – watched live, was worth suffering a little discomfort for. During an hour-and-a-half, thousands of costumed actors, choristers and soldiers brought Iranian history to life. The unfolding of the procession, and the dress, weapons and routines of the performers, had all been minutely researched and prepared, over several years, by the Army's Historical Service, and the execution of the spectacle had been entrusted to the Army, under the control of its Commander-in-Chief, General Fathollah Minbachian.

Ancient Persia opened the march in the person of a standard-bearer, wearing a tiger-skin and brandishing, on a staff, the mythical apron of Kaveh – the legendary blacksmith, who raised the people against a foreign tyrant and liberated the country. Then came fourteen detachments, each perfectly representing a substantial period of Iran's history: there were Medean soldiers, Cyrus' infantry, the horsemen and chariots of the Achemenides and so on. The siege and conquest of

Babylon was portrayed, then the imperial fleet, which was defeated at Salamis, and the Parthian cavalry, which crushed the Roman legions and preserved Asia from Rome's domination ... then on to the armies of Abbas I (1587 – 1629 a.d.) the infantry and cavalry of Nadir, who conquered India, the army of the Qadjars and, finally, the troops of the Pahlavi period. Units of the Imperial Guard, which was itself a replica of Darius' "Immortals", were followed by the boys and girls of the "army of knowledge", symbolising the Shah's "white revolution", which brought the parade to a close. Meanwhile, jets of the Iranian "Golden Crown" squadron – the impressive winners of international competitions – performed their remarkable aerial acrobatics and painted the green, white and red of the nation's tricolor-flag, in the sky.

The guests returned delighted and dazzled, if somewhat exhausted by the heat, and compliments, richly deserved and doubtless sincere, rained down. The Shah was clearly proud and pronounced himself satisfied with the expertise of the Army, in putting on this great show, as conceived and executed entirely by Iranians.

Today, all of the uniforms, costumes, antique weapons and period-copies, which the Army looked after, are exhibited in a museum, housed in the ancient palace of Saad-Abad, to the north of the Iranian capital. Even "the revolution" came, at last, to respect the symbols of history, which, at first, it denied and of which it attempted to erase the memory.

After an informal lunch, the afternoon of 14th October was given over to visiting Persepolis and the neighbouring tombs of the Achemenid Kings, for which the guests wore casual clothes. The King of Norway took with him an assistant, carrying a detailed map of the ruins. Queen Fabiola of

34

Belgium and the Japanese Princes could not be parted from their cameras. Prince Michael of Greece was much sought after, by his cousins, for his historical knowledge. He acted as an extempore guide, describing the subtleties of the architecture and history of the monuments.

At eight-o-clock, that evening, the gala-dinner – the most sumptuous and controversial of all the festival's gatherings – was due to begin. The diners, all in evening dress arrived outside the dining-tent, ready for the feast, and were welcomed by the Imperial Couple. Maxim's had prepared the repast, and two hundred waiters from *Potel et Chabot* were ready to serve it. Two waiters of the Imperial household would serve the Shah, who was known to be sensitive about such matters.

After the aperitif, the guests sat down, in order of precedence, according to the strict protocol of the Imperial Court. The Queen of Denmark was placed on the Shah's right, and, on his left, the Shahbanou and then Fabiola of the Belgians. In the place of honour, was seated the old Emperor of Ethiopia, with the King of Denmark on his left. The gentlemen being much more numerous than the ladies, mainly because so many Arab princes had come alone, it was not possible to respect the classical convention of seating the sexes alternately. That's why the Prince of Monaco, the Duke of Edinburgh, Prince Bernhard of the Netherlands, the Crown Prince of Sweden, vice-President Agnew and the Polish President were all sitting next to each other. When Prince Bernhard asked the Duke of Edinburgh why there was no woman between them, the Duke is said to have replied with one of his characteristic jokes:
"Because we are the only male queens."

Naturally, the menu was exceptional: quails' eggs garnished with Persian caviar; lobster mousse with a Nantua sauce; lamb flamed in alcohol; peacock stuffed with foie-gras and served in its plumage – its marvellous, iridescent tail fully spread. Accompanying all this, was a salad, called (no-one seemed to know why) "Alexandre Dumas", and then came the cheeses, a salad of figs and raspberries, a champagne sorbet and, since it was also the Shahbanou's thirty-third birthday, a vast cake, weighing thirty-three kilos (5 stone) was carried in by two head waiters. Next coffee and tea were served, and, later, the liqueurs.

Commencing the toasts, the Shah spoke briefly and gravely:

"The present gathering, of so many of the world's prominent people, seems to me to augur well, for I feel that our meeting here links the history of the past with today's realities."

Emperor Haile Selassie replied on behalf of the assembled company:

"When the day comes for the history of Your country to be written, Your Imperial Majesty will undoubtedly see Yourself accorded an eminent place in it; for you have given renewed vigour to the nation by making way for the necessity of modernisation."

Ten years later, both men had lost their thrones and perished in tragic circumstances.

The evening concluded with a tremendous firework-display, launched from the ruins of the Palace of Darius.

The 15th October was more relaxed, but it had its practical side. Many guests re-visited Persepolis, and some went, as discreetly as possible, to Shiraz to see the monuments of the great "city of the roses". Some paid courtesy-visits to well-known people, but more numerous were the political meetings which took place. The Shah helped to organise these contacts. The Emperor of Ethiopia received Presidents Tito, of Yugoslavia, and Podgorny, of the USSR. King Hussein of Jordan convened an Arab summit. Constantine of Greece, who had been driven from his country by the "coup-of-the colonels", had a meeting with vice-President Spiro Agnew – himself of Greek extraction – in order to plead his cause.

That evening, there was a *son-et-lumière*, whose French commentary was written by the historian, André Castelot, and, after that, an informal dinner, featuring several Persian dishes, which the guests liked very much.

The following day, most of the guests left Shiraz, although some accompanied the Iranian Sovereigns to Teheran, in order to take part in further ceremonies.

On 17th October, at Teheran, two, great inaugurations took place, which brought to an end the festivities and the international gathering. First, the opening of the *Shahyad*, the memorial of the kings – a triumphal arch, nearly 200 feet high, designed by the young, Iranian architect, Hossein Amanat – marking the principal route into the capital, on the square of the same name. Beneath the square, disposed in chambers with a floor-space of 87 000 sq ft, a museum tracing the history of Iran, was officially opened, at the same time.

After that, came the opening of Teheran's huge, Olympic complex, incorporating a stadium to hold 100 000 people. This had been designed by the architect Abdol-Aziz Farmanfarmayan, and largely built and fitted out by French companies. Some years later, this complex, and its Olympic Village, hosted the Asian Games, at which Iran came third, just behind China and Japan, and as a result of which Iran was able to initiate the process of applying to hold the Olympic Games of 1988 … which were held at Seoul.

On this occasion, a section of the international press hastened to accuse the Shah of megalomania. What need did Iran have of sporting facilities, suitable for developed countries, and of an Olympic bid, during the 'eighties?

Some years later, when a museum of contemporary art was opened in Teheran, and the works of numerous, famous, foreign painters and sculptors were exhibited, the same section of the press was even more scathing. It was the only museum of this kind, and on such a scale, between the Mediterranean and Japan. Acquiring such collections of western art, and exhibiting them together with the works of Iranian artists – so these journalists alleged – was to dedicate a museum to the latter and could only be yet another sign of the Shah's "megalomania". However, all the world's great museums possess impressive collections of Iranian art and craft, which, very often, they acquired by dubious means, and no-one thinks of saying anything about that.

"Isn't there something racist about that?" Mohammad Reza Pahlavi would subsequently ask.

That year of celebrations saw a marvellous increase in the completion of development-projects, in Iran - everyone wanted to indicate having played a part in the historic event – and some of the more important ones were declared open by the Shah and Shahbanou. Reference has often been made to the building of 2 500 village-schools, most of which were donated – and built according to plans graciously provided by the State – by private individuals, who wished to commemorate the name of a dear-departed one, by attaching it to a village-school in their area.

Numerous tourist-facilities were also completed that year, such as a Sheraton, in Teheran, and another in Ispahan – the one called "Cyrus-the-Great"- a new, grand hotel at Shiraz (part of the intercontinental chain called "Darius-the-Great") a palace not far from Persepolis, "Cyrus-the-Great", where some of the guests had stayed, and the motorway from Shiraz to Persepolis.

On 28th April 1971, in one of the ceremonies of the Year of Celebration, the Shah had opened the sporting complex at Shiraz University. As he left the sporting complex, after the ceremony, Mohammad Reza Pahlavi was obviously happy, almost radiant. The halls-of-residence were at least 500 yards away.

"Let's go and visit the halls," he said to me (I was then the Rector of the University) and, instead of walking, as expected, towards his residence, the Eram Palace, he changed direction, saying to his entourage, *"we're going to pay a visit to the students."*

Everyone panicked: the Provincial Governor and the local Savak-chief stepped forward. *"It's not planned, Sire,"* said the Governor.

"We've only secured the gardens," added the Savak-chief.

The Shah looked disdainful, and we went on. The others followed; but, with a gesture of his hands, the Shah stopped them, and we crossed the "secured", empty gardens. As we went, he talked about architecture and praised the style of the students' accommodation, "modern, but so suited to the climate and the surroundings – so Iranian!"

He spoke of his hope that work on the enormous, new university would progress rapidly: *"that will be the Persepolis of our times."*

We went into the first building and climbed a little stair to the raised ground-floor. We could hear the noise of conversation coming from a room.

"*Let's go in!*"

According to tradition, the Shah is in his own home, wherever he may be. I knocked at the door, which was soon opened. Two, young students were sitting on the floor, one with his back against the bed, the other leaning against the wall. Between them, lay books, notes and a small tea-pot. Their amazement can be imagined. They did not know what to do or say.

"*We've come to ask for your news and how you are – it's about time for the exams - you're getting ready for them, are you?*"

Moved to tears, one of them got up, threw himself at the Shah's feet and embraced his knees – a sign of tribal respect. Smiling, the Shah raised him by both hands. The other took the Sovereign's hand, held it briefly and then touched his shoulder.

"*Would you like some tea?*"

"*No, thank you – I'm sure that it's very good.*"

He asked them about their studies. They were studying for bachelor's degrees in Chemistry.

"*There's a profession which will be useful to the country's future!*"

Next, he asked them where they came from. The door remained open. Hearing the sound of voices, I suppose – if not, I can't think why – dozens of students came out of their rooms to see what was going on, and all started shouting, "*long live the King!*"

He shook their hands and spoke kindly to everyone. Soon, the corridor was packed, and we retraced our steps, surrounded by a joyous, chanting crowd of students, some of whom were in their pyjamas! The windows of the other halls opened – more shouts – the Shah laughed. After a few paces, he halted and said to the young folk, *"We mustn't stop you working – thank you for your welcome – go back now."*

"We want to come with you – thank you for coming to see us," said some.

"But we'll go back in – back in!"

The students – now more than a hundred of them, I guess – came to a halt, still crying, *"long live the King!"* and we rejoined the group of prominenti.

"You see," he said to them, half joking, half scornful, *"we're still alive."*

On 7th May, following complete restoration, the immense, Imperial Palace of Golestan, which was under construction, by the Qadjar dynasty, throughout the 19th century, and the much more modest Marmar Palace – residence and work-place of the reigning Sovereign's father, Reza-Shah – were declared national museums and opened to the public, in the presence of the King.

On 28th June, the Sovereign opened the irrigation-system associated with the dams, which an Irano-Soviet consortium had built on the frontier-river Arax. This network had cost Iran a thousand millions of dollars. On 26th September, he inaugurated the Norouzlou Dam in Western Azerbaidjan. The following day, five years after work had begun there, the dam "Chapour I", near Mahabad in Kurdistan, was ceremonially declared operational. Chapour I provided irrigation for 50 000 acres of additional land, and an annual generating-capacity of 24 million kWh of electricity. The day after that, was the inauguration of the "Cyrus-the-Great" Dam, also in Kurdistan. This barrage, built in four years, rendered 235 000 acres culvable and generated 56 million kWh annually. Including the electrical equipment, it cost four hundred millions of dollars. On the same day, the Shah and the President of Turkey jointly opened the railway line linking the rail-networks of their two countries.

On 24th September, before departing on a tour of the western provinces, Mohammad Reza Pahlavi – accompanied, this time, by Shahbanou Farah – presided at a ceremony to open the academic year at the University of Teheran, and inaugurated the new buildings housing the University's central library, which puts at the reader's disposal 600 000 books, a large collection of Persian manuscripts, many of them unique, and 1800 periodicals from all over the world.

The Head Librarian, Professor Iradj Afshar, had suggested organising, for the occasion, a great exhibition about authors of contemporary, popular literature, featuring, especially, four writers, two of whom, Djalal Al-Ahmad and Samad Behrangui, were considered to be "accursed". The Savak forbade the publication and sale of their books, which thus became cult-objects for rebellious, young people. Some foreign newspapers had even accused the Savak of assassinating Behrangui – not that anyone could think how such an act as this (which was obviously disguised) could have served the Savak's purposes.

Having been appointed Rector of the University, three months before, I had – with the Shah's full support – been promoting the process of making the greatest academic institution in the country truly democratic. The majority of posts had been made elective and, above all, the nomination and promotion to the administration of retired teaching-staff had been entrusted to a scrutiny-committee, which was directly elected, by secret ballot of the professors and lecturers of each faculty. The Government opposed this system: Prime Minister Hoveyda, intellectual though he was, became dictatorial and mistrustful towards the universities, where he was far from popular, and he fought vigorously against it; but the Sovereign's support ensured that the reform was introduced and successfully implemented.

I put forward the proposal for this exhibition, which he would open, to the Shah, and he accepted it enthusiastically at once. The Savak raised an uproar, and hostile letters came from the office of the Prime Minister, who was President of the University's Administrative Council. Opposition, from both quarters, was submitted to the Shah, who invariably replied:

"I am not minutely concerned with, nor do I wish to interfere in, the affairs of the University, which are a matter for the Rector."

This, redolent as it was of his amused complicity, provided me with deaf ears.

When the exhibition was opened, the Shah viewed it at length, openly pausing before the photos, memorabilia, books and manuscripts of the two, proscribed authors and allowing himself to be filmed and photographed with their works in his hand. A full hour followed, during which he visited, and was enchanted with, the library - its beautiful and well-equipped building, designed by the architect, Abdolaziz Farmanfarmayan - and its impressive collections of books, manuscripts and periodicals.

As he left – demonstrating his obsession with things grand and imposing - he asked me, *"what status does this library, as one of the world's institutions of this kind, give us?"*

I did not know, except, as I told him, that it was one of the most impressive and best equipped. Then he added, with a wide smile, which the press-photographers immortalised, *"we've given them a good hiding, haven't we?"*

Thousands of people visited the exhibition. The day after the opening, the books of the two authors re-appeared in the windows of the book-shops.

On 7th November, the Shah and Shahbanou inaugurated the capital's public library, and, on 14th, at Nazi-Abad, in the south of Teheran, the Prime Minister opened a social-housing development of 470 flats, which included a sports-centre, accommodating five thousand people, and a cultural facility.

On 17th November, in the province of Khuzistan, the Sovereigns attended the start-up of a large oil-refinery, with a daily capacity of 183 000 barrels, and of the largest gas-pumping station in the world ...

These were just some of the projects, among hundreds of others, which made the Year of Celebration a "great leap-forward" for Iran, demonstrating its economic vitality and dynamism and showing its will to draw upon new sources of collective imagination and creativity, while renewing its millennial traditions.

Elsewhere in the world, in more than forty countries, committees were set up to organise celebrations of the 2 500th anniversary of the founding of the Persian Empire. These committees were almost always chaired by Heads-of-State – exceptionally, by their wives, as in the United States and France – and numerous learned, or popular, works, dealing with the history, art, culture and civilisation of Iran, were published, and launched at the conferences, seminars, colloquia and exhibitions, which they organised. The celebration was thus to be an immense operation to promote the country, and the effort made, by the world's governments – from friend and ally, Pakistan, which declared the festival a national holiday, to distant Iceland, via the "great powers", especially the USSR – to take part in it, was certainly a tribute to Iran, and, above all, a sign that her rise to power in the international community was being recognised and that she was being accepted as a country, which was moving forward and would figure more and more in the calculations of global politics. National pride could not but be flattered.

In parallel with the festival at Persepolis, from 13th October, a great, international conference on Persian Studies was held at Shiraz, and the main building of the University's halls-of-residence, which, with its amphitheatre, restaurant and meeting-rooms, had been built by the architect Mohammad Reza Moghtader and company, hosted its plenary and committee sessions.

Opening the conference, the Shah opportunely recalled that all of these ceremonies were designed "to promote Iran's great culture".

"All political and military dominance," he continued, *"inevitably comes to an end; but the radiance of a culture, and its values, are eternal. In the course of our multi-millennial history, our best soldiers have been the men and women who nurtured the durability of our culture and transmitted it, ever more influentially, from generation to generation."*

Four hundred experts, of whom three hundred had come from forty-four foreign countries, took part in the conference, whose President was Chodja-ol-dine Chafa, cultural counsellor to the Imperial Court. A thousand studies and research-papers were presented, a list of which was published, shortly afterwards, in a 240-page volume, by the Pahlavi National Library. Publishing all the contributions had to be phased over the production of a hundred volumes, of 500 pages each, which added unprecedentedly to scholarship in the field of Iranian culture and civilisation. The revolution's henchmen sequestered this precious, scientific treasure, in its entirety, when they attacked the Library in February 1979, and no-one knows what happened to it after that.

The celebration of "the year of Cyrus-the-Great", as Iranians habitually call it, was, more than anything, a triumph of organisation. Everything went without the slightest hitch. The Iranians, who implemented the plans, ensured that it would be so. Providing security for so many of the world's prominent people was an enormous challenge, but it was taken up successfully. Three security-cordons were thrown around the guests at Persepolis: lodging these in a big hotel certainly made it easier to protect them; and the natural isolation of the camp was also a positive factor. Besides, the presence of so many Communist Heads-of-State, and of Government, tended to deter the subversive groups, which were rampaging around Iran, and other countries. They were hardly going to endanger the lives of those who were controlling them.

Teheran was different. Spectacular attacks, launched while the world's celebrities were there, watched by hundreds of journalists and thousands of tourists, would certainly have had a devastating effect on the regime. They were attempted, but they were thwarted. The first was a scheme to blow up, forty miles from the capital, the high-tension lines carrying electricity from the Amir-Kabir Dam, thus depriving the city of power during the celebrations. Helicopter-surveillance, by General Khosrodad's airborne division, alerted the security-services and the plan was foiled. Three other big explosions were planned - one at the moment of the inauguration of the Teheran Olympic Complex, in the presence of 100 000 spectators (the scale of the casualties may be imagined) and another, at the Memorial of the Kings, whose mighty charge was not defused until ten minutes before it was due to go off. It was the Savak, which managed to stop these attacks in time. The third, on 18th October, was a bomb, big enough to kill any number of passers-by, which was discovered by a night-watchman at the entry to the campus of Teheran University and disarmed in time by a specialist officer of the National Police.

If it had not been for the camp at Persepolis and the banquet by Maxim's – just when specialist publications were studying the refined cuisine, throughout history, of the Imperial Court – and if it had not been for the two hundred waiters from *Potel et Chabot*, which the Imperial Court, and a few of the country's big hotels, could easily have provided, then Iranian opinion would scarcely have been upset by the event, and the objective would have been fully attained. Iran was continuing to celebrate the quality of its elites and the success of its organisation, and attempting to display its achievements.

The French menu for the grand banquet, and the two hundred waiters, flown in by special flight, had been the trees, which hid the wood, a mistake, or worse, an offence, and the way the media handled it aggravated the consequences.

Thirty years later, whenever the revolution of 1978-9 is mentioned, those festivities are re-visited – the tents, the banquet, *Maxim's* menus and those two hundred people hired from *Potel et Chabot* – and nothing else. It's not good faith, but it is good warfare – a disinformation-technique.

How much did the festivities cost? Wildly varying figures,

and often the most fantastic of these, have been quoted. Between twelve million dollars (the amount given, at a press-conference on 24th October 1971, by the Minister to the Imperial Court, Amir Assadollah Alam) and a thousand millions, if not more. If we include the great dams, which were opened, the motorway and its road-houses, the 2 500 rural schools and all the projects, great and small, which contributed to that celebration, like the Central Library of Teheran University and the capital's large, public library, even this figure would be greatly exceeded, but only if we are going to reproach Imperial Iran for her policies of modernisation and development.

Nonetheless, it seems, the bill for the camp and the banquet will have to remain a mystery. Not even the revolutionaries were able to produce documentation on the subject. The Shah took care of everything. Even though he hadn't liked the camp-idea and would have preferred to use conveniently-placed hostelries, he allowed himself to be convinced and regretted it later. Probably – and several people have told me this since – he didn't know about the non-Iranian menu of imported food. This may have been only a detail of the problem, but it was a political error. Still less, they say, did he know about the hiring of catering staff, whom he saw at the reception, apparently with astonishment, for the first time; but the damage was done.

As the year of celebration ended, Mohammad Reza Pahlavi, the man, appeared at his zenith, featuring all the contradictions, which would condition his attitude to the revolution, seven years later. Iran would experience a few euphoric years. The demonstration of his power and the achievement of his ambitions would not only reveal his weaknesses, but stir up anxieties in the region and among his allies. The embryo of the destabilisation of 1978 would come to birth, but the country's leaders, first among them the Shah, paid no attention to it until it was too late. Their awakening was rude and lethal.

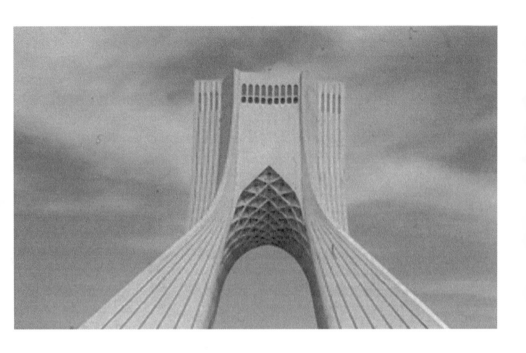

17th October 1971
The opening of the Shahyad, memorial of the kings,
dedicated to Cyrus the Great – a triumphal arch,
nearly 200 feet high
designed by Hossein Amanat.
Below ground level - a museum,
with a floor-space of 87 000 sq ft.,
showing the history of Iran

Part One

T U R M O I L

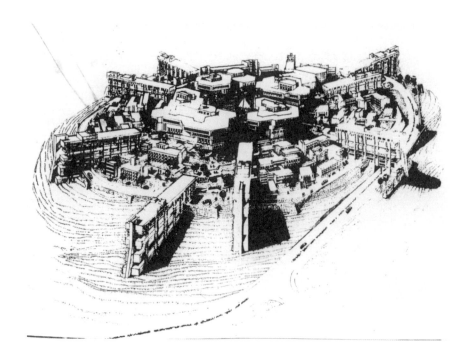

Persepolis in the 20th century: this was the Shah's vision of the
campus of Shiraz University, a scale model of which is shown
here. Much of the project was completed before the Revolution.
(Mr and Mrs Andref's Collection)

Chapter II

*"Iran is an island of stability in one of the
world's most disturbed regions"*

31st December 1977 – 1st January 1978

At 8.00 pm, on 31st December 1977, the Shah and
Shahbanou gave a state-dinner, at the Niavaran Palace,
on the heights to the north of the Iranian capital, for
the President of the United States of America, Jimmy Carter,
and his wife.

The American, presidential couple, accompanied by a prodigious entourage, had arrived in Teheran early that afternoon.

Protocol had demanded a traditional welcome, at Mehrabad
International Airport - with a guard of honour, national
anthems, and the presence of civil and military dignitaries,
including senior members of the diplomatic corps – as for any
state-visit.

At the main entry to Teheran, President Carter was presented
with the Keys to the City, while, all around Shahyad Square,
where the ceremony was taking place, school-children, nume-

rous labourers (sent by their trade-unions) boy-scouts and very large numbers of onlookers – for a great many people had come – showed their enthusiasm and waved miniature American and Iranian flags.

The Shah and the American President then departed, by helicopter, for the palace, where the conversation, just between the two of them, lasted more than three hours. As for the Shahbanou and Mrs Carter, they went to visit the Reza Abassi Museum of Safavid art, a facility, which was not yet completely finished and, on that account, not open to the public.

Apparently, Mrs Carter had mentioned to Ardeshir Zahedi, the Iranian ambassador, at Washington, that she would like to see some Persian miniatures, and it was on his insistence that the American President's wife was taken to this uncompleted site, where, nevertheless, there were hundreds of very fine pieces of that sort. I'm told that the visit was short and quite unconvivial.

Mrs Carter knew nothing of the history of Iran, and even less about Safavid miniatures. Mina Sadegh, Curatress of the Museum, and a perfect English-speaker, did her best to interest Mrs Carter in the collections on view. It would probably have been better if they had taken the "First Lady" to one of Teheran's many hundreds of trinket-shops!

Apart from Franklin D. Roosevelt's attendance, at Teheran in 1943, at the tripartite conference between him, Winston Churchill and Joseph Stalin, Jimmy Carter's visit to Iran was the third, by an American president, to the country. General Eisenhower came to Teheran in December 1959, and Richard Nixon in May 1972.

The peculiar importance of Jimmy Carter's state-visit may

be explained as follows. At that time, Iran was considered, by international public opinion, to be an unconditional ally of the United States. In fact, although the grave crisis of the 'sixties – when John F. Kennedy tried to topple the Shah, in a coup d'État led by the Head of the Savak, General Bakhtiar – was already forgotten, relations between the two countries had, since the beginning of the subsequent decade, continually generated a certain friction.

As early as August 1966, the United States' ambassador to Teheran, Armine Meyer, had notified his government that the Shah was "seeking freedom of movement". Iran had begun, progressively, to diversify its sources of supply for arms and military equipment, not only by approaching other countries in the "free world", but also by concluding important contracts with the Soviet Union. It had even initiated a programme to develop a national armaments-industry, the declared aim of which was to match the level achieved, in this sector, by Israel.

The country's financial resources and, even more so, the skill of Iranian engineers and technicians, were equal to this ambition, and there was nothing illegitimate about it; but the CIA saw it as a sign of "dangerous megalomania", and the Treasury Secretary, William Simon, had gone so far as to refer in public, to the Shah, as "crazy". One wonders whether such epithets as "dangerous megalomaniac" and "crazy" would have been applied to a western, or to an Israeli, leader, for pursuing such a course.

Some other things had also seriously annoyed the United States: the Shah had protested vehemently about the poor quality and excessive cost of certain military equipment provided by the United States; and this had immediately unleashed an anti-Iran campaign in Congress, where the lobby of the armaments-industry has long been powerful, and in certain organs of the press.

The Iranian proposal, that the security of the Persian Gulf and the Indian Ocean should be the responsibility of the countries with coasts on these waters, pre-supposed the withdrawal of American forces from the region. This, and another proposal, which called for the complete de-nuclearisation of the zone, and was aimed, of course, at Israel, succeeded in irritating, and even worrying, Washington as well as Tel Aviv.

The Yom Kippur War, in October 1973, also contributed to a deterioration in the climate of confidence between the two countries. Some months before the Syrians and Egyptians launched that operation – the only military action, by the Arabs, in their long confrontation with Israel, which ever met with any success – President Sadat broke his journey, from Karachi to Cairo, with a stopover in Teheran. Mohammad Reza Pahlavi, who was in the provinces, interrupted his tour and went to Teheran International Airport, where the two men were alone in conversation for more than three hours.

No particular reason could be found to explain this unscheduled meeting, and none was given. Had the Rais, perhaps, confided his plans to the Shah, on that occasion? Later, this would be considered a certainty, and the Sovereign would be blamed for failing to alert Washington.

Israel was a friend and ally of Iran, which angered certain Arab countries; but Iranian diplomacy did not, on this account, lend any less support to the cause of Palestinian nationalism, although it did condemn outright the acts of terrorism committed, in the name of that cause, by radical groups.

Besides, Iran was one of the victims of such acts, if for different reasons.

During the months preceding the Yom Kippur War, the Shah was often heard to refer to the need for a "balanced peace", between Arabs and Israelis, which would begin between Egypt, the natural leader of the Arab camp, and the Hebrew State.

"To achieve this," he used to say, "it is necessary that the Arabs modify their view of themselves as permanently humiliated losers and recover their sense of honour."

On the eve of the Egyptian attack, which was to be a complete surprise for the Israelis and the Americans – hence its early success - Anwar El Sadat went to Teheran to meet Mohammad Reza Pahlavi. This journey was meant to be totally secret, but, as now seems probable, the American and Israeli intelligence-services may have got wind of it.

The two men had a long conversation at the Shah's summer palace, Saad-Abad. It was the ambassador, Aslan Afshar, being then in the capital, where he had no official function, who went to collect the Rais from the airport.

What did they say to each other? No-one knows whether they talked about the imminent attack on Israel, or whether Sadat sought to secure the Shah's support, although one might suppose so; for, as soon as the Egyptian attack was launched, the Shah authorised the passage of Soviet heavy-transport aircraft through Iranian air-space, in order to bring munitions to Cairo, and ignored Washington's, and Tel Aviv's, protests on this score. Then, he granted emergency aid of a thousand million dollars to Egypt. Iran thus played an important part in the Egyptians' semi-success, which Arab public-opinion pronounced a victory and the first ever achieved against the Hebrew State and its shielding allies, the Americans. Thus, the conditions for a "balanced peace" with honour were met and led to the Treaty of Camp David, in the preparation of which document, with the utmost discretion, Mohammad Reza Pahlavi and his emissaries played an active part.

The agreement concluded at Algiers, in 1975, between Iran and Iraq, put an end to decades of tension between the two countries, and the rigour with which both parties subsequently honoured it, in the letter and in the spirit, might well have provided another reason for some to look askance at the Shah. Both the United States and the USSR had thereby lost a pretext to intrude into the affairs of the region. Israel, what's more - as soon as her Iranian ally seemed to be about to let her down - imagined all the might of the Iraqi army swinging round to attack the Hebrew State.

Iran and its Sovereign were never forgiven for taking these initiatives: people were quick to think that the Shah could, and should, have alerted the Americans, and that he had failed to do so. They decided that Iran should not have opened its airspace to Soviet aircraft, nor given emergency-aid to Egypt. In addition to this, the Americans were suspicious of the Shah, simply because his initiatives gave rise to extreme sensitivity in relations between Teheran and Tel Aviv. When the Islamic Revolution began, Israel failed to support Iran; and only General Rabin – a national hero, former and future Prime Minister, great visionary that he was – vigorously but in vain, opposed this failure, which he judged to be suicidal. As for President Sadat, he was an honourable man, who never forgot the loyalty of Mohammad Reza Pahlavi.

Iran's attitude during the Oil Crisis and its confrontation

with the oil-multinationals, which – with the backing of King Faisal of Saudi Arabia, before he was assassinated in 1975 – the Shah undertook, also helped to range against him those influential, American elements, which are linked together by certain think-tanks and pressure-groups, and which play a decisive role in determining the policy of the United States.

Influential Democrats, such as the senators, Edward Kennedy and Frank Church, as well as that guru of American diplomacy, George Ball, and Republicans – who were supposedly closer to the Shah – like William Simon, James Schlesinger and, before long, Donald Rumsfeld, waged, from then on, a high-profile campaign against "the ambitions of Iran". Henry Kissinger, himself, who was thought to be a personal friend of the Imperial Family, and who behaved as such during the Sovereign's exile, expressed the same opinion, saying, in 1974, to members of the American National Security Council:

"Some of us think that the Shah ought to change his policy, or have it changed for him."

He was received, in November of that same year – with every mark of respect and exceptional sympathy - in a three-day visit to Teheran. Did the Shah know then about those ambivalent stances of Kissinger's, which someone's indiscretions would expose during the 'eighties? It seems unlikely, despite the Shah's information-network in the United States.

Collating all the reliable studies published in recent years, both in Europe and the United States, indicates that the irreversible decision, to begin the process of destabilising Iran, was taken in 1977. That's when thinking turned into action, but the sources of ill feeling and active disapproval had continued to swell in the interim.

As much during the election-campaign, as after their

coming to power, President Jimmy Carter and his circle scarcely bothered to conceal their aversion to the Imperial regime, whose opponents of every stripe they openly encouraged and financed, so that the climate of relations between the two countries became decidedly oppressive.

The efforts of Ardeshir Zahedi, Iran's ambassador to Washington - who was much liked by everyone there for his friendly nature, his sumptuous receptions and gifts – two semi-official visits to America by the Shahbanou – who had a long, private interview with Jimmy Carter at the White House – and the appointment, shortly before, as the Head of the Iranian Government, of Djamchid Amouzegar – an honest, if unimaginative, technocrat and hard worker, who, it was said, met with the approval of American Democrats – alleviated this atmosphere slightly.

Mohammad Reza Pahlavi should not have been taken in by this, however. Even though this alleviation of the diplomatic atmosphere led, in November 1977, to a state-visit to the United States, by the Imperial Couple, its results were, on the whole, bad.

This visit made a big impression on the Sovereign, but he did not realise, at the time, what political consequences it would impose.

Some weeks before his death, while I was visiting him in Cairo, he referred to it at some length, and with annoyance, tinged with sadness. On the eve of their official arrival in Washington, the Imperial Couple stopped for the night at Williamsburg, where some five hundred, Iranian students had gathered to demonstrate their loyalty to the Shah. As was his custom, the Sovereign was going to speak with them. At a distance, there was another group of people wearing masks, "for fear of the Savak", as they claimed, but none of them spoke Farsee – which prompts the assumption that they were not Iranian. Waving the red flag, with its hammer and sickle emblem, these people shouted insults at the Shah. It was a small group of protesters, but it was they – and not the others – who became the focus of all the press and television reports. The following day, the news was full of the tale that several hundreds of people had mounted a demonstration hostile to the Shah.

On that day, 16th November, several thousands of Iranians arrived, from all over America – many bringing their families – to assemble near the White House and show their sympathy for the Shah. The police kept them as far away as possible, but allowed a small number of opponents to approach the railings of the Presidential Palace, close to where the Sovereign's helicopter was going to land for the official welcome. At the exact moment, when courtesies were being exchanged on the White House lawn, these people produced sticks and bicycle chains and set upon the others. The police fired tear-gas grenades into the crowd. Thus, the whole world was able to watch riotous scenes, on television, as an accompaniment to the arrival of the Imperial Couple. The Shah, meanwhile, was genuinely moved by the welcoming words of President Carter, who seemed to feel likewise. Recalling this episode, Mohammad Reza Pahlavi said to me, " it was choreographed like a Hollywood film, in order to misinform the public."

According to the press, the conversation between the two Heads of State took place in a pleasant atmosphere, and the Shah impressed the American President, on this their first meeting, with his homilies about geopolitical problems. The following state-dinner was luxury itself, and the table-talk made, by the tenant of the White House, was complimentary to the guest of the moment, to the point of eulogy, but this did not prevent an official of the State Department from declaring, on the same day, "if the Shah thinks he's going to get everything he wants in the way of munitions, he's got another think coming."

That's American diplomacy for you!

All the same, at the close of the Sovereigns' official stay, President and Mrs Carter agreed to pay a state-visit to Iran, where they eventually arrived on 31st December 1977.

By order of His Imperial Majesty the Shahinshah Aryamehr
And
Of Her Imperial Majesty the Shahbanou of Iran
In honour of His Excellency
The President of the United States of America
Mister, and Mistress, Jimmy Carter

The Grand Master of Imperial Protocol
Begs ...
To be so good as to attend for dinner on 31st December 1977
At eight-o-clock in the evening
Dress: dark suit – long gown
At the Niavaran Palace

Such was the wording of the invitation, to attend the state-dinner, which was received by more than 120 prospective guests.

The Niavaran Palace, standing in extensive grounds to the north of the Iranian capital, was, after a fashion, the winter-residence of the Imperial Couple and their children. It had three main buildings and several smaller ones. The most prominent of the three, larger houses had been built a hundred years before by King Qadjar Naser-El-Dine Shah, who, however, had spent little time there. The entire first floor was given over to the Shah's office – a huge suite, in the form of a cross, with breathtaking views - to the south, of Teheran, and, to the north, of the Elbrouz mountains – which also housed the administrative machinery of the Protocol Service, numerous waiting-rooms, the offices of the Minister to the Court, and the Grand Master of Protocol, and rooms occupied by various civilian, and military, aides-de-camp ...

When she became the Shahbanou, Farah Diba had the ground floor renovated, in the Qadjarian style, under the direction of interior decoratrix, Manijeh Torfeh. The result was an array of interconnecting, small salons, hung with Persian miniatures and XIXth century paintings. These rooms were used, from time to time, for private receptions. The film-maker, Abbas Kiarostami, made a documentary about the progress of this notable, architectural restoration, which was shown recently in Paris for the Iranian community there.

A small, single-storey house, which was built by the last of the Qadjar Sovereigns, Ahmad Shah, as a kind of folly, had been, for a number of years, the residence of the Crown Prince.

The building, where the reception took place, had been built in the early 'sixties. It was the work of the architect, Abdol-Aziz Farmanfarmayan – himself a Qadjar prince. The international media had often presented it as a "palace of one thousand and one nights". They had even equipped it with a heli-pad on the roof!

In fact, it was a big, detached house, of a kind very common in the west, which many American and European millionaires, or Hollywood stars, would have thought too small; but the

Shah had always opposed the idea of building a great Imperial palace at Farah-Abad - whose name, by the way, was that of the 19th century park, and had nothing to do with the Shahbanou – because he thought the expense superfluous.

"Our prestige," he once said, "is not to be seen in palaces, but in Iran's indispensable projects."

This "palace of a thousand and one nights" was arranged around a great hall, on the ground floor. Radiating from this were a reception-room, a small dining-room, another dining-room – for official dinners seating up to 140 guests – and a small sitting-room.

The only real luxuries were a cinema, of somewhat modest dimensions, and a very large and beautiful private library, which the Shahbanou had added later.

The two upper floors, both arranged, similarly, around the great hall – which extended to the full height of the building – consisted of the family's private apartments. The Shah and Shahbanou each had an office there. The roof of the hall could be opened, which was the building's only idiosyncrasy, but it was never used. The heli-port, with room for two machines, was in the northern corner of the palace gardens.

The protocol for state-dinners was fairly strict. Members of the Imperial Family were invited, together with ministers and military chiefs, accompanied by their wives, or husbands – for there had been female ministers since the 'sixties - and court-dignitaries. According to the guest of honour, some foreign diplomats and two or three, other, Iranian personalities would be added to the list. The principal members of the delegation, accompanying the visiting Head-of-State, would also be invited, of course.

For President and Mrs Carter, these arrangements had been changed. On the suggestion of the Shahbanou, there would be no members of the Imperial Family present, the number of ministers and military chiefs would be cut down and the order was given, most particularly, not to invite General Nassiri, Head of the Savak. To compensate for this, invitations would be sent to well-known intellectuals and academics, including a famous cinematographer, who was considered to be a rebel even though he was on good terms with the regime, two conductors and the head of the armaments-industry. The idea was to provide company, which was more representative of civil society.

The great swarm of journalists, which followed the American President, had all been invited to an alternative dinner at a grand hotel in the capital – all, that is, with the notable exception of Pierre Salinger, John F. Kennedy's former spokesman, who would later publish a detailed account of the state-dinner, in a newspaper of record.

All of the other guests arrived before the guests-of-honour. Champagne, whisky, fruit-juices and canapés, with salmon or caviar, were served in the entrance-hall, and the mood was jolly, if not joyful. On the contrary to what the great, international press wrote about it, the waiters were not dressed in livery, nor sporting wigs, nor were the Iranian dignitaries wearing "gold-encrusted uniforms, under constellations of medals". The gentlemen wore dark town-clothes – with which decorations are never worn – as the photographs of the banquet amply testify.

At exactly eight-o-clock, the Iranian Sovereigns, the American presidential couple, Prime Minister Djamchid Amouzegar, with his wife, and the Minister to the Imperial

Court, Amir Abbas Hoveyda, betook themselves to the salon for the presentation of the guests to Mr and Mrs Carter. Protocol had been modified at this point also: usually, the Shah presented Iranian prominenti, by stating their functions, and their wives, by simply adding "Mrs". This time, he introduced each person by name, frequently adding a short comment designed to amuse and put at ease. If some guest, who was not a member of the regime, was unknown to him, the Shahbanou, beside him, or the Grand Master of Protocol, to his rear, whispered the appropriate appellation.

When, for example, it was my turn, the Shah, who evidently recognised me, said to the President, "... he's the head of a group, which is studying the country's problems – leader of those intellectuals who are queuing up to harass me," which was a bit rich; but it made everybody laugh. Pierre Salinger did not have to be presented, because he was accompanying the President. Of him, the Shah said, "I read Mr Salinger every week, in the *Express*; so I know a great deal about what's going on in the United States."

About Admiral Ardalan, head of the armaments-industry, he added the remark that the Admiral was "a scientist, and not just a soldier, who has a doctorate in technology from a great, American university."

Once presented, the guests found their places in the great dining-room and remained standing, behind their chairs, waiting for the Sovereigns and the Carters and admiring the table's pretty, floral decorations. The napkins were embroidered. The table-ware was Limoges porcelain. The glasses were Baccarat crystal.

A little before nine-o-clock, everyone sat down and the meal could begin. A menu was placed before each guest. It was written in French and Farsee.

It appears that the American officers of protocol had expressed astonishment and had protested, because the menu was not in English, both of the languages used being equally foreign to the guest-of-honour. They were told that it had been traditional at court, since the 19th century, for French to be the only foreign language officially in use.

We began with a variety of Iranian hors-d'oeuvres, notably, fine, imperial caviar-pearls; then there were kebabs, Iranian-style rice, garnished with partridges, and some salads. Next, the lights were lowered a little, and a procession of waiters entered bearing the glaces-flambées. The banquet ended with a fruit-salad. The courses were accompanied, respectively, by Iranian vodka, a Château-Talbot 1972 and Dom-Pérignon.

Throughout the dinner, a small orchestra, installed along-side, played short pieces from Verdi, Chopin, Mozart, Bernstein and the Iranian composer, Hechmat Sandjari.

After we had eaten, it was time for the speeches, which would transform the occasion at once into an event to make the world's chancelleries and press-offices hum. No text had been distributed beforehand, because Mohammad Reza Pahlavi was going to speak in English, which nearly all the Iranian guests understood - so it didn't seem necessary – and the Americans hardly needed it.

The Shah's speech was conventional: he referred to the history of relations between the two countries and the "unfor-gettable" role played by the United States in sustaining Iran through certain, great crises of the past. Then he praised "the special qualities of the great, American nation, which was held always in high regard, particularly for its love of liberty and its humanitarian sentiments."

At one point, he adopted an almost sentimental tone: "in our country, according to ancient tradition, the visit of the first guest of the new year is an omen for the rest of the year; and, as surely as the new year rejoices invariably in the coming of spring, our guest this evening is a person whose good will and action presage excellent fortune for the coming months."

Then he raised his glass and invited all present to drink to the prosperity of the United States, to friendship between the two countries and to the health of the President and Mrs Carter. Everyone rose, made the appropriate gesture and applauded. Then the orchestra played the American national anthem.

At first, Jimmy Carter's reply was just as conventional. The length of his visit to Teheran was supposed to be less than twelve hours, and he had expected to be gone before midnight, to celebrate the new year aboard the presidential aircraft, "Air Force One". This "minimal" programme had also been announced to the public. The opposition to the Shah, which, ever after, would be encouraged, largely and overtly, by the US-embassy, took this as an opportunity to spread the word that the brevity of the visit was its essential feature and proof of the Americans' disavowal of the Sovereign. During the cocktail-party which preceded the dinner, the Americans present had expressed the same sentiment, in muted tones: one of them said to me, "the shortness of this visit, and the fact that the President will not be spending the night in Teheran, are a matter of regret, but he's already forcing himself."

This, translated from the language of diplomacy, meant that Carter wanted to make as little of the visit as possible. All the members of the American delegation thought they knew that the President's speech would be succinct and would not express any support for the Shah.

Indeed, that was how Jimmy Carter's reply began. In his familiar, flat, monotonous voice, he reviewed Irano-American relations and – with reference to humanitarianism and human rights - mentioned the great, Iranian poet, Saadi. It was neat, professional and designed not to displease the Iranian opposition; but, all of a sudden, his tone changed.

"Iran," he said, "owes its existence as an island of peace and stability, in one of the world's most troubled regions, to the Shah's great qualities as a leader, and this bears witness, Your Majesty, to Your abilities as a Head-of-State and to the respect and admiration accorded You by Your people."

The President went on to say, "it is important to us to have the benefit of the sureness of Your judgement and the sagacity of Your counsel," and he affirmed as follows: "No other country in the world is closer to ours in the matter of assuring our military security; there is no other country with which we are having closer consultations about the regional problems before us; and there is no other leader, towards whom I feel deeper gratitude or greater personal affection."

In conclusion, President Carter, in his role as self-proclaimed defender of human rights, even paid resounding tribute to the efforts, made by Iran and her Sovereign, to strengthen democracy in the country and make human rights respected there. Then, in his turn, he raised the toast to the prosperity of Iran and of her Shah and Shahbanou. Everyone rose, applauding, and the orchestra played the Imperial anthem.

Progressively, as President Carter enunciated these final paragraphs, expressions of surprise and amazement appeared on the faces of the American officials, as all the trans-Atlantic commentators would subsequently affirm. Even the few western diplomats present could not conceal the shock. As for the Shah, his usually impassive features were softened by a barely perceptible smile of amused satisfaction.

After the Iranian, national anthem had been played, Jimmy Carter took the Shah's hand in both of his and shook it warmly. The Shah now beamed without restraint. No other Head-of-State – and certainly no other American President – had ever shown him such cordiality, or (why not say it?) such flattery!

Following the dinner, the guests were ushered into the theatre, which opened on the palace' entrance-hall, for a programme of traditional, Iranian songs and dances, performed by Ministry of Culture's troupe of artists. Everyone was gay and admiring. Then came the evening's latest surprise: it was announced that President and Mrs Carter had decided to stay longer and spend the night of New Year's Eve in Teheran.

The decision had been taken just before dinner, and, in two hours, the private library had been re-arranged for a party, and a number of young couples, of the Shahbabou's entourage, had been brought in – all more-or-less dressed to go to the city's New Year parties, of which there were a great many – to brighten the atmosphere.

As soon as the performance, in the theatre, finished – and it was then a quarter past eleven – the waiters re-appeared, everyone was served with champagne and, on the stroke of midnight, a toast was drunk to the New Year. The Shah hugged Rossalyn Carter, and the American President hugged the Shahbanou. The Shah led Mrs Carter on to the dance-floor, although he was, as always, somewhat reserved, and the President led out the Shahbanou. Numerous pictures were taken by American and Iranian photographers. Then the Shah and the President slipped away. An hour-and-a-half later, the company was going to get the third surprise of the evening.

Protocol normally required that the revellers could not depart until after the guest of honour and the Imperial Couple retired, but officers of protocol fanned out among the guests to let them know, discreetly, that, although Their Majesties were happy for them to stay, the official party was over, and that the guests should feel free to leave the palace – which many of them, notably including the Prime Minister and his wife, and the Minister to the Imperial Court, duly did. Most of the non-governmental people stayed, however, and it is to some of these that I owe the story of what followed, for my wife and I slipped away also.

A little after half-past-one in the morning, the Shah and President Carter re-appeared, accompanied by King Hussein of Jordan! The Shah had kept the Jordanian Sovereign's presence in Teheran (he was a frequent visitor, it is true, to the Iranian capital) as a surprise for the American President, and this had apparently made quite an impression on Jimmy Carter.

Ever since the signing of the Treaty of Camp David, and the establishment of the peaceful relations, which the Shah had favoured, between Israel and Egypt, Carter had made every effort, in his desired role as peacemaker of the region, to bring about an accord between the Hebrew State and Jordan. This meeting, as everyone quickly realised, should be seen in that context.

The appearance of the two Kings and the President was warmly applauded by the remaining company, and then dancing, drinking and nibbling petit-fours continued. Eventually, the presidential couple, King Hussein and the Iranian Sovereigns retired, followed by all the remainder of the guests.

The Carters had to resume their journey, in order to arrive in New Delhi by the end of the morning; and so, after a short rest, they left for Teheran International Airport, at 6.00 am. Naturally, the streets of the capital were almost deserted. The schools, offices and places-of-business, in general, would not start to open until after eight-o-clock, and, consequently, there were very few police about. Besides, no-one – or almost no-one – knew when the American delegation would set out. Many, great, western newspapers wrote, nevertheless, on the following day, that the official cortege passed through parts of Teheran, which were "all locked up and emptied of people, by order of the Savak"!

President Carter's visit was supposed to have been shorter, by several hours. He was not supposed to stay the night in Teheran nor, above all, express any political support for the Shah – all the observers wrote so at the time, and have said so since. The occasion had become a considerable triumph for the Iranian Sovereign.

The commentators wrote that Jimmy Carter's courteous and friendly words (but was it not rather a matter of an exceptional and earnest tribute?) were intended "to prove to the Shah that a Democrat President could be just as firm a friend as a Republican President", but how convincing is this? The alternation of parties does not change the diplomatic orientation of the United States that much. The process of toppling the Shah had been envisaged and initiated in 1974, under a Republican administration. We know this now for certain. Numerous, published documents and studies bear witness to the fact, even if it was not until the beginning of the Carter administration that the decision was made to take concerted action by evoking problems related to human rights. Another explanation seems much more plausible. When he arrived in Teheran, Jimmy Carter had no intention of staying longer than the few hours required by the barest courtesy, but, in those few hours, the politically more experienced Shah – a greater master of international diplomacy – won him over and changed his mind. Carter then went over the heads of his advisers, all of whom were openly against the Shah, added those celebrated phrases to his speech – to the visible astonishment of the American diplomats present – and decided to prolong his stay.

It was only a temporary stay-of-execution, however. It would have been invaluable, if all had been well with the country's internal politics, or if the momentum of those politics had not provided the opportunity for destabilisation launched from without.

Indeed, the lustre of that evening, which seemed so idyllic at the time, was dimmed and tarnished only three days later.

An embargo had been placed, on the publication in the local press, of photos of the evening's dancing. Instead, Carter's speech, which had so perplexed the political opposition, was exploited to the full. The photographs, nevertheless, circulated throughout Iran, and especially in Qom, whence the Grand Ayatollah Shariat-Madari – first in Iran's Shiite hierarchy and the figurehead of a movement-for-change, which was gathering pace (Khomeyni had not then emerged from obscurity) telephoned me to vent his extreme displeasure and to protest about the photos, which showed "his cousin" – the Shahbanou being a "sayed", that is, a descendant, like the Grand Ayatollah, of the Prophet Mohammed – dancing with President Carter.

"It's not up to me," he said, "to tell her what she may, or

may not, do; but one should, at least, consider appearances, respect conventions and refrain from shocking Muslim public opinion."

Naturally, I passed on the message, Shariat-Madari being too important a person - playing an ever more essential role – to be ignored, but the lady in question did not give me the impression that she appreciated his admonition. Meanwhile, the photos continued to appear everywhere and were exploited without compunction.

Less than a week later, the real trouble began.

Chapter III

"The caravan passes and the dogs bark"

January 1978 to June 1978

In the days following the departure of the American President, the Iranian capital's political microcosm was divided between those, who appreciated the thought that the Imperial power had been considerably reinforced, and those, of the opposition, who evidently felt thwarted and let down.

On 8th January, an event occurred, which I look back on today as the detonator – the actual origin of the revolutionary process.

Teheran's, great evening-newspaper, *Ettela'at*, published an article over the name of "Rachidi Motlagh" – a pseudonym, which would soon set everybody wondering – all about the Ayatollah Rouhollah Khomeyni, who had been in exile in Iraq ever since he took part in the agitation of 1963, against the two mainstays of the "white revolution", agrarian reform and female emancipation.

Indeed, for some weeks, pamphlets and tapes from Najjaf, where the Ayatollah lived – and whose tone was pugnacious, if not insulting, towards the Monarch - had been appearing in certain circles in Teheran and Qom; but the chief spokesman, and head, of the politico-religious movement for regime-change in Iran, was still the prelate of Qom – the Grand Ayatollah Shariat-Madari. Khomeyni was then almost unknown to, or practically forgotten by, the wider public. This article, which portrayed Khomeyni as a major figure, was a maladroit absurdity, and, in the hours following its publication, hardly anyone seemed to notice it, but certain people must have been astonished to see it in print.

What did it say about Rouhollah Khomeyni? It said that he came originally from India, which was quite true, that his wife had been a street-dancer, which was false (she was the irreproachable child of an honourable, middle-class family) that he was an ignoramus, which Iranians, and everyone else, would soon see for themselves, and that, in his youth, he had evinced the morals of a catamite, which was unverifiable and, anyway, a private matter. In short, it was mixture of truth and lies. The article also accused Rouhollah Khomeyni of being, or of having been, an agent of foreign intelligence-services.

Indeed, he had belonged to the entourage of a cleric called Sayed Abolghassem Kachani, who was a confidant of the British and opposed to the nationalist chief, Mossadegh, and who, later on, during the rule of Colonel Nasser, received funds from the Egyptian secret service, to undermine the Shah. Kachani was certainly no stranger to intrigue and manipulation. Moreover, according to sources recorded at the independent, "Centre Européen d'Information" (CEI) the relationship between Kachani's circle and East Germany had ceased to be a mystery during the early 'seventies, and some specialised publications, in the West, had mentioned it before that.

The CIA learned of it, in 1961, from Colonel Goleniewski, the second-in-command of Soviet counter-espionage in Poland, who defected to the West on 25th December 1960: a CIA-report from that period, declassified in 2000, and obtained from the CEI, tells us that "Ayatollah Khomeyni was one of Moscow's five sources of intelligence at the heart of the Shiite hierarchy." Almost certainly, this information was never communicated to the Iranians. On the contrary, the Americans may have used it themselves, in 1978, to control Khomeyni.

Colonel Goleniewski's defection resulted in the unmasking, by the western powers, of several dozen Soviet agents, some of them very highly placed, and, in recognition of his services, the US-Congress took the unusual step of granting him American citizenship. A large number of studies have been written about him, since then, both in English and in French.

Accusations, relating to Khomeyni's relations with various other secret services, rely on more fragmentary evidence, but they are not, on that account, to be regarded as untrue. The point, however, is that the publication of the article in question, on 8th January 1978, made the grave error of exhibiting Khomeyni – an intelligence asset both of the East and of the West - as the regime's principal target.

It seems to have been smuggled into, if not imposed upon, the newspaper, which printed it: twenty-two years later, questions are still being asked about this in the many works, which continue to appear, about the Shah and the Iranian revolution. However, detailed enquiries, with many corroborations, now make it possible to explain how it happened.

The idea was suggested to the Shah by Amir Abbas Hoveyda, Minister to the Imperial Court, while Mohammad Reza Pahlavi was being harassed by propaganda issuing from the exiled cleric. He must have said something like, "why not retaliate by revealing Khomeyni's true past and character?"

"Why not, indeed!" would have been the reply.

This response was taken to be an agreement and then transformed into a command. The composition of the article was entrusted to a well-known journalist, who now lives abroad under cover, without giving him any accurate data to work on. Consequently, he merely repeated what everyone knew, adding various malevolent rumours, and sent the article to Hoveyda, who passed it to the Minister for Information, Darioush Homayoun, with the "command" to get it published in a prominent journal.

Homayoun acknowledges having received it, and having seen it, but denies having read it before it was published. He was more concerned about finding a newspaper to place it in: the two main morning-dailies were out of the question. The principal one, *Ayandegan*, had been founded, and was edited, by Homayoun himself. A talented journalist, when appointed Information Minister, he continued, in reality, as editor, publishing unsigned editorials, which were easily recognisable as his. Thus, to have published the article in *Ayandegan* would have been to proclaim its importance in an official manner. The other main morning paper, *Rastakhiz*, was the organ of the political party, which had been formed a few years before, on the initiative of the Shah. It was unsuitable for the same reason.

The choice, therefore, was between the two main evening dailies. *Keyhan* was edited by Senator Mesbah-Zadeh – an influential character, who had access to Prime Minister

Amouzegar, and to the Sovereign, and who would have been able to persuade the Shah to annul the "order", which had, in fact, never been given. This left *Ettela'at*, a prestigious journal, founded fifty years before by the Massoudi family, and which had been edited, until his recent death, by the mighty Abbas Massoudi, First Vice-President of the Senate.

Since his demise, his chain of papers had been directed by his son, Farhad, who did not wield great influence or political experience, and upon whom Hoveyda, while he was Prime Minister, had even succeeded in imposing a chief editor, who would comply with his own wishes.

Farhad Massoudi held out for forty-eight hours, by which time the Savak got wind of the matter, its chief, General Nassiri, having been given to understand that an order had been issued. Restricted in his capacity, Nassiri did not enquire further. He was there to take orders, not give advice. Of course, he could seek to verify orders coming from the Prime Minister, who was theoretically his direct superior, or even check with the Shah; but he didn't – even though his deputy, Parviz Sabeti, who was responsible for internal security, was highly critical of the article, which he adjudged "counter-productive and mis-timed". No-one took any notice. The young Massoudi tried to contact the Sovereign, but didn't manage it and gave up; and so, on 8th January, the article appeared. The Prime Minister, who knew nothing about the matter, and the Shah, who had not read the text in advance, only found out what the article said, after it had been printed and circulated throughout the country.

The launching of Rouhollah Khomeyni had begun, and it is hard to accept that Amir Abbas Hoveyda, an intelligent man and no servant of foreign powers, had begun it himself. It cannot be ruled out that he was manipulated by members of his staff, or that he acted thoughtlessly, but he loved this kind of intrigue, often having articles or pieces of gossip published, in this or that journal, in order to discomfit political adversaries or potential competitors. Chodja-Ol-Dine, the Shah's cultural counsellor, wrote to me recently, saying that this episode turned into a provocation, because it was a "banana-skin". He was not wrong.

Besieged by negative reactions, after the article's publication, Mohammad Reza Pahlavi, unconsciously or not, took responsibility, as was his habit. However, when, a few months later, under the military government, he had Hoveyda imprisoned – albeit for a grave infraction – he may have been exacting payment for the affair of this article, as well as for later offences.

The city of Qom - the Mullah's main training-centre, where theology-students attend Koran-schools (some of them modernised) rather than western-style universities - has always been a hotbed of agitation; and it was here that the demonstrations began, as soon as the article had been read. The first serious incident, the following day, was on a trifling scale, but the police, in attempting to disperse the crowd with inadequate resources, injured some of the demonstrators - one of them so badly that he later died.

Three of the Shiite world-community's most important leaders lived, at that time, in Qom. The international press called them "the triumvirate of Qom". Pre-eminent among them was the powerful and influential Grand Ayatollah Shariat-Madari, who had become the head of the Iranian, popular movement, and remained so until just before the return of Khomeyni.

The top of the Shiite hierarchy was, nevertheless, deeply divided, as it had always been - ever since 1502, in fact, when this minority-branch of Islam was proclaimed, for strictly political reasons, the state-religion – but, as ancient tradition demanded, faced with what they considered to be a slur on a key-cleric, the clergy now closed ranks.

Ayatollah Shariat-Madari knew Khomeyni very well and despised him, but this did not stop him demanding that, in order to promote reconciliation and head off rising agitation, the government should make its excuses or, at least, express its regrets. The response was clumsy. Very probably with the Shah's approval, a reply was issued to the effect that the press was free, the authorities had no part in the publication of the article, and there was, therefore, no need for an apology. This was just not credible.

Unrest was very limited and localised, and the government had two choices: either it could react firmly – start arresting people en masse and nip insurgency in the bud – or it could go along with Ayatollah Shariat-Madari and take the path of appeasement. In the event, thinking that time was on its side, it chose neither of these. Another mistake! The underground forces, which were going to organise the destabilisation of the regime and the fall of the Shah, were already at work, and the government's hesitation was going to be *their* trump-card. A calm *did* follow the demonstrations at Qom, but it was going to be temporary.

The authorities then decided to take the initiative at grass-roots level and, through Rastakhiz – the sole political party – organise a big demonstration, on 26th January, at Tabriz, the capital of Azerbaidjan and Ayatollah Shariat-Madari's birth-place. This was agitation on a considerable scale, bringing together three hundred thousand people in the great square at Tabriz, before a platform, set up outside the City Hall, where the Prime Minister, Djamchid Amouzegar, the General Secretary of the Party and numerous prominenti would address them. The Head of Government gave a very rousing speech – a bit too rousing, perhaps – and the Sovereign's name was warmly acclaimed. Enthusiasm was at its height, when the poorly and all-too-rapidly constructed platform partially collapsed. No-one was hurt, even slightly, but the superstitious crowd naturally saw in the occurrence, *a sign!*

Confronted with this show of popular force in favour of the government, the clerics adopted the tactic of the "quarantaine". According to Muslim custom, every death is commemorated with a religious ceremony, forty days after the decease. Ayatollah Shariat-Madari therefore invited his compatriots to celebrate the fortieth day after the death of the victim of the demonstration at Qom, and a gathering took place at Tabriz on 18th February. On the eve of the ceremony, by order of the provincial authorities, the mosque, where the obsequies were due to take place, was closed. The following morning, some hours before the crowd was expected to muster, the Chief-of-Police in Tabriz received a phone-call from General Nassiri, Head of the Savak, ordering him to re-open the mosque. To this, the local Police-Chief replied, very respectfully, firstly, that he could only take orders from his direct superior, the National Chief-of-Police – and not from the Savak - and secondly, that to countermand a written order, he had to have a written counter-order.

It was a matter of rivalry between the two police-forces. Evidently, the counter-order, permitting the re-opening of the great mosque, arrived too late: General Nassiri had to ask the Prime Minister, who felt it prudent to refer the matter to the Shah, and, while time was lost in hesitation, demonstrators and police clashed outside the mosque. The headquarters of Rastakhiz, which were almost unprotected, were taken by storm and sacked. A bloody riot ensued. The police, who were ill-equipped for crowd-control, were obliged to use weapons, wounding many and killing some. The cruel spiral of protest and repression had begun and led straight to revolution.

The strictly ordered life of the Shah and his Court continued undeviatingly. No-one at the top of the state-hierarchy apprehended the extent of the crisis. It was thought that the incidents were minor. Everything continued as though nothing was happening. Mohammad Reza Pahlavi, who was not then affected at all by the symptoms of the disease, which would soon carry him off, followed his extremely precise programme. He rose early; he took ten minutes exercise in his room; then he scanned the Iranian and international press – the *New York Times*, the *Washington Post*, *Le Monde*, *Le Figaro*, *The Times*, *L'Express*, *Newsweek* and *Time Magazine* – and reports from the security services.

At exactly ten-o-clock, he went to his office, where he at once received the Grand Master of Imperial Protocol, in order to discuss his schedule and sort out a few diplomatic matters – usually to do with official visits. A few months before, the Sovereign had re-organised the Diplomatic Service, whose head, the much criticised, former ambassador to Japan, Hormoz Gharib, had then been replaced in the traditional manner (from the ranks of senior diplomats) by Amir Aslan Afshar. Afshar had been ambassador to Washington, Bonn and Vienna, and then kept for a while in reserve. He had a solid reputation for probity, sincerity and rectitude, and his appointment was widely welcomed. He proceeded to re-shape Imperial Protocol and quickly rooted out certain abuses.

After the Grand Master of Imperial Protocol, it was the turn of the Minister to the Imperial Court – at this time, Amir Abbas Hoveyda – who dealt with various matters in his sphere of competence, in consultation with the Shah; after which it the audiences began.

These lasted about thirty minutes each – some a little more, some a little less – according to their importance. The last hour of the Shah's morning was always spent with the Minister for Foreign Affairs or, if he was away on one of his frequent trips, with his first deputy. It was, by then, about a-quarter-past-one, whereupon the Shah returned to his residence to lunch with the Shahbanou. However, if she was late (she was much less organised than he was) he would eat without waiting for her.

It was always a light meal, because, although the Shah was a lover of good food, he only ate sparingly and hardly ever drank. After lunch, he lay down for a while on a sofa and listened to classical, or mood-, music, before returning, at three, to his office, to give further audiences, until half-past-six or seven-o-clock. As a rule, he dined between eight and eight-thirty, after which – if he had no official or private reception to attend – his favourite relaxation consisted of watching adventure-films, historical dramas or comedies. This routine was often upset by receptions, political crises or travelling, which left him little time to devote to sport, except at the weekends, or when playing with the children.

Curiously, the chain of events, which would change the fate of the Imperial Family and the country, had no effect on the schedule and habits of the Court, until September. The

Shah did lots of work, but only within the context of his usual programme, and saw no-one other than his officials. Every evening, the Court relaxed and enjoyed itself, sometimes playing games for an hour or two, after dinner. The collected testimony affirms that the demonstrations, and clashes with the forces of order, which were already the main subject of dinner-conversation in the city, or at embassy-receptions, were hardly ever mentioned at Court. Did the courtiers not know about these things, or not care?

After the riot at Qom, "the Group studying the problems of Iran" – a think-tank and policy-centre set up four years earlier on the personal initiative of the Sovereign, and consisting of a thousand members from the University, the senior judiciary and big business, who, inhabitants of the upper-crust that they were, often thought of themselves as "His Majesty's Opposition" – sent the Monarch a detailed report on the gravity of the situation and the hardening of attitudes among the regime's religious opponents. Having argued that all Iran's revolutions, in the past two centuries, had arisen from unrest among the clergy, the report proceeded to insist on the necessity of starting a dialogue with the clerics – and especially with Ayatollah Shariat-Madari. The article in *Ettela'at*, criticising Khomeyni, was described as a serious, political error.

The King immediately set up a secret commission to study and evaluate the report. It included General Nassiri, Head of the Savak, and his deputy, Parviz Sabeti, a minister nominated by the Head of Government, the Ayatollah Sayed Hassan Emami – a prelate close to the Shah and the capital's religious leader – and numerous other, official, civilian and military figures. Professor Kazem Vadii, a sociologist and principal author of the report, and I, as well as the President of "The Group", were included also. Nosratollah Moinian, Head of the Imperial Cabinet, was the Chairman. After two, stormy sessions, the commission issued a report about "the Group's" anxieties, calling them "imaginary". With the exception of some paid foreigners, this report went on, the Iranian clergy remained loyal to His Majesty, and the current trouble was all due to "Toudeh", Iran's underground, Communist Party!

Ayatollah Sayed Hassan Emami would not associate himself with this verdict, and Parviz Sabeti said, while the report was being signed, that its conclusions ought to be qualified, but, apparently, only his direct superior's opinion counted.

Equally, it was in terms of intervention by foreign agitators, secretly infiltrating the country, that the Government's Minister for Relations with Parliament explained the events at Tabriz. It is true that several Lebanese and Libyans, who had passed through Palestinian training-camps, had been arrested at Tabriz, but their presence, if it explained anything, certainly did not account for the scale of the agitation.

The "Study-Group" then took the step of going public with its findings, and, a week later, its view of the deeper causes of the troubles at Tabriz, was published. There were regional origins, it said – especially mistakes by local government in Tabriz – and there were national ones, such as the flawed, economic policy, which had impoverished part of the population of the towns, by creating around them industries, which were not integrated with the general activity of the Province. Foreign intrigues, it concluded, were certainly present, but they were made possible by a harmful and gloomy economic climate: emergency talks with the clergy were necessary, at once. Nothing constructive was done. The Shah did not react at all. The organ of the only political party, Rastakhiz, and the state-radio, apparently inspired by the Government, the

Minister to the Court and, especially, the Chief of the Savak, launched a vehement attack on the "Study-Group". The municipal council of Tabriz called us, in an official resolution, "a Group of political agitators"; but our "Group of agitators" included most of the rectors and professors of the universities, the Public Chief Prosecutor, several past Presidents of the Supreme Court, the President of the Iranian Bar, celebrated writers, artists and researchers, a Cabinet Minister, one of the Imperial Family's two solicitors and even the Shah's personal physician!

Meanwhile, the unrest got worse.

In the spring of 1978, the Shah and Shahbanou, accompanied by Minister for Foreign Affairs, and Mrs, Khalatbari, and the Grand Master of Protocol, Amir Aslan Afshar, made two visits abroad: the first was to Poland and Czechoslovakia, and the second to Hungary and Bulgaria. My wife and I were also in the party, which received a magnificent welcome wherever it went. The socialist countries were good economic and commercial partners with Iran, and they were doing all they could to strengthen their ties with Teheran, by flattering Iran's leaders – sometimes embarrassingly – and, especially, of course, the Shah.

Before we went, I asked the Department of Imperial Protocol to give me a long audience with the Shah. The Department replied that it would arrange for this "quiet audience" to take place on the 'plane between Teheran and Warsaw. We took off at 10.30 am, aboard "Shahine", the Imperial Boeing 707, flown by the Sovereign in person, whereupon all the afore-mentioned travelling-companions met in the aircraft's saloon.

The King joined us a few minutes later and flipped through the Iranian, and some foreign, newspapers, for a quarter-of-an-hour or so. The others were chatting or reading. The atmosphere, as always, on the Sovereign's travels, was relaxed. The he got up, said to me, "come on then," and led the way into his adjoining office.

The aircraft, like all aeroplanes fitted out for Heads-of-State, contained a small saloon, a dining-room, an office, a bedroom – furnished for the Imperial Couple – and two compartments for the entourage, protocol-advisers, security, journalists, interpreters et al.

To start with, he said to me, "this is an important trip we're taking: of course we have ideological differences, and we have to watch out, but I don't see why we shouldn't get on well with the Eastern Bloc and do well out of it."

"They know now," he went on, "that we are stable and reliable, and they are quite at ease."

Then he smiled and added, "at least, let us say, 'at ease, officially' – these are completely trustworthy economic partners, and we can play them off against the West - without that, we would never have been able to build the steel-complex at Isphahan, the machine-tool factory at Arak or the tractor-works at Tabriz …"

"Do you remember how the Americans and the World Bank tried to blackmail us over that steel-complex?"

"Those times are gone – we can't be blackmailed or threatened now – we are strong enough to say 'no', and they constantly pay greater attention to what we say."

"Compared to the others, you are young: you have never known difficult times – or the humiliation we have had to put up with."

Those were his politics, in their entirety, and all his dreams, which would soon be broken, precisely because his ambitions became intolerable for both sides.

After this long, moving monologue, he rang a bell, ordered two whiskies and fell silent. He waited, looked out of the porthole and then looked at me, tapping his fingers on the little desk, dreaming, perhaps. Whisky, ice and soda were placed on the table. He made as if to drink, but didn't let the liquor touch his lips, then, regarding me closely, he said:

"But we are here to listen to what you have to say, however I may know, or guess, what you have in mind."

I told him about the ever more anxious reports of the "Study-Group" and about the press-campaign they had sparked off, concerning the events at Tabriz. I remarked that public opinion was getting fearful.

"Sire," I said, "the time has certainly come to strike at the root of this malaise by proceeding with some profound, political reforms.

"If Your Majesty actually desires that his son should reign after him, it is now that action should be taken."

I was forgetting that the Shah had an incurable illness. I begged him to excuse my bluntness, but I saw that he was at once adopting the stubbornly defensive stance, which, in such situations, was his habitual attitude.

"I know, I know," he replied, " you're talking about corruption: how it horrifies me – but it's nothing new in our society!

"I know there are people in my circle, who are not beyond reproach in this regard; but, as you know, I have no direct influence over the civil administration and cannot act as I would wish.

"Where I do have powers, in the army, I root out corruption ruthlessly.

"Apart from that, the Imperial Commission of Control is doing all it can."

"Your Majesty," I persisted, "all these general measures against corruption change nothing, even if they are shown on television and broadcast on the radio [the Imperial Commission's proceedings, which were the subject of public ridicule, were transmitted live] because people simply don't believe in them, or that they represent a genuine desire to suppress profiteering.

"What is needed is a clean break, between your circle and the country's affairs, and those people who provide easy targets, not just for professional agitators, but also for genuinely disgusted members of the public.

"If nothing is done, urgently, about this, the chances are that the institution of monarchy, and the Sovereign himself, will find themselves in very grave danger."

I was struck dumb, for a moment, by the Shah's reply:
"Naturally, this is not something, which can be repeated, but, as long as the Americans support me, I can do, or say, whatever I like – I'm irremovable."

Eventually, I said, "certainly, Sire, the Americans will support you, as long as Iran is an 'island of peace and stability,' as President Carter put it; but, what if, as result of our internal problems, the Americans change their policy and abandon us?"

The Shah stated finally:
"The Americans will never abandon me."

This was clearly false, even at the time. The Shah believed that he was indispensable and therefore invulnerable, but he was going to realise, bit-by-bit, that real, internal unrest was being exploited, encouraged, financed and organised by those very people whom he believed were his unfailing friends – not because of his weaknesses, but because of his strength – because of the rising power of Iran and her ambitions, which were already thought of as "intolerable" and "megalomaniac".

We conversed, after that, about more or less innocuous subjects, until it was announced that lunch was served. Then he got up – so did I – and, as he was going to wash his hands, which he always did before eating, he said, with much tenderness in his voice, "don't worry – I shall come through this crisis, as I have come through so many in the past!"

A few days later, somewhere near Bratislava, we were observing some military manoeuvres, which were a demonstration, with live ammunition, of the latest weaponry. Iran had decided to diversify her sources of military equipment – in order to reduce her dependence on the West, especially on the United States – and had begun to build up a competitive armaments-industry of her own; but she was also seeking arms-suppliers in the Eastern Bloc. The Czechs were interested in this and were presenting their finest products.

After a close-up presentation, as we all stood up on the platform (which had been specially erected to a considerable height) in order to watch the manoeuvres, the Shahbanou said to her husband, "I hate this kind of event and everything, which reminds me of war.

"One day, you may have to exercise your function as Commander-in-Chief of the Imperial Army – God grant that that day never comes!"

People did not know then that the Shah was seriously ill. Today, that strange little aside takes on quite a different sense.

During the winter, a few months before, to mark "tree-day", the Shah was visiting the 100 000 acres of conifers planted to the west of the capital, when he said to the Minister for Agriculture and the Environment, "take good care of these trees – I hope to live long enough to see a beautiful forest here."

Everyone thought that Mohammad Reza Pahlavi was simply enjoying one of his little quips – as the Minister, Hadi Hedayati, who was standing next to the King, told me later – no-one paid any attention to it, but, perhaps he did sometimes betray that he knew he had this disease.

As the spring passed, and summer began, life at Court went on as normal, and the King and the Shahbanou continued to make public appearances, visiting events and opening new projects. Public opinion remained, for the most part, solidly behind him, and his popularity was not undermined, but the increasingly anguished expectation of a reaction from him – of a decisive move to take things in hand and introduce reforms – was perceptible enough.

Towards the end of May, the Shahbanou took a break between organised ceremonies and paid a long visit, almost without security, to one of the capital's supermarkets, where she made some purchases. The crowd could hardly believe its eyes, but it gave her a friendly welcome with much applause and many handshakes. There was not the slightest hostility or reserve. A few days later, there was another impromptu visit, lasting five hours, to the southern quarters of the city, using an unmarked minibus, belonging to the Imperial Guard. Only General Neshat, Commander of the "Immortals", and Colonel Nevissi, an officer of the Guard, both in civilian dress, and a few assistants, were with the Shahbanou. The route was selected, as they went, according to the suggestions of a young, Teheran-City councillor, Mohammad Reza Taghizadeh.

During the first twenty minutes of the trip, the party was listening closely to a presentation, by professor Kazem Vadii, which was based on several reports from our Study-Group, about the capital's problems. In a few well-aimed phrases, he explained, to the Shahbanou, exactly the strategic role, which Teheran would eventually play in the coming upheavals, and described the measures, which urgently needed to be taken. The accuracy of his predictions was in vain: not one of his suggestions was put into effect.

As they went from one quarter to another, they received an enthusiastic response: hundreds of people chanted, and acclaimed, the name of the Shah; women embraced the Shahbanou; many made requests for assistance, hurriedly scribbling notes, on this or that subject, and passing them to her... a section of the middle-class was already beginning to challenge the regime, at this time, but the lower classes remained loyal to the Sovereign and had no inhibitions about showing it. That's how it was, right up to the end.

On 14th May, Amir Assadollah Alam – perhaps the Shah's only true friend and confidant – died of cancer, in New York.

Amir Assadollah Alam, an agricultural engineer by training – when only twenty-six, just after the war – had then become the youngest minister in Iran's constitutional history and begun his ascent to the summit of the political hierarchy. When he was Prime Minister, in 1962, he did not hesitate to order the arrest of a certain Rouhollah Khomeyni, who was then an obscure mullah, fomenting – with the aid of Toudeh, the Iranian Communist Party, and Egyptian funding – a revolt against agricultural reform and the political emancipation of women. He was Minister to the Court, from 1965, but, losing touch, little-by-little, with affairs of state (owing to his sickness) he was replaced in this post, in the summer of 1977, by Amir Abbas Hoveyda. He was certainly a controversial figure and he attracted criticism: he might easily be compared with the Duc de Morny, Napoleon III's half-brother, who had the same weaknesses and the same statesman-like pragmatism. It has often been said that, if he had been at Mohammad Reza Pahlavi's side, during the turmoil of 1978, the collapse of the regime could have been avoided. His death, at the height of the crisis, not long after the decease of former Prime Minister Eghbal and old General Yazdanpanah (the last surviving companion of Reza Shah) deprived the Sovereign of the last of the men he really trusted. More and more, he gave the impression that he had no confidence in anybody. It was a heavy, psychological and political blow for a figure who, despite his pretensions to the contrary, was ever more isolated.

Between March and June, there were many demonstrations at Tabriz and Qom, and even in Teheran, but their size remained limited, and Ayatollah Shariat-Madari was thought of as the leader of a politico-religious movement, which was still far from challenging the regime. In spite of the blunder, represented by the *Ettela'at* article, Rouhollah Khomeyni's influence appeared to be very small.

On 10th May, during the demonstrations at Qom, the forces-of-order pursued a group of rioters right into the residence of Ayatollah Shariat-Madari. Was this an accident, or was it engineered? Feelings ran high, and all the more so, because two had been killed in the course of skirmishes in the city-streets. In the hours which followed and having learned something, from the error made in publishing that notorious article about Khomeyni, Prime Minister Amouzegar apologised to the Grand Ayatollah for this "involuntary violation" of his home, and the Ayattolah made an appeal for reconciliation.

While numerous "political" prisoners – often people who had been arrested, tried and imprisoned for politically-motivated, terrorist acts – were released under amnesty or reductions of sentence, the government also proceeded to arrest some three hundred leaders of the urban riots. Since these were people with no profile on the political scene, their arrest created no reaction, either within the country or in the international press, despite the latter's increasing scrutiny of events in Iran. A distinct lull intervened throughout the nation. The Shah made several announcements about the necessity for liberalising political life. The regime made concessions, and various political groupings – especially those claiming to honour the spirit of the former Prime Minister and hero of oil-nationalisation, Mohammad Mossadegh, who had died in 1967 – stepped out of the shadows and expressed themselves freely.

As these months went by, and the opportunity to orientate matters differently passed, Mohammad Reza Pahlavi, seemed to become ever more detached from the requirements of the time. He knew, of course, that his days were numbered and he wanted to complete his task – to the limit of his dreams

– to lead Iran, "irreversibly", as he often said, to a higher level of economic and social development, from which a "retreat" would be impossible. On this account, he neglected "administrative back-up" and day-to-day management. He should have recruited a man, or men, who would have held the country together and taken it in hand - reformed it in a calm and orderly manner, opened a genuine dialogue with the clergy and the political factions -and cleared the air; who would, in short, have drawn the teeth of the international intrigues, which were rapidly becoming a conspiracy against the stability and progress of Iran.

Prime Minister Djamchid Amouzegar, that honest technocrat, who would have made an excellent Finance-Minister and had distinguished himself in the councils of OPEC, was not a great politician. He spent all his time examining details and failing to grasp principles. Amir Abbas Hoveyda, an instrument of the regime for many years, was a good tactician but too unpopular: as Minister to the Court, he pulled every string, and used the networks he set up, to intrigue against, and weaken, any successor. It was a recipe for paralysis.

The Shah pronounced himself proud of the country's balance and confident in the future; and he was right. At the end of the spring of 1978, nothing had yet been lost: Iran gave a constant impression of solidity, which inspired both respect and confidence.

Indeed, at the beginning of that spring, the annual average earnings of an Iranian were $2 540, as opposed to $160 twenty-five years before. Moreover, the forecasts of international organisations, and of the most reliable research-institutes, predicted that this figure would exceed $10 000 in the year 2000, which is approximately that of Spain today.

Iran also had full employment – such that there was a shortage of labour – which drew nearly a million, foreign workers, of all grades, from all quarters – Asians, Americans, Europeans – all living here in freedom and security.

The rial, the national currency, had been stable for fifteen years. Reserves of foreign currency were greater, in 1975, than those of the Netherlands, Belgium, Italy and Spain combined. As a creditor-country, Iran had made preliminary steps towards becoming a member of the OECD.

In 1977, the volume of Iranian, public investment abroad – which has sometimes been quoted as the Shah's personal fortune – exceeded $20 billion, and was spread across such a variety of sectors as oil, petrochemicals, banking, nuclear power and car-making.

The country's social security system, started by the Ghavam government in 1946 and gradually developed ever since, was hailed, by the ILO, as the best in the third world and a model of its kind.

The Iranian National Oil Company (INOC) was classed, by the American *Fortune-Magazine*, as twenty-eighth in the world in 1973, but had moved up to third place, the following year. Just before the revolution, the volume of oil extracted reached six-and-half million barrels per day. The capacity of Iran's refineries was forty million tonnes per annum, so that the country was not just exporting "crude", but fractionated products also. As a result, Iran was, in 1977, the second-most-prolific, oil-exporting country on Earth, with 270 million tonnes of oil-exports, and was, incontestably, the leading light of OPEC. Its oil-terminal on Kharg Island was the largest tanker-port in the world.

In 1977, cement-production exceeded ten million tonnes, steel-production reached six million tonnes and was due to triple in the next five years. That same year, 100 000 vehicles were built, and a volume of a million vehicles, some of them for export, was expected before the end of the century.

In the energy-sector, the capacity of Iran's power-stations (all categories combined) was 7 500 MWh, in 1977, against 850 MWh, in 1963. Four, large nuclear power-stations were under construction. Two of these had already achieved 80% of their total capacity, which was 4 000 MWh. Complete energy-independence was very close.

Between 1963 and 1978, the rate of increase in the number of pupils in nursery-schools was 1 350%. In primary schools, it was 560%, at intermediate level (course-selection) it was 263%, at secondary level, 331% and, in the technical and professional colleges, 1 550%. At the end of May 1978, when the school-year ended, Iran had passed more than 10 million pupils from nursery- to secondary schools. Illiteracy would have been completely eliminated in the course of the 'eighties. The twenty universities, and one hundred and thirty-five colleges of further education, had more than 200 000 students, almost all of them benefiting from bursaries or study-grants. Iranian universities – especially Teheran, Shiraz, Melli and Isphahan – had attained international recognition and drew many foreign students from all over the world.

Every quarter, if not every month, in the past three years, Iran had opened a new and splendid museum, cultural centre, library or sports-complex - all being the fruits of the efforts made in the past ten years.

Even in the agricultural sector, where development was slower, the thirteen, great dams, completed by 1963, which had allowed the irrigation of nearly two million acres of new farm-land, had, among other factors – and in spite of population-growth and a rise in per capita consumption – made Iran more than 90% self-sufficient in food. Even this deficit was seen as undesirable, but the country's revenues easily covered it.

The Iranian army was rated as one of the world's most powerful, and its air-force among the five best, so that Iran was indeed a pillar of the defence of the free world against Communism and Soviet expansion. This was what had led the Sovereign to promote, ever more insistently, the evacuation of foreign troops from the region, its de-nuclearisation and the formation of an alliance, for the defence of the Indian Ocean and the Persian Gulf, composed only of countries with coasts on those waters. This, in turn, was one of the more spectacular aspects of an active diplomacy, in favour of a policy of national independence (very reminiscent of de Gaulle) which had put some governments' noses out of joint.

Iran sparkled from all these facets, and Mohammad Reza Pahlavi – proud of his country's progress and expertise – was highly conscious of the fact. He knew intimately about these advantages and , indeed, many others, thinking in terms of economic growth, GDP, development-factors and the macroeconomy, and dreaming of a better distribution of the planet's riches, of the Third World taking off and the battle against poverty. He had his eyes fixed on the horizon, and he was ever more detached from the here-and-now; but he was sure that his efforts – those of his country, in fact - would dazzle the world. During the past three or four years, he had spoken increasingly of the need for western-style democracy, without, unfortunately, initiating the political reform and the orderly transfer of power, which were indispensable to it – even though he knew that the effect, of political liberalisation in progress, would be to silence some of his critics abroad. He thought of himself as solid and permanent fixture, but he had badly underestimated the danger. He thought of his position as unassailable, because Iran was on the verge of becoming the Japan of the Middle East, the beacon country of the region – not excluding comparison with a highly developed Israel – and the leading technological, scientific, economic and financial power in the Muslim world. However, it was precisely because of these achievements – or "megalomania" and "folie-de-grandeur", as they were called in the West – that he and his country were going to be destabilised. He mistrusted those, within the country, who (in his view) denied this evidence of progress, by concentrating on everyday difficulties and on so-and-so's corruption or incompetence, instead of thinking only in terms of a radiant, long-term perspective.

In the spring of 1978, at the celebrations for "Women's Day", in the imposing, covered stadium of the capital's sports-complex, before more than ten thousand enthusiastic Iranians, he called his critics "reactionaries", "stick-in-the-muds" and "fossils", and, in a thinly veiled reference to the clergy, he said:

"The caravan passes and the dogs bark."

Perhaps, people read too much into this, but it was taken as a threat. In Teheran, it was seen as a sign of hardening attitudes, of a forthcoming, vigorous stroke, and many trembled; but nothing happened. These harsh and wounding words were no more than straws in the wind.

In those last weeks, the Shah still held all the trumps, but he would not play them by rousing the politicians and functionaries from their immobility. It seemed as though he thought untoward events were like road-accidents, just as Louis XVI, Nicholas II or Haile Selassie, in similar circumstances, seemed to think. A few months later, in Morocco, Hassan II spoke to him about this lost year:

"Reza, shall I tell you what was your biggest mistake?" asked the Moroccan Sovereign, in the presence of a small, intimate circle, which included Amir Aslan Afshar, "you loved Iran more than the Iranians!"

"But for whom was I preparing Iran, if not for my people, for the Iranians, so that they could live happily in a prosperous country?" was the reply.

Autumn 1977 – Bouchehr Naval Base – Right (not in uniform)
Colonel Djahanbini, the Shah's personal body-guard.
(Admiral Deyhimi Collection)

Chapter IV

"No-one can depose me: I have the support of the majority, of all the labourers and of 700 000 soldiers"

June 1978

June began with a period of relative calm. The political life, especially of Teheran, was rife with rumours of change; but that was routine.

As was his wont, the Shah departed for an inspection-tour of Khorassan Province. No sooner had he arrived at the holy city of Meched, where stands the tomb of the Imam Reza – the subject of particular veneration in Iran - than Mohamad Reza Pahlavi was struck by the extraordinary warmth of his popular welcome. There were tens of thousands cheering in the streets, as he passed through, almost invariably standing upright, in his convertible limousine, to acknowledge their acclamations. After the traditional pilgrimage, in a ceremonial hall of the shrine's museum, he gave audience to fifty mullahs, some of whom were important men. All kissed his hand, to pay him homage; for was he not the Sovereign of the only Shia-majority in the Muslim world? And he was especially courteous, speaking of his attachment to the faith and his strong regard for the Imam Reza.

On the afternoon of the 10th, he paid a short visit to an
industrial complex, where, again, the workers' greeting was
deliriously enthusiastic, and his response, albeit brief, was
correspondingly so. Then, on to the inspection of a military
base. Returning by helicopter to his palace at Malek-Abad, he
over-flew the building-site of the new campus for Meched's
Ferdowsi University.

"Tomorrow afternoon, I shall receive the lecturers," he told
his entourage.

"But it's not in the programme, Sire," replied Governor
Valian, "and how can we get these hundreds of people
together, in just a few hours?

"Besides," he went on, "we're not sure about some of
them."

"Just do it!" the Sovereign retorted drily.

That evening, Parviz Amouzegar, the Rector – no relation
to the Prime Minister – was informed, and he spent the whole
night arranging the audience, contacting every one of the
professors, researchers and lecturers, without exception.

The morning of the 11th saw the Governor and a Savak
officer presenting the Rector with a list of twenty members
of staff who were, they said, "undesirable", from the point of
view of security, and should not be received; but the Rector
would have none of it:

"There will be no exceptions," he replied, "or I shall go and
present my respects to His Majesty, alone!"

"But you did that already, at the airport," argued the officials.

"Take it or leave it!" snapped Parviz Amouzegar.

In a quandary, the Governor submitted the matter to the
King, who flew into an unexpectedly violent rage.

"At what point," he demanded, "did you dare to decide

whom I may or may not receive?

"How dare you dictate my conduct to me?

"We shall proceed according to the Rector's wishes!"

That afternoon, in the palace-gardens, with no security-control at all, he received a thousand university-staff, who had come in their own cars.

Mohammad Reza Pahlavi was vigorously applauded and wreathed in smiles. The Rector only said, "Sire, we are happy to be with you."

"The same goes for me," returned the Shah, before going on to speak of his great pleasure upon seeing the new campus from the air and promising a longer visit when he next came to Meched. Then he mixed with the crowd, chatting with all and sundry, making jokes and sometimes laughing loudly.

Dr. Morteza Rouhani, first on the list of "undesirables" – because he was a notorious dissident and brother-in-law of Ali Shariati, a fundamentalist theoretician and opinion-former among Islamic radicals – asked the Shah privately to tell the University to give him a bigger flat.

"There are three of us," he said, "and our son is already a grown-up, young man, who wants to have his friends round, which makes 650 sq ft really too small."

The Shah replied: "There's nothing I can do, Doctor, because 215 sq ft per person is the norm for tied accommo-dation.

"Soon, no doubt, you will build a lovely house for your-self."

Then he added, with a laugh, "but take care that your son doesn't waste too much time with his pals – studies must come first!"

Everyone laughed to hear this, and the Doctor bowed respectfully to the King, who shook his hand. A few months later, he was Khomeyni's Health Minister.

The audience continued for three hours. As he left the academics, who applauded him at length, the Shah said to the Governor, with a mocking smile, "if only all the agitators were like that!"

On 14th June, at 10.15 am, in his small, private office, at the Niavaran Palace, the Shah received the Prime Minister, Djamchid Amouzegar, and Lieutenant General Nasser Moghaddam, Head of the Second Bureau of the General Staff, for the presentation of the latter as the new Chief of the Savak – replacing General Nassiri.

The ceremony only lasted two minutes. There were no photographers or cameras present, as is the way with military matters. The Prime Minister pronounced the usual formula:
"Sire, I have the honour of presenting General Nasser Moghaddam, as Secretary of State to the Council and Chief of the Savak."
The Sovereign shook hands with the General, who was in uniform, and said to him, "I'm sure you know your job."
That was it.

The two visitors left the office at once. A few seconds later, the Sovereign took the lift to the ground floor.

This substitution was one of the most important developments in that crucial year, but it came too late.

The Shah's choice had been delayed for several days, as he hesitated between two candidates: the other possibility had been Major General Ali Motazed, the Savak number two, who had special responsibility for foreign intelligence and counter-espionage. Lieutenant General Nasser Moghaddam had served in the Savak, at first, under the irreproachable General Pakravan, whose disciple he prided himself on being, and then at the beginning of Nassiri's period of office. He had been directing the Second Bureau of the General Staff for several years.

Both were known for their integrity, competence and respect for the law. Ali Motazed, although theoretically General Nassiri's direct deputy, was not thought to have been associated with the excesses, of which the latter was accused. His services were credited with the remarkable successes achieved in the battle against Soviet-Communist intelligence. It was also recognised that his agents had thoroughly infiltrated the Palestinian networks, which were breeding grounds for extremist opposition and terrorism in Iran. So well had this been managed, that the Israeli Mossad came to the Savak to ask for information. Indeed, the two services had been collaborating for a long time. On the other hand, it was felt that he was not well versed in domestic affairs. Amir Abbas Hoveyda, Minister to the Imperial Court, when consulted by the Shah, had strongly recommended Ali Motazed's candidacy –not that Motazed seemed to appreciate this very much – because he thought him the more tractable. He knew, especially, that General Moghaddam held a particularly negative and critical view of his performance, at the head of government, considering him to be one of those, who were principally to blame for the crisis, which was sweeping the country, and barely hiding his dislike.

Nasser Moghaddam, although a veteran of Savak, was looked upon as an outsider. He seemed to be well liked by the

Americans, but, mainly, he had a good network of personal contacts in the intellectual and religious circles, where the trouble was. Therefore the Shah plumped for him.

Curiously, Hoveyda's insistent support had counted against General Motazed. The Shah was becoming increasingly distrustful of the man, who had been his Prime Minister for thirteen years, and blamed him for several things – notably that ill-advised article about Rouhollah Khomeyni. Nevertheless, in the presence of his Minister to the Court, he gave the impression that he appreciated the suggestion, and Amir Abbas Hoveyda, thinking that the decision had been taken, told Ali Motazed about it, so that, on the evening of the 13th, the Major General was expecting a telephone-call from the Palace, or from the Prime Minister, to fix the time for his presentation – for Nassiri had cleared his desk that morning. Some of his friends had even gathered at his house to celebrate his appointment, and, towards eight-o-clock, a superb bouquet of flowers, accompanied by a particularly cordial note – Hoveyda knew how to do some things properly – was delivered to Motazed, by way of congratulation; but the 'phone did not ring.

That same day, it was announced that General Nassiri had been appointed as Ambassador to Pakistan, to which Islamabad's agreement had been obtained within forty-eight hours. Ali Motazed was appointed as Ambassador to Syria. Damascus had hesitated a little, it seems, before agreeing to this; and one can see why – not least because the Ambassador-in-post, after years of discord between the two countries, was a diplomat of the highest rank and very far from the world of intelligence-gathering, which suited the Syrians very well. He was also known to have been sympathetic towards Mossadegh's National Front, which had not hampered his career. This appointment saved the life of Ali Motazed. When the revolution came, he fled straight to London, asked for political asylum and got it. He died there, some years later, after a long illness.

The new chief of the Savak, General Moghaddam, had come from nowhere: only a few weeks before, he had been sure his career was over!

In April 1978, following the riots in Tabriz, General Moghaddam had telephoned me, saying he wanted to meet me discreetly, that day, for a long talk. This was an unusual development, in spite of our friendly, almost familial, relationship. He was, after all, a high-ranking army-officer. We agreed to have lunch at the restaurant attached to the Reza Abbassi Museum. He arrived at noon, in civilian clothes, bringing with him a memorandum, twenty-three pages long, about the crisis – whose gravity was now apparent to all – and asked me to read it, which I did. It was brutally frank. Nothing was missed out. It dealt, in damning detail, with corrupt practices among named people of the Shah's immediate circle – most notably, three members of the Sovereign's family (a cousin and two close friends of the Shahbanou) the CEO of the biggest public-sector company and two or three of the Court's most senior officials. It described the racket organised by the corporate-business association, during the premiership of Hoveyda (who himself, the General emphasised, had not been completely honest) extortion by General Nassiri, the real reasons for the price-rises, which had progressively disadvantaged and alienated the middle-classes, and the catastrophic results of the ballooning quarrel with the clergy. It concluded that dramatic measures must be taken, "at once, if not sooner"!

He begged me for my honest opinion. Indeed, as I then

said, the document was only stating – frankly and with names added – what two, other memorandums, sent to the Sovereign during the previous three years, had already said about the reasons for domestic unrest. One had come from the "Group for Studying the Problems of Iran", of which I was the Chairman, and the other - which Nasser Moghaddam had probably helped to produce – had come from the Chief of the General Staff; but neither of these had adopted the harshness of tone of the document before us, whose list of people "to be eliminated" included the names of figures at the very summit of government. It was extraordinarily audacious.

Having finished reading the document, I got up and embraced the General.

"I congratulate you," I said, rather emotionally, "but you know what a risk you're taking?"

"Yes, I do," he replied, "my colleagues and I finished this report a week ago; but how can we submit it directly to the King?

"I would be placed under close arrest, right away, and no-one would even know.

"Of course, I take complete responsibility for this document, but would you, could you, get it to the Shahbanou?"

I had been appointed, by the King, as chairman of her staff-committee, a few months before.

"Could you ask her to give it to the Sovereign?" he went on, "that way I would have witnesses."

I did not hesitate to agree. I wrote a short note to the Shahbanou and sealed it, with the report, carefully into an envelope, which I consigned to a despatch-rider. The General and I parted a little before 3.00 pm.

A little after 6.00 pm, the Shahbanou telephoned.

"Have you read the document you sent me?" she asked.

"Yes, I have," I said, "the General asked me to, and it's because I know what's in it, that I sent it immediately to Your Majesty."

"I would have preferred that you had not read it," rejoined the Shahbanou, thinking perhaps of those "friends" and contacts of hers, who were especially deeply implicated.

"The General beseeched me to read it," I explained again, "in order to ask my advice".
"Having read it, I thought it my duty to communicate it to Your Majesty."

The Shahbanou insisted: "There are things in this document, which it would be much better for you not to know."

I immediately regretted, and always shall greatly regret, having been so thoughtless as to reply: "Your Majesty may not recognise it, but what's written about certain people in that report, is no more than a small fraction of what people are saying, rightly or wrongly, in every tea-house."

The Shahbanou banged the telephone down – but she sent the report to the Shah – and General Moghaddam was not "placed under close arrest". He was not even sacked, and I still believe that his pitilessly detailed text was a solemn warning to the Shah from the Americans – or those, at least, among the American military, who were anxious about the destruction Washington was planning for Iran – in that tragic spring of 1978.

The Kennedy White-House had already tried to topple

the Shah, in a coup by the Savak-chief - at that time, General Teymour Bakhtiar – but the Sovereign got word of it, from a personal informant and, so it seems, from some high-ranking, American soldiers. The very unpopular Bakhtiar was quickly removed, and energetic, economic, social and political measures were taken, to restore the situation and silence the critics. Was it the case, for a second time, that someone was trying to warn the Shah about the urgent necessity for internal, political measures to shore up his regime and thwart an international conspiracy? I cannot answer this question with certainty, but it's worth asking.

Nasser Moghaddam was a perfectly honest man, a good father – which quality is valued by Iranians – and a fine professional. Certainly, the inertia of the Imperial regime disappointed him. After 12th February 1979, Mehdi Bazargan, Khomeyni's Prime Minister – perhaps encouraged by his American friends – asked him to remain at his post. He was installed in an out-of-the-way office, disguised as a fictional agency of public works, whence he tried, for some days, to limit damage to the organisation, which he had cleaned up and re-oriented. He was arrested and assassinated soon afterwards on Khomeyni's personal order. He knew too much. When interrogated about the matter by journalists, Mehdi Bazargan claimed that he first heard about the General's death, over the radio!

By transferring General Nassiri – a blinkered man with a loathsome reputation, but unconditionally, even blindly, loyal – the Shah was right in believing that he had made an impor-tant political gesture.

The new chief of the Special Services was immediately

ordered to re-organise and cleanse the force and, most importantly, to renew its dialogue – as enjoyed during the time of General Pakravan – with non-governmental society; with the intellectuals, the small shop-keepers and the clergy, in order to improve its image.

Some months previously, in September 1977, the Sovereign had appointed the ambassador, Amir Aslan Afshar, as Grand Master of Imperial Protocol, with precise instructions to re-organise and "purify" that strategic institution, albeit whose political importance was on an altogether different scale to that of the Special Services. In spite of Amir Abbas Hoveyda's constant advice not to "get into a scrap with the Imperial Family by cutting down on their privileges", Aslan Afshar went ahead and succeeded. The Court's way of working, and of relating to the public, was modified, and the abuses, which no-one could ignore and which tarnished the Court's image, were suppressed. The results were convincing.

The Sovereign thought he could operate through General Moghaddam with the same finesse, but time was of the essence, and none of the measures recommended in the General's report were immediately implemented. Mohammad Reza Pahlavi did take sensible action eventually and believed he saw corresponding positive effects.

The Government continued to liberalise political mechanisms, some contacts were made with the clergy, the Shah thought that he had de-fused the crisis, but he had still not grasped its dimensions nor its foreign origins.

That morning (14th June) at half-past-ten, the King was

due to open the Annual Conference of the Group Studying the Problems of Iran. A thousand attendees – academics, well known artists and writers, numerous magistrates, lawyers, businessmen, a minister in office (Karim Motamedi of Posts and Telecommunications) and the Governor of a Province – the elite of the nation – had gathered.

The late-spring sunshine was pleasantly warm, and the Palace-gardens, where the conference-goers met, were shady and full of flowers. The atmosphere was idyllic.

Form demanded that I, as Chairman of the Group, await the Sovereign at the doors to the lift, on the ground floor of the Palace.

He was smiling and very relaxed, shaking my hand and saying, "well, I hope you're satisfied!" which was an allusion to the already famous appointment he had just finalised, upstairs.

"I think Your Majesty made the right choice."

We emerged from the Palace.

Numerous journalists and photographers, from the national press, were there, drawn to this event, as always; but, this time, reporters from several, foreign newspapers and broadcast-channels were present also.

Seeing the numbers of people attending, the Shah broke into a wide grin and said to me, "who says that the intellectuals don't like us?"
He was genuinely happy. Seeing him arrive, everyone began to applaud, which he acknowledged with a wave. Then

he asked, "what are you going to say?"

"Some very important things," I replied, "which I have been charged with conveying, overtly and publicly, to Your Majesty's attention."

"And I shall reply," he said.

I fulfilled the mandate, my friends had given me, to the best of my ability. I began by stating that "the stability and unity of Iran depends upon co-operation between the religious authorities and the monarchy," which, at that time, was still a bold proposition. Then I spoke of growing discontent, of the need to root out corruption and of the importance of reforming the political administration. I talked about liberalisation, the difficulties created by the single Party and the urgency of creating a dialogue with the opposition.

The text had been prepared in advance and approved by the Group's steering committee. I continued, "those who surround Your Majesty, and are closest to You, ought to be exemplars of moral rectitude, virtue and integrity."

This too was unusual, and it was a crystal-clear allusion to certain individuals, who would be profoundly displeased by it. The crowd applauded.

"Let the nation," I concluded, "renew its confidence in the King, to direct us at this decisive turning-point, deal with the problems of the present and prepare for the future!"

The Monarch took this very well. He began: "I am gratified to see you here again in such strength."

He promised that he would do everything in his power, to ensure the country's development towards liberalisation, and that a dialogue would be instituted "with those who have something to say". Then he mingled with the attendees, asking questions and shaking hands. He told one lady-professor of his regret that there were not enough women on the staff. To the Public Prosecutor of the Supreme Court, he expressed the desire to see justice strengthened and become more active.

The gathering lasted more than an hour, and a recording of it was broadcast, on radio and television, a little later, towards 1.00 pm, and again, in the evening. The national press hailed it as a sign of liberalisation and of the reforming zeal of Mohammad Reza Pahlavi.

But what did he mean by a dialogue with "those who have something to say"? Whom was he thinking of, and what would the dialogue be about?

The opposition, which the international press called "secular", was very heterogeneous and un-representative. Over the years, every attempt had been made to extinguish it.

It consisted of the senior civil servants, merchants and some of the capital's clerics, who were grouped, rather restlessly, around the former Prime Minister, who had held office in the 'sixties, Ali Amini. This extremely rich and ambitious aristocrat wished, and hoped, to return to power. He had close contacts with the American Democratic Party and did all he could to capitalise on them, which was quite enough to make the Shah mistrust him.

The Nationalist faction was made up of those who claimed to uphold the lively and venerable memory of Mohammad Mossadegh, the Prime Minister who, in the 'fifties, had nationalised the oil-industry. In his early years the Shah had supported him. This faction had a certain prestige, but it had almost no organisation, and liberalisation of the political climate had only sharpened the rivalry, not to say animosity, between its leading figures. Professor Gholam Hossein Sadighi, Mossadegh's spiritual heir, whom the Shah called upon, a few months later, kept himself strictly apart from all political activity and concentrated entirely on his highly respected Institute of Social Studies and Research. Mehdi Bazargan, future Prime Minister under Khomeyni, had founded an Islamic movement, but declared himself to be also a follower of Mossadegh. He repelled the more secular nationalists, whose analysis of the great man's policies was more accurate. That leaves us with the triumvirate composed of Karim Sandjabi, former minister and former senior member of the Faculty of Law, of Shapour Bakhtiar and of Darioush Forouhar. These put themselves forward as a new version of the National Front, which was, in itself, a miscellaneous assemblage, founded long before by Mossadegh.

Some time before the present, Karim Sandjabi – an inveterate accumulator of offices and board-member of numerous, public agencies – laid plans to acquire an important post. Unwisely, the Shah rejected him and made of him an embittered man. Shapour Bakhtiar sat on the administrative councils of several companies, which were either semi-public or belonged to the Pahlavi Foundation. Forouhar, undoubtedly the most principled of the three, was a prosperous lawyer, who had become the legal adviser to the Ministry of Labour, and to the Sepah Bank, which administered the Imperial Army's pension-fund.

Sandjabi and Forouhar were household names. They had a certain reputation. Bakhtiar was practically unknown. If he had not been a relative of the Shahbanou, he would have been completely anonymous. As he himself said, his political party, Iran, only had two members!

Other figures from this movement had merged into national, political life, over the years, or succeeded brilliantly in business, after quitting public affairs. Some of the "Mossadeghis", many of them valuable men, had no wish to do more than play a part in the framework of the regime.

With so much fragmentation, there was no possibility of prompt action. It was never possible to overcome certain ill-feelings, even to the extent of showing a little courtesy during prayers. It was difficult, if not impossible, to have a dialogue with all of them as a group, but it would have been very easy to de-fuse their discontent. Mohammad Reza Pahlavi, robed, scornfully, in his dignity, was wrong, at this time, not to make, or rather, cause to have made, in their direction, the gestures of recognition, which would have radicalised them. A few months later, they were going to show their incompetence by collaborating with Ayatollah Khomeyni, whom they served for several weeks, before being humiliated, swept aside and expelled, even liquidated.

In the absence of a credible, secular opposition, the Shiite, religious hierarchy transformed itself, as so often in the past, into the voice of that part of public opinion, which wanted political change. In the Sovereign's immediate circle, the importance of the role the clergy had begun to play – and the manner in which this role might be exploited by certain forces – was still being ignored, even at this time. Prime Minister Amouzegar, himself from a middle-class family steeped in Persian culture and tradition, seemed to be totally unaware of it. The Minister to the Imperial Court, Amir Abbas Hoveyda, had casual contacts with certain mullahs, which he used, as was his wont, to try to "buy" the consciences of some; but the time had passed for manoeuvres of that sort.

Since the spring of 1978, the holy city of Qom had become, not only the centre for politico-religious agitation, but also the favoured destination of numerous politicians from the fringes of power and of official, or self-appointed, emissaries from the Imperial family, the Savak and the Government.

There, a trio of Grand Ayatollahs, thought of as "role-models" and "opinion-formers", held sway – at their head, the Ayatollah Sayed Kazem Shariat-Madari, who was considered, by Iran's resident, Shiite dignitaries, to be the supreme head of the sect. His prestige and influence among the Shiite community, both in Iran, where 80% of the population were Shiites, and abroad, were beyond compare, except with that of one other, great, religious figure. This was Ayatollah Khoi, also (like Shariat-Madari) originally from Azerbaidjan, who was then living at Najjaf, in Iraq.

Shariat-Madari was born at Tabriz, where he lived until the collapse, in 1946, of the two puppet-republics set up by Moscow in Azerbaidjan and a small part of Kurdistan. Having played a very active part in organising the resistance to the invaders and in offering sage advice to his compatriots, he had risked his liberty, and even his life, with utter contempt for danger. This glorious record, together with his knowledge and his natural modesty, made him very welcome at Qom, where he was elevated to the status of "model" – a great man, respected by all.

When the previous leaders of world-Shiism, the Grand Ayatollahs Boroudjerdi, who lived at Qom, and Hakim, who

119

lived at Najjaf, died, Shariat-Madari became the undisputed head of the Shia, although he refused to be invested with any kind of public dignity. He had a great gentleness, a mischievous glance, a great intelligence and he knew how to listen. He was punctiliously patriotic, tolerant and aware of social and cultural problems. There is no doubt that he was among the great dignitaries of Shiism, and the best informed, not only about world affairs, but also about the windings of national politics. He was able to use all the important sources of information, either in Farsee or in Arabic, in which he was fluent, for, in that troubled year, his secretariat's press-service made daily translations for him of all the main articles in *The Times*, *The Guardian*, *Le Monde* and the *Washington Post*. In addition, he frequently quoted from the words of this or that well-known commentator of the British, American, and even the Russian, radio-services.

At the time I'm speaking of, he headed a remarkable organisation. Thousands of Iranian, and more than three hundred foreign, students were taking courses in Islamic theology and philosophy in his schools at Qom. He also controlled an important network of mullahs, who had qualified in the city and then fanned out into every part of Iran, but especially into Azerbaidjan, where he was idolised, and into communities where the Azeri dialect was spoken.

He had thus established himself as an obvious dialogue-partner for the Imperial regime, and the Prime Minister sent him an emissary, but the latter was received only by Shariat-Madari's son-in-law and one of his colleagues. The Minister to the Imperial Court's emissary was, it appears, simply dismissed. General Moghaddam, once he was promoted to the head of the Savak, penetrated Qom's supreme sanctum and had discourse with the immediate circle of the "big-three" clerics. Djafar Behbahanian, who was in charge of the Shah's private fortune – and supposed, therefore, to be reliable - went discreetly to Qom and was received by Ayatollah Shariat-Madari, who told me later that he had not been quite sure whether Behbahanian had been despatched officially to see him, or whether he had come on his own initiative. The prelate also said that he was quite certain that his messages to the Sovereign had not been conveyed.

"They didn't dare," he told me," so what was the point of all those visits?"

I had enjoyed excellent contacts, for some time, with the Ayatollah and several other Shiite dignitaries, using as inter-mediaries the professors of Teheran University's Departments of Theology, Philosophy, Literature and the Humanities, whose researches and relationships often took them to Qom, and I put these contacts to good use by keeping the Shah informed about what was being said, in high places, in Qom. He charged me, therefore, in May 1978, to go discreetly and see the Ayatollah Shariat-Madari.

"Tell him," he said, "that you come on my behalf, and make it clear that you come to listen attentively to what he has to say – apart from any general rhetoric which he may reel off – and that you will repeat his proposals to me, and no-one else."

That was how the Shah initiated a dialogue, although not exactly negotiations, with the Head of the Shiite hierarchy. He believed that he had just made a breakthrough. Well, he had, and he hadn't.

An eminent professor of the University of Teheran, who frequented Qom, undertook to arrange the meeting, which had to take place in secret. The Ayatollah would receive me, at 9.00 pm, at the house of one of his relatives, which was adjacent to his own and which he could enter via an internal door. The city was almost deserted at that hour and my colleague's old car passed unnoticed. After the conventional greetings, the Ayatollah excused himself for not receiving me at his own house.

"I do not possess a sufficiently comfortable lounge," he said.

I told him that the Shah had asked me to see him and to listen, most attentively, to what he had to say.

"You know," I said, "that His Majesty has the highest regard for you and accords much importance to your views on national problems; for, like all Iranians, he has not forgotten what you did for the unity of the country, during the crisis in Azerbaidjan."

The Ayatollah smiled: evidently, the Shah had not commissioned me to present any proposals to him. Nevertheless, conversations have to be begun and, for that purpose, the atmosphere lightened. I was not paying a courtesy-visit, but representing the Shah to the country's leading, religious authority.

"I continually send messages to His Majesty," he replied: "the clergy has always been the refuge and support of the people during periods of unrest.

"That was the case in 1906-1907* when, thanks to a popular alliance of liberal and forward-looking clerics, the absolute power of the Qadjars** was abolished and the constitution proclaimed.

"The same conditions are occurring today: once again, no attention is being given to the causes of discontent."

---

* i.e during Iran's Constitutional Revolution.
** The reigning dynasty, 1796 –1925.

Then he cited the city of Qom as an example: "this city has nearly two-hundred thousand inhabitants, and, every Friday, between one- and two-hundred thousand people come here on pilgrimage – many more than that during religious festivals or periods of mourning.

"Well, in a country, where such great projects are being completed – as I would not deny for a moment that they are – almost nothing is being done for Qom; and the reason for this is that, in the circle surrounding the Shah, it is thought that Qom is not loved by the Shah, because it has always been a hotbed of opposition.

"You see, we have no drinking-water; we don't have enough bridges or relief-roads to take heavy traffic north-and-south, avoiding the constantly congested city-centre; there aren't enough tied-dwellings for civil servants or sufficient accommodation for pilgrims; the road-surfaces are in a regrettable state – there are even some hazardous stretches close the Shrine: all of this could have been remedied at the cost of few millions; but what would it matter that our pilgrims could happily stay in the city and perform their ritual ablutions, if the *Washington Post* had nothing significant to say about it?"

I interrupted the Ayatollah, at this point, to remind him that, during the four-and-a-half years, when I was Minister of Development and Housing, shafts had been sunk in the river's flood-plain to supplement the provision of drinking-water to the city; thirty housing-units had been built for Qom's civil-servants, and that the city's access-routes were under re-construction.

"I know that," he retorted bitterly, "but that's almost all that happened.

"Compare it with what's been done at Meched!"*

---

* Meched – pronounced "Machhad", in Farsee, is a holy city of north-west Iran, where stands the tomb of Imam Reza, the eighth Imam of the Shia and elder brother of Fatemeh-Masoumeh, who lies buried at Qom

"I'm told," he went on, " that Meched, in just a few years, has become one of the most beautiful and best-equipped cities in the Muslim world.

"Surely her little sister also deserves some attention!"

I conceded this and said I was sure that the Shah would give the appropriate instructions to his government; but this was no more than an introduction to the matter – a plea from general circumstances. Some of the Ayatollah's other proposals were more like alarm-signals. He kept insisting on the urgent necessity of "ensuring that the entire, Royal Family, and the Ministers and senior figures of the government and the Court, conducted themselves blamelessly".

"I know very well," he added at one point, "that we tend to talk about, those who are not impeccable, and to forget about the others; but isn't this normal?

"Is it not even just?

"Truly, those who are honest and serve their country well, are only doing their duty.

"I know too that there are profiteers in every country, and that the media, which criticise us, would perhaps be better employed in clearing up their own back-yards; but we are weak, and they are strong.

"We do not possess great organs of international communication; so the criticisms we level at the United States, at France, the Soviet Union or Great Britain, do not carry like the criticisms levelled at us.

"We must try, therefore, to be strong and, above all, united.

"We must ensure that the ruling class attracts the support of the people, and is rooted in the people.

"If not, the country will be overturned.

"The worst is to be feared."

So much for the generalities, which, as I knew all too well, were rigorous requirements of Iranian, polite society! Now, we had to go on talking, gradually establishing the bases for actual negotiation, before attempting to strike an accord.

To allow us to speak privately, the Ayatollah's relative, and my colleague, had retired together as the first cups of tea were poured. Both expected a sequel to our conversation, and, indeed, something was decided: namely, I should suggest to the Shah that he make a pilgrimage to Qom, which he had not visited for years, even though he went, once or twice every year, to Meched. A chance encounter with the prelate, inside the shrine, before, and after, going through the motions appropriate to the political landscape, might thus have healed the rift between the crown and the religious hierarchy and brought about a return to the traditional policy of the Shahs, a practised, until the beginning of the 'sixties, by Mohammad Reza Pahlavi himself.

However, we were no longer in this kind of situation – a fact, which I ignored during the session. I therefore took leave of the Ayatollah, promising to convey his invitation to the Sovereign and to return soon for a resumption of our exchange of views.

Towards the end of the spring, a relative calm returned to Iran. The political fabric seemed to relax. Opponents of the regime began to put their case openly, and numerous detai-nees, who had been imprisoned for acts of political violence, including attempted murder and armed raids on banks, were set free. The Chief of the Savak – hate-figure of the Iranian opposition, and of the international press – had been packed off to Pakistan, and his successor was thoroughly presentable. Also, the Shah had established a dialogue with the head of the

Shiite hierarchy. He felt that he had made concessions, but he could not pretend that intrigues, aimed at exploiting weak points in the domestic situation, were as prevalent as ever.

Elements of the international press – particularly France's *Le Monde* – kept up their campaign against Iran and the Shah, while diplomats from the US-embassy at Teheran plotted openly against the Sovereign and incited the opposition. Proof of this was provided by documents seized from the American embassy and published, by the revolutionaries, after the hostage-taking, which began on 4th November 1979 and went on for four hundred and forty-four days. Chief among the conspirators was the First Political Secretary, George Lambrakis, whom the Shah would later expose, in his memoirs. The British were more discreet, but were doing the same, and the BBC, which was much listened-to in Iran, gradually became the voice of the radical opposition. Even the Germans, closeted in the cultural section of their embassy, held "poetry-readings", with a few second- or third-rate quasi-poets, which were really political meetings, at which the regime was savagely attacked. On the Sovereign's orders, Iranian diplomats refrained from commenting on any of this.

Many of those attending opposition-meetings in Teheran were people who spoke only Arabic. These were Palestinian guerrillas or activists, who would soon draw attention to themselves. The police, and other security-services, were ordered to place them under surveillance, but this damaged the "liberal" image, which the Shah was trying to project.

"Measures, which were supposed to meet with general approval, were, yet again, taken as no more than a sign of weakness, on my part," the Shah told me later, in exile.

Eventually, he decided to indicate that liberalisation had reached its limits, and, on 26th June 1978, in the American magazine, *Newsweek*, he wrote that "the unholy alliance between the Red and the Black is contrary to nature," adding, " no-one is going to depose me: I have the support of the majority of the people, of all the labourers and of seven-hundred thousand soldiers."

Official propaganda obliged by echoing these sentiments for the benefit of Iranian public opinion.

Mohammad Reza Pahlavi still had many trumps in his hand. He was still in a position of strength. He had enjoyed several weeks of relative respite and would have more – sufficient to bring about changes, which would have shored up his regime.

After giving vent to these sentiments, in *Newsweek*, the Shah left, with the Imperial Family, for Nowchahr, on the coast of the Caspian Sea, to take his annual, summer-holidays.

14th June 1978

Niavaran Palace – the Shah receives the Conference of members of
the Group Studying the Problems of Iran.
Houchang Nahavandi is addressing the Sovereign.

(Author's Collection)

Chapter V

"Oh, that old man!"

1st July 1978 to 25th August 1978

Nowchahr, a commercial port and holiday-resort on the Caspian Sea, also featured the Imperial Family's summer-residence, for which the word "palace" was sometimes used. This wooden building, standing partly on stilts, looked down, in one direction, on the inner harbour of the port, and in the other, on the Nowchahr roadstead. Its main element was a wide terrace, around which were grouped a salon more than 200 sq ft, where the King received visitors, two smaller rooms used, during the day – one for the officers of the guard, and the other as a waiting room – and four bedrooms. It was furnished in a modern style with tasteful simplicity.

Here, the Shah's daily programme was lighter. There were no officials in attendance, and it was the officers of the guard, in summer-dress, who greeted visitors and ushered them to the salon to be given audience. The staff, wearing shirts-without-ties, served melon, water-melon or fruit juice to people awaiting audience, instead of the usual tea and dry cake. The King was taking a break, receiving visitors for only about three hours per day – between ten and one – and spending about as long looking through official reports and the international press. He would read, or skip through, a few books, almost always in French. He played a lot with the children, did some water-skiing and diving and swam a little. He listened to music a great deal. Life was relaxed and security light.

The Shah and Shahbanou used to go to Nowchahr, accompanied by some of the latter's friends, who, being younger than the Sovereign, helped to liven things up. Some of the Queen's female friends, Mohammad Reza Pahlavi didn't like at all. He had difficulty hiding his contempt; but he tolerated them with apparent indifference and by showing consideration for their husbands. These ladies were frequently the target of jokes, and sometimes of more malicious allusions; but that only seemed to amuse him. These guests stayed in a wing of the Hotel Tchalous, a few miles away, and came over to the Imperial residence, a little before noon, each day. The security-staff slept in simple, but comfortable, barrack-huts.

At the beginning of the summer, in 1971, when I had just been appointed Rector of the University of Tehcran, I was received at Nowchahr, in this capacity, by the Sovereign, who asked me suddenly, "do you manage to sleep well at night?"
"Oh, yes, Your Majesty," I replied, "very well."
"No sleeping tablets?" he asked again.
"Certainly not!" I said.
"I'm sorry to say," he rejoined, "that I've had to take them for years; but here, and at Shiraz, I always sleep well, without taking anything."

This must have been one of the Caspian coast's great attractions for the Shah.

From time to time, one or another of the Shah's friends – such as Professor Adle, for example, the celebrated Iranian surgeon – went to Nowchahr for the weekend, and, after dinner, the elder folk would play cards, without stakes, while the younger ones danced on the terrace.

When there were distinguished, foreign guests – King Hussein of Jordan often came; then there were ex-King Constantine of Greece and his wife, the Princes of the House of Savoy, the heir-to-the-throne of Morocco (now King Mohammed VI) the Academician Maurice Druon and so on – they were put up, not far away, in the luxurious villa of the Shahbanou's uncle, Mohammad Ali Ghotbi, who, if he was there, obligingly went back to Teheran or found somewhere else to stay.

The holidays of the summer of 1978, began relatively peacefully for the Shah, who believed that he had de-fused the crisis, and for the Imperial Family. There was almost no change to the usual routine. The Shah had rather more visitors than previously, and the Shahbanou, who had taken a complete break in preceding years, also began to give audiences, in order to keep pace with events.

It was up to me to keep up our contacts in Qom - especially with Ayatollah Shariat-Madari – and then to report my long conversations with the prelate, to the Shah. This I did, for the first time, at the beginning of July, just after the Imperial Family's arrival at Nowchahr. The Sovereign listened to me attentively. I had made notes of everything and recounted it faithfully. When I had finished, he exclaimed, "oh, that old man!" and passed to discussing other matters. Before I left, he added, "of course, you'll have to keep on going to see him," and so I did. However, the "old man" deserved more than that exclamation.

At the next encounter, I conveyed the Sovereign's compliments to the prelate and told him that the Shah attached great
importance to knowing the Ayatollah's views on the problems
of the time, although Mohammad Reza Pahlavi had said
nothing of the sort. All the same, it was significant that the
Shah wanted to pursue this dialogue with the country's principal, religious leader, who, in turn, asked me to convey his
gratitude to His Majesty. Both were pretending, but a channel
of communication worth exploring remained open.

The situation had not changed noticeably since my previous
meeting with the Ayatollah. No political decision of importance had been made. The Shah, his popularity intact, was still
the master of the game, and people were waiting to see what
he would do. The capital was rife with rumours concerning
the future direction of the government and what political
moves the Shah might make, such as a thorough ministerial
re-shuffle, or even a change of Prime Minister; for, indeed,
the latter had remained somewhat inert, sometimes giving the
impression merely of expediting current affairs, rather than
governing.

The dissidents had begun to express themselves without
restraint, and American diplomats spread out in political
circles, fomenting protest ever more boldly. Through their
traditionally much listened-to programmes in Farsee, the great
radio-networks of the West pursued their campaign against
the Shah. The domestic situation continued to deteriorate,
but life went on with a certain nonchalance. A major political
initiative was required, and it had to come from the Shah, but
what should it be?

Every passing day was another day lost. The closure of the
universities and schools, for the summer, and the torpor of the

holidays, had provided a respite, and the Shah, at Nowchahr, was serene. He was consulting.

Those who were preparing for radical change were about to strike decisively against the established order, and the Sovereign was certainly quite unaware of this. Despite all the frightening reports and warnings, he continued to be confident, above all, in the support of the Americans. He never dreamt that they, and their allies, would turn on him and betray him.

Of all this, I could say nothing to the Ayatollah.

After the usual greetings, Ayatollah Shariat-Madari taxed me with it, however: "but what is going on in Teheran," he asked, "what is His Majesty doing, why doesn't he act?"

Then, as I had feared he would, the prelate began to complain about the situation from a personal perspective, and at considerable length:
"If you want to know why people are irritated," he said, " look at the case of Ayadi!"*
"Perhaps he is an excellent doctor," Shariat-Madari conti-nued, " but you know as well as anyone that he is a Baha'i."**
"His Majesty has every right to choose his own doctor, of course, but it's quite unacceptable that this man should be

---

* Inspector-General of Medicine, Karim Ayadi, trained at the Military School of Medicine at Lyon. He had been the Shah's personal physician for many years.
** Baha'ism is the religion of the disciples of Baha-Allah, who was born at Teheran, in 1817, and died at Saint Jean d'Acre, in 1892. It spread through many countries, but especially through Iran, where it originated. Baha'ism has no public ceremonies nor sacraments. It aims at a synthesis of other religions and preaches universalism. The Muslim, religious authorities have always considered it to be an apostate and diabolical sect.

photographed, as happened recently, in the shrine of the Imam Reza, just behind the Shah, in the process of praying – or, rather, pretending to pray, since he's not a Muslim.

"I assure you that many Muslims were profoundly shocked by this," he went on, "but do you dare to tell His Majesty about it?"

"I shall, if you want me to," I said.

"I certainly do," he snapped, "and tell the Shah that we have a centre for investigating, and compiling information on, the adherents of this sect.

"We've got them all on file."

He then moved on to a more sensitive matter, regarding the conduct of one of the Shah's sisters. Having named her, he made some severe comments about her behaviour, her affairs and her interference in politics. He recounted some of her untimely, high-profile appearances at the functions of international organisations, where, he said, "she has no business – we've got ministers for that," adding, "I've sent the Sovereign several letters, warning him about this, but I don't know if they were ever received.

"I can't just ring him up and give him a moral lecture, although, God knows, he needs it; so, do you dare to take this message?"

He then reeled off a mass of detailed facts – with dates and places and the names of witnesses – about this person.

"At your express request," I replied, "I'll tell him."

Obviously, I had to take notes: scribbling furiously, I added, "I'll do it."

He looked at me quizzically, with a dubious irony, and asked, "you give me your word?"

"I do," I said.

"This a very delicate situation for you," he continued, "very difficult, but I can record all these facts and testimonies, on tape, with exact references.

"You take the cassette to His Majesty and – this is all I ask of you – make sure he listens to the whole thing, in your presence."

To ensure confidentiality, this conversation was taking place late in the evening. It had not begun until nine-o-clock. A Colonel of the Guard had driven me to Qom, in an unmarked car – to the house of my colleague, who was our principal intermediary with the Shiite hierarchy. The three of us then drove on to the Ayatollah's house, where the officer had to wait outside in the car. When the prelate joined us, my colleague, having paid his respects, retired to a nearby room, leaving us alone.

It was late at night, when we got back to Teheran.

About ten-o-clock the following morning, I rang Nowchahr to ask for an audience, which was then scheduled for ten the next day. The Shah showed his concern by sending a special flight to take me to the coast.

As I arrived at the Palace, I met General Moghaddam, the Chief of the Savak, which was odd, because this was not "soldiers' day", but he only smiled courteously and said, "your audience is going to put mine back by at least an hour, but, no doubt, there are good reasons for it.

"Just look at this file," he went on, showing me a small suit-case, "it's full of very frightening reports.

"I know you can speak fairly freely to His Majesty: achieve something, if you can, in your audience, by persuading him that he must act with extreme speed!

"Time is against us now.

"You know I wouldn't come here to tittle-tattle to the King about so-and-so's conjugal infidelities or the indiscretions of such-and-such.

"The Savak is doing its duty, at last, and it has some truths to tell the Shah."

I went in at once.

I reported my latest conversation with the Ayatollah to the Shah, mentioning notably the allusions to Inspector-General Ayadi.

"What rubbish!" Mohammad Reza Pahlavi said, "Ayadi is an atheist."

"What matters, Majesty," I insisted, " is not what he is, but what people think he is."

"That's the sort of remark Machiavelli used to make, to phase his listeners."
"Yes, Majesty, maybe it is."

Under enormous embarrassment, I then broached the matter of his sister and reported what the prelate had said. He heard me in silence, until I had finished, and then asked: "and you – do you believe what he claimed?"

It was a most delicate situation. I was faced with a

dilemma, from which it would be very difficult to extract myself. If I said "yes", I would give serious offence, and for extremely embarrassing reasons, to someone very close to the Sovereign. On the other hand, knowing that the monarch was not entirely ignorant of what I had just explained, I could only be accounted a hypocrite, or an imbecile, if I said "no"; and it was not in my nature to allow this.

"Majesty," I said, "I am only a messenger: it's not up to me to evaluate the words, which it is my duty to report to you, as they were spoken to me by the Ayatollah."

He gave me a strange smile, as though I had wounded him, and we left the matter there. As I was leaving, he said, "naturally, you will maintain the contact."

On leaving the salon, where I had been received, I met the Shahbanou just coming out of her private apartment. We went out together on to the great terrace, where I told her briefly about my meeting with the prelate, minimising my account of what he had said about her sister-in-law. She made no comment about the matter, even though the two women were not really on friendly terms.

During the afternoon of the same day, I had a telephone-call from General Moghaddam, who had also just returned from Nowchahr. He told me that the Shah had given him instructions, regarding several problems in Azerbaidjan-Province, and had asked him to brief me about them. I daresay that the Sovereign had let him know that I was acting as an intermediary in a dialogue with the Ayatollah Shariat-Madari; but neither of us mentioned that. The current problems the General referred to, were quickly dealt with, either by him, or through his mediation.

Next, I had to request another interview with the prelate, which I could have done, at once; but haste would have been construed as a sign of weakness, and, the country being in so parlous a condition, it was most important that the Sovereign should not lose face. I therefore waited for a week.

It was at this moment that an Imperial order was issued, naming Professor Abbas Safavian as "personal physician to His Majesty the Shah-in-Shah Aryamehr". Professor Safavian had trained in France. He had been a house-doctor in several Paris hospitals, run his own clinic and acquired the highest qualifications, before becoming Head of the Faculty of Medicine at the University of Melli – the capital's second university – and then its Rector. Besides being a renowned practitioner, he was also well known as a good Muslim and as the physician to several, important, religious figures. Like all those, who had been anti-communist during their youth, in the 'fifties, he had shared the patriotic, Nationalist dream represented in Mohammad Mossadegh – the man who had fought the British and the Communists. As a vice-President of the "Group for the study of Iranian problems", the professor was thought of as a reformist. Since 1976 – although this was not known until later – he had been part of the medical team treating the Shah for an illness, which was rigorously kept secret. In appointing him officially as his personal physician, the Shah had killed two birds with one stone. In the preceding months, Professor Safavian had been seen frequently at the palace, sometimes ostensibly to examine the Shahbanou – who was hardly in need of such attention – and sometimes under the pretext of giving an opinion on the condition of the Queen Mother, who had her own doctors. These visits could have awakened suspicions, and started rumours, about the state-of-health of Mohammad Reza Pahlavi; so, in appointing him officially, the Shah made his visits unremarkable, because it was quite normal for his doctor to see him frequently. At the same time, it was a gesture to the high clergy and to Ayatollah Shariat-Madari. The elderly Inspector-General Ayadi was clearly not given the sack, but he was asked to be discreet, while a good Muslim, with liberal, reforming ideas, was appointed to a confidential position. It can be assumed that this decision did not go unmarked.

Having waited a week, for the sake of appearances, and having requested and been granted another meeting with the Ayatollah, I found myself again at Qom – as always, in secrecy and after nightfall - facing the Shiite hierarchy's most influential dignitary and spokesman. It seemed to me that our conversations had developed sufficiently to permit the negotiation of an accord between the Sovereign and the clergy. The Shah had not asked me to go so far, but the fact, that he had urged me so keenly to follow through, allowed me to consider that I should. I knew that his pride and habitual reserve inhibited his expressing the wish. He was still all-powerful and believed that he was still master of the political game. Some other leading figures had been approached, all of whom had referred the matter to Ayatollah Shariat-Madari – the man regarded, by a large body of public opinion, as its representative, and with whose co-operation it might be possible to rectify the domestic situation.

Straightaway, when we met, he thanked me concerning some decisions taken, in Azerbaidjan, to resolve some current problems there, which he had raised with me:

"I don't know if you have any influence with His Majesty," he went on, "but at least I'm now sure that you have been passing on my messages."

Without alluding at all to his remarks about Inspector-General Ayadi, I then asked him, "incidentally, did you know that the King has a new, personal physician?"

"Oh, yes," he replied," and I have allowed myself to mention publicly that he is a fine practitioner and a good Muslim."

The psychological ground having been thus cleared, I could proceed further:

"Public opinion is waiting," I ventured, "with growing impatience, for some important policy-decision from His Majesty – something, which would create a new, political order, as I call it.

"His Majesty has not asked me directly to put this to you," I continued, "but I believe that he would be glad to know your views on how the situation might be rectified."

There was a long silence. Then, he said, "repression achieves nothing conclusive.

"What we need is an exemplary recognition, at the highest level, that lamentable errors have been made and must be corrected without delay.

"In a word," he went on, "it is necessary to make good, sincere policy and avoid dependence on oppression by the police.

"We have a constitution, which ought to be honoured and applied both in the spirit and the letter, and a Sovereign, who ought to act as an impartial judge, completely detached from factional interests.

"Indeed, he's throwing himself away, at the moment; he is terribly exposed.

"Power used in this way has a very bad effect on the one who is using it.

"Over the years, I often used to advise him to dissociate himself from the parties, but he wouldn't listen; and so I have kept my counsel to myself.

"However, since you ask for it, please convey yet another message to the Sovereign: I am convinced that the time has come for him to take a radical decision, in order to change the course of events.

"He is still in a position of strength, and the situation can be managed without any appearance of retreat; but, if the King fails to take this decision within the next few weeks, he will soon lose everything.

"Events will occur in such a way that reasonable people will lose control of them; and," he concluded, "you know as well as I do, that, if fratricidal chaos descends on Iran, its only beneficiaries will be foreign powers, especially our mighty neighbour to the north."

"So what are you recommending," I pursued, "a change of cabinet?"

"At least that," he rejoined, "Amouzegar is honest enough, but he is no statesman – certainly a change-of-cabinet."

I probed further: "whom would you pick as Prime Minister?"

He gave me some names, the first of which was that of Ali Amini, the super-rich financier, who was said to be a liberal and who had been a minister under Ghavam, Mossadegh and General Zahedi, before becoming ambassador to Washington and then (owing to pressure from the American Democrats, who were then in power) Prime Minister. For some months, Ali Amini had been dashing about everywhere, attending meetings, filling his house with distinguished Teheranis and visiting Qom. I knew that he had been to see the Ayatollah. I knew also that the Shah – to put it mildly – did not like him much. For one thing, as everyone knew, he mistrusted "men from Washington". Recently, Ali Amini had requested an audience with the Shah – just before he went to Nowchahr - but the Shah had not replied.

"And then," said the Ayatollah, "if that's not enough, tell him that he must take 'a capital decision'."

"What decision is that?" I inquired.
"Oh," he replied, "His Majesty is very intelligent: he will understand."

With that, he launched into philosophical considerations, with quotations from the Koran and anecdotes from the lives of the Imams and the life of the Prophet, concerning justice, equity and balance in matters of human conduct.

Having returned to Teheran, I went, on the day-after-next, to Nowchahr, where, notes in hand, I gave a completely faithful account of my conversation with the prelate. When Ali Amini was mentioned, the Sovereign got very annoyed, saying, "I know, I know – that's what they all want – to bring back the man who proclaimed our country's weakness, the man who knows how to use his mullah's manners to get round the Ayatollah."*

Events would soon befall, which would push Mohammad Reza Pahlavi into making decisions, which would only aggravate the crisis.

The summer-respite was not used profitably, as it might have been, to initiate a political process from a position of

* Before going to Paris to study economics and law – just after the First World War, that was – Ali Amini had trained for a year, in Islamic theology and law, at Najjaf, in Iraq.

strength. Insist, though the Savak-chief might, on such an initiative, nothing was done. A dialogue was under way with the head of the Shiite hierarchy, but it was not made use of beyond the introduction of a few perfunctory measures. The Amouzegar-government expedited current affairs, just as it had since its formation, without flair or fumble. The Shah, as he viewed political developments, constantly said that he had made up his mind to liberalise the system; and this would still have been easy to do, if only he had agreed to the moral regeneration, which would have satisfied the public's demand for virtue among the political class, but which would have meant lopping off several rotten branches.

During this time, virulent opposition expressed itself more and more overtly, but without uttering threats towards the monarchy or the Shah's person, and western embassies – especially that of the USA – pushed publicly for the radicalisation of the protest movement.

On 5th August, while the nation was celebrating the anniversary of the proclamation of the Constitution in 1906 (a nodal point in the development of an authentic, national reform-movement) the Shah solemnly announced that the next legislative-assembly elections, due in June 1979, would be open to all candidates. Thus, anyone not nominated by Rastakhiz – the Party the Shah had created not long before – "might," he added, "present themselves under the banner of their choice."

This announcement marked the end of the single-party system, which had never worked anyway, in Iran; and, as part of a coherent programme of reforms, this decision – which had been desired both by the Shiite hierarchy and by public opinion at large – would have had a hugely beneficial effect.

As an isolated act, however, it was thought to be no more than a sign of weakness.

On 11th August, the beginning of the Fast of Ramadan, some rather small demonstrations took place in Isphahan. Only a few hundred people took part in these events, but they were extremely violent and several cultural institutions were pillaged and set on fire. Then, for the first time, slogans were heard attacking the Shah. The police were poorly prepared for violence of this kind and could do little or nothing. This was the start of a planned radicalisation.

The Prime Minister, with the Sovereign's approval, no doubt, declared martial law in the Empire's former capital, which was a great, beautiful and prosperous city of more than a million inhabitants, rich in historic monuments. Both Chambers of Parliament were recalled from the summer-recess, to sit in emergency-session, and overwhelmingly approved the government's initiative. Several army-units were parachuted into Isphahan, to occupy sensitive areas, near monuments frequented by tourists, and the city's military governor took to marching through the streets and the mazes of the bazaars, in full dress-uniform. It's hard to see what the regime hoped to achieve by staging this show of force. What could its strategy have been?

On 14th August, the Group for Studying the Problems of Iran issued a long communiqué – which was published in the press, but censored by state-broadcasting – about the riots in Isphahan, the origin of the unrest and the need to arrest the movement towards extremism. The three, leading figures of the National Front expressed their doubts about the wisdom of the policy being followed and called for strict adherence to the constitution; but they did not condemn the violence outright.

On 19th August, a Thursday, in the early afternoon, a fire gutted the Rex Cinema at Abadan, Iran's chief centre for the oil-industry. Our hundred and seventy-seven people were killed, either by asphyxia or burns. Being a matinee-performance, on the eve of the weekend, the film-show was being attended by many mothers and children. All the exits to the building had been carefully blocked, in advance, with the result that neither the town's fire-brigade, nor the firemen from the oil-refineries were able to save a single soul. It was an unforgettable atrocity; and, from the very beginning of the enquiry, there could be no doubt that it was an act of criminal intent; but who could have done it and to gain what, exactly?

The regime made as little as possible of the matter, as though it were an everyday event, and the media were required to take the same line; but this attitude only amazed and scandalized people further. The Sovereigns remained at Nowchahr, and not even the Prime Minister, nor any minister, went to the place of the tragedy. If one believes the Shahbanou's memoirs[*] on this subject, she was actively discouraged from going. Why? The Imperial Family had always participated in national grief as a stringent requirement of public duty, showing compassion and bringing aid and comfort to the afflicted. In this case, the Shahbanou did instruct her cabinet to give assistance to some of the families who asked for it, but privately and discreetly, so that the gesture had no political impact whatever.

Later, a single explanation was given, in private, to the effect that the regime did not wish to spoil the ceremonies marking the twenty-fifth anniversary of the fall of Mossadegh, and the return of the Shah, in 1953! In those days of tension and opposition, the government kept on holding celebrations,

---

[*] Editions XO, Paris 2003.

making shows of force and staging demonstrations of support for the Sovereign.

The first reaction came a few hours after the death-toll was known, but before it was recognised beyond doubt that the Abadan inferno had been no accident, from the Ayatollah Khomeyni: "it is certain," he proclaimed, in a communiqué, "that this inhumane and un-Muslim act cannot be imputed to the Shah's opponents, however some indications might be used to attempt to smear the Islamic movement with the guilt thereof."

But no-one had been accused, at that point. Why this sudden protestation of innocence? In any event, little attention was paid to it.

A few days later, the police-investigation placed responsibility for the crime squarely on the followers of Rouhollah Khomeyni. The perpetrators, having fled to Iraq, where the Ayatollah was, were arrested there, and Iran made application for their extradition; but the authorities, anxious to appease the clergy, declined to publish the charges, however damning they might have been. They did not wish to embarrass the clerics. Rouhollah Khomeyni need not have bothered to make his cautionary remark.

The international press, starting with some Parisian newspapers, then accused the Savak of being behind this awful outrage, without, however, explaining how the deed could have been thought to serve the interests of the Imperial regime.

"It was an infamous calumny," the Shah said later, but he did not dare to reveal the truth of the matter, which he knew full well would not be believed.

The Abadan disaster and the campaign, thus begun, to diabolise the regime, were a turning-point in the operation to destabilise Iran. Three years later, the authorities of the

Islamic Republic vindicated the mass-murder, presenting it as "fundamentally revolutionary" and "Islamic in nature". We had to wait more than a decade before western studies on the Iranian revolution began to ask questions. Similar attacks, carried out in Algeria and Egypt – and, more recently, in the United States and elsewhere – by Islamists, prove, if proof were needed, that such acts are standard "tactics and techniques of the Islamic revolution", to use the terms employed by the commander-in-chief of the "guardians of the revolution".

Islamists thus began using the terrorist technique of mass-assassination, which they have continued to employ ever since.

On the morning of 20th August, the Shah, exhibiting profound distress and anxiety, received hourly updates on the scale of the tragedy. Why did he authorise, as he did, the government's inaction and the media's minimisation of the attack?

The Imperial Couple were due to go back to Teheran, at the beginning of the afternoon, to attend the Queen Mother's great dinner in celebration of 20th August, and then return to Nowchahr for another couple of weeks. Several of their companions were to remain at Nowchahr to await their return; but so anxious was the Shah about the turn events had taken, that he decided to cut short the holiday and remain in the capital.

On that 20th August, for the celebration of Mossadegh's fall and the Shah's return, in 1953, several thousand people, including parliamentarians, local councillors, ministers, civil-servants and members of community-organisations had been rounded up by the Rastakhiz – of which this would be the last sign of life – to demonstrate in the capital. The atmosphere was not exactly gay, but the crowd, in Mokhber-ol-Dowleh Square, was not exactly sparse either. Orators re-affirmed their fidelity to the Sovereign. The Prime Minister, in a lyrical speech – of the sort, which he had perfected, and which was applauded at great length – brought proceedings to a serene end, whereupon the demonstration dispersed without incident.

During the event, I was standing next to Mehrdad Pahlbod, the Shah's brother-in-law and quasi-permanent Minister of Culture (which office he had held for nearly fifteen years) His wife, the Sovereign's elder sister – Princess Shams – was surely one of the least criticised of the members of the Imperial Family. She never meddled in politics, but busied herself with the "Red Lion and Sun" (the Iranian equivalent of the Red Cross) and, a little more seriously, with the Society for the Prevention of Cruelty to Animals, being the president of both organisations. She had even built a refuge for abandoned cats and dogs at her home. A few years earlier, she had converted to Catholicism and built a small chapel in the garden of her palace some forty miles from Teheran. This was all a bit odd, but she wasn't taken to task for it. People merely thought her rather eccentric.

Mehrdad Pahlbod was a distinguished-looking character, a civil engineer by training, and a musicologist. He had spent a long career in fine-arts administration, before being appointed as minister by Hassan-Ali Mansour in 1964. He was rather discreet, always well-dressed and spoke several languages, but he lived in fear, on the one hand, of offending his august brother-in-law and, on the other, of being accused of abusing his position, which had given him great reserve. He rarely said anything at ministerial meetings, or expressed an opinion about anybody.

At 11.00 am, as the demo was breaking up, he invited me to take tea with him at his office, which was close by. We had been ministers together, in the same cabinets, and, afterwards we had got on well, as Minister and Rector, co-operating in various common projects.

"There won't be anyone there on a Friday," he said, referring to the weekly day of rest, "and we can have a quiet chat, without the 'phone ringing."

At the Ministry, the skeleton-staff provided us with cups of tea. Mehrdad Pahlbod was noticeably preoccupied: "what's going on, Mr Nahavandi," he asked, "what do you think of the Abadan-fire?

"It seems," he went on, "that there are a great many dead."

No-one knew the exact number, at that time.

"Her Highness," continued Pahlbod, referring to his wife, as always, by her title, "has cried a lot; but was it an intentional act, do you think?"

I told him frankly that I knew nothing about the matter, but that criminal intent could not be ruled out. Then we talked about the political situation and the latest rumours, until, suddenly, Pahlbod's reserve ruptured and he burst out, "Amouzegar is not the man for this situation: he spends an inordinate time on insignificant details and avoids discussing things with anyone: His Majesty must act firmly!"

"You're close to him," I replied, "why don't you talk to him?"

"I wouldn't venture to propose such a thing," he said, "I never speak unless spoken to, and he never asks me about anything besides family-matters or the Roudaki."

The Roudaki was Teheran's opera-house.

"But I've noticed," concluded Pahlbod, "that you talk to him quite a lot nowadays."

"True enough," I said, "I'll see what I can do."

"Will you be our next Prime Minister?" Pahlbod asked, "everyone thinks you will."

I smiled a little at this and countered, "why don't you ask Her Highness to have a word with the Shah?
"After all, she's his big sister and he respects her a lot."

"Agreed," replied Pahlbod, confirming what everyone thought, "but she never discusses politics with His Majesty."

We chatted about this and that until about a quarter-past-twelve, when I made to go. At the door of his office, he asked suddenly, " are we going to have a revolution?"

"No, no!" I assured him, quite sincerely, "His Majesty is in control of the situation – the army is strong."

"I hope you're right," he returned; and then he asked me a question, which I thought particularly strange: "what's the Shahbanou's political position?"

"Exactly that of His Majesty the Shah," I retorted, "I've no doubt of that."

"Don't be so sure!" he said.
At eight-o-clock that evening, the Queen Mother, "Tadj-ol-Molouk", in Farsee, gave her usual, grand dinner in comme-moration of the day.

Twice a year, on 20th August and 31st October (Crown-Prince Reza's birthday) the Queen Mother gave huge receptions at her Palace, "to mark," as she said, "the two dates of the re-birth of the Pahlavi."

On 20th August, the event was held in the wonderful Palace-gardens, and about a thousand people were brought in – not only serving-officials and their wives, or husbands, but also former functionaries, some of them very old, who had served under the Queen Mother's husband. There were also Qadjar princes – her father had been a general under the last dynasty – aged poets and various unfashionable or forgotten artists.

The octogenarian Queen Mother had spent most of her time, in recent years, sitting in a salon, carefully made-up, bedizened with jewels and sometimes dozing off. It was the chief-officer of her household who received the guests. The Shah and Shahbanou, and a few close friends, went to keep her company. Some official figures, whom she did not remember, came to present their respects.

As always, the reception was sumptuous, the buffets were beautifully laid out and the quality of the food and drink was exceptional. Two orchestras, one Iranian and one western, played alternately. Gentlemen wore evening dress and ladies wore gowns and jewels, which would have been the envy of the finest receptions in Paris or Rome. That evening, little was said about events at Abadan. Some ambassadors didn't even know about it, not having heard any broadcasts in Farsee, because no newspapers came out on a Friday.

The Shah mingled with the guests, as was his wont. He seemed relaxed; but he was wearing his habitual mask, through which no hint of his real, inner misgivings could penetrate.

At a quarter-to-nine, just before dinner was served, a footman ushered six, prominent people into one of the Palace's salons. The Shah stood up to shake hands with them, but now the mask ha fallen and his disquiet was obvious.

"What's the news from Abadan?" he asked.

"We still don't know how many died," was the response.

"It's dreadful!" exclaimed the Shah.

"And there were certainly many children among them," the report continued, "just as you'd expect on a Thursday afternoon, when nearly every seat is booked.
"We still don't know," the speaker went on, "whether it was an attack or an accident."

"But who would have barricaded the exits?" interpolated the Sovereign.

"I expect we shall soon know," came the reply.

Then the Shah invited those present to listen to an audio-tape of a press-interview, given the same day, in which he re-affirmed his commitment to liberalisation and directed some didactic criticism at the countries of the West. It was his usual line.
"What do you think?" he asked.

Prime Minister Amouzegar contented himself with a brief compliment, but Hoveyda (Minister to the Imperial Court) launched into a tirade of flattery, ending with "... full of frank and telling phrases, which will address every anxiety and silence every critic," which he evidently did not himself believe; but such speeches had become a habit with him. Once a lucid intellectual, he had been conditioned by the political game and become the Empire's leading flatterer.

It was then a quarter-past-nine, and the Sovereign said wearily, "let's have dinner."

He put on his smile-of-convenience and led the little group back into the throng. After dinner, he talked at length with the great writer, Ali Dashti, one of Iran's true Arabists and the author of a celebrated, iconoclastic biography* of the Prophet Mohammed.

A former ambassador to Arab countries, and a co-opted Senator, Ali Dashti was rightly considered to be an authority on Arab and Islamic history.

Towards ten-o-clock, there was the traditional fire-work display, which was as splendid as any the Iranian masters-of-the-art had produced over the centuries. The whole city watched it.

A few days later, when the scale of the Abadan-tragedy became common knowledge, radical opponents of the regime would denounce and exploit this glittering reception with its fire-work display.

"While an entire city wept," they would say, "there were dancing and fire-works at Court."

Thus, another grave error was committed. If only one had taken the initiative, cancelled the ostentatious fête and fire-works and declared a national day-of-mourning! The blow would soon fall hard upon the regime, and everyone would quickly regret, and deplore, the bad management of this affair;

---

* After the revolution, and then in his nineties, Ali Dashti was arrested, for having written this book, tortured and put to death. His body was dumped in a gutter near his home.

but history cannot be re-made.

The mass-assassination of Abadan opened the revolution's bloody phase and unleashed the western media against Iran and the Shah. At once, the tone of the principal radio-channels, broadcasting in Farsee, changed perceptibly: the Voice of America, the Voice of Israel and, especially, the BBC virtually became the voice of the revolution, moving from criticism, to overt incitement of revolt, and from biased reporting, to outright disinformation.

On 23rd August, the Ayatollah Khomeyni, whose name was beginning to be well known and frequently mentioned, squared up, for the first time, to the monarchic regime, and the Shah personally, and spoke of an Islamic Republic. On the same day, a small group of extremists set fire to the covered vegetable-market, in Teheran. The authorities' reaction was nugatory.

Apparently, the Shah had already made the decision, to change the government, and had been consulting discreetly on the subject since Saturday 21st. Meanwhile he authorised Amouzegar to carry out a modest, ministerial re-shuffle, with the object of stopping the rumours and keeping options open.

On the morning of 22nd August, I received a summons to go to the Palace, at half-past-four that afternoon. I had not requested an audience: I was told, I was to be consulted about political developments and my views on how best to deal with the crisis. I prepared a few notes, but nearly everything I would need was already written up in the latest reports of the Study Group, whose President I was. All I had to do was present a resume of the Group's many warnings, over the years, and of its proposals for alternative solutions to current economic, social and political policies.

The Sovereign greeted me very cordially. He usually welcomed visitors standing up. Sometimes he exploited this position to make some preliminary moves, which could be rather uncomfortable, but I got used to it. Exceptions to this rule were the Prime Minister, high-ranking religious dignitaries and foreigners.

This time, he invited me to sit down, not in front of his desk, but in a room at one corner of the suite. He sat down opposite me, looked at me for a moment and then rang for a servant to bring us two cups of tea. When the servant noticed this departure from protocol, he gazed at me in astonishment. Oh, the games and the subtleties of the Court! In his eyes, my status had just changed, and this circumstance would be commented upon in the ante-chambers, giving rise to rumours...

When two orderlies had served the tea (the king always had to be served separately) the Sovereign revealed his perspective of the general situation. It might be serious, he thought, but was by no means desperate. He still preserved, at that time, the over-proud self-assurance and dynamism, which would fall from him in the coming weeks.

"If you had to deal with the situation, which we see before us today," he asked me, "what solutions would you put forward?"

I started by analysing the domestic causes of popular discontent, which were being exploited by foreign forces. These were the corruption of a tiny minority of the ruling class, inflationary pressures, administrative slackness, some particularly unpopular measures taken by the Hoveyda and Amouzegar governments, a lack of actual dialogue with the religious hierarchy, persistent rumours concerning the Savak – despite General Moghaddam's reforms – and the organisation and policy of the Pahlavi Foundation* and some of its daughter-agencies.

He listened intently and did not interrupt. Then I listed the solutions, which, in my view, a new government ought to apply with all expedition: "to begin with," I said, it ought to seek emergency powers from Parliament for six months.

"Above all," I went on, "what we need is moral regeneration: some members of the Imperial Family" – and here I gave him the names of two of his brothers and one of his sisters, but the Sovereign did not react in any way to hearing them mentioned; his expression remained just as before – "should receive 'His Majesty's command' to leave the country.

"The holders of the principal posts of public responsibility – about three hundred people – should not only be competent, but also of unimpeachable probity, and that means dismissing certain people who think they are above the law."

I may have been wrong to cite anecdotes I had heard, one about a high-ranking officer of state, who had been seen drunk, recently, in one of the capital's Greek restaurants, and one about a provincial governor, who had engaged in a shouting-match, with the occupants of a neighbouring table, in a fashionable night-club; "but these facts," I added immediately, in a mild tone, "which might pass quite unnoticed in those countries, which wag their fingers at us, make a terrible

---

* The Pahlavi Foundation was a charitable and cultural institution, dependent on the Crown and benefiting from semi-public status and certain other privileges.

impression on public opinion here."

In fact, the rumour-mill had amplified these two incidents, which the regime's enemies had then taken up and used to do a lot of damage to the State's image.

A long-term programme would be necessary, I said, to contain inflation, but it could be begun by abolishing some effective monopolies, in the private sector, which were sources of abuse and rumours of abuse, thereby restoring vigour to private enterprise. In this connection, I referred to the Corporate Chambers, set up by Hoveyda, as "a gangrene, which was well on its way to contaminating the entire social structure".

"They should be dissolved forthwith," I insisted, "they have done nothing but undermine the bazaars and alienate the middle-classes, while their infringements of the law have been dismissed as 'corporate' and placed under amnesty."

All told, I continued, there were more than 180 000 civil cases, which would be impossible to clear at once, waiting to go before the courts: "small businessmen and craftsmen are beside themselves," I insisted.

I also envisaged an urgent programme to clean up the southern quarters of Teheran and the outer suburbs of Tabriz, Shiraz, Isphahan, Abadan, Khorramchahr, Ahwaz and several other big towns.

"We should return to the traditional solar calendar," I said, "and scrap 'daylight-saving' changes to the clocks, which have upset people no end.

"Just because they have them in the West, to save energy," I demanded, "why should we have to put up with them?"

Then I explained that, although I saw the Savak retaining its powers and responsibilities relating to intelligence and counter-espionage, I thought that essential responsibility for internal security should be transferred to the civil police, and a wide consultation conducted to ensure that this transfer would not endanger the security of the State.

I told the Sovereign that, if he entrusted me with forming a government, I would shortly present a cabinet to Parliament, armed with a succinct and rigorous programme. Some of the names I put forward astonished him: there were those, who had been dismissed, but had remained loyal – and were known for their authoritativeness and probity – as well as admirals and generals, on active service or retired. I think he was expecting a solid phalanx of academics and technocrats.

I opined that the domestic situation was still under control, but that, should the need arise, we should not hesitate to declare martial law, for three months perhaps, in order to show subversive elements that the time for "fooling around" was past. Straight away, however, I said, we should resolutely tread the path of democratisation, which would have no meaning or effect unless it was trodden with firmness and moral authority. In this connection, I went on, elections to the two chambers of Parliament, and the municipal elections, should not be held without the participation of all those dissidents who recognised the principles of the constitution.

"Eveything can still be saved," I said, by way of conclusion, and I believed it then, as I believe it now, that, if this programme had been implemented at once, Iran would have had a revolution of a productive kind, putting an end – in good conscience before the jury of international opinion – to the intrigues of foreign powers.

The Shah heard me out, for over an hour. Sometimes he posed questions and took notes. When I had finished, he thanked me politely and, as I took my leave, said with a smile, "I'll think about it."

In the next few hours, I picked up several scraps of gossip about the comments, which he had made to his entourage, about my long presentation: "Nahavandi wants to close the night-clubs ... he's going to declare martial law ... he wants to purge three hundred people"!

I would rather have had sarcasm.

Some days later, my friends reproached me hotly for having been too frank: "you have to handle the King very carefully," they said; but they were wrong. I knew my chances were slim; but, if he had asked me to form a cabinet, I would have had to be able to act freely, and not find myself clashing and horse-trading with him – and especially with his entourage – from the first days of the first measures, onwards.

At lunch, on 20th September 1979, at the Villa of Roses in Cuernavaca, the Shahbanou and Mrs Pirnia (his family-doctor) being also there, the King told me suddenly: "if I'd appointed you as Prime Minister, last year, you would have been assassinated."

Was this his way of apologising? Who, I wonder, might have assassinated me – the dissidents – the profiteers I had intended to dump – or foreign agents? But that was not the time for such a discussion: I refrained from replying, and we spoke of other things.

On 25th August, less than a week after re-shuffling his

cabinet, Amouzegar was asked for his resignation, but remained, in a caretaker-capacity until his successor should be appointed.

The Shah's "think about it" had just ended. On 27th, a Saturday – the beginning of the week in Iran – Djafar Charif Emami, the septuagenarian President of the Senate, of the Pahlavi Foundation, of the Bank for Industrial Development and Mining, of countless industrial, commercial and financial companies, and who was, furthermore, the Most Serene Grand Master of the Grand Lodge of Iran, was asked to form the new government.

Chapter VI

"But what did I do to them?"

25th August to 8th September 1978

On returning to Teheran, the Imperial Family, was provisionally installed at the White Palace of Saad-Abad, in the hills to the north of the city.

Mohammad Reza Pahlavi hated air-conditioning, and, at the end of that August, it was still torrid in the capital, and at the Niavaran Palace, which was too close to the arid slopes of the Elbrouz, in a landscape with few trees; but Saad-Abad, which had a great park, where several members of the family kept permanent residences, was different. The Imperial Couple always stayed in the big house - built in the 'thirties, with a façade of white stone (hence its name) – although it was stretching the definition of the word to call it a "palace". It was smaller and less luxurious than the Niavaran, but the temperature there was quite bearable at this time – even pleasant – during the day, and cool in the evenings.

On Thursday 25th, towards 10 am, I went to the palace to see the Shahbanou, whose chief-of-staff I still was. As a rule, she did not receive visitors on Thursdays, and I did not have an appointment, but I wanted to see what was going on, and I was quite sure that she would agree to see me for a few minutes, when she emerged from her private apartment. On arrival, I was ushered into a waiting-room, where I informed a valet that I would like to have a few words with the Shahbanou.

The Shah received "military men", twice a week – and mainly on Thursdays – so I was not surprised to meet the Chief of the General Staff, as well as General Moghaddam – Head of the Savak – and one or two other soldiers, at that point. Everyone there already knew about Amouzegar's resignation and, although it had not been publicised, about the appointment of Charif Emami also, and they were discussing these matters freely, when I joined them. General Moghaddam had just come out of the Shah's office: he seemed agitated, and asked me if I could arrange an interview for him with the Shahbanou. He wanted to speak to her right away, he said, and insisted that I should be there when he did. I called the Shahbanou on an internal 'phone and heard her say, very cordially, that she would see us in a few minutes. We went up to the first floor, to the Shahbanou's small office there. On the stairs, the General said to me, "I want to have a witness at this interview."

"Your Majesty will understand," the General said, after the civilities, "that I was more restrained, than I am being now, in the comments I have just made to His Majesty, the Shah-in-Shah Aryamehr [as was the official title] about the choice of Charif Emami as Prime Minister.

"I permit myself to intercede with you about this appointment," he went on, "because it is the worst which could possibly have been made, at this critical juncture in the nation's affairs.

"Charif Emami," the General averred, "is not the man for

this situation: not only does he have no following, popular or otherwise, but he has an abominable reputation.

"His appointment as Prime Minister – it is my duty to tell you – is nothing less than catastrophic: he will lead us straight into the abyss; but there's still time to stop it.

"Please, Your Majesty," he concluded, "persuade the Shah-in-Shah to re-consider!"

This surreal scene is graven forever on my memory. The three of us stood – the General, to attention – as the Shahbanou picked up the telephone and spoke to the Shah.

"Sire," she said – for that's how she addressed him in public (in private, she usually called him "Madi", a diminutive of "Mohammad Reza Pahlavi") – "Sire, your chief of the Savak is here, begging me to throw myself at your feet and implore you by no means to make Mr Charif Emami your Head of Government.

"His reputation is execrable," she continued, "and he's the most dangerous choice you could have made at this time."

Then, for several minutes, the Shahbanou said nothing, as she listened to what was being said at the other end of the line, and which we, of course, could not hear. Eventually, she replaced the receiver and said, "unfortunately, there's nothing to be done about it, as far as I can see."

Once outside the Shahbanou's office, General Moghaddam gave free rein to his anger and concern: "I just can't believe it," he groaned, "how can the Shah be so ill-informed?

"Charif Emami!" he exclaimed, "there will be a general insurrection within two months!"

"I've done all I can," the General ended, "to stop the worst from happening – you are my witness to that – and even now I beg you to keep trying."

We parted, and I went back to the Shahbanou's office, where she was once more on the 'phone: "I've been trying His Majesty again with this," she said, after hanging up, "but there's nothing to be done, nothing at all; he's made up his mind."

"Couldn't we keep Amouzegar?" I pleaded, "his resignation could be refused.

"He's on good terms with the Americans," I argued, "and his reputation for integrity is rock-solid.

"He's not incapable of leading a more political government and inspiring confidence!"

The Shahbanou only shook her head sadly.

Djafar Charif Emami had trained as an engineer in Germany and began his career working for Iranian Railways. During the war, the Allies imprisoned him, as a "subversive", which gave him a certain prestige and impelled him towards the followers of Mossadegh. According to Ardeshir Zahedi, son of the general who led the battle against "the old lion" in 1953, Emami was among those, who acted as intermediaries in the nationalist-chief's honourable, and rather spectacular, capitulation to the new regime. From that time on, he threw himself into politics and business, excelling in combining, and intriguing between, the two. Malicious murmurers referred to him as Mr 5%.

He was the son of a minor mullah, which facilitated his relations with some clerical circles; and he bragged of his contacts with former Mossadegh-supporters, who had been converted, like him, into wealthy businessmen or directors of great, public enterprises. At the end of the 'sixties, under pressure from the Sovereign, the various Masonic orders in Iran had been united in the Grand Iranian Lodge, and Djafar Charif Emami – although only a new member at that time – was installed as its Most Serene Grand Master, and constantly re-affirmed, against all Masonic tradition, in that office.

By the middle of the 'sixties, he had already been Prime Minister and been deposed by popular disapproval within a year of taking office. So why choose him?

The Shah could have kept Amouzegar on as Prime Minister. He was a lacklustre politician, it is true, but he had integrity and he could have been guided towards including in his team men capable of setting things to rights. That would have been the least bad solution, I think, and the Shah later regretted failing to apply it.

"That was a regrettable error on my part," he wrote, "I was wrong to distance myself from that well-disposed and disinterested man."

He could have created a government for order and reform, which would have reached an accord with the religious hierarchy, integrated the Mossadegh-partisans into political life and stood up to pressures from abroad. There were plenty of people who could have carried out such policies, but he probably felt that they would force him to make too many concessions and to sacrifice politically those whom he wanted to protect. It then became necessary to strike a firmer posture towards the westerners – Washington, London and Paris – but he hesitated. He still had confidence in his American "friends", and so, in trying to give away nothing, he lost everything.

In picking Djafar Charif Emami, whom he thought of as a subtle intriguer, he chose the man least suited to the situation. This was no time for keeping up appearances. Hardly two weeks had gone by before he realised he had made a mistake.

A year later, at Cairo, he said to me, "it was that wretched Hoveyda who made me do it: 'Charif Emami,' he explained, 'has got really excellent contacts with the Russians, and that's what matters when it comes down to it; but, besides that, he has the ear of the top clerics: he's just the man for this situation.'

"Poor old Hoveyda," the Shah continued, "gave me so many assurances of this that I believed it; but it was just when I appointed Charif Emami, as Prime Minister, that the oil-workers, stirred up by the Communists, started their strikes, whereupon I quickly saw that Emami's good relations with Qom were more apparent than real."

That's the short explanation. It was probably at this moment that the Shahbanou began to look at some solutions of her own – without the Shah's knowledge – to apply to the crisis; for it was only a few days later that she met secretly with Shapour Bakhtiar and started the process, which would culminate, at the end of December, in his being appointed Head of the Government.

On Thursday 25th August, the appointment of Charif Emami was semi-official, and, that evening, he commenced his "consultations".

During my second, and brief, conversation with her, that morning, the Shahbanou let me know that I was going to be called to join the Cabinet.

"Mr. Charif Emami cannot deal with a situation of which he has no understanding," I told her: "I beg of you, do something to stop me having to serve in his government!" and she promised me she would do all she could to get me off the hook.

That same Thursday, a little before noon, and having just left the Shahbanou, I ran into Amir Abbas Hoveyda, as he was emerging from one of the Saad-Abad park's walks. Being Minister to the Imperial Court, he had an official residence close to the palace – one, which, incidentally, he had had converted, while he was Prime Minister, to serve as accommodation for the government's guests – and it was thither that he now invited me, with the greatest amiability, "to chat for a moment". I agreed, and we went up to a small sitting-room on the first floor, where we soon fell to discussing the change, which was taking place at the head of the government.

"I suppose you've taken account of the fact," I said, "that the choice of Charif Emami will precipitate us into chaos."

He burst out laughing, and replied, "I don't know, perhaps it's not such a bad decision!"
"Besides," he went on, "aren't you going to join the government?"

"I've heard it whispered," I said.

"Well, it whispered a very good thing, believe me!" he rejoined, "and I shall make sure that it becomes a reality."

"Mister Hoveyda," I replied, very deliberately, with the emphasis on the Mister, "we've been working together for our country for fifteen years, and, during that time, you've done me many good turns.

"This time," I went on, "I beg you to take pity and stay out of it: it will do no good, if I join a government which is heading straight for an impasse."

"Who knows, my dear chap?" retorted Hoveyda, "it's not certain that he will fail; besides, you see, I'm going to found a great, political party and take a hand myself!"

"Then," he finished, " everything will change and everything will work out."

We talked for some time about events, and I reproached him for intervening in favour of certain members of the Imperial Family – to get them privileges and preferments – for which public opinion always blamed the Sovereign.

"No," he exclaimed, "you don't understand: when they got what they wanted, they stopped dragging me back; and then, you see, I could get on with my work!"

I thought then of another conversation, four years earlier, in the garden of his own villa on the Caspian coast, where no-one could overhear us. He had always known that I was critical of his politics, but a strange rapport had grown between us. It was composed of political mistrust mingled with personal confidence. Raising the matter of his favours to two friends of the Imperial Family – one, a favourite of the Shah's, the other, a favourite of the Shahbanou's – he had said to me, sadly, and with scorn, "I have to throw them bones in order to buy peace."

"But you know," I had returned, alluding, of course, to the Emperor, "who will be reproached for this, at the end of the day!"

Hoveyda knew very well what I meant, but he didn't like what I was saying and changed the subject.

All day, on the Friday, Charif Emami tried to put together a team – around the three ministers (Foreign Affairs, Justice and one other) whom the King insisted he should include.

To the Ministry of Foreign Affairs, the Shah appointed Amir Khosrow Afshar, a former ambassador to Bonn, London and Paris. He was an elegant diplomat, experienced and culti-vated, who was regarded as one of the most brilliant agents in the Service; but, in recent years, he had remained somewhat aloof. If one believes the newspaper controlled by Amir Assadolah Alam, who was certainly the Sovereign's only, real confidant, the Shah was irritated by Afshar's "self importance, not to say, 'arrogance'". However, such was the gravity of the situation, that the Sovereign was obliged to call upon someone he treated as "pretentious". It was an excellent choice, but it should have been made earlier.

The Professor of Penal Law, Mohammad Baheri, was the Shah's appointee to the Ministry of Justice. In his youth, Baheri had been a militant of the extreme Left, but, having obtained a doctorate from the Faculty of Laws at the Sorbonne, he had become an ally of Assadollah Alam and, in the early 'sixties, had been his Secretary of State, and then Minister of Justice. His appointment, in those days, was badly received, although he soon became very popular with the judiciary, owing to his bold reforms of the judicial apparatus and his through knowledge of case-law.

He was in Europe, when Emami was forming a govern-ment, and the latter had made some effort to resist recalling him. A few weeks before, Baheri had written a long letter to *Le Monde*, responding to the paper's campaign against the Shah; and the opposition had been greatly irritated, when the editor published extensive extracts from it. The new Prime Minister cited this irritation in an attempt to avoid appointing Baheri, but the Shah would have none of it, and Baheri was proclaimed, on Saturday 27th, as Minister of Justice, even though he didn't get back to Teheran until two days later. A few weeks later, he left the Cabinet, over policy-disagreements with Emami.

The third "obligatory minister" was me.

How could I get out of being a minister and of being consigned to that prison-ship?

I let it be thought that I had left Teheran and that no-one knew where I could be reached. When the vice-President of the Senate, Mohammad Sadjadi – who was about to replace Emami as the head of the second chamber – called me, on the morning of Friday the 26th, to discuss, on Emami's behalf, the composition of the new Cabinet, he heard my wife say that I was away; but the old Senator only congratulated her on her husband's imminent entry into government and lavished lyrical praise on the political capacities of the latter's new boss-designate.

The 26th passed. Several, personal, or political, friends, from whom I had not hidden my continuing presence in the city, called me or came round to see me. Some tried to persuade me to take the post – word having gone round that I was up for a Ministry – saying that the situation was serious and that I ought to try to influence the government from within. Others wanted me to refuse, pointing out that the new Prime

Minister's character and reputation were such a handicap, that I ought to be thinking of my own future and holding myself in reserve for the nation.

Fate would decide the course of events. On Saturday 27th, thinking that the new Cabinet would have been formed the previous evening, I went to my office as usual. As a precaution, I told my secretary to reply to all enquiries by saying that I wasn't there. Minutes later, she let me know that Charif Emami was on the 'phone and that he knew I was in the building.

At that moment, I was in a meeting – arranged a fortnight before – with Professor Hamid Zahedi, a former senior-member of the Faculty of Law and Secretary-General of the Universities' Co-ordination Council. We were discussing, within the context of our membership of the Study Group, a report on the reform of higher education. I asked him to stay and monitor my conversation with Emami. I wanted a witness.

After the civilities – naturally, I congratulated the Prime Minister and wished him every success – Emami told me that he'd been trying to contact me for forty-eight hours, in order to bring me "some good news", because he had "been thinking" of me. I thanked him very warmly, but declined his offer, saying I believed that "I would be more useful outside, rather than inside, the government".

"We all have to make sacrifices at this time," he insisted, "I have had to force myself, quite brutally, to accept the heavy burden of power."

I learned later that he was telling the truth – that he had agonised over the decision.

"But, as you know," he continued, "the country is going through a dangerous crisis: our nation is in peril, and I consider that you are indispensable.

"Such is your prestige among intellectuals," he went on, "and in our erupting universities, that you will have a key-ministry – that of Science and Higher Education – with extended powers and extra funding.

"Also," he said, "you will be able to bring in a law, which, I believe, is very close to your heart, to establish the autonomy of the universities.

"I wish to tell you expressly that I am completely in agreement with this," he vowed.

I refused again, with all the necessary courtesy, and, weary of battle, Charif Emami hung up. Professor Zahedi was not slow to express his displeasure: "You should have taken it," he said, "I can guess why you didn't, but you would be influential inside the government – you could shape policy or, at least, prevent errors – and what about the autonomy of the universities, which you could bring in?"

Gossip about the 'phone-call, which I had just received – and the content of which everyone could guess – had already spread round the office. There was a knock at the door, and in came Ahmad Araghi, one of my colleagues, and a venerable, religious man, who had kept me in touch with Golpayegani, one of the senior ayatollahs at Qom. Carefully and reverently, he bore a copy of the Koran in both hands.

"I have come to make you swear that you will on no account take a post in the Cabinet," he said, "Qom would not understand it."

"That man," he continued, "is bringing misfortune upon the nation again, just as he did in the past."

I told him that I had just refused the offer and – with a smile – that he would not have to bring the Koran into it. Less than ten minutes had gone by, when my secretary, a little overcome by the situation, came to tell me that the Shahbanou herself was on the line, and demanding to speak to me without delay. In the event, she spoke to me very kindly, begging me to reconsider the refusal I had just given Charif Emami, and it was clear enough that the latter had already telephoned the Sovereigns about it.

"Your Majesty will permit me to express my surprise," I said, "that it was no more than forty-eight hours ago, when You wished to assure me that You would do all in Your power to prevent my being shipped out on a political adventure, which was doomed to failure."

"Circumstances have changed," she replied, "I am now in His Majesty's apartment; and he demands that you join this government immediately, because it needs, and will be greatly strengthened by, your presence."

"His Majesty understands, " I rejoined, "that I cannot imbue Mr Charif Emami with qualities which he does not possess, nor prevent certain disaster."

There was a long silence, then the Shahbanou again, now more forcefully: "understand this, His Majesty is asking you to make a personal sacrifice; if you agree to make it, he will never forget that you did."

The Shahbanou was very good at hiding her uneasiness, but I could tell from her voice how pained and anxious she was.

I said: "so His Majesty is asking me to commit political suicide, is he?

Another silence – with a certain amount of whispering – then the voice of the Shahbanou again: "leave your office, put on your morning-dress and come to the palace – the new government will be presented at ten-o-clock."

It was an Imperial command – and a cry for help.

"But I'll never make it," I protested, "the traffic ..."

"He awaits you!" she snapped.

The Cabinet-members were a mixed bunch. Apart from the Minister of Defence, the irremovable General Azimi, who had been there for years, three of them – as I have said – were suggested, or imposed, by the Shah. The two others, Khosrow Afshar and Mohammad Baheri, had also required further palace-intervention, I learned, to get them to accept their posts – which was a quite unheard-of proceeding. That aside, all present enjoyed solid reputations for integrity; but there were other, more important considerations, as a last-minute incident showed.

The President of the National Telecommunications Service had been called as Minister for Posts and Telecommunications; and there he was, in the great hall of the palace, being congratulated by everyone on his entry into government. As the party moved towards the saloon, where the presentation was due to take place, however, the Prime Minister was called to the telephone. After a few moments, he returned, wearing an embarrassed frown, took the Telecoms Minister-designate by the arm and spoke a few quiet sentences in his ear. The latter then took himself off, without a word and white with anger. The two men had not even shaken hands. A palpable air of mystery and unease descended.

A little later, it became known that Charif Emami had just been informed of the Minister-designate's adherence – real or imagined – to the Church of the Bahai, which the mullahs so despised, and that he had dismissed his prospective Telecoms Minister for that reason.

Almost twenty-five years later, and although I hardly knew the man and never saw him again, I often find myself imagining the humiliation, resentment and, no doubt, rebelliousness, he must have felt, as he left the palace, like a miscreant in the eyes of the world, walked across that enormous garden and then had to face the hundred-or-so journalists who were massed around the great gate.

During the presentation, Karim Motamedi, the discreet and irreproachable Telecoms-Minister of Hoveyda's last Cabinet, and, later, in the Amouzegar-government, was appointed to Charif Emami's Telecoms-Ministry. When Amouzegar was sacked, Motamedi had gone off to relax in his native province of Mazandaran, where he heard, on the radio, that he had just been presented, in the capacity of Telecoms-Minister, at the palace in Teheran. The police then received the order to trace him and, that evening, sent him a message to return at once to the capital, which he did.

The ceremony was short enough. The Shah, in civilian dress, wore a serene, but rather haughty, expression, without his usual, sociable smile. Usually, he said a few words to each new Minister, outlining his priorities. This time, he contented himself with shaking hands and saying simply, to each one, "you know what you have to do!"

Then he wished everyone good luck and withdrew. There was no official photograph of the Shah and his new government. Numerous, foreign journalists and cameramen had gathered in front of the palace, for the occasion, and some Iranian press-men were even allowed to attend the ceremony, but "photo-op" was there none.

As we left the palace, we were told that the first council of government would take place in an hour. There was hardly time to change back into ordinary clothes.

I was on my way to the Presidential Offices, in my ministerial car, when I heard an extraordinary communiqué, on the radio, from the new Prime Minister. First, he announced that the country was in danger; then he evoked "the sacred union", proclaimed a time of "national reconciliation" and looked forward to the coming elections. The communiqué was dated, that same day, in the reckoning of the solar calendar counted from the Hegira ("The Flight"). This betokened the abandonment of the Imperial Calendar, which had been imposed, by law, a few years before, and of which Djafar Charif Emami – then President of the Senate – had been one of the most ardent exponents.

The radio announcement went straight on to reveal that all casinos and gaming-houses throughout the country, would be closed forthwith. There were fewer than a dozen such places in Iran, and all of them belonged to the Pahlavi Foundation, of which Charif Emami was still the President. Thus, he was closing the gambling-outlets, which he himself had opened. There was much scoffing about these "measures for public propriety", as the announcement called them, and it was soon clear that they were virtually all Emami had to offer. By rebuffing a Minister-designate, on grounds of supposed Bahai-connections, and then announcing one or two superficial reforms, the poor man must have thought that he could win the confidence of the clergy and of public opinion - because his government never attempted anything else – and, a few hours later, his "measures for public propriety" were utterly forgotten.

The first council-of-ministers showed us how little consistency the government possessed. It was made up, it is true, of honest and, in some cases, competent, men; but, although it was intended specifically to engage with the public, it was never able to agree on what to do about any of the essential problems, nor even to define precisely what those problems were.

Opening the session, the prime Minister invoked the Lord God and prayed to Him to take us under his protection. Then, a copy of the Koran was brought in and everyone stood to hear a sermon preached about loyalty to the nation and the necessity of serving the country to the full extent of our powers. This was another innovation, intended, I assume, to impress the mullahs.

Next, Mr Charif Emami demanded of his ministers that they all prepare plans, during the coming week, of programmes for their respective ministries. These, he said, would be debated in council and ultimately included in a general plan of action, which would then be presented to Parliament. Thus, the Prime Minister – who, admittedly, had not wanted to head this government – indirectly made a terrible admission: he did not have the faintest idea of what to do! I immediately said that discussing and collating the detailed programmes of each ministry would waste precious time, because the country was awaiting an urgent programme of clear and precise proposals for reform, which should be presented to the Lower House the following day, and to the Senate as soon as possible afterwards.

"Public opinion needs a psychological jolt," I added.

Minister for Foreign Affairs, Khosrow Afshar, supported me warmly and at once, concluding with words addressed, in a trenchant tone, to the Prime Minister: "this, Sir, is no time to sit around chatting!"

"We all know how serious the situation is," retorted the Prime Minister, "and I more than anyone; but we must not rush into things too fast: we must put together, with care, a complete programme, which everyone can understand, covering agriculture, industry, commerce, housing, infrastructure, justice and so on – I see no necessity for slap-dash emergency-measures."

It was thus decided that the Cabinet would meet again, "only a week" later, and that each minister would then present a project for his department. Thereupon, during the course of a second week, the council discussed only very minor matters, while the situation grew daily more alarming. I well remember, for example, a discussion, of Byzantine complexity, which consumed about three hours, on the types and power-ratings of tractors to be used, according to its particular climate and soil conditions, in each province!

Some of my more savvy, ministerial colleagues, simply observed a distant and mournful silence. In the fortnight, during which this went on, the country slid progressively into chaos.

The grand event, which marked the end of the summer in Iran, was the Festival of Shiraz, presided over by the Shahbanou. Among the numerous, national ensembles, great artists attended, from all over the world. I remember Bejart, Stockhausen, Arthur Rubinstein and Karajan, coming to the festival and performing in the magical settings of the ruins at Persepolis or the palace and gardens at Shiraz. Unfortunately, artists and groups of a lower standard – some of them rather questionable, to be frank – were invited too, without any clear justification. "Media-coverage abroad" was often mentioned by the festival's steering-committee, which, however, was dependent upon Iranian, national radio and television for its principal outlet, if not for its very existence.

Domestically, the festival was very controversial. Most of the intelligentsia were openly hostile towards it, as much because of its high cost, as because of its excessively occidental flavour and the subordinate role it gave to Iranian culture. The people of Shiraz complained that it interfered with their daily lives; but is this not always the case with events of this kind, in a big city?

Surprisingly – and this is to employ a euphemism - the Shah wasn't very keen on it either. He always paid a long visit to Shiraz at the end of the summer, but he attended only the festival's closing ceremony, and, with his wife, one other performance; and this was for the peculiar reason that he wanted to scotch rumours of an extra-marital affair and a quarrel with the Shahbanou. Once, while I was Rector of Shiraz University (1968 – 1971) we were walking in the garden of the Eram palace – a university-property, where he often stayed – and the Shah said to me, "I really don't see the point of this festival.

"It costs far too much," he went on, "and I don't think it produces anything.

"We invite mediocre artists no-one's ever heard of, and some of the plane-loads of journalists we bring over, stuff with caviar and heap with presents, spit all over us as soon as they get home; but the Shahbanou likes it, so what the hell?"

Then feeling, perhaps, that he had overdone it a bit, he added, "Mind you, this is just between us, you understand!"

In his notes, Ardeshir Zahedi – himself very critical of the festival – also reports unfavourable comments, by the Shah, about this event, which, nevertheless, he allowed to take place each year.

On 25th August 1977, the festival was punctuated by a heated incident. A small, totally unknown and, as the Sovereign called it, "talentless" troupe from the Balkans – God knows why they had been invited – put on a production, that evening, in the window of a car-showroom, on a main street, in the centre of Shiraz, in order, so they said, "to familiarise the public with modern art." In the mimes of the half-naked actors, astounded members of the public believed they were witnessing scenes of sodomy, and, indeed, the performance was not what you would call tasteful. Vigorous protests broke out, with cries of indignation; there was nearly a riot, and the police were obliged to intervene, partly to halt the production and partly to disperse the furious mob. The following day, preachers began to vent their emotions about the matter, in the city's mosques. The show was not staged again. Two days later, no-one in political circles was unaware that the Shah had heard about the incident, had become angry, had called those responsible "mindless, Leftist saboteurs" and had threatened them with criminal prosecution. However, things calmed down, and, out of affection or respect for his wife, I presume, he did, as usual, get over it. Later, he told the British Ambassador, Sir Anthony Parsons, who had just mentioned the incident, "after all, it was only a bit of theatre."

Ever since the Cabinet had been formed, the Prime Minister had been faced with what to do about this festival and the disturbance it might provoke. All the invitations had already been sent and enormous expense had already been incurred. If it were to be cancelled, there would be indemnities to pay. The bill would be very large indeed. As to the problem of maintaining order, the police and the Savak, when asked, replied that they were equal to the task. The army and the paramilitary police seemed to think the same. They all pledged their support and, they said, would work, if need be, together with the organisers. When asked for his opinion, the Shah left the decision to the Shahbanou and the Prime Minister.

One day, at the beginning of September, about 9.00 am, I received a 'phone-call, at my office, from Ayatollah Shariat-Madari.

"I'm told," he said, "that a decision is to be made about the Shiraz Festival: now I don't know much about things like this, but that incident, last year, was shocking and disgusting – I hope you know what I'm talking about.

"However," he went on, "please tell His Majesty, or whatever appropriate person, that to cancel it would be a serious mistake: the situation has reached such a pitch, that any concession now would be interpreted as a sign of weakness.

"Indeed, " the regime must exhibit firmness and authority from now on," he added and asked, "is the Prime Minister aware of this?"

I confessed that his complete frankness astonished me and told him that I respected his foresight and concurred with his analysis.

"You still don't know me very well," the Ayatollah rejoined, "but, assuming the festival goes ahead, the Shahbanou ought, on no account, to attend.

"Make the programme lighter," he insisted, "put on some dignified performances, especially Iranian ones, and have someone there to represent the government, such as the Minister of Culture.

"He's a well-respected man," added Shariat-Madari, alluding to Mohsen Foroughi's global reputation as an architect and archaeologist, "or you could even have His Majesty's brother-in-law."

(This was Mehrdad Pahlbod, Foroughi's predecessor as Minister of Culture)

"You can shorten it," he concluded, "and be careful, but don't cancel it!"

I called the Prime Minister without delay, and then the Shahbanou, and told them about the position being taken by the man who was still the leader and symbol, both of the secular opposition and the religious hierarchy. Two days later, a meeting, chaired by the Shahbanou, decided simply to cancel the festival and to do so on the sly: there was not even any official announcement. The press referred briefly to the matter, and the Prime Minister was said to have demonstrated his good will to certain mullahs – which ones I don't know – but it was just another useless retreat.

On 5th September, the President of the People's Republic of China, Hua Guo Feng, was ceremonially welcomed to Teheran. Since it was a state-visit, the Shah met his guest, in person, at the airport, with all the usual pomp, just as he had met President Carter, a few months before. During a long conference, President Hua promised his support to the Shah and warned him against joint, Soviet-American interference in Iran and their collusion in destabilising the country.

A little before this state-visit, a top-secret agreement had been signed by the recently-appointed Chief of the Iranian Secret Service, General Nasser Moghaddam, and his Chinese opposite-number, Qiao Shi, to oppose Soviet expansion in Afghanistan and to assist the still sporadic resistance, which was forming there. Western agencies found out about this new initiative of the Shah's, however; and this stiffened the Americans' resolve to dismantle his policy of independent action.

On the evening of 5th September, at eight-o-clock, one hundred and ten guests sat down to the state-dinner held in the Chinese President's honour. In accordance with his plan to open the Court to non-governmental society, the Grand Master of Protocol had invited one or two well-known provincials, a celebrated orchestral conductor and some businessmen, as well as the usual number of official figures - including, however, only one, Imperial Prince – such as the Prime Minister, the Minister to the Imperial Court and two other ministers and their wives. The businessmen, who had never sat at the King's table before, were full of surprise and pleasure at finding themselves there.

The Shah's speech was quite suitable – recalling the exceptional ancientry of the Chinese and Iranian civilisations and the age-old relations between them – and expressed hopes for the future. President Hua's reply took a more pragmatic turn, and he openly declared his support for Iran, which, amidst the ordeal the country was going through, might have been of some comfort to the Shah.

Thursday 7th September 1978, being the day of the feast marking the end of Ramadan, the two wings of the opposition – the religious and the secular, as represented, respectively, by Ayatollah Shariat-Madari and the leaders of the National Front – co-operated in organising a politico-religious demonstration in the northern suburbs of Teheran. After public prayers, the crowd of 100 000 people (according to the official count – twice that, according to the organisers) formed itself into a procession along Cyrus-the-Great-Avenue, one of the capital's main streets.

This was the first time that poster-portraits of Khomeyni appeared. They were scattered here and there above the crowd, but mainly near the end of the procession, where there were thought to be a few dozen Palestinians. The slogans being chanted were, however, not hostile to the Shah, nor to the monarchy: mainly, the cry was "down with corruption!" laced with allusion to a great variety of unpleasant fates, which were wished upon "the corrupt ones".

On the same day, and at much the same time – on the occasion of National Hospitals Day – the Shahbanou paid an impromptu visit to Teheran University's "Doctor-Eghbal Hospital", situated in a populous quarter of the city. As President of the University's Administrative Council, and the newly dubbed Minister of Sciences and Higher Education, naturally, I went with her.

We flew to the hospital's heliport, from the palace at Saad-Abad, to find a skeleton-staff on duty. Some doctors greeted the Shahbanou, and soon, everyone in that part of the city seemed to know she was there; for a crowd of five or six thousand people quickly massed outside. Radio and television had evidently been briefed, and, an hour later, when the Shahbanou went, on foot, to visit the Anti-Cancer Foundation, a few hundred yards away, the crowd, which had grown even larger, welcomed her with warmth and enthusiasm.

"Long live the King!" they cried in their thousands. It was a remarkable, and entirely spontaneous, demonstration. Brief announcements of the Shahbanou's visit had, admittedly, been broadcast, but only under strict censorship. There was nothing about the warm welcome she was receiving, no relay of the shouts of support for the Sovereign, no shots of the loyal throng.

That afternoon, the Prime Minister 'phoned to tell me of his displeasure. Why had the Shahbanou visited these hospitals, he wanted to know, on the very day "those gentlemen" had organised *their* demonstration, and why had I accompanied her?

"Because it was my duty," I told him, "and no more than common courtesy."

"Of course," the Head-of-Government replied drily, "but you should realise that the popular demonstration she provoked might upset the opposition." (!)

I learned soon afterwards that the Shah had been deeply moved by the sympathy for him, which had been expressed during that visit.

But how do we explain the Prime Minister's attitude? The broadcast-media had become outlets for opposition-propaganda, to such an extent that they were forbidden to cover a completely spontaneous, and extremely emotional, demonstration in favour of the King.

"As for, possibly, the most powerful propaganda-instrument of all, the television," the Shah wrote later, "I received, very belatedly, the proof that its staff at Teheran had been infiltrated by Communists."

However, Iranian TV had been controlled, from its very beginning, under discretionary powers vested in the Shahbanou's second-cousin, and foster-brother, Reza Ghotbi, whose competence and probity were never, otherwise, impugned by anyone.

That day of religious festival was fraught, more than anything, on a worldly and social level. It was a day for celebrating marriages and for merry-making thereafter. In the afternoon, my wife and I attended a wedding-reception for the daughter of my colleague and friend, Professor Davoud Kazemi, the former Rector of Ahwaz University, whom I had just appointed as my Under-Secretary. He was the brother of Mr Bagher Kazemi, who had been Foreign Minister under Mossadegh, and he himself was sympathetic to the nationalist ideas of "the old lion", which, clearly, had not tarnished the brilliance of his career.

Several well known members of the National Front were present at the wedding-ceremony, and, amid the hubbub of the reception, the political situation was vigorously discussed. Everyone was talking about the demonstration, that morning, on Cyrus-the-Great-Avenue, and commenting on its dignity and calm. The National Front people were impressed, also, by the size of the demonstration, which had greeted the Shahbanou's visit to the "Doctor-Eghbal Hospital", and I was asked many questions about that. Many were surprised that national broadcasting had done no more than refer briefly to the visit, in its flagship news-programmes of the early afternoon, and said nothing whatever about the even greater, popular gathering, which had taken place as a result.

Conversations were relaxed and friendly, and those who, a few days later, would take quite a different attitude – start proclaiming "the feebleness of a dying regime", become more radical, forget their secular convictions and, with American encouragement, flock to the banner of Khomeyni – were, for the moment, still speaking respectfully of the Sovereign.

Our colleague, Professor Karim Sandjabi, now Leader of the National Front, who had asked me several times, during the previous three years, to convey discreet offers of co-operation, if not of active service, to the Shah, now harangued me about the need for a Council of State, on the French model, in Iran.

"It should be suggested to His Majesty," he insisted, "because such an initiative would have a big impact on public opinion, provided, of course, that it is led by an independent and competent person, who could guarantee citizens' rights against infringement by the regime."

As a Professor-Emeritus of constitutional law, and a former senior member of the Faculty of Law, he thought that he himself would be suited to this post: it would represent a deserved return, for him, to the upper echelon of public life, and mean complete, political rehabilitation. When, a few days later, I told the Sovereign about this conversation, the situation had changed a great deal, and the balance of forces was altogether different. Karim Sandjabi, after persisting, for a while, with his vague attempts to succeed to the presidency of a secular, democratic republic, went to abase himself, before Khomeyni, at Neauphle-le-Château, abandoned everything he had stood for, and was later appointed – for a few days - by Khomeyni, as Foreign Minister of the Islamic Government, before being sacked, in disgrace, and going into exile, until the end of his days, in the United States of America.

He used to say, I hear, that he was deeply sorry for allowing himself to be used as a lever, to bring in an oppressive, Islamic regime, and as a cover – in spite of himself, maybe – for so many abominable crimes. Oh – belated and vain regrets!

That same Thursday, at the end of the afternoon, the followers of Ayatollah Khomeyni – some three to five thousand people – gathered in Jaleh Square in the east of the capital. The slogans were extremely violent, and, for the first time, the cry was heard, "death to the King!" Another gathering was announced, for the following day.

In the evening, the National Security Council, presided over by the Prime Minister, met and decided to ask the government to impose martial law on the capital, from the morning of the following day. Ministers were called immediately, from all over the city, to attend an extraordinary meeting of the council. My wife and I were at a reception, given by the Japanese ambassador and his wife, Mr and Mrs Ikawa, when the call came through, on the telephone in my official car, to go at once to the Presidency.

The meeting of the Council of Ministers, attended by most of the portfolio-holders and principal military chiefs, began at about seven-o-clock. Some members of the government, who had gone to the suburbs for a long week-end, turned up on time. Opening the session, Mr Charif Emami gave a brief report of the events of the day – the big demonstration in the morning, and the smaller, but more violent, one, in the afternoon. He referred to the slogans displayed at the latter, and added simply, "His Majesty is deeply uneasy."

He went on to tell us about the mass-demonstration, planned to take place – also in Jaleh Square – on the following day, and gave us these details: the demonstrators, led, and organised, by professional rioters, were planning to attack the Madjlis – the Chamber of Deputies – which lay about a mile-and-a-half from Jaleh Square. The idea was to take the building by storm and then proclaim a revolutionary, republican government.

This information, which seemed highly unlikely, was corroborated by the chiefs of the Savak, the National Police and the Second Bureau, who were all present, the first two as members of the National Security Council, and the third, as advisor to the Head of the General Staff of the Armed Forces. Consequently, the Prime Minister proposed that the Council proclaim martial law. Despite the urgency of the question, which no-one contested, someone objected that the government had not yet been presented to Parliament and had not, therefore, yet received the necessary vote of confidence. Would there be a precedent, he asked, for declaring martial law, under these circumstances?

After a brief debate, it was decided that the constitution would not be infringed: any government, it was thought, faced with such an imminent danger, had a right, as well as a duty, to act. It was, therefore, resolved unanimously to declare martial law, on the following day. The Council even decided, as a preventative measure, to extend the declaration to several other, big cities. General Gholam Ali Oveyssi, Commander-in-Chief of the Army, was appointed Administrator of Martial Law, in the capital.

Then the Prime Minister left the room briefly, and, from the next chamber, called the palace to tell the Sovereign what had been decided and to obtain confirmation of General Oveyssi's appointment.

According to Ardeshir Zahedi, Iran's ambassador to Washington, who was temporarily in Teheran and dining with the Sovereigns at the palace, that evening, the Shah thought about it for some time before giving his permission. He thought the measure was premature.

By about ten-o-clock, the meeting was drawing to a close, when General Gholam Reza Azhari, Head of the General Staff of the Armed Forces, asked to speak.

"The Army," he said, "will do its duty, I hardly need say; but I should mention that this is the evening of a Thursday, which, furthermore, is at the end of a feast-day."

"Therefore," went on the General, "most of our soldiers, officers and NCO's are on weekend-leave, at least until tomorrow evening, or even until Saturday morning.

"In the city, at the moment, we have only some reserve-

---

* Friday is the weekly feast-day in Muslim countries, but this Thursday, being the festival celebrating the end of Ramadan, was also a holiday.

units, which are sufficient for limited emergencies, but which,
I fear, will not provide the strength conveniently to control a
demonstration of the size envisaged.

"Besides that," he continued, "recourse to martial law
normally requires three or four days notice; but, since that is
not possible, I ask now that the proclamation of martial law,
for tomorrow morning, Friday, at six-o-clock, be announced
to the public immediately!"

Nothing could have been easier. All three TV-channels
were broadcasting until midnight, and national radio was
on the air twenty-four hours a day. Accordingly, the Prime
Minister made an executive decision to grant the General's
request and assigned Manoutchehr Azmoun, minister delegated to the Presidency of the Council, to order that radio and
television interrupt their programmes, as soon as possible,
with news of the proclamation of martial law, and that they
repeat this news every half-hour.

Martial law forbade public gatherings of more than five
persons: if the public had known about it, then, certainly,
far fewer would have gone to the demonstration, and the
number of casualties, civilian and military, would have been
much reduced; but the radio and TV-programmes were not
interrupted. Not only that, but news of the proclamation of
martial law was not broadcast at all, until it was announced,
on the radio, at six-o-clock, on the Friday morning, at the very
moment when martial law came into force, by which time
– the demonstration having been called at eight hours notice
- the crowd was already mustering in several quarters of the
city.

Did Manoutchehr Azmoun fail, on purpose, to convey
the order to the radio and TV-stations? Many have said

so. Certainly, in the days, which followed that Council of Ministers, the role of Azmoun – who was later assassinated, on Khomeyni's orders – was a matter of great controversy. I met him only once afterwards. It was soon after I was dismissed from the government, a few days later. I asked him what had gone wrong. He assured me, in considerable detail, that he had called the broadcasters to give them the Prime Minister's instruction. On the other hand, it is well known that he was at-daggers-drawn with the Controller of Broadcasting; and it was thought that he might have wanted the latter to get the blame; or did the broadcasters refuse to obey the instruction, or sabotage its implementation? These possibilities are not out of the question.

The Shah told me later, in Cairo, that, without having absolute proof, he did blame the broadcasters. Again, as he would later write, he bore a personal grudge against them, for their general attitude - and particularly against their Controller – but that was for other reasons, which I shall explain further on.

In spite of much investigation, I have not been able to come to any personal certitude about this essential matter. All I can say is that something went very wrong and that it was to have enormous repercussions.

From seven-o-clock that morning, Friday 8th September, lorries and other army-vehicles, equipped with loud-hailers and co-ordinated from helicopters, were deployed at road-junctions, and demonstrators were ordered to disperse. Meanwhile a crowd of up to thirty thousands, organised by riot-commandos and urged on by mullahs, many of whom were unknown (who were they, and where did they come from?) was set marching. The customary warnings stopped the mob at several points, but the forces of order were turned.

Unlike so many others, the Iranian army was not prepared or trained to deal with this kind of situation. Its mission was to defend the country, and preserve its territorial integrity, against attack from an external foe.

On this fatal day, its commanders made a grave error of judgement. They were probably badly informed. They believed that the deployment of a few hundred, regular soldiers and officers, who had received no training in riot-control, would be sufficient to keep the peace, and they over-estimated their strength. No call had been made for reinforcement by the recently formed anti-riot unit of the National Police, let alone by the army's own elite troops, such as the parachute–regiment or the Special Forces.

The soldiers on the spot received orders to fire volleys into the air, which they did. Then, seeing that they were being fired on from all sides - that there were armed and trained people among the rioters - and seeing their own comrades falling, dead or wounded, around them, they opened fire on the demonstrators. It was an appalling tragedy. The international press called it "Black Friday". The opposition-press called it "Red Friday". Soon afterwards, people were talking of thousands of dead among the demonstrators.

Two weeks later, on the basis of death-certificates and scrupulous cross-checks, the exact death-toll was established at 121 demonstrators and 70 police and soldiers. All told, 191 dead, including those who died, in hospital, of their wounds. It was a huge figure.

Several ministers, including me, proposed that the whole report, on this tragedy, should be published. At least, this would have shown that the figures being bruited about as rumours and peddled by sections of the foreign press, and which were growing larger by the day, were false. This report also established, in detail and without doubt, that elements in the crowd opened fire against the forces of order, whose casualties were all due to bullet-wounds. It also gave formal proof that there were, among the demonstrators, Palestinians, who had entered the country with "genuine" false papers, and whose presence in Teheran had been increasingly noticeable in previous weeks. Ballistics- and autopsy-reports showed, furthermore, that many casualties could not have been killed or wounded by the official forces - because the ammunition used was not regulation-issue – which indicates that rioting elements opened fire on the demonstrators also. The rooftops and apartment-windows of some buildings along the demons-tration-route, had been acquired to serve as vantage-points for these marksmen, many of whom came from abroad.

In July 1980, soon after my arrival in France, I received an astonishing, first-hand account of the events of that Friday, from one of my former colleagues at the Ministry of Development. This was someone, who, in 1978, had been an activist in the revolutionary movement. Like many others, he had suddenly abandoned the cause, when he realised its true purposes and character. The windows of his flat over-looked the route of the demonstration. He was contacted by a group of "Islamic-Marxists", who assigned to him two armed Palestinians. Posted at the windows, these two fired indiscri-minately, not only at the soldiers, but also, at random, into the crowd, simply to shed blood and create irreparable resentment. Other armed men, he told me, lay in ambush, throughout that quarter of the city, and opened fire in similar fashion.

Some days after "Black Friday", a certain Nasserieh, known as Ayatollah Allameh Nouri, was arrested. Numerous Arab passports were found at his home, together with a considerable sum of money and documents clearly indicating that the entire tragedy had been carefully organised. It had been a set-up. Some of these documents were published in the press. Then this person was freed, and the press fell silent. No more was said of Allameh Nouri, until he re-surfaced, after the triumph of the revolution, to be acclaimed, of course, as a hero. On the 20th anniversary of the massacre, he boasted, in the government newspapers of Teheran, about his role in the events of that fateful day.

The report, on Nouri's arrest in 1978, was never published. Certain army-chiefs had no wish to admit that seventy of their men had been murdered in this way. The matter of Allameh Nouri was hushed up on the orders of the Prime Minister, who – so he said – "did not want to embarrass the opposition and thereby impede the process of national reconciliation," which existed only in his imagination. What a waste!

Mohammad Reza Pahlavi was emotionally wrecked, if not psychologically broken, by the events of "Black Friday". He realised then, suddenly and brutally – or, at least, conceived doubts, which rapidly became certitude – that appointing Charif Emami had been a mistake and that the entire crisis had been badly handled. Nevertheless, he could not retract, because the government had not even been presented to Parliament, so he just went on trying to appear to be master of the situation. He was completely nonplussed, in particular – and this brought him to the verge of collapse – that some of his compatriots had cried, "death to the Shah!"

"But what did I do to them ... what did I do to them?" he said, from the evening of the 8th onwards, continually repeating it to numerous visitors, in the following days.

Iran – or a particular view of Iran – its grandeur and power, and its wish and will to play an important role, as a country, on the world-stage, had been his sole concern for years. Iran had been his only true love, an immense passion and the dream of all his waking moments. Suddenly, like de Gaulle in May 1968, he felt utterly betrayed, but, unlike the only statesman among his contemporaries for whom he had any real respect – and, indeed, a profound admiration – he was unable to get a grip on himself and sank like a stone.

Weighed down also by his illness, which no-one knew about at that time, he began his fall; but his hold on power was broken, more than anything, by the irremediable resignation, which set in after those tragic hours of 8th September 1978. His great dream was smashed, and his supreme love betrayed.

Chapter VII

"The Americans will never abandon me"

9th September to 6th October 1978

F rom 9th September, everyone tried to make sense of what had happened.

The Shah was profoundly affected by the extent of the disaster, the scale of the death-toll and the hatred shown towards him by some of the demonstrators: little-by-little, he slipped into a kind of resignation, as though events around him were no longer his concern. His actions, when he took any, were more and more delayed, disconnected from reality and sometimes decidedly odd. He had lost touch.

The high command of the army applied itself to an investigation: the scenes in Jaleh Square were analysed, and it was decided that we would all have to adapt to a new situation, in which an insurrection was being led by a minority of professionals. Some recalled that "The October Revolution", which had later been represented as a spontaneous mass-rising, had actually been just like this. The matter was given much study.

General Ali Neshat, Commander of the Imperial Guard, said to me, on the day after next: "what happened was frightful, because, owing to lack of time, the situation was poorly evaluated beforehand.

"If we had deployed units more suitable to the job, losses could have been minimised.

"But, just think," he went on, "of what would have happened, if the demonstrators had taken the Baharestan – the historic seat of Parliament, redolent with memories and symbolism!

"Of course, their revolutionary government would have been no more than a joke, but the army would have had to storm the place, inevitably causing many casualties.

"Blood would have flowed," he continued, "inside the 'House of the Nation'" – for so the building was called – "and caused such a stain as could never have been expunged."

He was right. The soldiers understood. We would have to change our methods.

From the morning of 9th September, therefore, the Head of Government – doubtless with the, at least, tacit agreement of the Shah, who, from now on, let him have his head – gave the order, to the Administrators of Martial Law, not to react to demonstrations. Martial law was not to be extended to any other cities. Lorry-loads of regular soldiers were placed on static guard, on some squares and road-junctions, in order to "reassure the population"! Then, as a "sign of goodwill", he told the leaders of the radical opposition about the instructions he had just given. By means of this absurd gesture, which had not been approved by the Council of Ministers – and which none of us would have agreed to – he reduced himself to impotence and deprived himself of every option. I'm told that the ambassadors of the USA and Britain congratulated him warmly on his decision – and I can well believe it!

On 10th September, two weeks after its formation, the Cabinet, which had already run out of steam, was at last presented to the Chambers and soon received an overwhelming vote of confidence, after a rather confused debate, which was transmitted live on national radio.

That same day, The Group Studying the Problems of Iran published a long communiqué denouncing the intention of extremists to negate liberties-for-women - as progressively obtained, over decades – by abolishing the statute of social and political equality. It condemned also the desire, as proclaimed by the same radicals, to challenge social legislation, in general, and the agrarian reforms, in particular, because they considered these to be contrary to Islam. The communiqué waned the government, in no uncertain terms, of the dangers of the process-in-train: "we must not allow all the social, political and economic rights, which women, labourers and peasants have acquired over the last fifteen years, to be swept aside!" the text concluded.

The afternoon (four-o-clock) editions of the capital's two, major dailies published this communiqué in its entirety.

There were three ministers in The Group – Kazem Vadii of Labour and Social Affairs, Karim Motamedi of Posts and Telecommunications and myself. The announcement was, therefore, clear enough that part of the Cabinet did not agree with the Cabinet's policies. Two other ministers would also endorse this document – Mohammad Baheri of Justice and Moghsen Foroughi of Culture.

At half-past-five, I had an audience with the Sovereign.

A footman ushered me into his office. Before even shaking hands, the Shah said, in a strange voice, "how dare you?"

I had no idea what he meant and was quite disconcerted; but he immediately added: "in times like these, it takes great courage to say what your Group has said.

"I've just read the papers," he continued, "and I have asked" – this word astonished me (usually, he said, "I have given the order") – "that your communiqué be broadcast live on radio and television."

Suddenly, I understood the degree to which he felt he had lost support – and was wrong to feel so – but he ploughed on: "have you heard their slogan?" Again, he did not wait for an answer, demanding, "but what have I done to them – tell me – what have I done to them?"

I told him that the cries of hatred came from a tiny minority and should not be taken as an expression of the sentiments of the Iranian people, who remained loyal to their King and asked only for the opportunity to prove it – all of which was still true.

However, it was for other reasons that I had requested the audience: a void had begun to form around him, and the "corrupt ones", among whom were members of his own family, were turning their coats and seeking guarantees elsewhere. He could feel that he was being forsaken.

Not only fidelity and decency, but also the welfare of the nation, demanded that one give him support during these difficult days. This I firmly believed, whatever the personal anguish his policies had caused me, and, in the years to come, I would always continue to believe it. He remained the fulcrum of an eventual recovery. To the *Observer* – a well-known British weekly – for this very reason, I said, "democracy in Iran will come through the Shah, or it will not come at all."

This little interview scandalised some progressive circles, at the time, but I believed that it was necessary to support the Shah, and build around him, if this absolutely indispensable evolution of politics, which needs tranquillity, peace and legality,
were to take place.

Thus, I took advantage of every pretext to go and see him, sustain him and, before long, simply to keep him company. At one point, I received a note from the Grand Master of Protocol, Aslan Afshar: "it's getting emptier and emptier – visitors are coming ever more rarely."

On this occasion, however, I had come on a specific errand. I wanted to lay before him the broad outline of a proposal for a law on the autonomy of universities, which I was preparing to present to Parliament soon. It was a revolutionary proposal, calling virtually for the complete internal control, of which all Iranian academics dreamed. He listened distractedly and gave his agreement.

Next, I told him about the changes I was going to implement, the following day, among the rectors and the managers of organisations, which were under the authority of my ministry and its under-secretaries.

"Before the Cabinet has agreed?" he asked.

"The academic year begins on the 21st," I said, "they need to be ready to get down to work."

He nodded. It was obvious that the matter did not interest him. He seemed distant. His mind was elsewhere. Suddenly, though, when I explained that I was about to replace an under-secretary, who was incompetent and always absent from the centre in his charge, the Shah burst out, "oh no, not him!"

Then I heard him enunciate, to my total amazement, a speech, which was an insult to Farsee slang. It was unthinkable that it could have come from a man whose language was always so refined, polished and courteous.

"If, with a bit of luck," he ranted, "we get this show back on the road, I know what I'm going to do with that sodding schemer.

"I know all about his little plots – and the ones he's hatching at the Palace – playing both ends against the middle, and you mustn't give him any excuse to play the victim: just keep an eye on him, if you can!"

Nevertheless, a few weeks later – at the request of the Shahbanou, it seems - he received this person for a quarter-of-an-hour.

My audience, this time, was somewhat brief - barely twenty minutes – and, as I rose to go, he asked me sharply, "what do you think of Charif Emami?"

It was an odd question. He never interrogated ministers about their boss, because he didn't want to weaken the latter's position.

"He's good at directing Council-meetings, Your Majesty," I ventured – which was true.

"Yes, he's certainly that," was the reply.

I think he was probably regretting his choice by then.

On the morning of the 11th, at half-past-eight, I was travelling in my staff-car along a section of Teheran's new ring-road, which the city-authorities had named "de Gaulle". National radio's morning news-bulletin, which I had been listening to, as usual, had finished a few minutes earlier. The car had just reached the turn-off for the centre of town, about ten minutes from the Ministry, when the telephone rang and was answered by my bodyguard. His face went white, his hand tensed. Then he said to me, in an emotional tone, "His Majesty wishes to speak to you."

Clearly, I thought, it could not be the Shah, in person: it must be the Palace' switchboard-operator; so I was not at all surprised. The King, of course, never called ministers on the telephone, and no-one ever called him, except for the Shahbanou, the Prime Minister, the Minister to the Imperial Court and, more rarely, the Head of the General Staff, if he had to react to a serious emergency; so I could hardly believe it, when, a moment later, I heard the King's voice. I was presenting my respects, but he wouldn't wait and almost shouted, "have you heard about this?"

I told him that I was in my car, and asked him, on that account, to allow me to speak to him in French.

"To what are you referring, Sire?" I enquired.

"They've just broadcast your communiqué," he snapped.

"As Your Majesty ordered, I believe," I said cautiously.

"Yes, I did," he replied, "but the song they put on right afterwards – they finished the communiqué so that it would be followed by this song."

I hadn't really noticed. Apparently it was a revolutionary ditty from the beginning of the century, with words by Bahar, the famous poet – a sort of Iranian version of *Le Temps des Cerises*. Using metaphors, it referred to the despotism of the King, at the time of the revolution of 1906: a nightingale dreamt it had the power to leave its cage and sing at liberty. It was not a forbidden song, although it was not often played – any more often than you're likely to hear *Le Temps des Cerises*, on French radio, even on a long car-journey – but the Shah was right: it was probably a provocation, for these were times of symbols and allusions.

"But what can I do, Sire?" I asked, "the radio is not my responsibility."

"Well – do something!" he insisted, "it's a scandal - it's sabotage – just when somebody's saying something sensible for once," and he hung up.

I was amazed. The Controller of national broadcasting was the Shahbanou's first cousin – her foster-brother – and, as a matter of principle, nothing was broadcast without his approval. The thing to have done would have been to call him from the palace; or, if not that, why not bring in the Prime Minister, who was the usual intermediary in such matters?

I reckoned that the Shah, whom everyone generally obeyed, no longer knew what to do, even about banal matters.

In the hours which followed, I learned that the Prime

Minister, whom the Shah had authorised to make any changes he thought necessary, had, as a precaution required by the Shahbanou's attachment to her foster-brother, sought the Sovereign's specific approval, two days before, for the replacement of Reza Ghotbi. The Shah had told him that such a move would embarrass his wife and added, "give Ghotbi a final warning: tell him he must get rid of all those Communists around him, who are running everything!"

Apparently, the Prime Minister then said, "but he doesn't even bother to reply to my telephone-calls."

Perhaps this explains why the Shah, feeling that he had got it wrong, had not called Charif Emami.

I couldn't decide what position to take in this affair. In the end, I called the Minister of Information, who was, in theory, Reza Ghotbi's superior, and told him what the Shah had said to me. My colleague said that he would try to obtain a meeting with Reza Ghotbi, "but," he added, "that will not be easy."

I learned, soon after, that causes for concern about Iranian Radio-Television, had been building up for two years. There had been an Indian documentary, albeit screened very late in the evening, about the training of guerrillas in India, and there had been an otherwise excellent series, about a Qadjar king of yore, in which he was unjustly ridiculed. There had been an outside-broadcast interview, in which, the Sovereign believed, he had been insulted; as also in an interview he had given to Barbara Walters, the well-known American journalist, which had gone badly wrong. Each time, the Shah commented publicly, and harshly, on the management of IRTV, but, out of regard for his wife, he never went further than that.

During the next week, the Prime Minister persuaded the Shah, on the grounds that it would appease public opinion, to replace Amir Abbas Hoveyda, as Minister to the Imperial Court, even though he owed his own appointment, as head of the executive, in large part, to the latter.

Ali Gholi Ardalan, former Minister of Foreign Affairs, former ambassador to Bonn, Moscow and the United Nations, and now in his eighties, was appointed to the Imperial Court, on the suggestion, it seems, of Ardeshir Zahedi. It was a choice, which depoliticised the function. Ardalan was from an illustrious Kurdish family, which was said to be descended from the Sassanids (the dynasty, which reigned in Iran from 224 a.d. to 651) He was a cultivated, multilingual diplomat, courteous and distant, who had retired at the end of the 'sixties. Since then he had divided his time between Iran and Europe, had published a noted volume about the "European Common Market" and had continued, with his wife, to live out a deservedly gilded old-age, frequenting the city's society-dinners and embassy-receptions. The general public had largely forgotten him, but his reputation was impeccable. When the Shah called upon him, he was most surprised and hesitated, telling the Sovereign that he didn't know much about the country's political life, the men in official positions or those leading the opposition; but the Shah said, "I need you, and the country needs you, in these dark times."

So he accepted. It would cost him several years in prison, after the revolution, and a particularly unpleasant death. General Hassan Pakravan, another prestigious and irreproachable retiree, was appointed his deputy.

Telling him of his decision to replace him, the Shah proposed to Hoveyda that he take up the post of ambassador to the King of the Belgians. Hoveyda turned it down flat, saying that he could not bear to leave the country, at such a difficult juncture, because he was no deserter. Would he have accepted a post as ambassador to Paris, Washington, London, Moscow even, or to the Vatican – that is to one of the posts usually proposed to former Prime Ministers? He may have regarded Brussels – in spite of his knowledge of, and love for, the place, having been a student there – as an inferior option. It is possible.

Two or three days after his dismissal, I called him on the telephone. He had already left his ministerial residence and was living in a large apartment, which he had bought and, so they tell me, had tastefully decorated. We chatted for a long time. He asked me where I was calling from. I told him I was in my ministerial office, adding, in French, with a laugh, "the poisoned chalice you gave me."

He laughed heartily. Then he said, "it doesn't have to be like that: one is always more useful when one has an important post and can influence events from the inside."

We promised to see each other again soon; but the course of events would pronounce otherwise.

The Prime Minister also proceeded, by virtue of the powers, which martial law conferred on the government, to have several former ministers, and various other prominenti, arrested. Some of them were clearly unpopular; but the government's powers were properly applicable only to "persons endangering public order and the security of the state", and it was not possible to see by what criteria these actions were taken. Troublemakers were roaming the streets with complete impunity. At a Council-meeting, the Minister of Justice, Mohammad Baheri, mentioned this. According to the Constitution, any prosecution against former ministers, for acts committed in the exercise of their former duties, should first receive the agreement of the Chamber of Deputies, and the accused should be judged by the Supreme Court. It was an arrangement inspired by the Belgian constitution. Baheri was in the process of preparing amendments to the law, which would simplify this complex procedure, so that the Chamber could delegate its powers, for a limited time, to an investigatory commission, composed of deputies and judges of the Supreme Court.

"Instead of imprisoning people for no clear reason," Baheri said, "and thereby making victims of them, would it not be better to present this reform to Parliament, as an emergency measure?

"That," he added, "would be an obvious sign of the government's intentions."

Several ministers, of which I was one, approved of this. The Prime Minister retorted, with irritation, that the matter was not on the agenda, that the public were demanding the rolling of heads, and that when appeasement had occurred, he would tell us.

That same week, the Prime Minister obtained "the head" of Reza Ghotbi. For the time being, it was Ghotbi's deputy who took over, and things continued as before, on the radio, and especially on TV.

Of course, these superficial measures – these last, "big decisions" taken, or obtained, by the Head of the Executive

– did nothing to appease the mounting tension. As ever, they were seen as signs of weakness. The situation continued to deteriorate.

On 11th September, Ayatollah Shariat-Madari proclaimed a national day of mourning for the victims of "Black Friday". Everything went off calmly and with dignity.

Theoretically, in Teheran and some provincial cities, martial law was still in force. The Shah had issued only one order – to avoid bloodshed. The Prime Minister was preoccupied with only one thing – to avoid upsetting dissidents, however radical. He did not have any other ideas about what to do. In the capital, on some of the squares, and in front of some public buildings, regular troops sat in their lorries; and the dissidents had been informed that the soldiers were under orders not to fire unless attacked. Some small groups of ultra-leftists now began to use another tactic: they would come and offer flowers, and even sweets, to the soldiers, while insulting and threatening their young officers and NCO's. This was particularly trying for both officers and men, and it sapped their morale. The soldiers saw that their superiors could be insulted, and even spat upon, with impunity. The officers and NCO's were demoralised, because they had been ordered to do nothing. Groups of dissidents went round to all the lorries, one by one, cursing the Shah and tearing up, or spitting on, photographs of him. How could it have been explained, to these young soldiers, many of them from the countryside, who had been trained to defend the nation and obey their commander-in-chief, that they were expected to put up with this in silence? It would have a disastrous psychological effect.

Wildcat-strikes began to break out here and there, especially in the oil-industry, organised by a small committee of
former Communists. The Prime Minister immediately agreed
to a 25% pay-rise in the oil-industry – a sector, whose workers
were already very well paid. In the Council of Ministers, he
declared that this commitment would not be honoured and
that its only purpose was to "soothe spirits and restore calm".
Nothing was done. The country began to slide into anarchy.

On 16th September, an earthquake devastated the oasis-
town of Tabass, to the south of Khorassan. 70% of the town
was destroyed. Early estimates put the number of casualties at
more than 3,000. The emergency-services of the "Red Lion-
and-Sun" (the Iranian Red Cross) supervised by the provincial Governor, the widely respected and experienced, Hassan
Hedjazi, were, however, soon on the scene.

As was his custom in such situations, the Shah decided at
once to go to the disaster-area. He was not about to repeat the
show of official indifference, which greeted the tragedy of the
Rex, at Abadan. According to some who were with him on the
'plane, he was obviously nervous, as they flew towards their
destination; but, if he feared hostile shouts, or even demonstrations, he said nothing about it; and, as it turned out, the
afflicted population welcomed him in the touching, traditional
manner. For more than three hours, the Sovereign toured the
streets of the wrecked town, listened to sorrowful accounts,
offered consolation to his countrymen, allowed himself to be
embraced by anyone – which was not at all his custom – took
children in his arms, gave suitable orders to the Governor, to
the President of the "Red Lion-and-Sun" and to the officers
of the emergency-services, and inspected the tents, which

had been erected for the homeless. His communion with his people was complete. Having arrived full of apprehension, he departed once more serene, at peace and deeply moved. He then made a brief pilgrimage to Meched – a surprise-visit, which was, nevertheless, met with a warm welcome from the populace there. In the mausoleum of the Imam Reza, he received a large number of mullahs, whom he told of his attachment to Islam, in an atmosphere quite devoid of hostility. Everyone kissed his hand and expressed loyalty to him. It was a total surprise: his popular capital, charisma and authority were completely intact; but he drew no lesson from it.

A few days later, the Shahbanou went to Tabass, but the inappropriate attitude of some of her entourage annoyed people, and the popular reaction was mixed. She herself was agitated, and – probably with wilful intent to discredit her - the radio relayed her touchy moments.

The government appointed a retired, general engineer to oversee the reconstruction of the devastated region. He was a former chief of military engineering, well-known for his piety and competence, and he went on site at once to get the operation started. It was already well under way, when some small groups of mullahs appeared from nowhere. They were certainly not from Meched, and the security-services knew nothing about them. They gave out sweets, some clothes and modest sums of money, to the survivors. After that, certain opposition-leaders asked for audiences with the Prime Minister, saying that, since the clergy was looking after the disaster-victims, why should they not be given a chance to do so. These "gentlemen" would, they said, be most appreciative of such a show of confidence.

Charif Emami's reaction was stupefying. He ordered his appointed, general engineer to pack up and return to Teheran.

The government's agents practically deserted the area. The opposition immediately accused the regime of criminal irres-ponsibility and negligence, and who could say they were wrong? The public were scandalised. All of this happened without the Shah's knowledge!

This was the context, that September, in which the Grand Master of Protocol, Aslan Afshar, received a remarkable tele-phone-call from the ambassador of the USSR, KGB-Colonel Vinogradov (who had previously been posted in Egypt, and is not to be confused with his namesake – Moscow's representa-tive in Paris, while de Gaulle was in power) Col. Vinogradov said that he would like to hold a dinner in honour of Farideh Diba, the Shahbanou's mother! It was a most unusual request, especially at this time, and in relation to a lady who, although she was the Shah's mother-in-law, had no political or diplo-matic profile.

The day before this 'phone-call, the ambassador had had a long interview with the Shah, at which the possibility of a state-visit to Iran, by Leonid Brezhnev, or of a state-visit to Moscow, by the Sovereign, had been raised. It might be surmised that Moscow envisaged a rapprochement with Teheran, if the Shah succeeded in unravelling the crisis, and was sketching out a route to that end. The Soviets, whose agents were playing a considerable role in the agitation, would thus appear to have been hedging their bets, and this symbolic invitation would have been part of the same subtle game.

The Shah agreed to the plan, and the dinner was quickly organised. It was a very smart and expensive affair, with every Russian refinement and courtesy - such as only the represen-tatives of Communist countries allowed themselves to put on – for sixteen guests, all of them Iranian. The invitees included

Aslan Afshar and his wife (daughter of former Prime Minister, Saed, and, since her mother was Russian, a fluent Russian-speaker) the Cultural Councillor to the Imperial Court, Chafa, and his wife, the Shahbanou's chief aide, Hossein Nasr, and his wife and Mrs Hachemi-Nejad, wife of the Head of the King's military household. I was the only member of the government to have been invited. The protocol-office called my secretary, beforehand, informing her that I was requested to cancel any other engagements, I might have that evening, and be absolutely sure to attend this dinner.

I went alone, since my wife happened to be in Paris. It was an awkward occasion, largely because we had to have constant recourse to interpreters. Only Mrs Afshar was at liberty to speak directly to our hosts, in Russian. The Soviets refused to speak French, or English, which were their guests' foreign languages. Hence, an interpreter had to be placed behind each guest. The meal was delicious, but seemed interminable, until, at last, His Excellency Vinogradov proposed a toast to the Sovereign, praising the Shah and Iran's progress, stability and international, political role, and expressing, in extravagant terms, the desire to develop Irano-Soviet relations. Mrs Diba remained seated as she returned thanks. Indeed, nothing had been said, to which she, specifically, was required to reply! The Soviet message was perfectly clear and, after the company had risen from the table, it was discussed further, in private, by the Soviet ambassador and Aslan Afshar, in relation to an eventual state-visit, either by Brezhnev to Teheran, or by the Shah to Moscow: "I'll get down to work on it," Vinogradov said.

He left soon afterwards for Moscow and did not return to Iran until after the fall of the Shah. Meanwhile, Moscow took care, officially, to appear neutral. It seems to be well attested, by each of the two, unconnected, military messengers concerned (who both confirmed this for me, although both of them wish to remain anonymous) that the Shah had received friendly overtures, a few weeks before, from Moscow. A significant increase in the purchase of armaments from the East (especially from the USSR) - a 30% increase was to be guaranteed - and a slight drop in dealings with the West, would produce, it was suggested, "a policy of the Indian variety, which," the Sovereign was also told, "would give Iran the means to pacify its unrest."

To both of these intermediaries, the Shah's reply was the same: "Iran cannot change its strategic alliances," he said, "forget this nonsense!"

The preferred allies, themselves, were less scrupulous.

In fact, Radio Moscow was the only influential, international station to observe strict neutrality - about the events, which were convulsing Iran - right up to 16th January 1979, when the Shah fled; but what need had Iranian Communists – or any of the Leftists, who were manipulated, more or less directly, from Moscow – of media-support from Soviet-satellite countries, when they could say what they liked, when they liked, on British, French, American and Israeli channels and in the western press?

As for Ambassador Vinogradov, it was found out later that he played an important part in the hostage-taking at the American Embassy in Teheran, which was certainly one of the more spectacular exploits of the special services of the USSR.

The end of the summer and the beginning of the autumn provided the Shah with several opportunities to appear at grand ceremonies. There were the state-opening of Parliament, the beginning of the university-term (albeit delayed, that year, by a fortnight) the dedication of a new year-group to the Military Academy and the end of the study-cycle at the Institute of Higher National-Defence Studies. There were plenty of them, that year, and it was expected that the Shah would take advantage of one, or another, of these events to make some statement, at last, about the national situation, speak words of guidance, point the way ... but he did none of these things. He did nothing!

The overwhelming majority of the public, traumatised though it was, had still not wavered; but the Prime Minister's cosmetic gestures – the ones which were not immediately forgotten, that is - continued without good effect, and the causes of domestic discontent remained. These were, most notably, the exactions of the corporate chambers, the threat of more than 100 000 legal actions – hanging, like a sword of Damocles, over small businessmen – restrictions on the construction of housing in towns – under the pretext of a new spatial-development plan, which had neither been published nor scheduled for publication – and the policy, announced by the previous government, concerning the compulsory acquisition of dwellings, which were empty or "insufficiently occupied". Hoveyda had received his thanks, and several others had been thrown into gaol, but the half-dozen, most hated, suspicious characters continued to swan around in their official capacities. Besides all this, everyone knew that the western powers – always considered, until now, to be the allies and supporters of the regime – were plotting against the Shah.

Caught between an ever more flaccid government, and an ever more sinewy opposition, people waited, watched and became more and more cautious. Who, they wondered, would win?

A Toxic Environment

The two Chambers had voted, in emergency session, to confirm both the appointment of the government and the proclamation, in the capital and some provincial cities, of martial law.

According to the constitution, at the end of September, the Shah should open the new, legislative session and give the King's Speech, which, traditionally, indicated the major policy-directions of the year to come.

Professor Safavian, one of the four medical practitioners attending the Shah – and who was now his official physician – had been away for some months on sabbatical leave, in Paris, returning, every month, during a weekend, on one excuse or another, to make a discreet visit to his "illustrious patient" and check up on his state of health. However, since his appointment as "personal physician to His Majesty", his visits began to occur in a more ordinary fashion, usually in the morning, before eight-o-clock, when he went to the Royal bed-room, and the Shah, in his dressing-gown, received him. They only ever discussed medical matters. On 19th September, the examination had been arranged for four in the afternoon. In the Sovereign's private apartment, Safavian now found the Shah, in his shirt-sleeves, with some papers in one hand and a pencil in the other. As the doctor came in, the Shah walked into the small room next to his bedroom. Safavian could see that he was reading and correcting a text, and recalled immediately that the Shah was due to open the new session of

Parliament on the following day. He guessed, therefore, that his patient was reading his speech and making alterations as they occurred to him. Like most of us, Safavian was worried about the political situation, and so, for once, he decided to mention it, and made careful note – "for the sake of history," he told me – of what was said.

"Before I proceed with the routine examination, Sire," he ventured, "may I talk to you, for a few moments, as an Iranian and a patriot?"

"Certainly, certainly," replied the Shah, "say what you have to say."

"The country is in a critical condition," rejoined Safavian, "the people are restless – it's like sailing a raging sea – public opinion, and most of the responsible intellectuals, of whom. I believe, I am one, are waiting for the captain of the ship to take things firmly in hand and state our course: there is a huge expectancy in the country.

"Break your silence, Your Majesty," he pleaded, " tell the people what is going on, and in no uncertain terms."

"Yes, of course," returned the Shah, "but one cannot deprive folk of their freedom of expression, can one?"

"Certainly not," argued Safavian, "but calm must be restored at once: we cannot regard bomb-attacks and acts of terror, like the burning of cinemas, hotels and cultural centres, as expressions of liberty, surely?

"I think we must place a premium on restoring order," the doctor went on, "and then proceed to sweeping constitutional reforms: Your Majesty is going to give an important speech tomorrow – would that not be a superb opportunity?

"We must cut the ground from under the feet of the agents of 'subversion'," Safavian insisted, using the French term, "most people are still loyal to you, and they will take courage, defend the nation and defend the King!"

Said the Shah: "but, these people who, you say, are patriotic and love their King, why do they not demonstrate?"

"Because they are stupefied by the government's attitude and the King's silence," the doctor replied, "they are awaiting a clear signal."

"What would you have me say?" the Sovereign asked, "what signal?"

"Sire," Safavian explained, "in many respects, our situation is very like that of France in May 1968: week after week, schools, universities and factories were on strike, and the country was paralysed - we're not at that stage yet, but it's not far off.
"In France, that spring," the doctor continued, "revolutionary groups had the upper hand everywhere, and constitutional, democratic order was in real danger – I was following developments hour-by-hour.
"De Gaulle was openly jeered and insulted, by the demonstrators; the media went over to the protest-movement, and national collapse, followed by a Leftist takeover, was feared.
"Wide swaths of the middle class, and the intellectuals – or those who call themselves intellectuals – could see no outcome but the General's resignation.
"Then," Safavian went on, "came his famous speech: 'in the present circumstances,' de Gaulle said, 'I cannot possibly resign'," and the doctor then quoted the General's words in their entirety, hoping to inspire the Shah, whom he knew to be a great admirer of de Gaulle.

"Just a few hours later," Safavian, concluding his story, added, "a million people turned out on the Champs Élysees, and, on the evening of 30th May 1968, it was the revolution, which collapsed – the entire dog's breakfast" – he actually used this phrase – "had been cleaned up."

"The people of Paris cried, 'long live de Gaulle!' and, well, Your Majesty knows the rest.

"Do the same, Sire – show your desire to beat this subversion and send the strong signal the world is waiting for!

"You'll see," Safavian finished, "the nation will follow you!"

"Yes – yes – yes," said the Shah, and then, after a very long silence, Safavian notes, his "illustrious patient" asked him to proceed with the scheduled examination.

The next morning, at ten-o-clock, the Shah went to open the Parliamentary session, in the imposing setting of the Palace of the Senate. Deputies and Senators wore their ceremonial gowns, and all the ministers were there, and ambassadors and army-chiefs, in dress-uniforms, studded with decorations. A great many foreign journalists crowded the benches reserved for the press.

According to the traditional proceeding, the Shah had to deliver his address, standing up, with the Shahbanou on his right, and slightly behind him, and, behind her, some members of the Imperial Family, the Minister to the Imperial Court and the Grand Master of Protocol.

The Imperial Couple drove to the Senate in a ceremonial coach, receiving, on the way, an affectionate greeting from people in the streets. When the Sovereigns entered the chamber, all present noticed, with astonishment, that only Mrs Diba came in with them. Everyone in the chamber rose and applauded, as was traditional, and the Shah invited them all to sit down. Then, to general amazement, he sat down himself and read his speech in that position. The text was all about the annual balance of payments. It was full of acronyms and numbers and larded with economic generalisations. There was no allusion whatever to the national, political situation. The speech was utterly disconnected from political reality. The applause, which accompanied it, was no more than polite. Disappointment spread like a virus.

Three-o-clock, on the afternoon of 21st September, was the time set for the traditional ceremony of dedication for the final-year group at the Military Academy – an institution created, with the help of French officers, at the beginning of the 'twenties, by Reza Shah, the Sovereign's father, on the pattern of the French, Military Academy at Saint Cyr, where Mohammad Reza Pahlavi had himself spent a year, after finishing his secondary education, and had obtained the rank of Second Lieutenant. He would sometimes joke about this, saying, "I am the Commander-in-Chief of an army, in which I am only a Second Lieutenant."

That, at any rate, is what they sometimes say he said, when addressed with compliments about his expertise, which was indeed surprising, on strategy and armaments. Not since the creation of the Academy had a Shah ever failed to preside over its dedication-ceremony.

Brigadier Manoutchehr Beyglari, the brilliant, Kurdish Commander of the Academy, presented the annual report, which, to everyone's surprise, took a decidedly political turn: "these young officers," Beyglari intoned, " who take their oath of loyalty today, are ready to defend King and Country, in whatever circumstances and whoever the enemy, be he outside Iran or within her borders."

As the General showed him round, the Shah bucked up considerably. For more than three hours he toured the buildings – dormitories, studies, libraries, canteens, the armoury, the lecture theatre and so on – talking with all and sundry. He sampled the that evening's menu, whose main course he found excellent and said, "of course, you knew that I was going to taste it: I just hope that the food is as good as this, every day!"

So friendly was the atmosphere, as I can personally attest, that the Shah was happier, than I had seen him, for months. As he left, he complimented the Commander of the Academy and then turned to the civilian-visitors. I was the only minister there, because a Council of the Cabinet, with all my colleagues present, was going on at the same time, whereas I, having taught economics at the Academy for several years, could not resist the chance to see the old place again.

The Shah said gravely, "with a magnificent army like this, how can we imagine, even for a moment, that 'those people' will ever succeed in de-stabilising the country?"

There are two, diametrically opposed, and equally correct, answers to this question.

The ceremony, marking the end of the study-cycle at the Institute of National Defence, took place two days later. Many non-governmental prominenti were present in the hall, and the atmosphere was less sympathetic. The shouts arising from a nearby demonstration were audible, which irritated the Shah.

After a hum-drum speech, diplomas were distributed, and then a small number of soldiers and civilians were ushered into the Institute's operations-room, where a case-study, produced during the year, was presented to the Shah. This year, the material concerned a hypothetical intervention of elite, Iranian troops, in Pakistan, to restore order there, following a Communist uprising. It was a simulacrum, on a larger scale, of the scenario, in which the Iranian Army had succeeded, quite remarkably, in the Sultanate of Oman, a few years before – and of that, in which it had failed, shortly afterwards, in Somalia – and it seemed plausible. It was certainly minutely researched and professionally put together. The Shah listened for a few minutes. Under the current domestic circumstances, however, in which the army was being prevented from restoring security and order, it seemed out of place, and the Shah began to show signs of nervousness, which was odd in a man normally so much the master of himself. From a small table, he picked up his "kepi" – which went with the army-uniform he was wearing – got up and left the room.

"What are we playing at?" he said loudly, just outside the door.

As a rule, the re-opening of the universities and institutes of higher education took place on the first Saturday of the autumn. I watched the situation getting worse by the day. On 1st October, there were some important demonstrations - at which the Sovereign was booed - in Teheran and several provincial cities. At Kachan, a secondary school, called "Pahlavi", had its name changed. The security-forces did not intervene anywhere. After a rapid telephone-consultation with the Rectors – all of whom approved my decision – I decided to postpone the beginning of term for two weeks. I also authorised the rectors to open their faculties thereafter, in stages. This avoided the initiation, throughout the country, of a new front to the current wave of unrest. I did not bother to consult, or even inform, the Prime Minister, whom I felt to be a lost cause. Three days later, General Oveyssi, Teheran's Administrator of Martial Law, thanked me warmly for my action: "that's been a relief," he told me on the telephone, "you have given us a small respite."

It was at this juncture, when everything looked about to topple, that, on the initiative of Senator Mostafa Tadjadod, founding president of the first, privately-owned bank in the country and one of Iranian Free-Masonry's most listened-to and influential figures, that a serious approach was made to Charif Emami, himself the Most Serene Grand Master of the Grand Lodge of Iran. The Senator, supported by several important "brethren" – three, very prominent, former minis-ters (of Foreign Affairs, Justice and the Interior, respectively) a Senator, who was a former Chief-of-Police and some busines-smen and heads of public organisations, who were important in financial circles – submitted, to the Most Serene Grand Master, the proposal for a meeting of powerful Free-Masons, at his own private residence, in order to undertake a large-scale operation to support the Shah. Substantial sums of money had been pledged, to counter the flood of funds being distributed and spent to sustain the subversion. The only religious digni-tary to belong to the Lodge, Ayatollah Hassan Emami, the capital's chief cleric, had also lent his support to Tadjadod's plan. The Prime Minister was firmly against it.

"That would only poison the climate further," he replied, "leave it to me to slacken the tension!"

He even added, without laughing, that a meeting of fifty people – all pretty well known – seemed to him to be incom-patible with martial law! Only activism against the regime would, apparently, be tolerated.

The day after this approach, the Most Serene Grand Master,

without consulting even the leading lights of the Grand Lodge of Iran, decided to put Iranian Masonry into abeyance, and discreetly informed "the gentlemen" of the radical opposition of what he had done.

As these weeks went on, the true nature of the events the country was living through, at last, began to dawn on the Shah. The orchestration and exploitation, of a wave of domestic discontent, by foreign powers, in order to destabilise and capsize Iran, became apparent to him, and he confessed to having under-estimated its power.

The cries of hostility, from a minority, towards him personally, had already upset him profoundly, but now he began to evaluate the dimensions of what was happening. He still could not believe that he had been betrayed by his foreign "friends and allies", the USA, Britain, Israel and, yes, even France.

The American Secretary of State, Dean Rusk, had told the Shah, some years previously, that, "after the President of the United States," and on that geo-strategic level, where political events and military problems converge, "you are the best-informed man in the world."

Iran's intelligence-services overseas did indeed function very well, and the Shah read the international press, and diplomatic dispatches, attentively. Above all, he had his own network of special correspondents, who kept him informed about what was going on in the USA, Britain and France. Regarding the Eastern Bloc, he placed confidence, not without justification, in the intelligence-services of Iran's allies.

Paradoxically, this man, who knew about the amorous adventures – sometimes the secret ones – of the world's great figures and, in amazing detail, about political intrigues in Paris, London and Washington, who noted every little weakness of the controllers of western governments and media, and often took advantage of his knowledge, in masterly style, to aid his country's diplomatic efforts, gave the impression that he could not take seriously the conspiracy being carried on, against his country and his person, in the world's principal centres of power.

Why not? Were any of the signs lacking? We now know that the idea of deposing the Shah was broached continually, from the mid-seventies on, in the National Security Council in Washington, by Henry Kissinger, whom the Shah thought of as a firm friend and who had often helped him over the years. Did the Shah really not know about this?

Iran's international ambitions, and rise to economic, technological, financial and military influence, were disquieting. Although an ally of Israel, Iran had not hesitated to bring decisive aid to Egypt, during the Yom Kippur War, the only conflict against the Arabs, which the Hebrew state was not able to win. President Sadat would not forget this, which was to his credit; but the Israelis would not forget it either. This switching of alliances, and the ambivalence of Iran – the only country in the region able to match itself against Israel – disquieted the leaders of the Hebrew state, especially those on the Right.

Throughout the years, during which he had been at the head of Iranian diplomacy, Ardeshir Zahedi, formerly the Shah's confidant and son-in-law, had progressively oriented Iranian policy in a less pro-Israeli direction. The ambassador, Hossein Montazem, who was at the Ministry, and in charge of Africa, during my time in government, described to me the directives, which were then being transmitted to Iran's representatives in the Muslim countries of that continent. Iran, I learned, practised a diplomacy of balance, which was, however, influenced by the unjust treatment being meted out to the people of

Palestine; so that, after the death of Nasser, Iran easily became a staunch friend and ally of the principal, Arab power, Egypt. When Hossein Montazem had himself been Iran's representative in two of these countries, he had passed on these same directives, bearing the same message.

The Israelis and the Americans could not but have known about this and been inconvenienced by it. Surely the Shah must have realised that there would be repercussions to this policy – and not just covert ones.

From 1975 onwards, even when the Republicans were in power in Washington, highly hostile attitudes proliferated there, towards Iran and her King. When Jimmy Carter came to power – and despite his pronouncements of 31st December 1977 – this hostility reached a climax, and Washington started acting on it, but the Shah hardly paid any attention.

Djamchid Gharib spent a large part of his diplomatic career in Turkey, where he was our ambassador, before he retired. In 1978, while spending his summer holidays there – for he knew the country perfectly and had many, Turkish, personal friends – he was told, by the two highest authorities in the Turkish government, that, according to their information, Washington was preparing a coup, in Iran, involving certain religious leaders; and they begged Djamchid Gharib to tell the Shah "that he ought not to trust the Americans". Secular Turkey was worried about the possibility of a theocratic government being installed in Iran. It was an important message, and, as soon as he returned to Teheran, Gharib asked for an audience with the Shah. He was kept waiting – he no longer had any official position, after all. He confided his information to Hoveyda, who offered to act as an intermediary. Gharib declined this offer, and, after several days, his persistence paid off. He was received, and relayed his message, in detail, to the King, including the identities of his informants. The Shah, annoyed, asked him, "whom have you told about this conversation of yours, in Ankara?"

"The Minister to the Court asked me about my business," replied the former diplomat, "and I declined to reveal it; but I said a word or two, without the least detail, to Nahavandi, and to my son-in-law, Doctor Shirvani,"

Shirvani was a professor at Teheran University and an elected Deputy.

"Forget this for ever," snapped the Shah commandingly, "and tell them to forget it too, for it is no more than drawing-room chatter!"

George Ball – that guru of American diplomacy and prominento of certain think-tanks and pressure-groups – once paid a long visit to Teheran, where, interestingly, the National Broadcasting Authority placed an office at his disposal. Once installed there, he played host to all the best-known dissidents and gave them encouragement. After he returned to Washington, he made public statements hostile and insulting to the Sovereign; but, for some reason, the Shah didn't seem to notice.

Count Alexandre de Marenches, Head of the French intelligence-services, was greatly admired by the Shah, who also thought of him as a friend. He too warned the Sovereign in no uncertain terms. Later, in his memoirs, the Count wrote, "one day, I mentioned to the Shah the names of those Americans, who had been assigned to plan his deposition and replacement.

"I had myself been present at a meeting, where one of the questions raised was 'how do we get rid of the Shah, and with whom shall we replace him?'

"The Shah was unwilling to believe me," de Marenches continues, "saying, 'I believe you about everything else, but not about this.'

"'But, Sire,' I said, 'why will you not believe me on this point also?'

"'Because,' he said, 'it would be stupid to replace me!'

"'I am the best defender of the west,' he went on, 'in this part of the world; I have the best army and the greatest power: the whole thing is so absurd, that I cannot possibly believe it.'"

Further on, Count de Marenches notes: "but the Americans had made their decision."

I mentioned the matter to the Sovereign once. I had no particular information – just an impression, vague but persistent, obtained from reading the international press and listening to recordings of George Ball's Teheran interviews. The Shah's response was clipped and dogmatic: "the Americans," he said, "will never abandon me."

There was a glaring error in his analysis; but what did the Americans have against him really? "Megalomania", they said; but all they meant by that was his country's rapid rise to power, his proposal to de-nuclearise the region – which was anathema to Israel – and his plan for a security-pact linking the countries with coasts on the Indian Ocean and the Persian Gulf, which would allow them to tackle common problems, themselves.

Then there were the big oil-multinationals, who would not

forgive him for the role he played in raising OPEC against them, and in which he had the support of King Feisal of Saudi Arabia – another modernising sovereign, and one who was assassinated, in 1975, in circumstances, which are still unclear.

Ever since then, in order to weaken the Shah, the universal propaganda-machine, creator of world-wide lies – and now in constant use – was set running. Domestic discontent was stirred up and amplified, and, a few weeks later, the successor, who, it was thought, would be more malleable, was fabricated. Being insignificant in himself, this person was just what was required to get rid of the troublemaker.

At Cairo, in 1980, a few days before his death, Mohammad Reza Pahlavi told me: "Hussein [of Jordan] was right: at the beginning of that autumn [1978] he rang me and said, 'what the Americans are doing in Iran is what they tried to do to me, five years ago [Black September 1973]'

"'But I held on,' Hussein continued, 'crushed the rebellion and forced the subversives to the negotiating-table.'

"'If,' he went on, 'you find you cannot give the orders, which meet the needs of the time, let me come to Iran, install myself in a little office next to yours, for three days, and speak for you, and in your name, to tell the military chiefs what to do!'

"'You'll see,' he concluded, 'everything will be all right, and the Americans will abandon their plans.'

"I was completely deceived," the Shah resumed, "by the American attitude, but, above all – above all – I did not wish to shed my people's blood: a King cannot act like a dictator, hanging on to power at all costs."

"Iran guaranteed order and security in the Persian Gulf."

The Shah pays a state-visit, which rapidly became a show of force,
to the Emirate of Kuwait. To the Shah's right, the Emir.
Directly behind the Shah, Ardeshir Zahedi,
then Minister for Foreign Affairs.
To Zahedi's right, Iranian Ambassador Reza Tadjbakhch.

(Ardeshir Zahedi Collection)

Chapter VIII

*"What do you expect a poor, grubby mullah
to do to me?"*

6th October to 6th Novembre 1978

C harif Emami, happy and smiling, at last! This was at the Council of Ministers of the beginning of October. Before even broaching the agenda, the Prime Minister announced "a very good piece of news" to his Cabinet-colleagues.

"Our ambassador in Baghdad has signalled us that Khomeyni has just left Najjaf for the Kuwaiti frontier," he began, "but the Kuwaitis will certainly not admit him, because they have a very strong Shiite community, which Khomeyni would not neglect to stir up, and we have sent them a despatch requesting that they do not grant him asylum.

"That only leaves him Syria or Libya," the PM continued, "Libya would be better, from our point of view, because it doesn't have automatic telephone-connections with us; but, either in Syria, or in Libya, he will be conspicuous."

"At this moment," Emami concluded, "we can finally enter into discussions with the moderate clergy."

What had happened was that, a few days previously - following an approach from the Iranian Embassy in Baghdad - the Iraqi government had firmly reminded Khomeyni of his conditions-of-stay, as a foreign national, and that these were incompatible with the inflammatory announcements, which he was continually making and which the international press were beginning to reproduce. Khomeyni had then announced that he was going to leave Iraq, in protest.

However, since he no longer had a valid passport – his old one having expired more than ten years before – he had to apply, at the Iranian Consulate in the neighbouring city of Kerbala, for a new one. His application was transmitted to the Iranian ambassador in Baghdad, who then asked his ministry, in Teheran, what he should do. Khomeyni was "becoming a nuisance", the ambassador had said. A decision was then made, by the Prime Minister, to grant the application for a new passport. It was not known whether the Shah had been consulted. He may have been, even if, at that time, he was leaving all policy-decisions to the PM.

Khomeyni's relations with foreign intelligence-services were well-known – notably those with East German agencies, which were doubtless acting on behalf of Moscow – and we had obtained proof of them in the early 'sixties, during the disturbances of those days, at Qom and Teheran, of which Khomeyni was a leading figure. Ten years later, in the early 'seventies, the independent "European Information Centre" (EIC) run by Pierre de Villemarest, had published, in its French bulletin, information about Khomeyni's contacts with the Eastern Bloc, including further details, which, later again, would have a very dramatic effect on everyone's political thinking.

On this occasion (1978/9) Khomeyni would be handled by a US-citizen of Iranian extraction, who was later identified by experts as a CIA-agent, directly under the orders of the Agency's Paris Centre[*]. His name was Ibrahim Yazdi[**].

The Emirate of Kuwait refused entry to the troublesome Ayatollah, as predicted; so that, at the moment when the Council of Ministers was meeting in Teheran, Khomeyni was still in Iraq, seeking a way to leave the country.

We could, I suppose, have refused to give him a new passport; but we didn't dare. Anyway, he would have been able to get one from Libya, or even Syria, we were told, in spite of the recent improvement in our relations with those countries. We could have asked Baghdad to keep him in Iraq and watch him, which would have been the best bet – and I even received proof, later on, that this could have been done – but nothing was done. We hoped that Khomeyni would proceed, under his own steam, to Damascus or Tripoli. We were fooling ourselves.

As soon as possible, at that session of the Council - despite the congratulatory smiles of my colleagues - I asked to speak.

---

[*] Pierre de Villemarest Archives.
[**] After the triumph of the revolution, Yazdi's career sparkled. He became Deputy Prime Minister and then Foreign Minister, and he even presided over early sessions of the Revolutionary Tribunal Of Teheran, which sent hundreds of people to be executed. He lives now in the USA, where his family is resident.

"I do not share this optimistic view," I said, "Khomeyni will not go to Syria or Libya, but to Paris."

"I should very much like to know," exuded the PM, tapping his finger on the table, "why you are always contradicting me!"

"Mr Prime Minister," I explained, "we must be logical: Khomeyni is after a platform, to launch his agitatory propaganda, and he will not find it in the Middle East, nor yet in Bonn or Rome.

"He can't go to the USA – they couldn't admit him – and, if he went to London, he would be accused, here, of anglophilia.

"That leaves Paris, the capital of liberty – the capital of revolution – where there is an important group of Iranians, hostile to His Majesty, who will welcome him – let's face it! – with open arms."

"The Savak has told me otherwise," retorted the PM, "and so has the Foreign Minister: may we at least know the source of your information and how you obtained it?"

"By good sense," I ended, "and a kind of intuition."

At this point, Khosrow Afshar, the Foreign Minister, in person, spoke up!

"I beg your pardon, Mr Prime Minister," he said, "but the Foreign Ministry has never told you that Khomeyni will not go to Paris; and, for my part, I do not find the Science-Minister's reasoning to be devoid of logic."

All this went into the minutes of the Council-session and was published at Teheran with the kind of comments, which may be imagined. I was right, and wrong, at the same time. Khomeyni did not go to Paris under his own steam. He probably didn't even know where it was on the map, let alone anything about its historic role in the development of ideas around the world. He was taken to Paris.

As *Libération*-journalist, Dominique Lorenz, wrote, twenty years later, in his much read book*, about several important affairs of recent decades, including the goings-on at Neauphle-le-Château – the Americans, "having picked Khomeyni to overthrow the Shah, had to get him out of Iraq, clothe him with respectability and set him up in Paris, a succession of events, which could not have occurred, if the leadership in France had been against it."

Several studies have confirmed this since.

Having arrived in Paris, Rouhollah Khomeyni was installed in a villa at Neauphle-le-Château, where his image underwent a complete makeover. He was of Indian extraction – nothing wrong with that, of course - the son of an immigrant fortune-teller, who, early last century, entered the service of a feudal landowner, in the region of Khomeyn, and was killed in a brawl, when the future Ayatollah was two, or three, years old.

At Neauphle-le-Château, India was air-brushed from the picture, and Khomeyni's father became *"the Headman of the Community of Khomeyn"* – a title invented in Paris – *"who* (furthermore!) *was assassinated by the evil henchmen of Reza Shah,"* in defiance of the fact that the Sovereign's father was no more than twenty years old, at the time, and was then serving as an obscure soldier. In this new picture, Khomeyni's

* "Une guerre" ("One War"), Éditions des Arènes, Paris, 1997.

life became *"a career of struggle against imperialism"*.

The truth was that, until 1962, he was a mullah of no great note, and the only political affiliation, which can be ascribed to him, was his connection with the followers of a cleric, who was opposed to Mossadegh's nationalisation of the oil-industry. At the beginning of the 'sixties, he did emerge as the leader of a protest-movement, against agrarian reform and the emancipation of women, which – as some of Nasser's principal aides later attested – was financed and guided by Nasser's Egypt and the intelligence-services of the Eastern-Bloc; but, apart from that, and his role as a mullah, Khomeyni is known to have engaged in only one other activity, during the years after the Second World War, and this was to do with running a small transport-enterprise. Again, there's nothing wrong with that, but it's not particularly heroic and not at all anti-imperialist.

Khomeyni was also allocated "a son and martyr, assassi-nated, through hatred and vengeance, by order of the Shah, in 1978". This "son and martyr" died, of bulimia with cardiac complications, in 1977, while Iran was still at peace, and his father was totally forgotten at home and had never been heard of abroad.

Above all, they made of Khomeyni *"a brilliant philosopher and theologian"*, although his writings were quite unknown, which is not surprising: when extracts were published after the triumph of the revolution, they were found to be laughable; but then it was too late.

In the course of the one hundred and twelve days Khomeyni spent at Neauphle-le-Château, he gave one hundred and thirty-two interviews and made fifty public announcements. He said the sort of things people like to listen to – about freedom, human rights and democracy. It is now irrefutably proven, from statements made by his entourage and published in Teheran itself, that these declarations to the national press were not composed by him, but by an advisory committee, presided over by Yazdi. Khomeyni merely allowed his advisers to embellish them with his photograph or endorsed them by reading them to camera.

Some journalists, including Pierre de Villemarest and Oriana Fallaci, saw through the trickery; but de Villemarest's articles were suppressed, and Fallaci was excluded from Khomeyni's villa for alleged "impertinence". For the sake of history, they later published damning accounts. The memoirs, or witness-statements, of some of Khomeyni's advisers – such as the barrister, Nazih, or mullah Montazeri – also reveal much about this episode; but they were slow in coming.

In this way, in a few weeks, the global propaganda-machine transformed an obscure and uncultivated old mullah – however forcefully animated by hatred and ambition, and however well-preserved – into a figure of international dimensions. It even went so far as to give him the title of "Imam", which was nothing short of blasphemy, to most Muslim authorities, and was contrary also to all Shiite tradition.

The world-wide disinformation-system has often used such procedures since then. Certainly the truth is available today – for those who seek it – but, since the objectives, which were researched and fixed by the puppet-masters of the operation, have been attained, is not the work, of making the truth available, nothing more than an academic exercise? Those, who seek and find the truth, will decide. However, radical

Islamism, until now sporadic and marginal, has, by the means described, *already* made its entrance on to the international stage.

As the holder of a valid, Iranian passport, Rouhollah Khomeyni did not need a visa to enter France; nor did he need to apply for political asylum, for the duration of his "exile in France", as, twenty years later, President Valéry Giscard d'Estaing suggested that he did, despite having previously admitted otherwise. It is also false to pretend that Teheran requested Khomeyni's extradition, as an adviser at the Quai d'Orsay (the French Foreign Office) recently wrote.

Political asylum was neither requested nor given. Khomeyni was a very special visitor, who was treated, from the first, in France, as a VIP – if that is not understating the case. Thus, from 6th October 1978, Paris became the headquarters of the Iranian revolution, and the base for a campaign of subversion against a country, which had been a friend and ally of France, since the reign of Henry IV.

Two days after Khomeyni's arrival in Paris, I was received for a brief audience with the Shah. I asked him if the government intended to ask the French authorities to hold Khomeyni to the condition usually imposed on foreign visitors to any country; namely, the requirement that they desist and abstain from meddling in the internal affairs of *any* other country. He shrugged and said, "Giscard telephoned me with the same question, to which I replied that it made no difference to me."

He fell silent, and then added, "What do you expect a poor, grubby mullah to do to me?"

Nevertheless, the Quai d'Orsay is nothing if not prudent: the French ambassador to Teheran, Raoul Delay, sought confirmation, from the Prime Minister, that he had "no objection to Khomeyni's staying in France". Some political circles in Iran suffered from the illusion that the smoothness of Franco-Iranian relations was a guarantee against Khomeyni's subversive schemes. It was an illusion, which was soon to be shattered.

Everything had been well prepared – and well in advance – for Khomeyni's stay in Paris. Two squads of armed police were detailed to protect him; but he was still mistrustful, in spite of everything, and asked for Algerian, and some Palestinian, agents to be added to the detachment. The authorities agreed. The villa was provided also with a state-of-the-art radio-transmitter. Pierre de Villemarest, the first journalist to meet Khomeyni, after he settled at Neauphle-le-Château, was shocked by what he saw. As a well-known, former member, from its inception, of the French Resistance, and of the French intelligence-services, he felt impelled to report his surprise and disquiet to the Ministry of the Interior; but, he subsequently wrote, "they told me to occupy myself with something else."

Around the small villa occupied by Khomeyni, the agents of many of the world's secret services were gathered as thickly as the autumn leaves. The CIA, the MI6, the KGB and the SDECE were all there. The CIA had even rented the house next door. According to most of the published witness-statements, the East Germans were in charge of most of the radio-transmissions; and, on at least one occasion, eight thousand cassettes of the Ayatollah's speeches were sent, direct to Teheran, by

---

* So we are told by Count Alexandre de Marenches, the archives of Pierre de Villemarest and several journalists of the time.

diplomatic bag. Agents of the Iranian special services, who had themselves infiltrated Khomeyni's entourage, alerted the government to this and proposed that we seize the tapes, in a feigned error, at Teheran International Airport, and publicise their seizure, even if it meant apologising afterwards to the ambassador concerned; but the Shah raised formal objection to the plan. Diplomatic immunity was sacrosanct, he said.

The mobilisation of the media, in favour of Rouhollah Khomeyni, was remarkable and highly effective. The BBC, which was much listened-to in Iran, was transformed into the voice of the revolution and transmitted, in advance, the times and places of the principal demonstrations taking place in Teheran. The Voice of America – in a manner hardly less blatant – and the Voice of Israel, another channel Iranians listen to a lot, both did the same – not to mention the three networks, which were then publicly owned, of French television.

The eight-o-clock news was even delayed, one evening, on one of these TV-networks, in order – so it was explained – to include the Ayatollah making one of his announcements, when he had "finished saying his evening prayer". Of course, at that season of the year, when the sun sets early, that famous prayer would have been over and done with more than two hours before. The idea was to inflate the importance, in the public mind, of Rouhollah Khomeyni.

A media-bubble was launched, in the press, and on the radio and television, of the entire world, reflecting an aggrandised and distorted image of this rather insignificant person. The message, proclaiming Khomeyni to be a historic figure with a heroic background, was everywhere. In Teheran, the crowds, discovering the "global importance" of this character, paraded his portrait. In the west, this illusory importance was then augmented by Khomeyni's obvious "popularity" in the streets of the Iranian capital. The Ayatollah Shariat-Madari, until then the uncontested leader of a less-than-radical protest-movement, was gradually pushed into the shadows of a lesser status.

Committees-of-support for the Ayatollah (Khomeyni) were created, in Paris, and animated by the usual claque of Left-Bank radicals, led by Michel Foucault, Jean-Paul Sartre and Simone de Beauvoir. *Libération* – though still with a small circulation – *Le Nouvel Observateur*, and especially, *Le Monde*, cranked up the "committees"-project. In an editorial, entitled, "The Return of the Divine", which was widely distributed in Iran, André Fontaine compared Khomeyni to John-Paul II, heaping praise upon the former without reserve. The philosopher, Jacques Madaule, referring to Khomeyni's role, asked if his movement did not "open the gates of the future of humanity".

Gabriel Matzneff, however credulous of certain details, described the scenario unfolding before his eyes with greater lucidity: "If a bishop of the Russian Orthodox Church was staying in Paris," he wrote, "and suddenly started pronouncing anathemas against Mr Brezhnev – calling insistently on his countrymen to rise against the Soviet regime – there would be a general uproar against *him*.

"The Left would drag obscurantist, barbarian popes through the mud, and our Minister of the Interior would take immediate measures to reduce the untimely prelate to silence."

But the Socialist Party, led, at that time by François Mitterrand, supported the movement and even organised a public demonstration in its honour. Later on, it actually sent an official delegation to Teheran, to show solidarity with the revolutionary regime's operation to take American diplomats hostage.

241

There were a few dissonant voices, but they were quickly drowned by the immense clamour of enthusiasm.

After the triumph of the revolution, Mehdi Bazargan, having become Prime Minister of the new, Islamic Republic, thanked the media of the west – and particularly the BBC and *Le Monde* – for their support for the "Imam" and their role in precipitating the revolution.

At Teheran, it was, of course, impossible to ignore the scale of this conjuring-trick, but the regime's attitude was curious. Some ministers proposed protests and retaliatory measures, but the Prime Minister, with the Shah's approval – it is true – opposed this course: "we are not going to exacerbate the situation," he kept saying.

The Iranian secret services were completely up-to-date with events among the immediate followers of Khomeyni, and the Shah received detailed reports, on the subject, from the Savak and the Second Bureau. He took notice of then, at first. Then he ignored them. He had withdrawn from the scene. Unusually, at this time, he received, in audience - on two occasions - our Military Attaché in Paris, Colonel Hassan Aghilipour. The Colonel told him about certain pieces of information, which he had received from French sources, and which did not accord with the line being taken officially, by the government. These sources, he said, were getting more and more worried about the way things were going. The Shah listened, and then charged the Colonel to see to it personally that no attack was made on Rouhollah Khomeyni! It seems that some such action had been proposed to him. He added, "the blame for it would fall on my shoulders."

Just once, however, during this period, the Sovereign decided to react. He told the Grand Master of Protocol to summon the British Ambassador, Sir Anthony Parsons, and tell him personally of his astonishment and confusion concerning the vehement tone of the BBC and its role in the process, which was unfolding. Naturally, Sir Anthony understood the nature of this approach and that it had come from the Shah himself. The ambassador's reply was simple. The BBC was an independent organisation, he said, and Her Majesty's Government, having no power to intervene, could do nothing about the matter. This may have been true of the BBC's domestic services, but everyone knew that programmes beamed abroad – almost all of them organised by people who were not British subjects – were under the control of the government and the secret services. It's the same everywhere these days. Sir Anthony did say, nevertheless, that he would transmit these observations to London.

A few days later, Parsons telephoned ambassador Afshar to tell him that, the day before, the leaders of the IRA had been interviewed on a domestic channel of the BBC: "you see," he said, "even terrorists can express their opposition to the government on our televisions.

"How can we possibly intervene to moderate the BBC's criticism of Iran?"

Aslan Afshar's official approach had not concerned British television, however, or the domestic programmes of the BBC, but its radio-broadcasts in Farsee. The bad faith of Parsons' reply was so evident to the Shah, when he was told about it, that he asked for the matter to be dropped.

The personal relations between the Shah and President Valery Giscard d'Estaing might, perhaps, have had some kind of influence on the French government's official attitude to Iran, during this period, and the unreserved support it gave to Rouhollah Khomeyni: did they greatly accentuate the official tendency? Such effects have often been described. Indeed, there have been many other cases, in which personal resentment has influenced the course of political events.

The Shah had known Valery Giscard d'Estaing, for years – almost since the latter joined the government of Michel Debré as Minister of Finance. In that capacity, Giscard paid a ministerial visit to Iran, which was a great success. Mohammad Reza Pahlavi appreciated the Frenchman's cultivation and intelligence and thought he would have a splendid career, even if, during the presidential elections of 1974, which took him to the Élysée Palace, Teheran sometimes gave the impression that it preferred his rival, Jacques Chaban-Delmas.

The Iranian Sovereigns' state-visit to France, in June 1974, had been a triumph, so exceptional was the welcome. Important economic accords followed: Iran agreed to invest a thousand millions of dollars in France, and the French agreed to participate in the development of Iran's nuclear industry. Iran invested in "Euro-diffusion",and there were a number of other joint-projects.

Strikingly, on 17th February 1975, President Giscard, while on holiday at Courchevel, went over to St. Moritz to visit the King, who was there for a few days skiing. Perhaps this was where things started to go wrong. Having arrived by helicopter, the French President had to wait several minutes before being met. He took offence, they say, and bore a grudge against the Sovereign ever after. A year later, President Giscard and his suite paid a state-visit to Iran, during which certain questions of protocol arose. A "Miss Giscard" was accompanying her parents, together with her "future fiancé", a Mr Gérard Montassier. Regarding the seating-plan for the state-dinner, French protocol would have Mr Montassier placed high up the table, next to the Presidential Couple's daughter. Hormoz Gharib, then Grand Master of Protocol, found this quite unacceptable, saying, "a 'future fiance' has no status in protocol and cannot, therefore, take precedence over Iranian dignitaries and French officials."

Faced with French intransigence on this question, Gharib made the blunder of remarking that he would refer it to His Majesty, who, when briefly asked about it, grew irritated and said to the high official, "what has that to do with me?

"Apply the rules of protocol!"

Gharib therefore refused the French request, going so far as to say, "His Majesty will not authorise me to infringe the rules in that way."

So it was, that, at the banquet of one hundred and thirty covers, Gérard Montassier found himself sitting at the end of the table.

After the repast, the Giscards returned to their apartments in Golestan – the Versailles of Teheran – and talked the matter over. According to some authors, the President was already cross, because he didn't like the presents the Imperial Couple had given him, and had called the Sovereign "an upstart"; but we shall never know for sure what was said around the table that night, as is so often the case with consequential conversations in the world's plush residences. However, this is what was reported to the Shah the following morning. On the next day after that, the little world of the Court, which was addicted to such chatter, talked of nothing else: it was impossible to tell whether the rumour was true or not, but everyone wanted to explore the idea and add his, or her, comments. Incontestably, however, a certain chill settled over the latter part of the presidential visit to Iran.

Dominique Lorenz suggests another explanation. During October 1977, Giscard paid another visit to Teheran. To all appearances, his mission was to warn the Shah that France and the USA would abandon him unless he and his ÒPEC-friends revised their attitude to the western powers. Perhaps the Shah underestimated the cogency of this warning. At any rate, he refused to give way.

Whatever the hypothesis adopted, and none excludes the others, summit-relations between the two countries never reached the same heights again. A climate of antipathy established itself between the two men. The Shah would not utter the name of the French President, unless – not being ignorant of the President's true origins – he called him only "Giscard", without the aristocratic suffix. At Court, naturally, everyone did the same.

When he was in exile in Morocco, a journalist asked him about this, and he replied indirectly, "I don't think Charles de Gaulle would have done anything like that; but – him – he's not in the same league!"

On 9th May 1980, when I visited the Shah, I asked him the main question directly.

"Just gossip!" he said, "I think that Giscard is above all that.

"At Teheran," he continued, "for all I know, his visit went off very well; whereas, at St Moritz, I don't know that he was kept waiting.

"If he *was*, then I'm sorry – he was early though."

The installation of Rouhollah Khomeyni at Neauphle-le-Château marked the beginning of the final phase of the destabilisation of Iran, which had not yet been called "a revolution".

The Shah was hesitant and confused, although he was still following events. Meanwhile, the Prime Minister, to whom he had ceded complete latitude in the direction of affairs, was completely out of touch with them. The army was becoming demoralised. The regime's concessions only made its opponents bolder and more demanding. Since repression was almost non-existent, there were no martyrs. Hence, the professional organisers, who would direct the subversion from now on, came up with ideas, for fake corpses and false funerals, which would later be described, and the theory of which would be developed, by the Commander-in-Chief of the Revolutionary Guard. Lorries packed with regular troops stood in the streets symbolising a near-imaginary, military administration; but what could one *not* attribute to them, if one wished to whip up blood-lust and had the willing assistance of the western media to do it with? Some senior officers and politicians suggested to the government that it take the empty coffins by force, while they were being paraded in the streets, and then expose the deception to the press. The reply was in the negative: "it would serve no purpose," they were told, "people would only claim that it was a Savak trick."

It was under these conditions that the high command of the army – certainly not without the Shah's knowledge – devised a rescue-plan.

On the afternoon 7th October, the re-opening of the universities took place. This was, in each institution, a solemn ceremony, which had been performed, in the same way, for forty years. At a quarter-to-three, the Shah and Shahbanou arrived, by helicopter, at the central campus of Teheran University, where they received an enthusiastic welcome from staff and students alike. The applause was not stage-managed, but entirely spontaneous. The Rector, Abdollah Sheybani, gave the annual report, and then one of the year's graduates made a speech. For some reason the Rector had replaced the usual musical interlude with a poetry-reading. It was a very beautiful, patriotic work by a young lecturer from the School of Literature, named Behzadi Andouhdjerdi, and one of the verses evoked the mystical bond between the Shah and his people. In effect, it was an alarm-call, and it was greeted with sudden, thunderous acclaim. Mohammad Reza Pahlavi was moved almost to tears. Then, as the Sovereign mounted the platform, to present various prizes and medals to the new graduates, he received a fine ovation. Public opinion – or a part of it – was sending him strong signals; but would he, or could he, still set his course by them?

For all the habitual impassivity of his face, one could see how weary he was. Nevertheless, he listened, with great courtesy, to what the graduates spoke to him about – usually requests for bursaries or intervention in personal problems – for, according to tradition, the Shah had a duty to listen to petitions and to give instructions for the resolution of any problems presented to him. Throughout, a vice-Rector stood, notebook in hand, discreetly in the background to record "His Majesty's orders", such as, "tell the Pahlavi Foundation to make this grant, and report on it to me!" or "the Minister of Sciences to resolve this problem and let me know the result." One student asked him to remit the sentence of one of his relatives who had been sentenced to imprisonment: "write to the Minister of Justice," the vice-Rector scribbled, "and ask that, if legally feasible, a request be presented to us soon."

This went on for nearly an hour, after which the Shah was physically exhausted, but rather cheerful. For many, he was still a source of help, and that reassured him.

After the ceremony, there was a small reception, at which he mixed with the company, shaking hands and making an effort to speak with everyone, but his weariness could not be concealed.

It was five-o-clock, when the Shah and Shahbanou left the University, and, at that moment, an officer of the guard notified me, without further details, that I was summoned to the palace at Saad-Abad for a Council-meeting at six-o-clock. This meant that I would have to drive several miles, in dense traffic, in the course of the next hour, and so I hurried off, telephoning to the office, from the car, to cancel a working-engagement.

The Council-meeting was strangely tense. At Saad-Abad, I found, with the PM, Mohammad Baheri, the Minister of Justice, Kazem Vadii, the Minister of Labour and Social Policy, and Manoutchehr Azmoun, Minister-without-Portfolio. Also attending, were a number of Generals – Azhari, then Head of the General Staff, Gharabaghi, Minister of the Interior, Oveyssi, Commander-in-Chief of the Army and Administrator of Martial Law in Teheran, Moghaddam, Head of the Savak, and Samadian, Head of the National Police. Later, we were joined by General Gangi, the Minister of Education.

The surprise was that the Shahbanou, Farah, was also

present and co-presided over the session, seated to the left of her imperial husband, at the top of a large table, in the palace' dining room. In this way, she made a kind of public entrance on to the Iranian political scene.

The Council began just after six-o-clock and went on until half-past-two in the morning (Sunday 8th October) To begin with the Shah spoke briefly: "every day," he said, "the situation becomes more serious and unruly; and this is why I wanted ministers with political responsibilities and principal, military chiefs to meet here today.

"We are here to decide what should be done, and what I should do," he went on, "and I must ask each of you to speak directly, clearly and frankly – brutally so, if necessary – and without ulterior motive."

Then he handed over to the head of the government, who provided a pessimistic analysis, complaining about everyone and everything, including some ministers who – it is true – had not turned up, and said that they were being "left behind by events".

"Nevertheless," he added with feeling, "I know how to do *my* duty!"

General Azhari, Head of the General Staff, advocated a policy of keeping order, as an "absolute priority", and some reforms. Manoutchehr Azmoun proposed the formation of a "revolutionary council", to be presided over by the Emperor himself.

"We are going to have to set some big precedents," he stressed, "with military tribunals applying procedures as in time of war, judging individuals in the teeth of public criticism and performing summary executions.

At this point, General Moghaddam, Head of the Savak, asked permission to interrupt Minister Azmoun and said calmly, "Sire, if we are going to hang some individuals in Sepah Square" – where executions were performed in the past – "I think that, in all justice, Mr Azmoun should be the first to swing!"

He wasn't joking – not even in bad taste – and a long silence fell, which the Shah broke, saying, with a taut smile, "enough badinage, gentlemen – please continue your presentation, Mr Azmoun!"

In turn, everyone present gave his analysis and made his proposals. Kazem Vadii coined a phrase, which impressed us all: "Sire, these events smell, more than anything of *oil*."

Towards nine-o-clock, we were called in to dinner, at some small tables in a waiting-room, and the Sovereigns and other attendees moved off there together.

The meal was relatively simple, with a good claret, which the Shah hardly touched. Because there were waiters present, the conversation consisted of small-talk only, and we chatted, among other things, of the ceremony at the University, that day and the warm welcome the Shah had received. Some tried to relax the atmosphere by telling jokes, but it didn't work. General Moghaddam and Manoutchehr Azmoun, who were both shot after the triumph of the revolution, avoided one another's eyes.

After dinner, discussion resumed , and, progressively, the sensible options became clear. The media would have to be taken in hand, especially the broadcast media; measures for keeping order in the big cities would have to be augmented; trouble-makers would have to be arrested - and the streets patrolled to prevent the development of mass-confrontations – and certain particularly corrupt officials would have to be brought before the courts.

To implement these measures – and especially certain, indispensable, political reforms – and to get talks started, from a firm, clear basis, with the clergy at Qom and the secular opposition, the government would be re-shuffled and reinforced by the co-option of some first-rate people. These measures, it was decided, would be brought in, in the morning.

However, during the course of the 8th October – and then the following day – no move was made to put any of these "urgent decisions" into practice. No ministerial re-shuffle was announced. Was there obstruction from the Shahbanou, who had said hardly a word at the meeting, or from the ambassadors of the west? Rumour again ran riot in political circles.

I asked for an urgent meeting with the Prime Minister, who was happy to see me first thing in the morning of the 10th. He seemed tired – somewhat haggard. I asked him point-blank, "what about our 'urgent decisions', Mr Prime Minister?"

In reply, he launched into rambling explanations, involving his experience of grave crises and – taking a cue from Vadii - intrigues among the oil-companies, and he invited me to be patient: "things will quieten down – I'm keeping an eye on them," he said, and we parted.

Back at my office, I composed a long letter of resignation, to the PM, which, for greater security from leaks, I was going to have typed, outside the ministry, by the secretary of one of my colleagues, Professor Rouhani Zadeh, Director of the Department of Nuclear Physics at the faculty of Sciences of Teheran University. In this letter, I chronicled events, since 27th August, and the half-measures, evasion and procrastination, with which the PM had responded to the ever-growing violence. I underlined one phrase, which I hoped would shock him: "where are we going?"

In short, I told him that present government-policy was heading for certain disaster, which could have tragic consequences for the nation. Rouhani Zadeh came to get the letter and promised to have it typed and bring the copy, at half-past-one, to the "Cercle Français", where we would have lunch together. This went according to plan. I then asked, as was customary, for an urgent audience with the Sovereign, which was granted, a few minutes later, for seven-o-clock that evening, in the office inside the King's private apartment.

At the restaurant, we were joined by Hamid Rahnema, a former Minister of Information, who was a good friend of mine, and a wise counsellor, and I read my letter to him. He said: "you don't think you're overdoing it, do you?"

I replied without, of course, mentioning the meeting at the palace – which was not referred to directly in the text – that I could no longer support the government's attitude. He laughed loudly and said, "What government – it doesn't really exist, does it?"

Seven-o-clock at the Niavaran palace: the small office was very dimly lit, but the Shah, his face seamed by fatigue, was nevertheless wearing dark-glasses. I excused myself for requesting an urgent audience. He said that, the state the country was in, he didn't blame me, adding, "What's going on?"

"Sire," I said, "you know what I think – I didn't join the government willingly – I did it out of patriotism and because you wanted me to; but my presence in it makes no sense at all now.
"Why have none of the decisions, reached the other night, been acted on?"

"They can't do anything any more," he replied.

"Well, perhaps, we ought to be looking elsewhere, then," I suggested

"Where?" queried the Shah.

"What about a government, including certain elements of the opposition, with the support of the army?" I ventured.

"And, if that doesn't work?" he asked.

"A military cabinet!" I said.

I told him that I had decided to leave the Cabinet, and he read my letter. At first he seemed shocked, then he commented: "you're taking quite a risk, writing this – no-one dares to say things like this any more."
He returned to his question, saying, "We'll look at both possibilities – check out the prospects for forming a coalition-government.
"This is not an invitation to form a government, but a request for information; but explore it in depth, use your contacts and be very discreet – the position of Charif Emami is not good, but it could be worse."

My letter of resignation reached the PM the following day. I was the first holder of a ministerial post to resign, without being ordered to, in 25 years. I had already distributed the text of the letter to leading members of the Group Studying the Problems of Iraq, and four, serving ministers received copies, because their attitude was so like mine, that I felt I should let them know my reasons for going.

Of course, there were leaks, and some newspapers printed stories featuring the main points of the document. Two days later, the big-circulation, English-language magazine, *Keyhan International*, analysed it in depth, beneath one of its front page headlines, which read, "Dramatic warning to PM!"

Meanwhile, I had set myself diligently to accomplish the information-gathering mission, which the Sovereign had assigned to me.

My first thought was of the three figures, who, officially, were directing the National Front. Of these, Karim Sandjabi was abroad, attending a meeting of the Socialist International, and Bakhtiar was already acting very much on his own. I discovered later why he was doing this. That left Dariouch Forouhar, to whom I then sent word that I wished to meet him.

At Forouhar's request, our encounter took place on what he called "neutral territory", and which, in fact, was the house of his deputy, Takmil Homayoun - a sociologist, who, while studying for his doctorate, in Israel, had married an Israeli girl. I knew him quite well, having had him as a student, while he was studying for his master's degree, at the end of the 'fifties. In order, no doubt, to cover himself, in the eyes of his supporters, Forouhar had also asked that his deputy be present throughout the meeting. I did not need to cover myself, in anyone's eyes, but I asked, nevertheless, that my colleague, Prof. Rouhani Zadeh, be there. He was himself well known, and accepted, in some opposition-circles. Thus, for more than three hours, we discussed matters, in the presence of two, silent observers. Takmil Homayoun took notes, from time to time. Rouhani Zadeh intervened on two or three occasions.

With Forouhar, and all the dissidents I met, I used the same, central argument: "the Sovereign really wants political evolution," I would say, "but, if you won't settle for a compromise, the opportunity this provides will be lost, through the inevitable intervention, in one form or another, of the army."

All of them, beginning with Forouhar, dreaded the latter eventuality, and their fear led them into great wisdom. It is obvious now that those who were directing the operation from abroad, were already working on the emasculation of the army, but this was not apparent then, either to the Shah, or to my negotiating partners, or to me, and so, my argument held. Several of my consultees were starting to be aware of two dangers, which were threatening their movement. One was the increasingly important role being played by the extreme left - the Toudeh, that is, or Iranian Communist Party, and an ultra-Leftist, Maoist-Trotskyite faction - and the other was the growing power of the fundamentalist, Islamic movement, which was being openly encouraged by certain English-speaking diplomats, who were accredited to Teheran.

My interlocutors, therefore, still preferred a constitutional solution, backed by the Shah and the clerics of Qom. Hence, I encountered a considerable amount of good will among them.

21st September 1971

The Shah and Shahbanou in academic dress: having officially opened
the new Central Library of Teheran University, the Royal Couple are
proceeding to a further part of the ceremony.

Left: Prime Minister Hoveyda
Right foreground: Houchang Nahavandi
(appointed Rector of the University, three months before)

Right background: (in military uniform) General Ali Neshat,
Commander of The Immortals.
(Photo courtesy of Mrs. Seda Aghassian)

12st October 1971

Solemn tribute to Cyrus the Great. Two-thousand-five-hundredth anniversary of the founding of the Empire.
(*Photo courtesy of Mehrdad Pahlbod*)

Princess Fawzieh of Egypt, the Shah's first wife. This photograph is
dedicated "to Ardeshir". *(Ardeshir Zahedi Collection)*

The Shah and Empress Soraya at the wedding-ceremony of Princess
Shahnaz and Ardeshir Zahedi. The Sovereign is signing the register.
Soraya was the great love of the Shah's life. *(Ardeshir Zahedi Collection)*

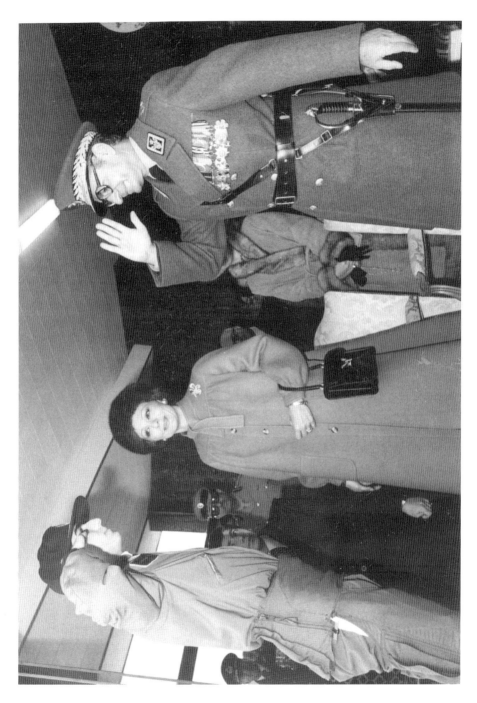

November 1977: Prince Reza receives his pilot's licence from the Sovereign. The Shahbanou stands beside her husband. *(T.S. Collection)*

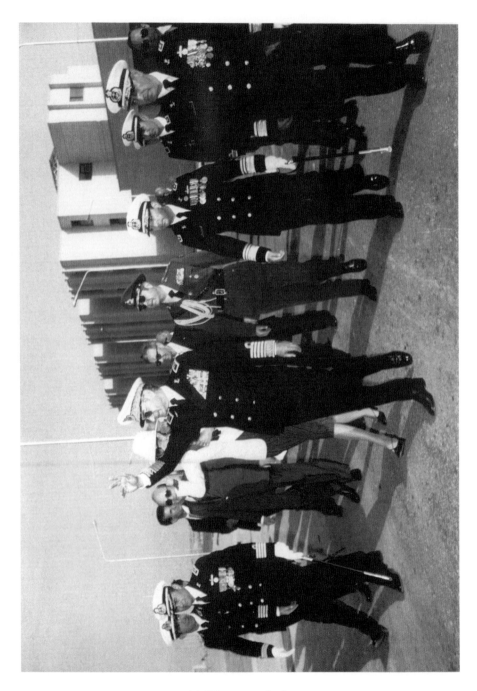

At Khorramshahr
(Admiral Deyhimi Collection)

Autumn 1977 – Bouchehr Naval Base – Right (not in uniform)
Colonel Djahanbini, the Shah's personal body-guard.
(Admiral Deyhimi Collection)

Autumn 1977, at Bouchehr Naval Base
(Admiral Deyhimi Collection)

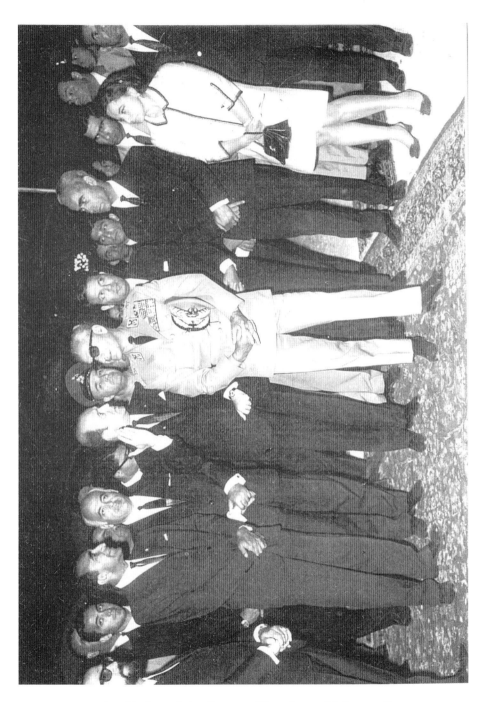

The Shah and the Rector, Houchang Nahavandi,
at the University of Shiraz *(Private Collection)*

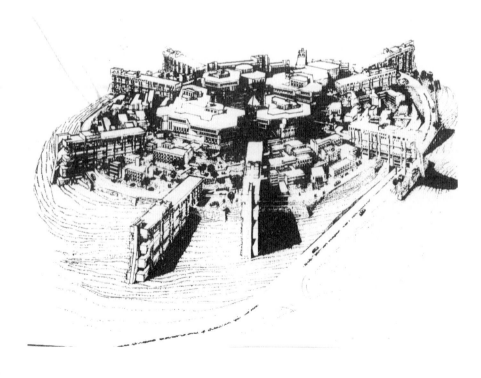

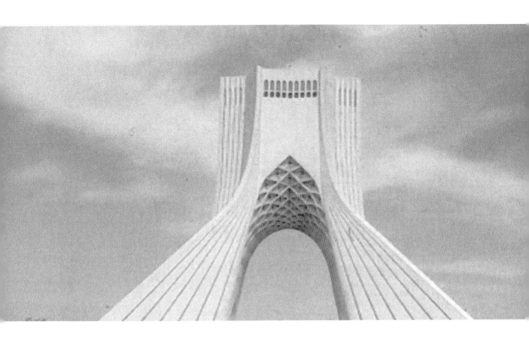

The Shahyad, memorial of the kings, dedicated to Cyrus the Great

—

a triumphal arch, nearly 200 feet high,
designed by Hossein Amanat.
Below ground level - a museum, with a floor-space of
87 000 sq ft., showing the history of Iran.
(All Rights Reserved)

FACING PAGE

above
18th October 1971 – Inauguration of Teheran's Olympic Complex,
designed and built, by Abdol Aziz Farmanfamanian and company,
around a central, 100 000-capacity stadium,
which remains one of Asia's premier venues.
(Farmarfamanian Collection)

below
Persepolis in the 20th century: this was the Shah's vision of the
campus of Shiraz University, a scale model of which is shown here.
Much of the project was completed before the Revolution.
(Mr and Mrs Andref's Collection)

20th August 1978 – Mokhber-Ol-Dowleh Square, Teheran.
Celebration of the twenty-fifth anniversary of the Shah's returning
to Iran following the downfall of Mossadegh. *(T.S. Collection)*

September 1978 – the Shah visiting Tabass, which had been stricken by an earthquake on 16th September 1978. *(T.S. Collection)*

Rector Pouyan presents the good wishes of Melli University's teaching-staff to the Shah and Shahbanou. Behind the Sovereign, Rector Nahavandi. *(Dr Parviz Pouyan's Collection)*

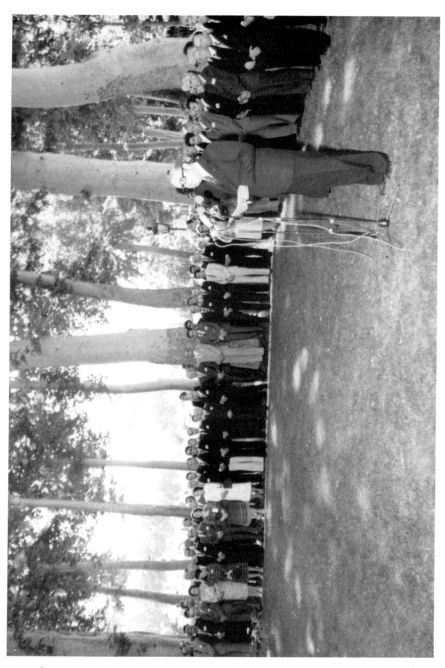

14th June 1978 – Niavaran Palace – the Shah receives the Conference of members of the Group Studying the Problems of Iran. Houchang Nahavandi is addressing the Sovereign. *(Author's Collection)*

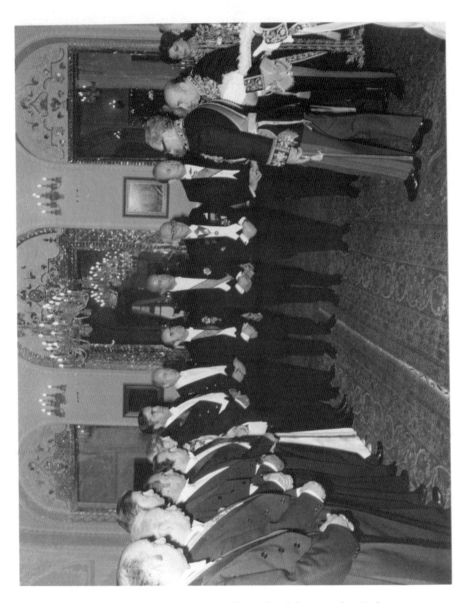

Ceremonial presentation of good wishes at the Palace.
Behind the Sovereign, Prime Minister Amir Abbas Hoveyda.
On the Sovereign's right, the author.
(Dr Parviz Pouyan's Collection)

The Shah, Richard Nixon and Secretary of State, William Rodgers.
Behind, Henry Kissinger.

(Ardeshir Zahedi Collection)

Teheran, 31st December 1977: surprise visit, arranged by the Iranian
Diplomatic Service, of King Hussein of Jordan to President Carter.
Behind King Hussein, Ardeshir Zahedi, Iranian Ambassador to the
USA. Left, William Sullivan, US-Ambassador to Teheran.

(Ardeshir Zahedi Collection)

Henry Kissinger, the Shah and Ardeshir Zahedi.

(Ardeshir Zahedi Collection)

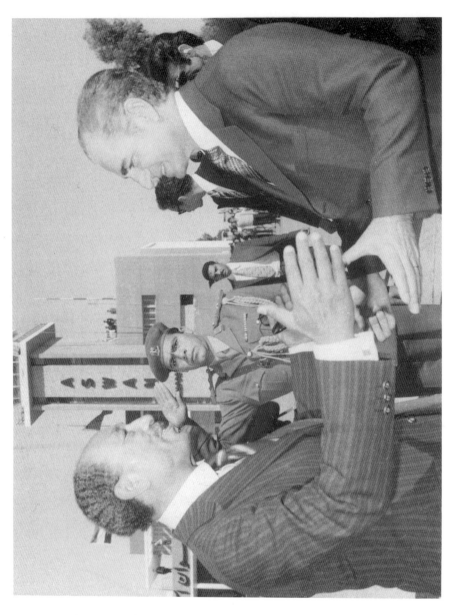

Aswan – the Shah visits President Sadat, in 1977.

(T.S. Collection)

Teheran – 5th September 1978 – The Shah receiving the President of the
Chinese People's Republic, Hua Guo Feng, at Mehrabad International
Airport. This was the last visit to Iran, by a foreign Head-of-State,
before the Revolution. *(T.S. Collection)*

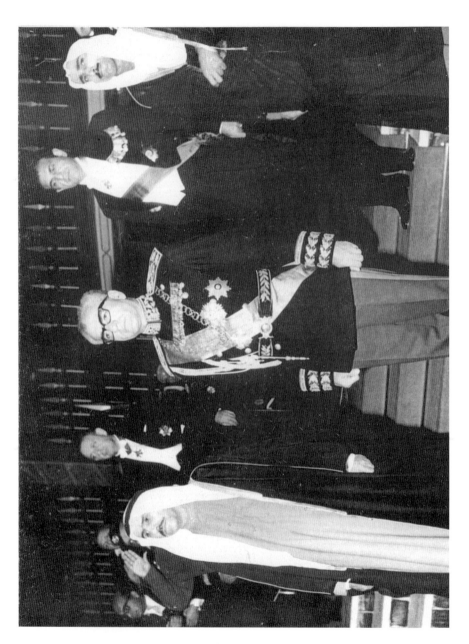

The Shah pays a state-visit to the Emirate of Kuwait. A show of force.
Behind the Sovereign and the Emir, Ardeshir Zahedi (then Minister of
Foreign Affairs) and the Iranian Ambassador, Tadjbakhch.
(Ardeshir Zahedi Collection)

The Shah's last visit to India. From left to right: Ambassador Aslan Afshar, Houchang Nahavandi, the Shah, the Indian President and his wife, the Shahbanou and the Indian Prime Minister.
(T.S. Collection)

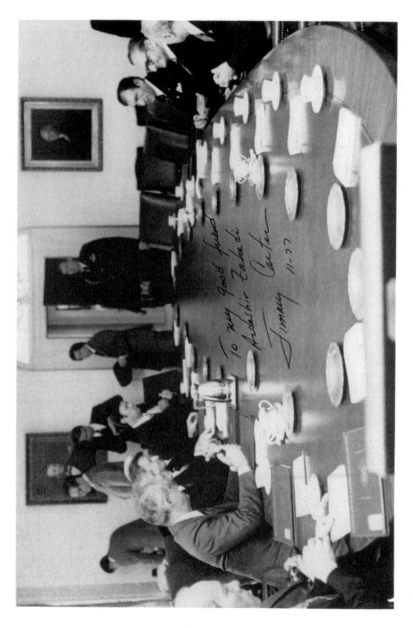

November 1977 – The White House, Washington DC – a meeting
between the Shah and President Carter. Ardeshir Zahedi, who was then
the Iranian Ambassador, and to whom Jimmy Carter presented this
photograph, is shown to the right of the Sovereign. To the left of the
Shah, is shown Abbas Khalatbari, the Iranian Foreign Minister. Sitting
next to, and beyond, President Carter, is Zbigniew K. Brzezinski.
(Ardeshir Zahedi Collection)

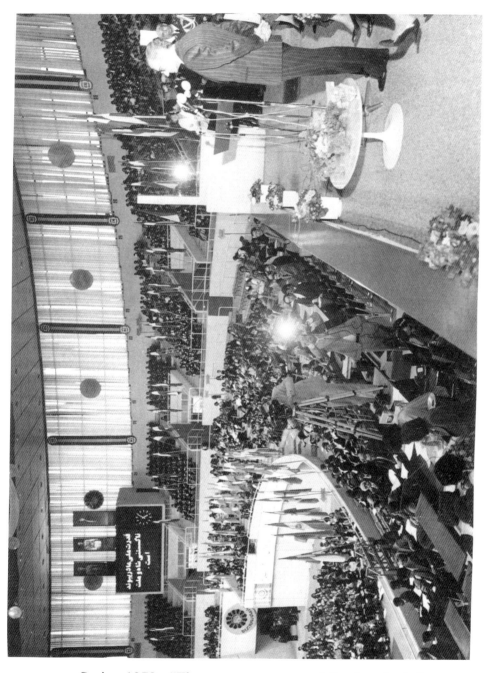

Spring 1978: "The caravan passes and the dogs bark,"
said the Shah, at a large public meeting.

(T.S. Collection)

Arranging the Imperial Couple's stay in Mexico: Ardeshir
Zahedi went, in person, to Mexico and was invited to dinner
by President Lopes Portillo (right) who presented him with the
Mexican Government's written agreement.

(Ardeshir Zahedi Collection)

29th July 1980 – Cairo – The Shah's Funeral. Behind the Shahbanou and President Sadat, are ranged the Imperial Family, almost in its entirety.

(Ardeshir Zahedi Collection)

محمدرضا پهلوی

پاسخ به تاریخ

به جناب هوشنگ نهاوندی اهدا گردید

نهم خرداد ۲۵۳۹

Title Page of "A Reply To History", dedicated to Houchang Nahavandi, and signed by the Shah. Calligraphy is an art much prized by the Iranians. Experts will note the beauty of the Shah's writing.

At length, most of the nebulous branches of the dissident movement had been consulted. I spoke to representatives of the Movement for the Liberation of Iran - led by Mehdi Bazargan, Khomeyni's future Prime-Minister - to people from the Iranian Human Rights Association, to followers of former Prime Minister Mossadegh - who retained great, moral authority, despite their, in many cases, advanced years - and also to Ali Amini, who seemed to be on everyone's, and no-one's, side.

The discussions were not easy, but a programme capable of satisfying everyone, including the Ayatollah Shariat-Madari, was at last hammered out.

The Priority, which all accepted, was a return to peace and order. Everybody agreed to put out clear calls for such a return, so that, as soon as it was achieved, the government could proceed rapidly to lift the sanctions of martial law (which was, in theory, in force) recognise opposition-parties, reform the Savak, dissolve the Corporate Chambers, re-structure the Pahlavi Foundation and distance itself from certain members of the Imperial Family, who would then be persuaded to go and live in Europe.

Eventually, at a further stage, a steering-committee would be formed to conduct elections to the legislative assemblies. This committee would be chaired by a senior judge of the Supreme Court and would include representatives of the secular and religious factions of the dissident movement. Several leading figures of the nationalist factions, and some other folk, whose great age was matched (in many cases) only by the weight of their moral authority, also agreed to join the Cabinet. Thus, the ministries of National Education, Commerce and Justice would all be given to well-known dissidents, and that of Information would be allotted to someone, who seemed to be on everyone's side, and none.

Apportioning the Ministry of the Interior was especially ticklish and gave rise to some sharp exchanges. Agreement was reached, in the end, to confer it on His Excellency Djavad Sadre, who had held this portfolio some years before, but had been pushed out, by Amir Abbas Hoveyda, for being too independent and frank-speaking. The dissidents further acknowledged that the portfolios of Defence and Foreign Affairs should be held at the discretion of the Sovereign, and that three high-ranking military men (two admirals and a general) would hold the posts of Minister of Industry, Minister of Development and Housing and Minister of Posts and Telecommunications, respectively.

The nomination for Minister of State in Charge of Relations with the Clergy, received the blessing of the Ayatollahs of Qom. It had become difficult for me to organise a meeting with Ayatollah Shariat-Madari, so he sent me three envoys, with plenipotentiary powers, to negotiate the details of the arrangement.

Ten days later, Isubmitted thje programme, and the lists of ministerial nominations, to the Shah.

In the meantime, the situation had developed considerably. Strike had succeeded strike in most sections of the economy, and industrial action was now affecting some ministries. Riots and skirmishes were becoming ever more commonplace. In the capital, life became increasingly difficult. Charif Emami no longer possessed any authority. Some ministers resigned, and others waited, in deserted offices, for they knew not what.

The Shah listened to me for an hour-and-a-half, discussed everything and wondered at some of the nominations. He laughed unrestrainedly about a retired admiral, who had become a dissident-leader, haggling over which post he should have: I had proposed Commerce, but he wanted Education, and I had given way. The Sovereign said, "I always knew he was an ass, but not that much of one: Commerce is a nice, restful ministry - Education is fraught with annoyances - but, things being as they are ..."

Finally, having touched on every aspect of the matter, the Shah gave me a long look. It could have been absent-minded - a sort of vacant stare - or a moment of intense, personal reflection. I was expecting him to ask outright whether it wasn't simply too late for any of this, because I was close too asking myself this very question; but he resumed, "perhaps things will get better: we *are* in talks with the Americans, and it is *they* who are behind all this unrest."

In fact, he had just recalled Ardeshir Zahedi, our ambassador in Washington, where, together with Foreign Minister, Khosrow Afshar, he had been pushing for a thoroughgoing clarification of the positions being taken by the White House and the State Department, but this came to nothing: as far as the West was concerned, the die had been cast.

Unlike his usual, distant self, the Shah thanked me warmly "for having carried out such a difficult mission so well". Certainly, he had just been presented, for the last time, with the concessions he would have to make, in domestic affairs, if there were to be any hope of saving his regime.

I took my leave. At the door of his office, I heard him say suddenly, "we've done some good work together; I shall think about this arrangement; I'll sleep on it."

Zahedi's arrival in Teheran unfolded in an odd manner. It was supposed to happen, as was customary, in a low key - like any ambassadorial consultation. However, in the arrivals-lounge, at Teheran International Airport, were waiting the Chief of the General Staff, the Foreign Minister, Oveyssi (the Administrator of Martial Law) and numerous, senior, military officers and political figures. They had all come to ask him to do something to save the country.

The following day, I telephoned him, and we met for breakfast, two days after that. A group of about fifty people - soldiers of the high command, senators, journalists and even some distinguished medical doctors - had crowded into the garden and reception-rooms of his house at Hessarak, and all of them were asking him to press the Sovereign to react, at long last, with the firmness, which a section of the public was demanding. In my view, this section - "the party of order" - was still in the majority, in Iran, at that time, and it was seeking a spokesman; but the game was already over. Nevertheless, Zahedi would do all he could to sustain the Shah, morally and psychologically, to the last day of his reign, and even during his exile.

The idea of turning to Ardeshir Zahedi, at this time, was going the rounds of all the political circles in the capital. Indeed, of all Iranian politicians, Zahedi was indisputably the most influential and highly regarded among the upper echelons of the army. He had excellent relations in American politics, albeit mainly among the Republicans, and an unequalled, international address-book, which he would soon use for the benefit of the Imperial Couple, during their tragic wanderings in exile. He had enjoyed good relations, for some years, with the people close to the National Front, and he had his connections among the clergy. All of this provided him with many cards to play in the circumstances the country was experiencing; but a large part of the Imperial Family and the Shahbanou's "friends" didn't like him - or feared him, rather. His plain-speaking made many tremble, because they knew that he would not hesitate to lop off rotten branches. The Savak - or some of their senior officers, at least - feared him also. All of these things should have meant that he would be called to take office.

For myself, I never heard anything on this subject, either from the Shah, or from the Shahbanou; but someone very close to the latter told me, at that time, that there were doubts about the way he might govern, and the effect his appointment might have upon the Democratic Party, in the USA. Was that all there was to it, I wonder?

Mohammad Reza Pahlavi's depressive condition was, from now on, visible. The mask often fell, for he was no longer master of himself. He who, up to this point, had faced events squarely, now fell into a state of discouragement and dejection. Up to now, he had believed in his destiny, in his friends abroad and in his people; but the moment had come, when all he could see around him was collapse. He was ill - which, still, nobody knew - and his terrible trials had exhausted him. Henceforth, the Shahbanou would play a very active, political role, even though, constitutionally, she had no role whatever.

Abruptly, the Prime Minister began to mention the Sovereign again, having previously reached the point of forgetting his existence. He, Charif Emami, had held talks with the "committees" of journalists, who were trying to take control of the capital's principal, daily newspapers. The result had been a joint-declaration, giving complete satisfaction to the latter, for it conceded editorial authority, and management, of the two, big, evening papers, *Keyhan* and *Ettela'at*, to them.

The members of these "committees" were all well-known for their excessive zeal in favour of the Imperial regime! Some of them, indeed, and not just the minor figures among them, were suspected of being Savak-informers. In fact, I believe that, in switching allegiance and embracing revolutionary extremism, they thought that they were securing an alternative future for themselves. Some of them soon regretted having done this, but not all.

When he heard the news, Khosrow Afshar, the Foreign Minister, having just returned from the USA, where he had been attending the General Assembly of the United Nations Organisation and meeting American politicians, rushed to the Prime Minister's house.

"You have been utterly thoughtless," he said to the PM, "how could you have ignored the fact that these newspapers are privately owned?

"By what right do you consign them to these 'committees' of revolutionary hooligans?

"Can you not foresee the political consequences of doing this?

"It's nothing short of treason!"

Charif Emami, when addressed in this fashion, which was not what he expected from an experienced diplomat - whose discourse was usually most restrained - replied to him in resigned tones.

"I thought it would calm them down," he said, "but I realise now that it served no purpose."

Having become aware of the despairing inactivity of his Prime Minister, and searching for a political solution to the crisis, Mohammad Reza Pahlavi asked the high command of the army to think about providing an outcome, which would be "both military and constitutional".

A policy for securing control of the country, and especially the capital, called "Operation Khach", was then conceived and implemented by a restricted group of officers, led by generals Khosrodad, Amine Afshar and Rahimi. General Oveyssi, Commander-in-Chief of the Army and Administrator of Martial Law in Teheran, evidently knew all about this, because the Sovereign asked him to be ready to head a constitutional, military government, as a way out of the impasse.

The object of Operation Khach was to alter, in a matter of hours, the balance of forces in the country - to enable the regime to negotiate with the opposition, from a position of authority - and to stop the psychological and political momentum of the subversion. On the "D-day" of this operation, immediately after the nomination of General Oveyssi - which would take place shortly before the imposition of a curfew, units of the Savak's intervention-force, based at Lavizan, of the National Police Guard, based at Echrat Abad, and of the airborne division, based at Baghe Shah - all composed of elite troops, held, until then, virtually apart from the conflict and in reserve - would proceed to arrest about four hundred leaders and organisers of the sedition. Most of these would be taken to the military section of Mehr Abad International Airport, or to the air-base at Dochan Tapeh. At each of these sites, two C-130, heavy-transport aircraft would be placed in readiness to carry the detainees to Khach - hence the code-name of the operation - which is a small city in the province of Baluchistan, on the Pakistani border, whose inhabitants are Sunnis. Rapidly and discreetly, the army had already refurbished and re-equipped the old barracks there, which had been disused for some years.

Supplies, bedding and an emergency task-force, for generating electricity, had already been transported to the camp.

The strike in the oil-industry, and in the distribution of electricity, was now causing inconvenience to the population, and some two dozen of its organisers had been identified. Military engineers and technicians would replace these strike-leaders as soon as they were arrested. National radio and television stations would be occupied and their output controlled. Television-news, for example, would be presented by young officers in the uniform of the Press Service of the General Staff. Opposition-leaders - those with whom negotiations were to be conducted - would not be removed to Khach, but held under house-arrest, or at the Army-Officers'Club, where they would be entertained as "guests of the government".

The spirit, in which this plan was conceived, was not aimed at creating a coup d'État, but at installing a government, which would restore order, uphold the law and provide security. The intervention of elite troops was to be of short duration, whereupon the regular troops, which were already stationed in the cities, would mount guard over sensitive locations.

It was envisaged that the military Prime Minister would be presented to the Chambers, and, having obtained their vote of confidence, would be accorded plenipotentiary powers for a limited period. No decision had been made concerning whether Parliament should be dissolved or allowed to run its normal term. General Oveyssi preferred the first option, the Shah, the second. In either event, to conform with the constitution, there would have to be an Imperial Ordinance, decreeing the date of the next elections, which would also reassure opinion at home, and make it clear abroad, that the state-of-emergency - for such it was - constituted no more than "shock-therapy" for overcoming the grave crisis, in which the country found itself. The army was completely operational, and the elite troops were well prepared for carrying out the tasks, which would be assigned to them.

The plan stood a serious chance of succeeding. Military intelligence-networks, were re-directed towards examining domestic subversion, and the police and the Savak were tracking the people marked for arrest. Moreover, the secret had been well kept and the plan would have the advantage of surprise. There was also Oveyssi's considerable reputation, as a strong-man, and as a member of a religious family of Qom, which would count, it was thought, very much in favour of success. He had been preparing, discreetly, for the formation of his government, by talking to certain Grand Ayatollahs and eliciting some assurances from that quarter. To avoid creating any rumour, which might be harmful to the existing cabinet's authority - such as it was - his political encounters took place late in the evening, after curfew. His chief information-officer, Brigadier-General Djavad Moin-Zadeh, went himself to find the people, whom his boss wanted to consult or meet, and, after the conversations were over, took them back to their homes. Oveyssi's team had to include civilians, to deal, especially, with foreign affairs and finance, but soldiers were in the majority, and most of these were high-ranking technicians, of which the army possessed a plentiful supply.

Towards the end of October, he let the Shah know that he was ready.

The 26th October was Mohammad Reza Pahlavi's 59th birthday. Traditionally, it was a day of ceremonies and festivities, with the solemn presentation of good wishes, in the morning, followed by a sporting festival in one of the city's great stadia. Since the completion of the capital's Olympic Complex, events of this kind had been held in the presence of a hundred-thousand people and were very like those which precede the Olympic Games. In the evening, guests were invited to a more intimate reception at the palace...

This year, the sporting festival was cancelled, for security reasons - in case of hostile demonstrations - and the reception was not held either. It seems that the Shah, in a state of complete dejection, had declined even to taste the birthday-cake, which was served after dinner.

The Council of Residents'Associations, a secular body deeply rooted in the city, and a number of large sporting-clubs had, however, decided to organise a patriotic, sporting festival, at the Mohammad Reza Shah Stadium, a huge hall in the centre of the capital, with twelve thousand seats. A literary figure, well known for his talents as an orator, some young champions and a President of the Association would speak. A sporting and musical programme was planned. What's more, this imposing show was intended as a riposte against those many demonstrations *against* the Sovereign, which were proceeding unhindered.

The PM was against it: "it would be a provocation," he said, and he invoked the very provisions of martial law, which proscribed assemblies of people, to ban it! The Shah was petitioned, on behalf of the organisers, but only said, "I am touched by this, but what good would it do?"

The idea was abandoned. The traditional ceremony of the presentation of good wishes was not cancelled, however: it began at nine-o-clock in the morning, in the hall of mirrors of the Golestan Palace, in the heart of the city. Fifteen minutes earlier, the King's helicopter touched down in the City Park, less than a mile away. The ceremony was a fixture, and announced in advance, and the route from the park was known to all. The placing of a guard of honour, which one had not wished more substantial than usual, gave notice of the procession's approach. A crowd of several thousands of people packed the pavements of Khayyam and Davar Avenues and Ark Square, by which the cortege would travel. The Shah rode in an armoured Rolls-Royce, with the usual escort of motorcyclists around the car. There was not the least demonstration - no cheers, no jeers, no whistles - only a heavy silence, both going and coming back. This reflected the view mainly taken by the public - amazement and expectancy. People were waiting for an end to disturbing events, and the winner of the confrontation. A little before nine-o-clock, the Shah, in full ceremonial garb, arrived, ashen-faced, at the palace. He was expecting, perhaps, signs of hostility, but not this silence - these questioning looks turned towards him.

He composed himself for a few moments, taking a cup of the sweet tea, which he loved. His face was sad and his posture stiff. Before he made his entry into the hall of mirrors, Aslan Afshar, who was walking, ceremoniously, in front of him, to announce him, slowed and fell back a pace, whispering in his ear, "smile, Sire, no-one must notice your sadness, especially today - you must inspire confidence."

Mohammad Reza Pahlavi replied, "you're right," and got a grip on himself. The appearance of a smile lit up his features. Once again, we could see the convenient mask.

The nation's different estates were received in turn. First came the dignitaries of the Court, then the Government and the Chambers, the Magistracy, Superior and General Military Officers, the Universities and "Civil Society", and lastly the "personalities", former Prime Ministers, other Ministers and Provincial Governors. Other than in the last two estates, there was no thinning of the ranks. It seems that the Shah was expecting a lot of absentees from among the university-staff, but they were nearly all there, and old Rector, Abdollah Sheybani's, good wishes - presented on behalf of all the capital's universities - were exceptionally warm, which evoked a very cordial response from the Shah. The number of the "personalities" was somewhat reduced. Usually, there would be a former Prime Minister, who would present good wishes on behalf of everybody, but none of the three former heads-of-government, who were still alive and living in the capital, turned up. Neither Ali Amini, who was so fond of publicised events, nor Amir Abbas Hoveyda, nor Djamchid Amouzegar had responded to their invitations. It was necessary to improvise and ask Abasgholi Golchaiian, who had been a minister in the 'thirties and 'forties, to speak for all, which the venerable old man carried off well enough.

Not having an official function any longer, I found myself among the "personalities". The Sovereign stopped in front of me and said, either sadly or ironically, "at least you're there."

The group of clergy from minority religions - Christians, Jews and Zoroastrians - was received separately, as was customary. Their greetings were especially affectionate. The threat of Islamic fanaticism had evidently not escaped their notice. Throughout the course of history, the King had always been the protector of minorities, and it was under the reigns of the Pahlavis, especially that of the reigning Shah, that these minorities had achieved positions, which were much envied in other countries. This the delegates knew, and they showed it.

The reception of this group made that of the Muslim clergy more delicate. Out of respect for them, and for tradition, the Shah invited them to sit on the chairs provided, as he had invited the delegates of the minority religions to sit, and to take tea. There were not very many of them. A celebrated preacher spoke of political matters and gave a plethora of advice. This annoyed the Shah, who cut the audience short.

As he left the Golestan, Mohammad Reza Pahlavi was clearly tired, and his expression reflected an immense sadness. He was probably bearing the weight of the terrible realisation that this would be his last visit to the historic place where, as a very young heir-to-the-throne, he had attended his father's coronation, and where, much later, he had taken part in his own and seen so many of the world's great men come and go.

I had to take to my bed, on Thursday 2nd November, because my spine was in a bad way, and there I was that evening, at about half-past-seven, when the Shahbanou rang.

"His Majesty is with me," she said, "and is following our conversation, so I am speaking both for him and for myself.

"According to the latest information," she went on, "Khomeyni's supporters are planning a riot in Teheran, next Tuesday.

"They intend to burn the cinemas, pillage the banks and provoke a massacre - especially in the University-quarter - precipitating, if they can, a full-blown, revolutionary situation.

"Some elements of the security-services, manipulated by foreign influences, can no longer be relied on.

"It is, therefore, absolutely necessary," she concluded, "that we form a government, which has the confidence of the opposition, before next Tuesday, in order to de-fuse the plot *politically.*"

I was stunned by this analysis. Order could not be restored by making further concessions, but how could I put it? They knew my position. I therefore merely explained that I appreciated the gravity of this news, but that I could not go anywhere, because I was unable to get out of bed.

"But you can telephone the leaders of the opposition," she pursued, " and ask them to form a government of national unity, making it clear that His Majesty will accept, as Prime Minister, whomsoever they put forward."

"But Your Majesty will understand," I rejoined," that what was still possible twenty days ago, is not so today.

Nevertheless, I acceded. The seriousness of the situation and the importance of the initiative, which I was going to undertake from my bed - since I couldn't move - seemed to me to require witnesses; so I asked "Mr Abdolkarim Lahidji, an eminent lawyer", one of the opposition leaders, and my friend Dr. Emami Ahari - who was then a confidant of Ayatollah Taleghani - to come to my house.

In their presence, I called, first, Shapour Bakhtiar, and talked to him, by my watch, for forty-five minutes. He was somewhat astonished - for which I learned the reasons later - and replied by giving me a detailed list of his grievances against "His so-called Majesty, the Shah", starting with twenty-five years of ostracism and ending with his arm being broken, during a recent demonstration, by "Savak's *agents provocateurs*".

"The Shah has wasted twenty-five years of our lives," insisted Bakhtiar, "preventing us from taking part in the life of the nation - and now he wants a decision within the hour!

"It's just not possible," he concluded, "Mr Sandjabi is in Paris, negotiating with Khomeyni, and I, with just Forouhar here, cannot take a decision."

After a few more lively exchanges, I told him, "I'm only passing on a message: if you like, I'll come to see you in the morning, although I have the greatest difficulty in walking, but then, at least, we would be able to speak face to face."

"Tomorrow is Friday," Bakhtiar protested, "and I'm off to Karadj" - a place in the suburbs of the capital - "for a picnic - so what's the hurry, anyway?"

"I'm afraid I must insist," I said, I can be at your house tomorrow morning at any hour you care to indicate."

"But we have all the time in the world!" cried Bakhtiar scornfully, "he [the Shah] made us wait twenty-five years; why shouldn't he wait a few days?"

He was getting really angry now. In fact, as I soon found out, he had been having talks with the Shahbanou, since September, and he himself wrote about this, later on. He may have thought that those talks (with the Shahbanou) had the Sovereign's blessing, and could not understand, therefore, why the Shah was now making *me* his messenger. As for the Shahbanou, it seems likely that, in calling me, she was merely doing as her husband asked, without mentioning her own initiative to him. The game, as they say, was rigged.

After this discouraging conversation, I rang Darioush Forouhar - then number three in the National Front - who, it is worth saying, was the one who had suffered most, of the three, during the quarter-of-a-century referred to by Bakhtiar. However, he lent me an attentive ear.

Then he said, "I understand the Imperial disquiet, but the present situation is the result of His Majesty's errors."

"I don't deny it," I said.

"I must tell you, now," Forouhar resumed, "that we can only take useful action and find a solution, if Messrs. Bakhtiar and Sandjabi are in agreement.

"If they are, then so am I.

"Unfortunately, Mr Bakhtiar will not accept an arrangement of any kind.

"At the moment, furthermore, his connections with the National Front have become tenuous.

"He must have some scheme in mind, but I'm damned if I know what it is."

We exchanged a few comments about various people, then he suggested that I try once more to strike an accord, in principle, with Mr Bakhtiar. There was nothing else I could do but telephone Mr Bakhtiar. again. His reply was the same and just as irritable.

Towards ten-o-clock, I called the palace.

In recent years, in Teheran, several works, published with the authorisation of the censor - and, therefore, necessarily biased and abridged - have related the events of those times, in great detail, and according to witness-statements taken, on the spot, or from the transcripts of the interrogation, in prison, of certain people; and all of these have accused the Shah of duplicity, in that, by engaging the opposition in talks about forming a coalition-Cabinet, he was only trying to pull the wool over their eyes, while, in reality, preparing for a *coup d'État*. Nothing, I believe, could be further from the truth. He was depressed and distraught and had no notion of what to do. He launched initiatives, but all of them were ineffectual. He didn't really take advantage of the army, and it seems probable that the mission he assigned to Oveyssi - just like the one he asked me to carry out - were no more than the flying of kites. He had lost his touch, and his mastery of events, and no longer had at his side - as he once had, in 1941, 1945/6 and 1963 - the strong men who could have supported him. He was worn out, at the end of his tether, and only hanging on out of a sense of duty. Michel Poniatowski, who visited him three times during the decisive months, or the Count de Marenches, will also bear witness to this, but only the Shahbanou knew the true state Mohammad Reza Pahlavi was in. She also tried a few things, but these were ineffective too.

The events, which the Shah dreaded would occur on the 7th November, broke out even sooner than he feared.

Chapter IX

"I have heard the voice of your revolution"

6th November 1978

Throughout Friday 3rd, and Saturday 4th, disorder continued in Teheran. On Sunday 5th, the demonstration, which had alerted the Palace - and which the BBC had announced in advance - had been well organised by Khomeyni's followers. It began in the morning, within, and, especially, in front of, the Central Campus of the University of Teheran, where all the foreign journalists present in the city, had also been gathered together.

Not only had the Shah formally forbidden the security-services to use their weapons, but neither the soldiery nor the police had performed any patrols. From the direction of the University, the huge crowd wound its way into the heart of the city, and no obstacle was placed in its path. Amidst the throng, it was possible to discern special units - led by individual commanders, many of whom were Palestinians - all armed to the teeth and intent on destroying and burning anything on their route.

Thousands of hotels, restaurants and shops had their windows smashed, and many banks, company-offices, cinemas, ministries and other official buildings were set on fire.

The Embassy of the United States was protected by troops, but the Ministry of Information and a British consular building were sacked. The scene was reminiscent of the barbarian invasion of Genghis Khan. In order to terrorise the population, the Islamists employed their usual tactics of indiscriminate destruction, without restraint.

That Sunday evening, Teheran presented the terrifying aspect of a city devastated by fires, some of which were still burning the following day.

Just before eight-o-clock, the lights came on all over the city (normally the strikers deprived the capital of electricity until ten-o-clock.) and an edited film about the events of the day was shown on the main, evening television-news. It showed scenes of government-oppression, such as soldiers firing into the crowd and bloody corpses. To make it look authentic they cut in a sequence of Rector Sheybani - who had indeed been admirably courageous - in the great gateway to the campus, exhorting the students not to take part in the violence. It was soon established that the film had been put together from foreign newsreels. The soldiers' uniforms, and the places depicted, were not Iranian. Naturally, the vandalism and fire-raising were not shown. Television-broadcasts like this, were relayed - and whipped up great emotion - throughout the world.

A quarter of a century later, they still put these newsreels on, to mark the anniversary of the revolution. There, people have recovered from their illusions. Now, they know; but, in the state it was in, at the time, public opinion was not about to ask why the electricity workers had suddenly restored power, nor why the soldiers in the film were all wearing unusual uniforms.

At the palace, the King had emerged from his torpor and was receiving regular reports, by telephone, on the situation in the capital. His orders were categorical: "Do not fire into the crowd - there must be no bloodshed - soldiers have no right to shoot unless they are themselves directly attacked."

Then he received the Prime Minister: Charif Emami had come unexpectedly to submit his resignation, which was immediately accepted. Thus Charif Emami's second cabinet was given the sack, just as his first had been, back in the 'sixties. On this occasion, he had practically ceased to exist as a politician. He had become a fictional character. During the short audience, the PM said to the King, "I'm just not in charge of anything any more and I no longer have any idea what to do."

Several important, senior officers, who were deeply upset and angered by the situation, and who found it hard to accept that the army should be reduced to doing nothing - that the country should be allowed to fall apart and the capital burn - had met in various rooms close to the Imperial Cabinet to ask the Grand Master of Protocol, if he would be so good as to tell the Sovereign that they were waiting upon His Majesty "for a firm and definitive decision". Aslan Afshar conveyed the message.

A little after 6.00 pm, the Grand Master of Protocol was summoned by the Shah, who had not left the telephone and seemed very emotional: "Tell General Oveyssi," he said, "to hold himself in readiness in his office and await a call from the palace."

Aslan Afshar understood what this meant, and hurried to execute the order at once: "I told this news to the senior officers present," he said later, " to their very great joy."

Several of them called their units immediately and told their seconds-in-command that the order had been given to launch the first stage of Operation Khach.

"At Lavizan," it was confided to me later, by the Commander of Special Forces, "I had six hundred men ready for anything, and I had even ordered them into their combat-transports - each group with its specific instructions."

At Baghe-Shah, General Khosrodad's paratroops were straightaway prepared for departure - each of the commanders knew what he had to do - and the Imperial Guard, although it was not intended to take part in the operation, was nevertheless brought to maximum alert. Mohammad Reza Pahlavi appeared suddenly to have got a grip on himself. He summoned the ambassadors of Britain and the United States and then, although there was a piercing chill in the air, went for a quick turn around the park. An endless, agonising wait commenced. One hour later, the ambassadors arrived. During this time, the Shah had talked at length with the Shahbanou.

Having completed these three interviews, the Shah summoned the Grand Master of Protocol once more and announced to him that he had decided to ask General Gholam

Reza Azhari, Chief of the General Staff of the Army, to form the new government.

"But what about Oveyssi?" a bemused Aslan Afshar enquired

"Telephone him and tell him that he can stand down," replied the Shah.

When the generals and other senior officers heard this news, "they were," Afshar later reported, "thunderstruck".

"Apparently," he notes, "the ambassadors of Britain and the United States dissuaded His Majesty from appointing General Oveyssi, because he would have acted with firmness and taken hold of the problem, which was exactly what the British and the Americans did not want."

When His Majesty was in exile in Morocco, he told me, "the British and American ambassadors thought that Oveyssi would over-react and aggravate the situation, and that we should appoint someone more moderate, who would appease the population, but I am quite sure that they [the British and the Americans] just wanted to get rid of me."

The position of the Shahbanou, who, to all appearances, was opposed to the nomination of Oveyssi, and to the taking of tough action, is harder to understand. Some of her circle, at Court, feared, or let it be thought that they feared, a recapitulation of the case of Pakistan., in which General Ayub Khan, and, later, General Zia-ul-Haq, had profited from situations of disorder, in order to gain power for themselves. They were forgetting, firstly, the complete loyalty, of the army, to its constitutional Commander-in-Chief, which proved itself throughout these events, and, secondly, the natural balance of forces within the population at large. A recently-published, authorised biography of the Shahbanou, recounting these times, insists that "Farah always preached the path of moderation". It is always possible to re-make history; but many have thought, said and written since, that firm action could have saved the country from tragedy, avoided hundreds of thousands of deaths and prevented the exodus, *en masse*, of her élites. I still think so today.

The appointment of General Azhari was notified to him that evening, and the General, who suffered from a heart-condition, had already stayed at his post beyond the normal age-limit of sixty-five years and had no political ambitions at all, mentioned his reservations, about it, to the Sovereign: "I am not the man for the job," he stated flatly.

The Shah's response left no room for doubt: "I'm not asking you, I'm giving you an order," he said.

The old man was true to his military discipline. He complied without another word.

The appointment was not officially announced until the following day, 6th November. Operation Khach was, of course, abandoned.

At the end of this trying day, the Shah said to his entourage, "tomorrow, I shall address the nation," and off he went.

On Monday 6th November, Mohammad Reza Pahlavi got to his office at exactly 10.00 am. He received, and conferred briefly with, the Minister to the Imperial Court. Then he summoned the Chamberlain of the Household, Manoutchehr Sanei, and said to him, "the National Radio-Television team should be arriving very shortly."

"It's already here, Sire," was the reply.

The Shah paced nervously across his huge office, waiting.

In the ante-chamber, there was speculation concerning who could have prepared a text for the media-appearance, since Chodja-Ol-Dine Chafa, the Sovereign's Cultural Counsellor, who was usually responsible for this sort of thing, had gone on a mission abroad. Three minutes later, the Shah called Sanei back: "Reza Ghotbi," the Sovereign said (referring to the former head of radio-television, who was also the Shahbanou's cousin and foster-brother) "is supposed to be bringing the text of our speech, but where is he?

Sanei knew nothing about this and said he would go and find out. A few minutes later, the Shah was informed that Reza Ghotbi was being received by the Shahbanou, together with Hossein Nasr, the head of her personal staff. The Sovereign's temper flared: "what are they doing in the Shahbanou's office?" he demanded, "it's *my* speech!"

Aslan Afshar, the Chamberlain's superior in the hierarchy, called the Shahbanou to convey her husband's thoughts. Several minutes then passed, before the Shahbanou, Ghotbi and Nasr at last arrived with the script and entered the Emperor's office. Afshar , who was also there, at this moment, noted all that was said and later published an account of it The Sovereign took the text, which Ghotbi had brought, and read it through.

"Oh, no!" he cried, "I can't say anything like that!"

"No, Majesty," returned Ghobi, "the time has come for you to align yourself with popular opinion and say things, which will please the people."

The Shahbanou and Nasr whole-heartedly agreed with him. The Shah had the radio-television team brought in and delivered the speech, as written, in its entirety.

Afshar recalls: "He himself told me, later, in Mexico, that he had sat down in his office and recorded the message - 'without changing a word -in a state of extreme fatigue' and with his 'throat constricted by sad emotions', because there was absolutely nothing else he could do."

Afterwards, the Shah deeply regretted it. The speech included the following: "I have made many mistakes ... but I have heard the voice of your revolution ... the course of events will have to change, I do not deny that ... and I have instructed the Head of the General Staff to form an entirely provisional government, with the object of restoring order, so that a civilian government can be formed and free elections held.

"I undertake henceforth to respect the constitution... the revolution of the Iranian people shall not, and cannot, ever have my approval."

It was a wretched speech, and it had disastrous effects. No-one remembered anything of its content except the single sentence, "I have heard the voice of your revolution". Never, until this moment, had the word "revolution" been uttered; but here it was, given official recognition, with all its connotations! The text also carried the implied admission that the Shah *had* violated the constitution - which he had sworn to uphold and guarantee. He had been made to confess to perjury.

Sir Anthony Parsons, the ambassador of Great Britain, wrote in his journal, at the time: "did the Shah really understand the implications of what he had said?" but these were the implications of what he had been *made* to say, even if he alone would have to take responsibility for them.

The transmitted message had none of the predicted effects, and the shift in public opinion, which the Shah had been persuaded to hope for, did not take place. It could have been obtained, if the tone and the words had been different, but not like this, as Mohammad Reza Pahlavi would rapidly, and bitterly, perceive. That evening, around seven, Aslan Afshar was working in his office at the palace, a mere three rooms away from the Emperor's suite of offices, when the door suddenly opened, without a knock or any prior announcement. There he saw the Shah, addressing him! He had never seen such a procedure: the Shah never went into the other offices of the palace. Naturally, he rose and bowed. The Sovereign gestured to him to sit down, which - even more astonished - he did, and then took a chair up to the Grand Master of Protocol's desk and sat down himself.

"Telephone Sullivan and Parsons," he said (meaning the ambassadors of the USA and Britain) "and ask them what they thought of the message I broadcast today," adding, "you will have to do it as though off your own bat, of course."

Afshar proceeded to do this, but only for form's sake. As for the two ambassadors, they too were at a loss to decide what the purpose of his call was.

William Sullivan replied that he had not yet seen the text,

because it was still being translated, both for him and for transmission to Washington. Of all the people, whom the Shah later believed had been in-the-know about this particular operation, it seems most probable that staff at the US-embassy knew about the tenor of the speech, before the text even came into the hands of the man who would have to read it out and take the consequences for doing so. However, the ambassador's response was prudently, and courteously, diplomatic.

As for Sir Anthony Parsons, he said much the same - that he had not yet had time to study the text - "but," he went on, "the eminent lawyer, Mr Abdolkarim Lahidji* has telephoned to say that he was very pleased with it."!

Having taken note of these reactions, Mohammad Reza Pahlavi said not a word, but gave a smile of infinite sadness. The man who, in the presence of the representatives of certain powers, displayed so much hauteur, if not disdain, in order to show - with all due courtesy - the status and potential of his country, which had "become an oak, and was no longer a rose", as he used to say, now recognised his enfeeblement and suffered profoundly from this recognition.

While I was with him, in Mexico, in September 1979, the Shah recalled this episode at some length.

"I was wrong," he said, "I placed my trust in people who were not worthy of it.

"For the most part, my speeches were not written, and I rarely even used notes, but, when I had to read a text, I studied

---

* One of the opposition's most visible, but not thought to be one of its most extreme, leaders.

it with care first, and usually modified it.

"On this occasion, I was harried in such a way that I didn't even have time properly to look through what I was going to say.

"That's why I stumbled over the words, so often, while I was reading it.

"I have to say, unfortunately, that, in this case, I was certainly betrayed, because I was obliged, in some way, to relinquish the ability to think and persuaded to say that which I did not wish to say and should not have said."

This accusation of treachery, against those who had suggested, prepared and made him read this, as it were, funeral oration for the monarchy, had already, and progressively, become an obsession with the Shah. He was persuaded - and not without cause - that this speech had been one of his worst, political mistakes.

Later again, in the spring of 1980, at Cairo, during the long conversations we had then, the Shah returned persistently to this matter. He was racked with remorse, especially for not having taken, at the right moment, certain measures of domestic policy, which would have disarmed his critics and made the public less susceptible to manipulation from abroad. He bitterly regretted having trusted the Americans and attributing a false rationale to their policy, but, above all, he was distraught at having abandoned his country to "gangs of criminals and looters". He had expressed these regrets to certain, foreign newspapers also, including a widely read Egyptian weekly, which President Sadat recommended to him.

Regarding the broadcast, he believed, "according to an

investigation which I have had made," he said, "that, as well as Ghotbi, and Nasr, several other people, who had been, for greater or lesser lengths of time, in orbit around the Shahbanou, contributed significantly to bringing all of this about - especially, one of the latter's close friends and two former leaders of the 'Confederation'*."

"There's nothing odd," the Shah continued, "about the fact that these two leading Confederationists should have been able to enter Iran without any trouble - nothing could have been more normal - for any Iranian could return to his country; and what did we have to fear from such people, however intelligent and brilliant they were?"

He knew all about them, of course, although he had never met them.

"But," he went on, "how should we explain the fact that one of them was helped so much, financially and politically, by Hoveyda, and the other acquired a strategic post in television?
"How do you explain the fact that [Charif Emami] was received several times at our house [at the palace, by the Shahbanou] without my knowing?"

There is nothing here but suppositions, however plausible; but he reserved a particular grudge for Reza Ghotbi, whom, it seems, he had thought well of, for a long time. During my first visit to Cairo, the four of us were at lunch - the Shah, the Shahbanou, Mrs Pirnia, the Imperial Family's doctor, and myself - in a saloon of the Koubbeh Palace, when a sentry came to tell the Shahbanou that she was wanted on the telephone.

---

* This "Confederation" was a small, extremist, Iranian youth-organisation, which, according to the Count de Marenches, was financed from American sources.

She excused herself and got up from the table. The King said, slightly nettled, "let us proceed with lunch, this will probably take some time!"

Twenty minutes later, she came back. The King did not get up, and so, as protocol demanded, neither did Mrs Pirnia or I. The Shahbanou then said, as sweetly as you like, "Reza Ghotbi sends you his regards."

A heavy blow of the Shah's fist upon the table made the crockery leap into the air, and a most unpleasant word was uttered. It was a painful scene, and the reaction was, perhaps, excessive.

However, to sum the account: the Shah did assent to deliver that dreadful speech; but did he not accept the consequences afterwards, with courage and dignity, even if part of the responsibility for them undeniably lay with those who had pushed this weary, distraught and suffering man to deliver it?

Chapter X

*"I have asked the head of the general staff to form
an entirely provisional government."*

6th - 8th November 1978

The entirely provisional government, which the head of the general staff had been assigned to form, was presented late in the night of the 6th and 7th of November. Most of its members were soldiers. However, several of them would be rapidly replaced by civilians, in order, so it would be said, to honour the spirit of appeasement..

General Azhari was little known to the public. He was a man of great cultivation, with an impeccable public and private life, honest and courteous. For several years, he represented Iran at CENTO (formerly Baghdad Pact) and even presided over its Military Co-ordination Committee; but his had never been the reputation of a mighty warrior, capable of facing down a revolutionary situation. He had said as much to the Sovereign, and only took the job of Prime Minister in obedience to orders, because a soldier always obeys a superior officer. He had only one superior officer, the Commander-in-Chief of the Armed Forces, but that was the Shah.

His appointment provoked no reaction against him personally. Even the regime's worst enemies could not reproach this soldier, whose life and past were without stain or the least sign of ambition. Members of his circle said that, despite his staying on as head of the general staff, beyond the usual age-limit, he had no other aspiration than to retire soon and, if possible, to be accredited as ambassador to a quiet country. Certainly, he would have been granted that. His predecessor had, after all, been accredited to Madrid, where he had been greatly appreciated. Nevertheless, Azhari braced up to the task.

In spite of the Shah's pusillanimous speech, the presence of soldiers in the government gave the rioters pause for thought, calm returned and life resumed its normal course. By the afternoon of 7th November, Teheran gave the impression of a city, where nothing in particular had happened, just a few hours before. It was the same in the provinces. The strikes came to an end, in the oil-industry, at the steelworks and at the power-stations; and, at the television studios, young officers in uniform replaced the usual presenters of the evening news. This was one of the few elements of Operation Khach, which were actually implemented. In the bazaars, a few recalcitrant merchants received visits from one or two officers of the army or the police, who, without needing to insist, invited them to re-open their shops.

At the ceremony of handing over power to the ministries, the soldierly ministers, not without some misgivings, presented themselves in uniform; but everywhere the staff was all present and the welcome was polite and eager, even warm.

Several eminent opposition-leaders called me. One colleague, who had been prominent in organising agitation at the University, talked to me at length about "his respect for His Majesty, personally," saying, "I do hope that *they* are not going to give me a hard time: if anything happens to me, promise me that you will get me out."

I joked a little, to reassure him, and told him that I had no idea what the government intended to do and that, if, for any reason, they should see fit to interrogate him, I would do what I could. Someone else, whom I hardly knew at all, passed a request through his cousins, who were close friends of our family, asking if he could come and stay at my house for a few days, which, he quite wrongly thought, would place him "under cover"! These two cousins subsequently fled to Paris. They will, no doubt, recognise themselves. Others came to see me to restore connections. My friend, Mohsen Foroughi, who had remained in the new government as Minister of Culture, told me, the following day, that numerous people had contacted him for similar reasons ...

In forty-eight hours, the opposition saw itself beaten into a position of weakness. The regime had, at last, scored a point.

On this 7th November, Prof. Abolghassem Banihachemi, vice-Principal of the Darius-The-Great Faculty of Medicine, at the University of Teheran, took a Sabena-flight from Vienna, where he was spending a sabbatical year, in order to pay a short visit to Teheran. On the 'plane, he sat next to a "very neatly-dressed and exceptionally courteous" mullah, who introduced himself as "Dr. Behechti". Naturally, the two compatriots got chatting, and this doctor of theology - a future, self-proclaimed

Ayatollah and strong-man, for two years, in the Islamic regime-to-be (before being assassinated in the course of an internal power-struggle) launched into a long diatribe against the Shah: "change is coming," he said, "soon we shall take power and build a new society."

On being asked for his opinion, the senior academic experienced a moment of doubt: "I thought for an instant," he told me later, "that this might be an *agent provocateur*."

Then he began his reply: "what you say does not make sense," he stated, "do you really think that the army will permit violence and disorder to triumph?"

"But it's all taken care of," replied the potential Ayatollah, "we have been given assurances ..."

On arrival at Athens airport, the passengers were informed that, owing to a technical fault, a relief-aircraft would come, from Brussels, to take them on to Teheran, and that their baggage was being disembarked. They were invited to take refreshments at the expense of the company.

"I'm going to get a paper," Behechti said.

Five or six minutes later, he returned, pale, and with lips-atremble, saying, "we have been betrayed - the army has taken power in Teheran - someone has just told me this, on the telephone.

"He," the doctor went on (referring to the Shah) "has turned the tables on us again, and everything is ruined, for another twenty years.

"I cannot continue this journey," he concluded, "I must go to Paris to consult various people and see Mr Khomeyni," which it appears he did.

Ten days later, he did come back to Teheran and become one of the principal actors in the events there, which, after the Shah's example, people henceforth began to call "the revolution".

Lieutenant General Djafarian, military governor of the province of Khouzistan, and the army's commander there - where there were two, mighty, armoured divisions - received a visit, on 7th November, at half-past-six in the morning, from the members of the oil-industry's strike-committee. They had heard "the news" and come to give themselves up.

"You know us, General," they said, "and we have confidence in your sense of honour.

"We also know that we shall now spend a long time in prison, so please take pity on our families and let them stay in their tied-accommodation, for our wives and children are in no way to blame."

The General gave them some breakfast - and his word as a soldier that that he would watch over, and ensure the safety and the well-being of, their families. Then he put the committee-members in two rooms at his HQ, placed a guard on them and sent to Teheran for further instructions.

The strikes had already ended.

Three days later, he received the order to release the prisoners, which he did at once. General Djafarian was shot, on 11th February 1979.

On Wednesday 8th November, at 10.15 am, at the Niavaran

Palace, an ad hoc Council met, chaired by the Shahbanou and the Minister to the Imperial Court, Ali Gholi Ardalan.

On the Prime Minister's insistence, it had been decided to undertake a thoroughgoing reorganisation of the Pahlavi Foundation - a measure, which I had advocated, to the Shah, at first, four months, and then again, two months, previously, and which the Shah had decided, each time, was too radical a departure. Mir Sayed Ahmad Emami, a senior judge, in his eighties, who had been Public Prosecutor of the Supreme Court under Mossadegh, now replaced Djafar Charif Emami as the head of the Foundation.

Also, a commission of enquiry was set up, into the personal fortunes of members of the Imperial Family, and presided over by a serving Justice of the Supreme Court.

Conveniently enough, the decisions, on these two initiatives, were taken in time for their announcement, on national radio-television, during mid-morning news-bulletins. Now, the members of the commission did not actually have the legal authority to pass judgement on the Sovereign himself, but the Shahbanou, doubtless with the prior agreement of her husband, decided that royal immunity would be waived, on this occasion, even though the commissioners themselves had asked for no more than a purely consultative role.

There was a lull. Then it was announced that the Shah was going to receive the commission.

Its members crossed the palace-gardens and climbed up through the ante-chambers, while the Shahbanou went straight to the Imperial Cabinet. Ten minutes later, all were assembled. The Shah looked haggard, and he was obviously ill-at-ease. He invited everyone to sit. Nosratollah Moinian, the chief of his staff, was there, and asked leave to withdraw.

"But why don't you stay?" the Sovereign said to him, in an indifferent tone, "your advice will be useful."

Moinian, knowing what was about to happen, pretended to have urgent business to attend to, gathered up his papers and disappeared. The Shah rang for a chamberlain and gave orders for tea to be served.

Arrayed around the Sovereign, were Ardalan, the Minister to the Imperial Court, and his deputy; then there were General Pakravan and the Mayor of the Capital, Djavad Chahrestani; also in the circle were the former Director of National radio-Television, Reza Ghotbi, Mehdi Pirasteh, the former ambassador to Baghdad, and later, to Brussels, who was also a former Minister of the Interior, and myself.

The Shah addressed us: "from all sides, he said, "I am being pressed to authorise the arrest of Hoveyda, under the powers allowed by martial law, because, they say, this would pacify public opinion.
"Let me ask you," he continued, "to give me your advice on this matter."

The Minister to the Imperial Court replied first, a note of distress in his voice, "I do not understand how one can arrest a former Prime Minister, who was in power for thirteen years."

"Thank you very much," returned the Shah.

General Pakravan and Reza Ghotbi approved the idea, in moderate terms, pointing out the exigencies of the time.

Neither of them was considered to be an enemy of the former PM - far from it. The Mayor of Teheran owed his entire career to Hoveyda, and had always been thought of as his protégé, so the vehemence of Chahrestani's attack upon him now was nothing less than astonishing Mehdi Pirasteh, who had been out of touch with current affairs for years, was a sworn and open foe of Amir Abbas Hoveyda. His intervention was less unpredictable.

I was asked last. As a declared and consistent political adversary of Hoveyda's, I was probably expected to share the majority view; but I invoked precisely this circumstance to justify abstention. Like the others, I too was honoured with an, albeit rather surprised, "thank you very much". The Shahbanou said nothing throughout. At some point, the 'phone rang. The Shah picked it up and listened, saying only, "hmmm."

The call lasted less than a minute.

"I've just been told, quite justifiably," reported the Shah, "that a decision on this question is urgently required."

Everyone wondered who the call was from. According to the Shahbanou's account, it was from General Moghaddam.

"Very well," the Shah concluded, when he had heard everyone, "unfortunately, we'll have to do it."

I implored the Sovereign, to give his former Prime Minister, and former Minister to the Court, some warning, saying, "even an arrest can be undergone without loss of dignity."

"That would not be easy for me," the Shah retorted, and, turning to his wife said, "you could do it, perhaps."

"Why me?" the Shahbanou replied angrily, "he was *your* Prime Minister, not mine!"

It was an unsightly tiff to have in front of others. The King rose and said simply, "it shall be done."

Everyone present took their leave and filed out of the Imperial Cabinet.

I learned soon afterwards that the Shah had telephoned Hoveyda himself, to explain that it was a matter of placing him under guard, in order to ensure his protection and satisfy public opinion. The conversation, I'm told was polite.

It was the deputy-Administrator of Martial Law in the capital, Lieutenant General Rahimi Laridjani, who received the order to secure the person of the former Prime Minister. Hoveyda, himself, set the rendez-vous for 6.00 pm, not at his home, but at the family seat, in Darrouss, where his mother lived. If he had been arrested in the eighteen-storey building, where he lived, the occasion might have caused something of a stir.

So that there would be witnesses to the circumstances of his arrest, Hoveyda caused to be present Nasser Yeganeh (the President of the Supreme Court) Dr. Djavad Said (President of the Chamber) and another former Prime Minister, whom he sometimes referred to as his "heir apparent", Abdol Madjid Madjidi. The General arrived at the appointed hour, accompanied by a few officers, who did not enter the house, and conducted Hoveyda to a villa, at Lavizan, which was usually kept for official guests of the Savak, and where, although effectively isolated, he was housed comfortably and treated respectfully. He was released from there, by the revolutionaries, on 12th February 1979.

The decision to arrest the former PM, "to reassure the opposition and pacify public opinion," could not have been taken, except by the Shah and, in the event, the Shahbanou as well, who was then playing a decisive, political role. The idea was to make a scapegoat of him. Amir Abbas Hoveyda, had certainly not been popular. He used to be fond of saying that power only exploited those who did not have it, but he was a man whom, more than anyone else I know, power transformed. He had been a true, sceptical, liberal-intellectual - a plain-speaking, cultivated and tolerant man. He had become a politician - possessed of personal integrity, certainly - but unscrupulous and blatantly amoral. He extended the network of his personal influence even into the police and the secret services and became quite formidable. I believe that the King began to find him so, in the middle of the 'seventies, although almost imperceptibly, at first.

The army did not care for him - to put it very mildly. In the middle of the decade, for example, a very well documented report from the Head of the General Staff - who was none other than General Azhari, who had just become Prime Minister - directly accused him of responsibility for the rise in popular discontent. Soon after, there was another report, from General Moghaddam - then Head of the Second Bureau, and, shortly afterwards, appointed chief of the Savak - which took an extremely hostile view of him. It is therefore probable, that it was from this quarter the strong pressures came, which worked upon the King, in order to make him place all the responsibility for the crisis, which was racking the country, upon Hoveyda.

Among Hoveyda's friends, Ardeshir Zahedi, the Sovereign's former son-in-law, and ambassador to Washington, was often accused of having instigated his arrest, but Zahedi, who had never concealed his reservations concerning Hoveyda's policies, denies it. He had suggested to the Shah - or so numerous people, who were close to the palace, at that time, have told me - that he banish Hoveyda from the capital, while assuring him of the means to live comfortably, in a kind of gilded exile. Rumour also had it, quite unverifiably, that the last two heads of government, Amouzegar and Charif Emami, had both persuaded the Shah to have Hoveyda arrested.

More recently, the King, himself, wanted to put the blame on Charif Emami - and not only for this - but also for having concealed things from him. It is a natural human trait, perhaps, which emerges as difficulties pile up, and Mohammad Reza Pahlavi did have a tendency to shift, or, to a greater or lesser extent, unload, responsibility on to others. Indeed, beside himself - and, in many areas, more so than himself - Hoveyda had been the most powerful man in the country for many years. Now he was paying for it, and very dearly. Nevertheless, I believe sincerely that, in spite of his ill-feelings towards Hoveyda, the Shah regretted until the end of his life, his decision, to have him arrested.

Once confined, Hoveyda never ceased to entertain the belief that he had the right to a magnificent trial, which would have had international repercussions, and he was preparing for it, asking, so I hear, Edgar Faure to conduct his defence, and receiving a reply in the affirmative. A well-known lawyer of Teheran, the barrister Assadollah Soufi, was also approached and set about preparing a dossier of the case for the defence, on the spot. Hoveyda was undoubtedly the best informed man in Iran. He knew the weaknesses of everyone, and especially those who, from being functionaries of the Imperial regime, had transformed themselves into incorrigible revolutionaries, and he thought that this would provide him with insurance. On the evening of 11th February 1979, he remained alone, at *his* villa, which the guards had then deserted. He could have escaped, gone under cover and fled the country, although he would certainly not have sought asylum at any foreign embassy, for he was too proud for that, but, like so many others, he had friends who would have helped him. Courageously, he decided to face it out, and was assassinated in a most cowardly fashion, on 7th April 1979.

The Azhari government maintained the illusion for three or four days, during which calm returned and normal life was resumed. The Shah seemed more relaxed, but, instead of engaging in lively discourse, and, above all, acting with alacrity and strength, the government rapidly became bogged down, and the effect of the measures of 8th November drained away.

Tremendous pressure was placed upon the Sovereign to espouse "moderation" and dissuade the Cabinet from acting firmly and from applying - if only temporarily - the provisions of martial law. The former Prime Minister, Ali Amini, who was well known for his American connections - especially with the Democratic Party - flanked by two, venerable nonagenarians (now elevated to the status of moral authorities) namely the former Rector of Teheran University, Ali Akbar Siassi, and Mohammad Ali Varasteh, who had been a minister in the 'forties, before serving under Mossadegh, now pestered the Shah and the Shahbanou "to take particular care to do nothing, which might antagonise dissident elements or ... Washington". The ambassadors of Britain and the USA acted to reinforce these exhortations, as did the Shahbanou and all her friends. Meanwhile, those who wished to resist this interpretation of "moderation" - that section of the army, and most of the general officers, who wanted to take action - were invited to "see reason".

There were some interesting, political somersaults: the Ayatollah Shariat-Madari, for example - more lucid than ever - made contact with me through the usual channels, saying, "implore His Majesty, on my behalf, to save the country and re-establish order!

"If he does not, a blood-bath awaits us.

"Arrest me and throw me into prison, if necessary, but act swiftly!"

I passed on this message to the King. There was a long silence. Then he said, "tell him we shall do what we can."

The leaders of the powerful Association of Officers and NCO's of the Reserve called a meeting at the house of General Hassan Arfa, who had been Head of the General Staff during the Second World War - another venerable old man - and delivered what amounted to an ultimatum to the Shah: "we shall go out into the streets," they said, "occupy the ministries and impose a policy of national salvation."

The General, for all that he had twice been an ambassador after passing the age-limit for army-service, was not very diplomatic and proposed himself as Prime Minister, if "those young soldiers" were not capable of doing anything. He said to the Sovereign, "I held my own against Communists and Russians, during the war, with a small, very poorly-equipped army.

"I can certainly take these hooligans in hand."

This made the King smile.

General Azhari at length presented himself before the Chambers. He recited some suitably moving anecdotes and referred, at once, to the Almighty, to religious problems and to the democratic ideals, to which the people had every right to aspire. Then he re-formed his Cabinet, making room for civilians. The Commanders-in-Chief of the Army, the Air-Force and the Navy, who had taken part as "super-ministers", were recalled, and emissaries were dispatched to reassure the leaders of the radical opposition and "dissipate their disquiet". The demonstrations resumed, then the strikes, then the violence and the fires, and then the lynchings began.

Other than in the field of economic planning, Mohammad Reza Pahlavi, was quite unaccustomed to governing in council. The essentials of domestic affairs, and the short-term management of the economy, were taken care of by the Prime Minister and the Government. The Sovereign involved himself very little or hardly at all. He kept himself informed - he certainly did that - but, when he had to take decisions himself - about oil-policy, national defence and great questions of diplomacy - he consulted widely, or pretended to do so (according to his detractors) before deciding. Faced with burgeoning agitation and violence, to which he had been led into awarding the title of "revolution", he was unable to change his habits. The only exception to this, I can think of, was the arrest of Amir Abbas Hoveyda, where the Shah, and the Shahbanou saw fit to gather a number of people and consult them about a decision, which had already been taken. Assailed by mounting dangers, isolated, assessing the situation wrongly - failing to admit that his foreign allies were fanning the flames and scheming to depose him - he lost his grip, realised that he had lost it, and panicked. He no longer trusted anyone and was unable to conceal the fact that he had not the least idea what to do.

As for the Shahbanou, she seemed more serene - receiving politicians and clerics and holding meetings - although the initiatives she tried to take were sometimes misinterpreted.

Outwardly, one thus gained the impression that the two members of the Royal Couple were not following the same political line; and this caused anguish at Court and plunged the political scene into turmoil.

The Shah and his government persisted in ignoring the support supplied, by Washington, Paris and London, to the agitation and violence in Iran, which support constituted overt, hostile interference. They made not the least protest about this, let alone taking any reprisal for it, although Teheran certainly had means at its disposal to react in these ways. The only departure from inaction, on the Shah's part, was to make sure that no attack was made on Khomeyni at Neauphle-le-Château!

Outraged by the BBC's attitude, and the regime's corresponding limpness, General Badrei, Commander of the Imperial Guard, imparted to the Shah, through Aslan Afshar, the information that he had the technical means necessary to jam these transmissions, and requested authorisation to do it.

"Tell Badrei that such an attitude would be beneath our dignity," the Sovereign retorted.

Ehsan Echraghi, a minor mullah of Qom, who was also

Khomeyni's son-in-law, and several other members of the latter's family, transmitted messages to the Shah, requesting that they be allowed to go to France. In essence, they feared that they would not be able to get passports. Not only was the Imperial Guard then assigned to get passports for these people, that very day, but also to offer them tourist-class 'plane-tickets. It's true!

Another, insignificant mullah, Sheikh Hossein Ali Montazeri, a future, self-proclaimed Grand Ayatollah, who was briefly thought of as Khomeyni's heir-apparent, regularly received a modest stipend from Mohammad Ali Ghotbi, the wealthy public-works entrepreneur, who was also the maternal uncle and foster-father of the Shahbanou (who lost her father when she was still a baby) It was, of course, quite customary in many rich families to pay for the upkeep of a few mullahs. Ghotbi was truly amazed, when "Sheikh Hossein Ali - such an amusing man, who often makes me laugh" (as he told me at the time) came to ask him for assistance to go and join Khomeyni in Paris. He made enquiries and was told, to his surprise, that, in fact, this "insignificant mullah" cut quite a figure, as a dissident, at Qom, and that he had been arrested, and released, two or three times, by the police. Nevertheless, Ghotbi got him a passport - which might easily have been refused - at short notice. Not only that, but he offered him his ticket and a small sum as well!

Two days later, Prof. Safavian, who had come from Paris to examine "his illustrious patient", took an Air-France flight, originating in the Far East, in order to return to the French capital. He found himself sitting next to two men, one, an Iranian businessman from New Delhi, who had been living in India for many years, and the other, a mullah with a lot of hand-luggage. After take-off, the businessman introduced himself and engaged his two fellow passengers in conversation. Like many Iranians, he tended to poke fun at mullahs and said to the cleric, "So you're off to Paris to find yourself a pretty French girl to marry, are you?"

This got the mullah going: after responding in the negative, he made jokes of his own, distributed sweets to all the nearby passengers - who were amazed at his behaviour - and took to clowning, which made all the travellers laugh, however embarrassedly. A cleric owes it to himself to preserve a dignified attitude. Towards the end of the six-hour journey, the mullah calmed down; but imagine the astonishment of the passengers, when they arrived, to find a delegation of French officials, some Iranians and a pack of journalists and television-reporters gathered to welcome the comic mullah! That evening, Safavian reports, the arrival of "Khomeyni's heir-apparent" was shown on TV. Here he was, the Grand Ayatollah Montazeri, the Imam of Neauphle-le-Château, dubbed the heir-apparent and proclaimed a Grand Ayatollah! The insignificant, clerical buffoon would soon return to Teheran, with Khomeyni, and play the part, which history has recorded.

After the third week in November, when the effect of the surprise-nomination of General Azhari wore off, and the wait-and-see immobility of the regime became evident, violent demonstrations began again. Lorries full of regular troops, were once again stationed at various points in the capital and in other big cities. The palace was protected by a discreet security-cordon, which the demonstrators had not hitherto approached; but the army had received the order not to react, unless attacked, and the protesters had all been informed of this. Fires and other sabotage therefore became commonplace.

From time to time, fake corpses were exhibited, and spurious funerals conducted, for the benefit of western television.

On 18th November, Shahbanou Farah nevertheless went to Karbala and Najjaf, two, holy cities in Iraq. Her chief-of-staff, Hossein Nasr, and Reza Ghotbi went with her. The Shahbanou's welcome in Baghdad, showed how afraid the Iraqi government was of the mounting religious fanaticism in Iran. The Iraqi vice-President received her at great length and assured her of his government's support. She was received also - a most notable event - by Ayatollah Khoi, the recognised leader of the Shiites world-wide, who gave her a message of good will for the Shah, in which he spoke of his "fervent prayers for the health of the Sovereign and for his success in the service of Islam and Iran". By any reckoning, this was a message of support, and obtaining it was a considerable success, which could have been suitably exploited. It was not. During the pilgrimage, the Shahbanou's retinue was said to have breached the strict observance of the rituals, and, although such breaches were not at all unusual, these were said to have been caught on television and to have given rise to adverse comment, both humorous and otherwise.

From the beginning of December, while the Shahbanou was increasing her quota of political audiences and working-meetings, the Sovereign decided that having a soldier as head-of-government, without any firm action or show of strength, was not producing results, and he began to seek another solution. Two, very venerable, ancients, Abdollah Entezam, who was in his eighties, and Mohammad Sorouri, who was past ninety, were asked to form a "united cabinet", but they refused. Prof. Mohammad Nassiri - no relation to the former head of the Savak - a renowned jurist, former head of the Faculty of Law, former Governor of the National Bank under Mossadegh and later a Minister of State, did the same.

I believe it was the Shah's despondency, and the effect of his illness on his psychological state, his successive failures and Anglo-American pressure, which had conspired to induce in him, since the end of November, a desire to leave the country - a desire, which would soon become common knowledge. For this reason, he began to engage in political consultations in other quarters.

On 3rd December, encouraged - if not obliged - to do so, by certain army-chiefs, Mohammad Reza Pahlavi made an unannounced visit to a cadet-training centre and to a nearby girls' high school. The young people welcomed him warmly, and the population of the neighbourhood, hearing that he was there, quickly rallied round. Cries of "long live the King!" rang out, and Mohammad Reza Pahlavi was deeply touched. His eyes moistened. They still loved him! That was his last public appearance. On 11th and 12th December, the Tassoua and Achousa days of Shiite mourning, hundreds of thousands marched through the streets of Teheran to demonstrate in favour of Ayatollah Khomeyni. The army wanted to forbid mass-demonstrations, and the organisers, who were approached beforehand by Generals Oveyssi, Rahimi and Khosrodad, were told, by them, of the possible consequences in no uncertain terms. This demonstration would be the red-line, the organisers heard, which should never be crossed; it would give rise to the feared blood-bath, which would, in turn, precipitate a *genuine*, military coup. They were even threatened with intervention by the parachute-brigade, from Shiraz, who had a formidable reputation, although they had taken no part in events so far. Teheran then buzzed with talk of parachutists jumping on the city, if the demonstration took place.

The soldiers were trying to inhibit the momentum of the radical opposition, to force it to retreat and thus reverse the current, so to speak, as a current, and they won their case. The organising committee, faced with a firmness, which seemed to them to be unshakeable, eventually agreed to content themselves with a lively, verbal protest. Patrols of the entire city, armoured vehicles and units of the riot-squad were then deployed. A unit of heavy tanks, based more than a hundred miles from Teheran, was ordered to move on the capital, and news of this was circulated in order to frighten potential rioters. It was psychological warfare. On the evening of the 10th, the ban was lifted, by formal order of the palace, and national radio announced - if there was any need to do so, since the BBC had already done it - that the demonstration would take place. The army had not dared to disobey.

It soon became apparent that the Shah had been forced to back down, yet again, by a string of characters, who were "anxious to pacify the public": there was that trio of worshipful sages, Amini, Siassi and Varasteh, among others; there had been further strong pressure from the British and American ambassadors; and the intrigues surrounding the Shahbanou also played a part. Speaking of this at Cairo, months later, the Shah told me, "Parsons [the British ambassador] even came to tell me that it would constitute a referendum, and that I should let it happen for that reason," adding, "another mistake, which I should not have made!"

At that time, the Shah believed that he could confer the leadership of a government of public security on some opposition figure, whom everyone knew, but who was not embroiled in the current agitation. There were some, of course, but who would have been so rash as to accept such a mission?

Thus it was that, on the advice of some close counsellors, and after long hesitation, he made contact with Prof. Gholam Hossein Sadighi - a former companion, and the spiritual successor, of Mossadegh - to ask him if he would be so good as to come and see him (for he feared a refusal) and possibly try to do something about forming a government of public security. The two men had not seen each other for a quarter-of-a-century, but they had begun to respect one another in recent years, and I think I know why this was.

Five years previously, when Prof. Sadighi was due for retirement, his faculty - and then the Council of the University, of which I was Rector - both decided unanimously, by secret ballot, to make him a professor emeritus. The ceremony, in which the charter conferring this title was to be presented, was, as always, to be a very solemn occasion and carried live on the radio. Sometimes these ceremonies were even broadcast on one of the national TV-channels. The recipient normally gave a speech - sometimes a long one. Three eminent academics were to be honoured, but Prof. Sadighi was easily the best known among them. Nationally, he was famous; so, naturally, it would fall to him to be the principal orator for the occasion. Owing to the expected attendance of Sadighi, therefore, the ceremony, which might otherwise have passed unnoticed, suddenly became a major, political event, eagerly awaited by the public.

I was put under a lot of pressure, by the Prime Minister

and the Savak. Hoveyda said to me, "what bee got into your bonnet over conferring an emeritus on this character?"

"But, Prime Minister," I said, "it will be an honour for the University."

"Well, we can't allow it," the heads of the government and the Savak said, in much the same words, "we shall cancel the broadcast and lay the matter before His Majesty, if necessary," and that's what both of them did.

The Shah's response was unambiguous: "don't interfere with the affairs of the University," he said, "they are the responsibility of the Rector."

Political and intellectual society held its breath. Were they going to allow the political heir of Mossadegh to speak on the radio, for half-an-hour? Reza Ghotbi, head of National Radio-Television, had, it seems, even taken special precautions to prevent any technical hitch, or other incident, which might interrupt transmission.

The ceremony took place, although, contrary to tradition, no minister of the government attended, and the Ferdowsi lecture theatre of the Faculty of Literature was full to bursting. Sadighi's speech was nobly cast, as a lecture on social and political morals, without the least flattery for anyone, or even any mention of, any individual politician. It was very warmly applauded, in the auditorium, and highly appreciated elsewhere.

Ever alert for intrigue, but genuinely curious also, the Shah too followed the speech. A few days later, at a public ceremony we were both attending, he said to me, "I saw, and heard, your friend, the other day: he spoke very well."

The next day, I conveyed "His Majesty's compliments", in suitable terms, to the person concerned. It was then that the old academic told me that he could guess what pressure I had been under and had not believed, until the very last minute, that they would let him speak live on television, adding, "please thank His Imperial Majesty, on my behalf, for his compliments and for his support to our university."

I believe that, since that incident, the two men had forgotten some of their animosity towards each other. At any rate, when Prof. Sadighi was approached by two emissaries from the Shah, his reply was characterised by noble sentiment: "I harbour no resentment towards the Sovereign," he said, "for the twenty-five years I have been kept at a distance by the regime.

"I also know that to agree to form a government at this time may cost me my reputation, but what good is prestige, if, when one's country is in danger, one cannot use it to try to save her?"

Now in his seventies, a former pupil of the Saint-Cloud College for Teachers in Higher Education and a Doctor of State-Administration at the Sorbonne, Prof. Sadighi was Minister of Posts and Telecommunications, then Minister of the Interior and then vice-President of the Council, under Mossadegh. When Mossadegh was put on trial, although he too was gaoled, he never ceased to express very great respect for the "old lion". This attitude earned him high regard, in his turn, even from the Prosecutor and the Shah. Most of Mossadegh's former colleagues, after all, had testified against him, ignominiously accepting their liberty in exchange. The order was given, to free Sadighi, because of his dignity. Thereafter, without ever having repudiated his political past, he kept his distance from partisan agitation and himself, in reserve, for the nation, refusing every favour and sinecure.

In 1957, at Teheran University, he founded, and directed with competence and authority, The Social Research Studies Institute, which rapidly gained international recognition. Gholam Hossein Sadighi enjoyed a great moral reputation among academics, intellectuals generally and the westernised middle-class, as well as among ordinary people.

His interview with the Shah went quite satisfactorily, as he told me at length the following day. The Shah had deployed all his talents to charm the venerable professor, assuring him, especially, of the complete availability and readiness of the forces of order and the army.

"I had no reason to disbelieve him, and I was touched by his sincerity and feeling," he told me.

The differences of the past were to be forgotten, in the interests of the country. Sadighi asked for a week to prepare a programme and a list of ministers. Several members of the National Front agreed to serve under him, and the followers of Ayatollah Shariat-Madari, whose influence was still considerable, supported him. Even some from Khomeyni's immediate circle did so. A large proportion of the public saw him as representing a great reforming transition towards observance of the constitution. He had, therefore, a genuine chance of succeeding, where others had failed.

When he returned to see the Shah, after a courtesy-visit to the Shahbanou, he made one condition - that the Sovereign leave Teheran, without quitting the country. In this way, he said, the head of the government would have his hands free.

In asking the Shah to remain in Iran, Sadighi was trying to preserve the unity of the army, which, he feared, might split. He suggested that the Shah go to the naval base at Bandar Abbas, where there was a fine house, sometimes used to lodge distinguished guests, and in which the Shah stayed during tours of inspection.

The Shah refused this condition, which did not conform with an Anglo-American requirement that he should leave the country! He had, perhaps, just missed another real opportunity.

Gholam Hossein Sadighi saw the King for the last time, four days before his final departure from Iran. He went to ask him, in the name of the general interest of the country, not to abandon her.

"I knew it would be no good," he said, soon after leaving the palace, "but I had to do my duty."

After the failure of the Sadighi-solution, the King turned to another long-term opponent, Mozaffar Baghai, another former lecturer and septuagenarian, long-since retired from Teheran University, who had been Mossadegh's closest companion for many years, before breaking with him, without ever being reconciled with the Shah. A redoubtable public speaker, with a socialist and secularist bent, he did not have the reputation and charisma of Sadighi, but his unblemished character, his academic standing and his austere, almost monastic, way-of-life, inspired respect. He also had a great many contacts.

In these times, when all the dissidents were being wooed,

and friends - even the most blameless and politically adroit - were being somewhat neglected, by the Shah and Shahbanou, Baghai could turn out to be an important asset.

Ardeshir Zahedi, who was, at the time, trying frantically to lay the dust of an anti-Iranian, and anti-Shah, stampede, in the wilds of Washington, had, so they say, encouraged this choice, as had some army-chiefs. Dr. Darioush Shirvani, a successful gynaecologist and a Deputy for the capital, knew Baghai well. He was asked to sound him out, and reported to the Shah the philosopher's great concern, about the upsurge of violence and fanaticism, and his desire to put a stop to it. An audience was arranged. Shirvani came with Baghai to the palace. Baghai was received, for more than two hours, by the Shah, who said to the Deputy, the following day, "Mozaffar is a patriot."

Baghai, the eternal dissident, had been asked to suggest a programme and prepare a list of ministers. Shirvani accompanied him again to the palace, to visit the Shahbanou, and attend a second audience with the Sovereign. Arrangements were made.

One evening, towards the end of December, an ultra-secret meeting was held at Shirvani's house. To avoid any hint of an indiscretion, he had given all his domestic staff the night off. Mrs. Shirvani herself prepared some refreshments for the attendees. Ardeshir Zahedi was there, with his right-hand man, Hossein Danechvar (who, however, was asked to sit in another room) Also there were General Rabii, Commander-in-Chief of the Air-Force, Shirvani and Baghai, whom the Deputy had gone personally to fetch. The four participants were discussing the finishing touches to "Operation Baghai", which involved asking the Shah to leave Teheran, but to remain in the country, at a well-furbished air-base, called Vahdati, at Hamadan, in the west.

Baghai's Cabinet would then demand full powers from the Chambers, before dissolving them and organising free and fair elections, as soon as calm had been restored, but, in any case, within six months, as the constitution required. By virtue of the decree of martial law, already proclaimed, and the full powers obtained, about four thousand individuals would then be arrested - according to a list already provided by elements of the secret services, which were opposed to the regime's "soft" policy. This would probably halt the agitation at a stroke, although freeing the vast majority from its effects would take rather longer.

"Who do you think is the first on the list?" Baghai asked, laughing, "well, I'll tell you, it's Behechti" - for, this time, Behechti had completed his journey to Teheran. He had arrived a few days before, and now figured as the principal leader of the rebellion.

In effect, they were going to carry out a beefed-up portion of Operation Khach, on behalf of a government of national security, led by an undoubted dissident. Baghai said he had obtained the support of the army and part of the Savak. General Rabii confirmed the support, and complete readiness, of the heads of all the armed forces, which, he said, would act within minutes of receiving Baghai's instructions.

"Has His Majesty approved this plan?" the two civilians wanted to know.

"He hasn't said no," replied Baghai, adding, "I told the King that I've got a ninety-percent chance of restoring calm and engaging a process of political normalisation.

"I asked him to give me a fortnight.

"If I fail, all he has to do is return to the capital, give me the sack and charge me with my crimes."

Well after midnight, the meeting broke up. Rabii ushered Baghai into his own car, but not without first standing to attention and presenting, as he would to a Prime Minister, his good wishes and assurances of loyalty.

The following day, Shapour Bakhtiar was nominated as the next Prime Minister.

In total bewilderment, Shirvani rang Zahedi, complaining, "we have been made fools of!" to which Zahedi replied, "you know who is responsible for this, don't you?"

Mozaffar Baghai was arrested a few months after the triumph of the revolution - not because of this episode, which is revealed here for the first time - but because of a placard of protest. He died in prison, under torture.

According to certain witness-statements, published in the USA, or reported to the author (by Senator Ali Rezai, by former minister Ghassem Ladjvardi and by the former Governor of the Central Bank, Meholi Samii) the Shah also made contact, at this time, with Allahyar-Saleh, another time-honoured companion of Mossadegh, who was respected by all; but the conversations came to nothing. I too met Allahyar-Saleh once, during those decisive weeks, in order to consult him. He was much shrunken in stature physically, but his concern for the future of the country, and his aversion to the rise of fanaticism, burned as fiercely as ever.

In the midst of these tense times, an influential figure in the Iranian, Jewish community, who was a friend of the family, relayed a message to me from ambassador Lubrani, head of the Israeli mission in Teheran. He wished to meet me urgently. Both of them came to my house, the following day, at 4.00

pm. I had not met Lubrani before, but I found him discreet and polite. Later, he would play a considerable part in the political affairs of his country. He wanted to ask me about the state of national affairs.

"Will the Shah hold on?" he asked.

Surprised, I explained to him the point of view, which I had been defending for months: "domestic reforms are desperately required," I said, "but they cannot be attempted until order is restored.

"The military government must show its authority, at last, and act swiftly and well; but, without the Shah, everything will collapse.

"We have to support him," I insisted, "and we shall do it against his wishes, if need be."

The ambassador listened to me, almost without reacting, while I said what I had to say. The interview lasted for an hour. As he was leaving, I had the feeling that the meeting had been quite useless. A few days later, Bakhtiar having become Prime Minister, Lubrani closed the Israeli embassy, on the orders of the Islamists, and sent his staff home. After the triumph of the revolution, Khomeyni offered the building to the PLO. In Israel, General Rabin was courageous enough to denounce the odd behaviour of the Israeli government in not supporting the Shah and in favouring, instead, the triumph of the Islamists; but that is another story.

On 21st December, while the demonstrations and violence were continuing, albeit on a limited scale, and Khomeyni's supporters continued to burn, pillage, destroy and shed blood without the slightest opposition - while the government was reduced to complete inaction - General Azhari had a serious heart-attack. Nevertheless, with great fortitude, he remained at his post, frequently resting on a camp-bed, in the prime ministerial office, and constantly attended by a military doctor.

The Shah, in a state of collapse and suffering, but retaining his dignity, now neither sought, nor looked forward to, anything but departure.

His Prime Minister, also calm and dignified in appearance, was putting up a struggle with his grave heart-condition and the problems of the nation, which had become like a ship crewed by drunkards, with no hand on the tiller. The country was indeed in chaos, especially the capital. There were strikes and petrol shortages, public services ceased to function, banks closed. There was insecurity on the streets. Old scores were settled. Aircraft bound for abroad were stormed on the tarmac. Large numbers of people began to flee, by road, towards the Turkish border, or take whatever passage they could get, southwards, across the Persian Gulf.

The different provinces were in different states. In Baluchistan, it was almost as quiet as ever - so also in the Kurdish and Turkmen provinces. In these places, the majority were Sunnis. The television teams did not bother to go there. The countryside generally was almost normal. Here and there, some farmers were demonstrating, not against the government, but against the great landowners, who had been dispossessed by agrarian reform, and now, having wrapped themselves in the Islamic flag, were attempting to get their lands back. However, counter-revolutionary peasant-revolts were of no interest to the foreign press.

Azerbeijan was also less disturbed than many other parts of the country. Here, the influence of Ayatollah Shariat-Madari was still the determining factor, and the great prelate, ever more disquieted by the turn events were taking, had taken steps to curb excesses.

In the north of the country, in the coastal provinces of the Caspian Sea, and in the urban centres of Mazanderan, which were traditionally Leftist in attitude - almost a fiefdom of the Communist Party - there were many disturbances. Violence was a daily occurrence there. At Guilan, where the mullahs had never had much influence, there was overall calm and life was going on normally.

Isphahan, Shiraz, Yezd, Kerman, and so on, were weltering in the same outpouring of violence as the capital. In Teheran, confrontations between anti-Khomeyni workers and peasants, and revolutionary, small shop-keepers and civil-servants, were particularly bloody.

The different, sociological sectors of the population were far less unanimous than the western press said. The functionaries - people receiving salaries from the taxpayer - and the folk from the bazaars, were on the streets, certainly; but the factory-workers of the west of the capital, many university employees and the peasants of the suburbs, were clearly hostile to the revolution.

The police, the riot-squad and the army remained disciplined and loyal to the King. Every attempt to foment mutiny among the armed forces failed, except one, affecting a few dozen aircraft-technicians, several of whom were quickly arrested by the military police. Here and there, policemen, and agents of the special services, reported the theft of uniforms from specialist tailors. It was also reported that basic soldiers' uniforms were being manufactured privately in certain workshops in the Sartchechmeh quarter. The Islamists were undoubtedly preparing the sudden appearance of fake soldiers and officers - just as they did, later, in Algeria - to sow further confusion. The western press would then be able to speak of military revolts; but events now moved so fast that such preparations were not necessary.

As a body, the army remained the last bastion of order. It required an enormous amount of manoeuvering, and a huge operation of intoxication, to get it merely to declare itself *neutral*, after the departure of the Shah. The Americans exerted all their influence to achieve this.

In truth, Iran had not been governed at all, for months, and every attempt to put things right had been stifled. The overwhelming majority of the population was weary, confused and passive, wishing only that all of this could be over, that normal life would return, that peace would descend, that they could breathe freely again.

Chapter XI

"The last Prime Minister of the Empire"

31st December 1978

I t was a chaotic situation:the Shah was depressed and exhausted, plots proliferated, and General Azhari's government was paralysed. While the Shah was having discussions with Sadighi - and then Baghai - other discussions were being held, in extreme secret, to form a Cabinet, which one does not venture to call "transitional", for the die was cast, and everyone knew that the end of the Shah was inevitable .

It was then that a man appeared on the political scene, whom no-one expected to see there: this was Shapour Bakhtiar. On 31st December 1978, the Shah asked him, officially, to form a government.

He was sixty-five, the son of the chieftain of a clan of one of the Bakhtiari tribes of central Iran, Sardar Fateh, whose career was cut short, soon after Shapour's birth. Having been defeated in a battle with regular troops, at Cholil, Sardar Fateh was condemned by a court martial and executed, for armed rebellion. This was in the time of Reza Shah, when he, the founder of the Pahlavi dynasty, was imposing order on a country, which badly needed it.

Although the other clan-chieftains of the tribe were officially not in sympathy with Fateh's action, they protected his young son, Shapour, and made sure he had the best possible education. Amir Mansour Khan, son of the tribal chief, Sardar Mohtachem, personally endowed him with a small inheritance - so some of his friends say.

Shapour Bakhtiar was sent, therefore, to Beirut, where he completed his secondary education, and then to France, where he became a Doctor of Law - the first of the Bakhtiaris ever to achieve such a distinction. He also married, while in France, took French nationality and joined the French army.

His return to Teheran was less than propitious and was a disappointment to him. He was unable to obtain a professorial post in the Faculty of Law and eventually got a job in the Ministry of Labour, which had just then been set up by Ahmad Ghavam. During the oil-crisis, he was the ministry's departmental director in the province of Khouzistan - an episode, which became the subject of lively controversy, when he was appointed Prime Minister - and, by the end of the Mossadegh-era, he had gone on to become under-Secretary of State for Labour.

Between 1953 and 1978, Bakhtiar - although he was never a noted leader of the National Front - was imprisoned briefly, twice, before obtaining seats on the boards of various government-bodies and enterprises, most notably, the Pahlavi Foundation.

His peculiar advantage in life was that he was a nephew of the Shahbanou's aunt, Mrs Louise Ghotbi, born Samsam

Bakhtiari, and that - so they say in the family - when he was young, he bore a striking resemblance to his late mother. Over the last twenty years, it was the Shahbanou's uncle, Mohammad Ali Ghotbi, who had discreetly protected Bakhtiar's peripatetic career.

Mohammad Ali Ghotbi divorced Louise Samsam Bakhtiari, just before the fall of the regime, and re-married shortly afterwards. He died in 1998, in Monte Carlo. However, it was the Ghotbi's son, Reza - the Shahbanou's foster-brother - who arranged for Shapour to have at least two interviews with his foster-sister, in, or after, September 1978.

The Ghotbi's villa, in a northern quarter of Teheran, was the setting of the first interview. Someone once wrote that it lasted six hours, but, according to the subsequent testimony of the owner of the property, if the villa had been emptied of staff and placed ready, for six hours, the duration of the talks would have been less - about two-and-a-half hours, apparently. Then the Shahbanou left, and his aunt, who had remained in the house, had a long conversation with Bakhtiar. At least one other meeting took place, a few days later. Did these encounters occur without the knowledge of the Shah? It's not hard to imagine that they did. There was an entire system, at the palace, for receiving visitors - some of them much more well-known than Bakhtiar - in extreme secrecy. President Sadat, King Hussein of Jordan, Yasser Arafat and certain Israeli leaders, among others, had been received by the Sovereign, in this way, in recent years, and news of these meetings had never leaked out.

Unlike some other leaders of the National Front, Bakhtiar was unknown to the public and could easily have passed unnoticed. In that same period, more than twenty religious dignitaries -

who would have been much more difficult to disguise - were received discreetly at the palace. One of these was received by the Shahbanou, and the others by the Shah, and no-one knew anything about it. All of these prominenti, including some very important people, had come to lend their support to the Shah and to ask him not to leave the country, but, like so many others, all these attempts failed. In disappointment or despair, some of these people would turn their coats, join the victors and make - as a few of them still are making - brilliant careers for themselves under the Islamist regime. Indeed, we can be sure that the meetings between the Shahbanou and Bakhtiar escaped the notice of the Shah.

There was a great sympathy between Bakhtiar and the Shahbanou. Bakhtiar never missed an opportunity, after the triumph of the revolution, to proclaim, and congratulate himself on the fact, that he had "thrown out the Shah"; but he spoke in quite different terms about the Shahbanou, praising "her liberal and progressive ideas" and "her taste for French poetry" - for she sent him a book of Paul Eluard's verse, as Bakhtiar himself wrote later.

From that time, in about September 1978, while Mohammad Reza Pahlavi was battling to come to terms with a crisis, which poisoned his every waking hour, the Shahbanou's little circle of friends started talking about "a social-democratic monarchy", as a possible solution to the unrest. At the same time, they started mentioning the code-name "cousin" - which was what they called Shapour Bakhtiar - in connection with a "providential man", who would bring in this new regime. Indeed, did not this "cousin" present himself everywhere as a "social-democrat"?

Was it a plot against the Shah, or against his wishes? I

don't really think so. It was parallel game, played by a few socialites, who had no grasp of the social and political realities of the country, who deceived themselves and, by increasing the regime's general loss-of-confidence, contributed to its enfeeblement, just when it needed cohesion and firmness, more than ever before.

Bakhtiar, for his part, thinking, perhaps, that the family-connection would not be enough, tried hard to engage the Shah's intentions directly. He once asked Djamchid Amouzegar, then an outgoing Prime Minister, in whom the Sovereign retained a certain confidence - considering him "an honest and wise man" - to recommend him to the Shah; and this Amouzegar did, during an audience at the beginning of December, before he finally left the country. Roughly at the same time, Ghobad Zafar, the well-known architect, and a man of importance among the Bakhtiaris - being a cousin to the former Empress Soraya - went to see the Grand Master of Imperial Protocol, Afshar, and asked him to deliver a note personally to the Shah, which the Grand Master did. The Shah asked for the note to be read to him. Ghobad Zafar himself presented Bakhtiar to the Sovereign, guaranteeing his loyalty to the crown and suggesting that he be called to take part in government.

Thus was fate sealed: the Shahbanou's clan had succeeded in putting Shapour Bakhtiar into the orbit of power. One evening in mid-December, after curfew, the chief of the Savak, General Moghaddam, went personally to fetch Bakhtiar, from his villa at Farmanieh, quite close to the palace, and take him to see the Sovereign. Bakhtiar was received, officially, and asked to prepare his proposals, but he was not then nominated as Prime Minister. It was a polite encounter and the first of several, which occurred before his nomination was announced. As the Shah had requested, Bakhtiar produced a detailed analysis of the domestic situation, which, however, made no allusion to the effect of foreign influences on the crisis. He added that he would always be at the Sovereign's disposal and that he would keep his distance from the rebellious elements inspired by Khomeyni, in which he wanted no part, "either theoretically or in practical, political terms".

Ten days passed while Bakhtiar put together most of his team, already conducting himself as a future head of government. The British Ambassador, Sir Anthony Parsons, mentions in his memoirs that he had lunch alone with Bakhtiar, on 18th December, and heard then about his plans. Bakhtiar did not know, of course, about the other negotiations, of the same kind, which were going on at the same time. He was quite sure that he would be nominated.

He was called to the palace again. The domestic situation was deteriorating. The Americans had stepped up their pressure on the Shah to leave the country. The Sovereign therefore enjoined Bakhtiar to act quickly. Later, Bakhtiar would write that he had withheld his answer for ten days, and Sir Anthony confirms this. At last, on 31st December, exactly a year after the sumptuous reception at Teheran, for President Carter, Shapour Bakhtiar was publicly nominated as Prime Minister and received his Imperial Warrant.

When he became head of government, the wider public knew almost nothing of him, and, to tell the truth, he had no qualifications for this exalted job. He had no political support, except that of the Shahbanou - who was about to leave the country - and that of his own circle of friends. The army-chiefs didn't like him, or just knew nothing about him, and his natural, political allies had repudiated him. He was said - rightly or wrongly - to be an atheist, so the clergy despised him. He was certainly ambitious, well educated and with pleasant manners; and he appeared to be an epicure, enjoying wines and fine cookery. His very "British" elegance reminded me of cavalry officers of the Indian Army. He had a penchant too for Persian, and French, poetry, many volumes of which adorned the impressive library of his beautiful villa, in the fashionable quarter of Farmanieh - and that was all!

He had been President, during the 'seventies, of the "French Circle" - that quintessential Teheran-club, so frequented by politicians and business-people - often inviting prominent men to his table. Usually these were the heads of public corporations, including some super-rich adherents of the National Front, but sometimes he entertained medical men. Besides this, little by little, he got the habit of drawing closer to political circles - to powerful, and useful, people. In this connection, when he was elected to the much prized presidency of "the Circle", General Nassiri, then chief of the Savak, personally intervened to dislodge him from this important, social position, which he only retained thanks to the friendly, but firm, intervention of the mighty Minister to the Court, Amir Assadollah Alam.

Apart from that, the man had hardly any more political past than he had political qualifications, and his sudden ascent to the summit of the hierarchy surprised many. In fact, the definitive choice of the Bakhtiar-option seemed to have been the result of a complex interplay of four forces.

First of all, the Shah, sick and distraught, was searching for a passable candidate, who would agree to his departure. All those whom he had previously sounded out, about taking the reins of government, had, as we have seen, refused to do it, if he left the country. Thus, it could have been Bakhtiar or anyone, provided that they let him go with some of his dignity intact.

Next, the Shahbanou, as she said publicly, was anxious to preserve the throne for her son. She was the only one who knew about her husband's illness - and that he might die at any time - and she also felt that, by saving the monarchy, she might ensure for herself, in the capacity of regent perhaps, some years of rule and power, supported by the eager circle, which a new boom in popularity would produce. This plan could only succeed if she had a man, who was a complete non-entity, at her side, and the entire army, and some fraction of the clergy, at her back. She judged Bakhtiar poorly and she too pushed him to the front of the stage.

After these, come the foreign powers - Washington, London and Paris - working together to push the Shah out of his homeland. The British, especially, saw in Bakhtiar a reliable man. One might also think - from the repeated journeys Michel Poniatowski made to Iran, and from the protection he enjoyed later in France - that this dual-national was being supported by the French government. However, at this advanced stage of the Iranian crisis, the game was already over as far as the western powers were concerned. They were all calling quite openly for the departure of Mohammad Reza Pahlavi, and had placed their bets on the advent of Khomeyni. Nothing in the published works, any more than from the cross-checking of the events, allows one to think that the West saw, in Bakhtiar, anything other than a transient figure of no great significance. They had found someone to hand over the keys to Khomeyni and the fundamentalists. Four years previously, when it was decided to hand over Vietnam to the Communists, this sad function had been confided to a certain General Minh. Bakhtiar was cast in the same role.

As for the man himself, he saw in this political farrago the chance of his life. It was his opportunity, at last, to play an important part, he thought, but the part was too big for him. He was more opportunist than ambitious, but he had previously tried to force destiny's hand by contacting American diplomats in Teheran with a view to winning their support - as attested by a volume of documents, published after the storming of the American embassy in November 1979, and which was embarrassing, in places, for Bakhtiar. He pressed himself, in particular, on the small circle of intimates, surrounding the Shahbanou, who profited from her strategic position, even though they was suspected, if not detested, by the Sovereign. For this circle, the "cousin" was a means of acceding, at last, to political power and of taking revenge on the Shah, from whom, at the end, it no longer hid its hatred and its desire to expel him from Iran. Thus, it was an exchange of services.

History tells us what happened. Shapour Bakhtiar dived into the whirlpool of power in a vulnerable state of disarray. Contrary to what he told the Shah, he did not have recourse to many "new faces" to form his government. His "eternal friends" deserted him. The political faction, of which he called himself president, within the National Front, only had two members. He said it himself. In the end, he had to call upon the high officials of the existing regime to fill most of the important posts, such as Foreign Affairs, Labour and, of course, Defence.

In reality, he was alone before even setting out on his mission. He even tried to negotiate with Khomeyni's followers to get himself nominated as the latter's Prime Minister!

He succeeded in collapsing in no time - an achievement for which he deserves recognition and will enter into history like a latter-day Erostrates.

On 6th January, the date of the presentation of the new cabinet to the Sovereign - in the waiting-room - and in such a way as to be heard by the footmen and other palace staff, Shapour Bakhtiar asked his ministers to refrain from bowing to the Sovereign in the traditional way. Not only that, but, on the same morning, he had caused the regulation portrait of the Shah to be removed from his presidential office, and replaced by a much larger one of Mossadegh.

During the presentation, the Shah, looking dejected, or absent, retained all his dignity, but he was clearly longing to get it over with. The new Prime Minister, striking a pose of unconcern for the television-cameras, looked at the ceiling. Some of his ministers declined to be photographed with the Sovereign. More than anyone, it was those who had been the regime's dignitaries who were embarrassed.

Paradoxically, with the exception of the Minister of Defence - General Chafeghat, the most becoming, if not deferential in his behaviour, was the Telecoms-Minister, Lotf-Ali Samimi, a member of the National Front, and the only declared dissident to have agreed to join the government.

The more unavoidable the departure of the Shah became, the more certain people tried to prevent it, sensing, as they did, that it would lead to the wrecking of Iran. The Sovereign's political influence had shrunk, chaos was everywhere and numerous official figures, with their usual promptness, either made themselves inconspicuous, beat a path to the door of the Shahbanou, or sought asylum abroad.

The Grand Master of Protocol, Amir Aslan Afshar, anxious to sustain the Shah's morale, and, above all, to occupy his days, granted requests for audiences from representatives of non-governmental society, such as the leaders of residents' associations - who were very influential in the capital - or retired generals, all of whom wanted to see the Sovereign and pledge him their support. The palace's antechambers filled, from then on, with people who knew little or nothing of the Court. Nearly all of them came to lavish their advice on the Shah, but, especially, they wanted to warn him against leaving the country and abandoning the army.

Much later, in Cairo, just before his death, Mohammad Reza Pahlavi mentioned these visits to me - these unexpected pledges of loyalty - regretting, intensely, that he had ignored them. It was at that moment, that an idea took root in some minds - an idea, which, today, seems silly or naive, but which was in the tradition of the relationship between the Shah and his compatriots. The first to broach it was Prof. Mohammad Baheri, the former Minister of Justice: "go and occupy the palace," he advised, "and stay there until the Sovereign agrees to stay in the country!"

Mossadegh himself had used this strategy twice, during the 'forties and 'fifties, once to get some fraudulent elections annulled, and again to get the campaign for the nationalisation of the oil-industry under way.

Many people were quickly seduced by this idea, especially

eminent academics. Mohammad Baheri even took it to the Grand Ayatollah Hadj Agha Ahmad Khonsari, the chief, and most influential cleric in the capital, and a leading light in the Shiite hierarchy. Would he agree, Baheri wanted to know, to allow several hundreds of people, from the quarters of the city, from the Bazaar and from non-governmental society in general, to come and pack themselves into his house, with a view to demanding that he intercede with the King to renounce leaving Iran? The Ayatollah was anxious about the course being taken by events, and said so, in private, but, to Baheri, he said: "you know that I steer clear of politics and of this distressing agitation."

"But you will not shut the door of your house to your fellow Muslims?" insisted Baheri.

"Certainly not," replied the Grand Prelate, "and, if necessary, I shall convey their wishes to the proper quarter."

It was a clear, and prudent, position, which also gave the go-ahead. A sum of 150 000 tomans (20 000 dollars of the time) was provided by two businessmen, who were also friends, and was entrusted to the Ayatollah's son for the funding of the operation - to buy one or two great tents, mobile heaters and food.

The convergence on the prelate's house - situated in the heart of Teheran's bazaar - was due to begin at dawn on 7th January. The occupation ("tahasson" in Farsee) and the march towards the home of one of the most important Shiite clerics, was thus due to be proclaimed, from the 7th, in order to create an event, which could save the day - always assuming the army took a more energetic posture.

With this in mind, a group of about a dozen academics, including two famous surgeons from the capital, some writers and other intellectuals went to the palace, on the evening of 6th January, and were received, a little after six-o-clock by the Shah and Shahbanou. Mohammad Baheri was there, and the Rector Ghassem Motamedi - both of whom now live undercover, outside Iran. All had taken care to put over-night bags in their cars, before setting out. In silence and with quaking heart, I listened, that evening, to an eminent professor of surgery, who had just set foot in the palace for the first time, addressing the Sovereign, in the following, deeply felt terms: "the Imperial Army is loyal to you," he said, "and it is the only power capable of maintaining the unity of the country and resisting extremist pressures.

"What will become of that army, if Your Majesty leaves Iran?" he went on, "it might break up or it might take over the state.

"In either event," he concluded, "Iran will be eclipsed by anarchy and chaos, unless Your Majesty heeds the interests of your nation, and your duty to history, which command you equally, Sire, to remain."

The Shahbanou was unable to restrain her tears, when a famous author recited, with great emotion, and in an almost theatrical tone, some verses, about the responsibilities of a sovereign to his people, by Ferdowsi*.

The Shah remained cold and distant. Sometimes he looked as though his mind was elsewhere, walled up, as he was, by

* Ferdowsi, 935 -1020 ad, was considered the greatest of all Persian poets and the bard of Iranian nationalism. Over more than thirty years, he composed "Shahnameh" - "The Book Of The Kings" - a poem of 60 000 verses, which standardised Farsee, just as "The Divine Comedy" standardised Italian.

his determination to conceal his feelings. He concluded the audience by thanking his visitors for braving the snowstorm to come and tell him about the concern, which they felt for their country and their Sovereign. His demeanour was strange, disconcerting.

No-one mentioned the formation of the new government, or the name of Shapour Bakhtiar. Everyone was obviously aware that this would embarrass the Shah. Having said what there was to say, and having heard the Sovereign's thanks, the time had come to raise the principal matter of the audience. Rector Motamedi, speaking very gently, to avoid shocking the Shah, said to him, "Sire, if you cannot now assure us that you will not leave Iran, we shall remain here until you do."

He also pointed out that other people, with the same object, would be arriving on the following day.

Mohammad Reza Pahlavi emerged suddenly from his torpor and retorted drily, "will you then teach me my duty?"

Then he rose, to signify that the audience was at an end. The Shahbanou, acknowledging the evident embarrassment of the company, said kindly, "Mind how you go, it's getting very cold, and we still have another group to see this evening."

The Sovereigns shook hands. The Shah re-assumed his haughty bearing, thanking everyone politely.

On three previous occasions, "occupation of the palace" - in order to express a request to the Head of State - had met with the, at least, tacit acquiescence of the incumbent. Twice, Mossadegh and his followers had protested successfully against existing governments, in this way; and once, opponents of the Nationalist chief had used the device effectively on him, when he was in power, but, on this occasion, it would have been unthinkable to try to impose oneself on the host and have oneself thrown out by the guards. The project had failed. The Shah's resolution to leave the country was, from now on, a recognised fact. Soon enough, we would understand the kind of pressures he had been exposed to, and which he no longer had any desire to resist.

The following morning, from 7.00 am, messengers despatched by Mohamad Baheri went to ask those, who were rallying at Ayatollah Khonsari's house, to re-trace their steps. Even at that early hour, a considerable number had come. Some wept, when they were told that they "were not wanted". It was clear what this message meant.

As they left the palace gardens, in the near-darkness occasioned by a strike at the power-stations, the party encountered ten-or-so Deputies, arriving for their audience. One of these was Hodjatoleslam Danechi, parliament's only mullah.

"Well then, he's going, is he?" they all wanted to know, including Danechi, who, however, answered himself.

"Don't worry," he said, "I know just what to say to talk him out of it."

Another naive illusion! After the regime fell, he was vilified for taking part in a "secret initiative", and shot, on the orders of Khomeyni.

The following day, Shapour Bakhtiar presented himself

before the Chamber and delivered a beautiful speech, proclaiming, with forceful conviction, that he would be faithful to the constitution, and therefore to the monarchy, and said not a word about the eventual departure of the Sovereign. However, he had adopted as his own the insistence, of London, Washington and Paris, that the Shah should leave the country forthwith. He was also negotiating, at this time, with Khomeyni's party, concerning his position in the coming regime, and he was sending letters to the "guest of Neauphle-le-Château", which would soon be made public, and in which he swore fealty to Khomeyni! The Shah had asked his Prime Minister to proceed quickly with obtaining a vote of confidence from the two Chambers, so that the Cabinet could be invested constitutionally and legitimately.

At the very moment, when the Prime Minister was presenting himself before Parliament, a document was published in Iran, which was highly compromising for him. It had been produced by Mozaffar Baghai, the prestigious, former companion of Mossadegh, and , in it, he accused Bakhtiar of "having been a British agent for many years". In fact, the communiqué revealed, when the oil-industry was nationalised, opening the files of the "PDG" (a local branch of the Anglo-Iranian Oil Company) had shown - and the documents were there to prove it - that Bakhtiar had been on the payroll of the British Company, and that, shortly afterwards, pressure had been brought to bear, on the Iranian government, to include him in the Iranian delegation to the annual, plenary session of the International Working Group - presumably to forestall any anti-British manoeuvers. Baghai was quite confident of his sources, because he himself chaired the commission, which seized the documents! When, moreover, Dr. Darioush Shirvani, an opposition Deputy, announced these facts, from the podium of the Chamber, for all Iran to hear - just as the new government's programme was being discussed - the scandal, a veritable bombshell, broke immediately and with terrible effect. The Prime Minister's lack of reaction only placed him under deeper suspicion. We know, of course, what the principal reason for the Deputy's ire was.

Certainly, the Shah knew, in detail, about this affair, but, curiously, he continued to exhibit apparent confidence in the man, whom he had just made Prime Minister and whom he had just invested with powers, which no-one, for many decades, had wielded before him - and this, at a time when the fate of the country was in such dire jeopardy! The explanation for his attitude seems to be two-fold: Bakhtiar was the only politician available, who did not want the Shah to remain in Iran, and the only civilian ambitious enough to accept the premiership at whatever cost. Besides, for the Shah, it was all over, nothing mattered any more!

This sense of utter defeat, giving rise to complete indifference, distraction and alienation, was noted also by Sir Anthony Parsons, on 8th January 1979, just after having seen the Shah, "calm and unconcerned, speaking of the country's affairs as though they were no longer any concern of his!"

That Monday, 8th January, the same people who had gone to the palace two evenings before, met for a long time, trying to prevail upon me to go again to see the Shah, hoping that he would confide privately to me things, which he would not reveal to a larger meeting, but I knew enough of the monarch's character to be of a different opinion. Nevertheless, I could not refuse to try one last time, and I felt freer to make the attempt, knowing that Shapour Bakhtiar had just obtained a vote of confidence in the Chamber, by 149 to 43, with 13 abstentions, and would soon receive another from the Senate.

The audience was granted for the 9th, at half-past-three, and then rescheduled for half-past-five. Night fell on a city deprived of electricity and invaded by a cold, grey mist. There were few cars about, if only because most of the petrol-stations were closed, but the old palace, which served as the Sovereign's office, and had its own generator, was, however, brilliantly illuminated, which gave it an unreal appearance. Not in the least did it resemble the bunker, surrounded by trenches, watch-towers and tanks, which the western press described! I even had the impression - which was sinister enough, under the circumstances - that a gala-evening was in progress.

Since I was a few minutes early, I wandered about the entrance to the first courtyard, where I had left my car, whereupon I soon realised why the time of my audience had been put back. In front of the stairs leading up to the Emperor's offices, I recognised the armoured Cadillac of the US-Ambassador - with its star-spangled banner on the front, right wing - and the no less characteristic Bentley of the Ambassador of Her Gracious Majesty, with the Union Flag on its bonnet.

In the corridors, footmen and guards were whispering in little groups. It was a strange atmosphere. I went into the civilian-chamberlains' room. In charge, that evening, was Manoutchehr Sanei, who was universally respected as a specialist in the first three centuries of Persian art - a man of distinction and courtesy - whom I found in the company of two or three other chamberlains, all eager for news. Each wore a suitably anxious expression, moved stealthily and asked the same question, in hushed tones, "will he go, or won't he?"

All of this was going on in a restrained, respectful way, as though in the house of a very sick, great man, who was asleep, and whom one must take care not to wake. A few moments later, a special bell was heard ringing from the Shah's office. An audience had just come to an end, and the Sovereign was calling for the next visitor. Manoutchehr Sanei led me, therefore, into the Shah's office and introduced me. It was a very large room, in the form of a short-stemmed cross. The northern arm, where stood the Sovereign's desk, looked out towards Mount Elbrouz; the southern arm had a view over the Chemiran Valley and the city of Teheran, extending beyond the park and the public gardens.

This southern branch was a salon, furnished in the Imperial style, into which the Shah usually conducted his important visitors, when he wanted to converse privately with them. In the centre of the cross was a huge table, decorated with flower-arrangements, which the Imperial gardeners renewed each day.

It was an imposing suite, with a marble floor covered with Persian carpets. The walls were hung with grey tapestries, soberly ornamented with ancient, Iranian weapons. A few pictures by Iranian masters added, here and there, a touch of colour. This decor was certainly not new to me, but, on this occasion - perhaps it was a premonition - I had a strong impression that I was seeing the place for the last time. The objects around me appeared in a bizarre light, like theatrical scenery, which was about to be removed.

I directed my steps towards the northern arm of the cross. The Shah was sitting behind his Imperial desk, with a globe, and two telephones, on his right. One of these was gilded, but was not made of solid gold as some pretended. There were no files on his desk-top, for he usually studied papers later in the

367

evening. Besides, he had not studied anything for several days. Alone on that expanse were a few coloured pencils, a pen and a paper-knife. On a small table stood a powerful radio-receiver, by means of which he could hear the national news-bulletins, and those put out by American and European radio-stations.

The Sovereign came towards me and shook my hand. As always he looked me in the eyes. Looking at him, I was suddenly struck by his terrible state of emaciation and the way his navy-blue suit hung from him. He was deathly pale, and his deeply-ringed eyes seemed lifeless. He offered me a chair and sat down himself, not behind, but beside his desk, facing me across a small table. He called for tea, which was promptly served. He didn't touch his, even after putting sugar in it. Naturally, I didn't drink mine either.

"It's best that I keep the telephone within reach," he said, "I have asked to be kept informed of developments hour-by-hour, and more often, if necessary."

Then he fell silent and waited for me to speak. This was not his custom, or even in accordance with the rules of politeness. It was the Sovereign's responsibility to start the conversation, but this was no time to stand on ceremony. Thus it was that a tragic conversation took place between, as it were, two deaf men.

I rehearsed once again the argument he knew: if the Sovereign left national territory, the army would no longer have a Commander-in-Chief and the government would fall fatally into the hands of adventurers and fanatics - many of them paid and guided from abroad - who would lead the country to chaos and ruin.

"Such will be the catastrophe," I said, "that everything,

which has been built up over the decades, will be torn down again."

The Shah got up and began to pace across the great room, running his fingers through his hair, something he only did when in a state of extreme agitation. I too rose, of course, but he gestured to me to sit down. Then he resumed his seat and said slowly, in a heavy, sad voice, "most of my visitors say something quite different to what your friends prophesy, and to what you yourself predict.

"From all sides, I am being advised to leave Iran, and by the new Head of Government, Bakhtiar, more than any.

"He assures me that my departure will make things easier - will facilitate appeasement.

"I have become, a complete spoilsport, it appears."

I knew where these counsels were coming from. I also knew that most of his visitors in recent days had been begging him to remain, and that this was the unanimous wish of the army, which remained loyal to him. The Shah tried to convince me, but he wasn't very good at it. It was necessary that I tell him, probably for the last time, what I had to tell him, so I ran over my thesis once more.

"I beg your pardon, Sire," I said, "you know I have never been a courtier, but, although it may seem needful that Your Majesty depart, for a while, from the capital, the destiny of the nation, of which you are still the master, is at hazard..."

He rested his hands on the back of an armchair and looked at me in such a way, that I could read nothing in his gaze but a profound internal tension. Then I mentioned a report, which I had presented some years before, and the reforms I had suggested, affirming my conviction that, if they had been carried out, we would not be where we were today.

"Still, that's all water under the bridge," I said, "today, it's obvious: there's nothing left to do, but to try to avoid the worst and save what is essential."

The Shah shook his head impatiently, saying, "you talk like the opposition, claiming that I haven't carried out any reforms - that I have refused to listen!"

I rejoined: "Is it possible to say, nowadays, Sire, that the opposition were wrong, when they warned Your Majesty against certain policies?
"In any event," I protested, "I dare hope that you have no doubts about my continuing loyalty and good faith."

"I am persuaded of it," he replied, "otherwise I would not have received you, but, please, do continue."

I repeated yet again my conviction that the Emperor should leave Teheran, but stay in Iran, in order to preserve intact the only remaining, solid institution - the armed forces. Perhaps, I said, he could install a Council of Regency and, if calm returned, envisage a political solution in line with the constitution. Prof. Sadighi had asked precisely this of him, just a few days before.

"Let's assume," he said, "that I quit the regime, but remain in Iran: where should I go - to Kich?"

"Perish the thought, Your Majesty!" I responded, "tourist-complexes, like Kich, attract endless criticism!
"Go away quietly, Sire," I urged him, "to a military base, among your soldiers, where you will be safe.

"Iranians, have always had the greatest respect for the army, of which you are the Commander-in-Chief: stay with the army, Sire!

"That, I believe, is the solution."

I proposed the naval base, at Bandar Abbas, where the Shah could choose, as a residence, either the house of the Commander-in-Chief of the Fleet (in the Persian Gulf and the Indian Ocean) where guests sometimes lodged, and in which he usually stayed, during his tours of inspection, or a villa belonging to his nephew, Commander Shafigh, a superior officer of the Imperial Marine. From there, if things got really bad (out of deference, "in case of necessity", is what I actually said) it would be easy enough to cross the Strait of Hormuz, by helicopter, to the Sultanate of Oman, a country with a debt of friendship to Iran. I had a fleeting impression that the Shah was wavering, and so I insisted, mentioning Kharg Island, where there was a naval base and an oil-terminal, and which was perhaps even better protected and more secure. At that point, the Sovereign made an astonishing remark: "Very well - if I leave Teheran, but remain on Iranian soil, how shall we organise the military honours-ceremony?"

I could hardly believe my ears and, for several agonising seconds, was unable to think of any reply. Finally, I said: "that's a detail, which Protocol will have no trouble sorting out."

"No, it's definitely impossible," he rejoined, "Sadighi made the same condition, you know; and I refused, because I can longer withstand the pressures, which have been brought to bear upon me."

In exile, he regretted it bitterly; but at that moment, he

was crushed and without will in the matter. Nevertheless, I continued.

"Do you speak, Sire, of the two ambassadors, to whom you have just given audience?"

"You saw them?" he asked.

"No, Sire, but I saw their cars outside - a Cadillac with the Stars-and-Stripes, and a Bentley bearing the Union Jack."

"Ah!" he exclaimed, "they put out the flags, did they?"

At that moment, I was quite sure that the Shah had made an irrevocable decision to leave Iran.

"Sire," I said, "you chose Shapour Bakhtiar as Prime Minister, even though he has less experience than Sadighi and, more importantly, he is less popular."

He made an evasive gesture.

"That's over and done with," he replied, "I designated Bakhtiar, and that's that; there's no going back on it - it's up to him to act now."

"Does Your Majesty have the least confidence in him?" I enquired.

"No," he said simply.

"But why did you designate him then?" I pressed.

"Because he was the only civilian, who would accept what I

would call a suicide-mission," he explained, "he is so ambitious that he wants to be Prime Minister, at any price: I should like to think that he might succeed - I wish he could - but what does it matter, if the last Prime Minister of the Empire is called Bakhtiar or something else?

It's all over, and nothing matters any more."

My deepest feeling, which I could not express, was entirely of regret and pity. At this moment, one of the two telephones began to ring. The Shah turned and answered it, then listened for several minutes. On the line - so he told me after the conversation - was the General Administrator of Martial Law in Teheran, reporting on certain operations for maintaining order.

"I must insist," the Shah retorted at last, a sudden vehemence in his voice, "blood must not be shed - not at any price.

"At any price, d'you hear?

"Take the necessary measures, but just make sure there are no wounded and, especially, no dead!"

He replaced the receiver, his face livid, murmuring, almost to himself, "I will not go down in history as a murderer of my own people!

"If they want power, very well, let them have it!

"I'm not going to hang on at the cost of hundreds of thousands of the lives of Iranians, like myself, who have as much right to life as I have."

He got up, moved towards me and held out his hand, which indicated to me that the audience was over. I think I was the last visitor of the day.

"Sire," I said, my voice shaking with emotion, "I beg of

you, leave Teheran, but not our country: do not abandon the army!"

The extended hand fell, and, for an instant, he regarded me gently with a look of such distress that it was impossible to return it. Then, clicking his heels together - which, for him, was a sign of extreme annoyance - he put his hand to his head, applying the index finger to his brow, saying, "can't you understand that I am unable to do anything more - that I have had all I can take - that I need to retreat, to see things from a distance, without being plagued and haunted and subjected to pressures, of all sorts, from all quarters?

"I must leave the country!"

"Has Your Majesty decided which country he will go to?"

"No," said the Shah, "we haven't decided yet, neither where nor when, but we're thinking about it and shall probably make these decisions very soon."

"This, then, will be the last time we shall see each other, Sire," I replied, "in Iran, at least."

The Shah's look became rather more distant: "I believe so," he said, "but we may see one another again, some time: God alone knows - may He be with you and keep you!"

The next day, I recounted this conversation concisely to the friends, who had persuaded me to go once more to see the Sovereign. I had already made notes, of the exchange - most of which I have just described - without delay, for the record..

I also took the step of informing certain reliable soldiers that, in my opinion, we could now discount the Sovereign from any move to stabilise the situation. In this vein, I notified admirals Ardalan and Deyhimi - both, today, in the USA - General Djavad Moin-Zadeh, head of military intelligence, who was then very active in attempting to mount a public-security operation - he died in 1998, in London - and, lastly, and in an extremely furtive manner, General Neshat, the recently-appointed Commander of the Imperial Guard.

As for the Sovereign, he continued to give audiences - not to officials, who now avoided him, for reasons one can imagine, and who no longer accounted to him for anything - but to numerous people from outside the government, who came simply to show their sympathy and loyalty.

"He planned to go to the USA, after a short stay in Cairo, to meet President Sadat," notes Aslan Afshar, and arrangements had indeed been sketched out, though not actually made, for such an itinerary.

His aircraft would land on the military airfield at Andrews Air-Force Base, where the house of one of the Shah's personal friends had been proposed, by the Shah himself, as his place of residence for the duration of his stay. Mohammad Reza Pahlavi expected to be able to negotiate, with the American leaders, a transformation of their attitude towards Iran - an illusion, which was not dispelled until the Guadeloupe Conference, beginning on 5th January, where the main, western powers decided definitively to support the Islamic revolution and favour radical change in Iran.

During these dramatic days, the Shahbanou also gave many audiences, but she spent a lot of time packing too.

Paradoxically, she did not exclude the possibility of staying in France, especially if her husband was going to the USA. The Empress of Iran, replacing Khomeyni on French territory, would have added spice to the story! She asked the writer and journalist, Jean-Michel Pedrazzani, the former chief-editor of RTL, who was also a press-baron and a friend of the family, to come urgently to Iran. She then requested that he sound out the French authorities regarding this plan. Evidently, they said no.

The demonstrations continued in Teheran, while, on the Shah's orders, the armed forces made themselves less and less visible. The capital was handed over to the revolutionaries. There were no corpses to exhibit to the crowds, to stir up their emotions - or to show to the western TV-crews, so that they could report "bloody repression" - so fake ones had to be manufactured. Funerals with cadaver-less coffins, filled with any old ballast - for they weren't empty, but carefully weighted - were systematically organised. Clothing, stained with dyes, resembling the blood of victims, was held up to the cameras. The revolutionary leaders admitted as much soon afterwards, calling this trickery "revolutionary tactics"; but who dared to doubt what they saw on "the news", at that time? The global propaganda-machine had been set running and would sweep away everything in its path.

Chapter XII

*"I entrust Iran to you and commend you
to God's protection."*

16th - 22th January 1979

S ince the nomination of Bakhtiar, the Shah appeared ever more detached and distant from the events, which were tormenting the country. His people, whose ingratitude mortified him, wished him to be gone. His allies abroad, disgruntled by the ambitions he vaunted for his country, were overtly undermining him. He was exhausted. Thus, he withdrew from the game - though not without a last discreet overture to Washington, which, having opted definitively for Khomeyni, brushed it casually aside.

Mohammad Reza Pahlavi's last fortnight in Iran would be the most trying of all. Having decided to go, he viewed his departure as inevitable, but, to maintain his sense of duty and dignity, he continued to keep up appearances, going regularly to his office, giving audiences and following a schedule.

His eldest daughter, Fahranaz, went to join her brother, Reza, the heir-to-the-throne, in the USA. Mrs Diba, the Shahbanou's mother, took the two younger siblings, Ali Reza and Leila, to

France. All the other members of the family had already gone. As a precaution, the mortal remains of the Shah's father and brother, which had been deposited in a mausoleum to the south of the capital, were removed to a place of safe-keeping. Equally, by personal order of the Shah, all the secret archives, as well as important files of the Imperial Cabinet, were transferred abroad, by special, military flight. Some of this material, which would be of incalculable worth to historians, is now in the USA, and some in Switzerland. As far as I know, the post-revolutionary regime has not sought to recover it, nor even acknowledged its disappearance, which is revealed for the first time, hereby, in this book. There are too many documents, compromising for the revolutionary leaders, in those files.

The Shahbanou, who had been a prime mover in the nomination of Bakhtiar, also continued to give audiences and organise working meetings. She was sorting out, furthermore, the family's personal affairs, and carefully collecting clothing, souvenirs, personal jewellery, some works of art and so on, which she sent, by military aircraft, to Europe. The Shah took no interest in these preparations. He did not even deign to reply, when she asked him whether they should take this or that object, or not. He was already far away.

He hardly ate anything any more, and, when he was obliged to take something, he always ate alone. Outside his office, and beyond the strict performance of his work, he lapsed into an uncanny speechlessness.

On the other hand, although the Imperial Couple could no longer conceal the imminence of their departure - for one thing, Washington was pro-claiming it publicly - they made every effort to keep the date a secret. This was not directly for reasons of security, but to avoid demonstrations by those who did not want them to leave. It would only take a few hundred people, at the airport, to upset, and possibly prevent, their embarkation, and they could hardly set the Imperial Guard on a crowd, which was demonstrating its loyalty to the King!

On 6th January 1979, at Guadeloupe, the four, great Western Powers had been assembled, since the previous evening, at the invitation of Valéry Giscard d'Estaing, to discuss the crisis in Iran. That day, Jimmy Carter, Helmut Schmidt, James Callaghan and the French president sealed the fate of Iran. Giscard spoke most passionately, of the four, against the Shah, although he denied this years later. If Mohammad Reza Pahlavi remained, he insisted, Iran would slide into civil war and an immense blood-bath; the Communists were becoming ever stronger; American officers stationed in Iran would be drawn into the conflict, and this would give the Soviets the excuse to intervene: Washington had to accept the prospect of change.

After the catastrophe, each of the participants at Guadeloupe naturally attempted to shift the blame on to each of the others. According to the French president, it was Jimmy Carter, who was the first to affirm: "the Shah cannot stay - the Iranian people don't want him any more - we have nothing to worry about".

One day, the archives will probably reveal the whole truth of this episode. However, cross-checking the subsequent, published, indiscreet references and settling of accounts, permits us to suspect that, although unanimity was reached in favour of Rouhollah Khomeyni's taking power, it was the German Chancellor, Helmut Schmidt, who was the least enthusiastic of the four, about it.

An urgent mission was then assigned to General Huyser, the American deputy-Commander-in-Chief of NATO, to speed up the Sovereign's exit. The General flew to Teheran and, to quote the Count de Marenches, "made a tour of the officers' mess-rooms", in order to dissuade the Iranian army from intervening in the crisis. He also met, at considerable length, the revolutionary leaders and, in company with the American ambassador, was granted an audience with the Shah. This interview was short and, it seems, barely polite.

"Both of them were only interested in finding out the date and time, at which I would leave," the Shah said later.

Apparently, the Sovereign had not even been informed of the American general's arrival. Huyser was, however, quite familiar with Iran, and his visit was no secret in the capital. Everyone was talking about it; but no-one told the Shah until the two Americans asked for an audience.

Ardeshir Zahedi, who was still nominally our ambassador to Washington, and who was still in Teheran, partly to organise an eventual transit, for the Shah, to the USA, and partly to find him another destination if that country wouldn't have him, was consulted about Huyser's presence in Iran and the prospect of according him an audience.

He was against the idea: "this chap," he said, "has come here without declared purpose or authorisation, which he has no business to do.

"Have him arrested for illegal entry, or, at least, expel him - that would be a nice, energetic move - for reasons connected with the restoration of order.

"Then we might be able to start negotiating from a position of strength."

Zahedi's courageous proposal was, of course, in total contradiction to the appointment of Bakhtiar, who had been brought in simply to organise the removal of the Shah, and the latter rejected it out of hand.

Some army-officers even put forward the idea of an attack on the American general, and of blaming it on the opposition. Perhaps it was a foolish idea, but anyway, the Shah formally proscribed it.

Huyser met all the revolutionary leaders at least three times. One of these meetings lasted ten hours. I called General Gharabaghi on this subject (he had been promoted to Head of the General Staff, after the military cabinet was dissolved) and told him of my apprehension about the rumours, which were circulating, concerning Huyser's manoeuvers.

"Don't worry," Gharabaghi replied, "General Huyser is my political adviser"!

Now, it has all come out - from the statements of numerous witnesses - that Huyser was "advising", in the name of the USA and the great, western powers, the formation of a Khomeyni-Bazargan government, inspired by Islam and backed firmly by the army. This was to happen, apparently, after the fall of the Shah and the proclamation of a republic, which would bring in democracy!

Huyser stayed in Iran for several days after the Shah had gone, and the officials from the US embassy even participated, during that time, in meetings to prepare for the coming, and the welcoming, of Khomeyni to Teheran. Under these conditions, the dismissal of General Alexander Haig, the Commander-in-Chief of NATO - and therefore Huyser's superior officer - for objecting to his deputy's being assigned this mission, passed almost unnoticed. Reagan's future Secretary of State was indeed hostile to the idea of lending any American, or western, support to the Iranian revolution.

François Charles-Roux, sometime French ambassador to Iran - and a man who knew the country well - was consulted by the Élysée Palace, at this time, and heard repeated there an expression of the French President's gratification concerning the judgement passed at Guadeloupe: "at last, with Khomeyni, we shall get stability in Iran!"

"They were bad ideas, which brought bad consequences," as Jane Kirkpatrick, the American ambassador and academic, later wrote.

Outside the time passed at his office, the Shah no longer had any files to study, nor did he any longer scrutinise the international press. Strangely too - according to the testimony of Prof. Safavian, who still examined him on some mornings - he was no longer *given* any newspapers other than *Libération*, which was then far more Leftist than it is now. Sometimes, he wandered alone through the palace.

"It made you want to weep, just to look at him," one officer of the guard, who was frequently assigned to ensure the internal security of the Imperial Residence, told me, "he used to look at us, but it was as though he didn't see us - as though he were somewhere else completely."

"Audiences", which fewer and fewer officials and prominenti attended, were henceforth accorded to "ordinary" folk, and were sometimes quite poignant. Once, the capital's butchers sent a large delegation to beg the Shah not to leave. Some of them, having little knowledge of protocol, did not even remove their hats. Told of this by the duty-chamberlain, who wanted to ask them to take their hats off, the Shah ordered him not to trouble them. Several of them, threw themselves, in tears, at the Sovereign's feet, crying, "don't go, don't leave us, don't make orphans of us!"

The Shah, with great gentleness, bid them rise, himself almost weeping, saying, "nothing is decided yet, and even if we go, we shall return: I find your faithfulness very moving."

One group of Deputies also went at it full tilt: "Sire, if you do not give us your assurance that you will stay in Iran, we shall oppose the vote of confidence in Bakhtiar."

"Don't do that," replied the Sovereign, "it is urgently necessary that we form a constitutional government."

Just as they were leaving, one Deputy, weeping, seized the King's hand and said, "where will Iran be without you?
"Do not abandon us!"

Moved but dignified, the Shah reassured him.

An old professor of law, who had come to the palace for the first time in his life, said to the Shah, "Sire, if you have no confidence in your guards, I shall come with a group of friends, and we shall protect you: we shall lie down outside your bedroom door, and your enemies shall not pass, except over our dead bodies.
"You will not be more secure in foreign countries than you are here."

At Cairo, shortly before his death, the Shah told me this story, not without emotion, adding, "the old man was right - after all we have had to put up with..."

There were certainly people who still loved him!

Having fixed the date of departure, and made all the arrangements, the Shahbanou decided, with her close friends, to organise a farewell-party, at the Imperial Family's hunting-lodge, at Khodjir, which was far enough away from the capital, isolated and quiet. When told of this the Grand Huntsman, Abolfath Atabay, who had served the last Qadjar King (died 1925) and the Sovereign's father, cried indignantly, "this is no time for an evening-do!

"How shall we ensure the safety of the Shahbanou and her guests?

"The peasants of the neighbourhood might come and demonstrate."

When the Shah was asked about it, he ordered that it be allowed to go ahead, saying that the guard would take adequate precautions. The group stayed at Khodjir for about thirty-six hours, in an atmosphere, which - according to an officer of the guard - although nostalgic, was by no means sad. Little was said of current affairs, and everyone made believe that Bakhtiar would somehow re-establish control, so that the Shahbanou, at least, could soon return. They ignored, or pretended to ignore, the presence of Huyser, in Teheran, and his manoeuvers. They ignored also, no doubt, that Bakhtiar was already attempting to negotiate with Khomeyni to ensure for himself a future with the coming regime. Only the officers and agents of the guard were nervous. So relaxed was the tenor of the gathering, that some were expressing, almost openly, their astonishment that the "poor, old Shah" should have been left on his own. The word "abandoned" was used. Nevertheless, it all passed off without incident, and Mohammad Reza Pahlavi passed those hours, even more alone, and a prey to his remorse and distress.

The Shahbanou returned to Teheran on the morning of the 14th.

On the morning of the 16th January, at ten-o-clock, the Sovereign, went once more to his office. He was perfectly serene and detached. He signed a few more documents and gave his last audiences. The final one, beginning a little after eleven, was for Prof. Mohammad Baheri, a former minister, who had come to ask the Shah, yet again, not to forsake his country, his people and his army. Mohammad Reza Pahlavi listened, said, "no date has been fixed yet," and thanked his visitor for having done so much in "these difficult days". Baheri believed that there was still hope. Thereupon, he downed a cup of tea, standing up, making of this a grand consummation of the final days. Then he called his Grand Master of Protocol and the duty-chamberlain, Manoutchehr Sanei, and said, "let's go!"

The palace was almost deserted, for the courtiers had shown themselves faithless, and now the minor personnel were alerted. No-one knew until the last minute. Everyone was shocked and stunned.

At the exit to the building, Janine Dowlatshahi, the palace librarian, tells us, everyone was there - the officials, the valets, the "gorillas", all the palace staff - and the Shahbanou lingered for a few moments, "all were sobbing, some loudly, others weeping silently; a few were exchanging remarks in low voices."

The Shah and Shahbanou shook hands with everybody and said their goodbyes. The Sovereign "had a cynical, world-weary air". He was asked, for the last time, not to go.

"I shall return," he said to some of them, to calm them down.

A Colonel of the guard, in uniform, casting military convention aside, fell at the Shah's feet, saying, "do not leave us, Sire - do not abandon your country!"

For an instant, the Sovereign froze, as though unable to move, but the Shahbanou, somewhat piqued, intervened, saying to the officer, "Don't bother His Majesty like this, can't you see you're embarrassing him?"

The Shah took advantage of her intervention to recover himself, extend both hands and raise the officer to his feet.

A small, disorganized crowd walked with the Imperial Couple as far as the heliport. It all lasted about an hour.

The Shah and Shabanou took a helicopter each, doubtless for security reasons. The Shah was accompanied, in his, by Aslan Afshar and Colonel Djahanbini, an officer of the guard. With the Shahbanou, went Mrs Pirnia (the family doctor) and Colonel Nevissi. The little gathering of staff pressed closely around the two helicopters. Twice, the King lowered a side-window, to tell the bystanders to move back, for the blades were turning faster and faster.

He travelled often enough by car to "sniff", as he used to say, "the air of the city", see the people at close quarters and watch their reactions; but he loved, sometimes, to look down on his capital and his country, from the sky. This would be the last time. In the helicopter, as they flew, he said not a single word. He was infinitely sad, but profoundly attentive. He scrutinised the city, as though looking for something. What was he thinking?

The helicopters, which had taken off almost at the same time, landed, a few minutes later, close to the modest, Imperial Pavilion at Mehrabad, the international airport of the Iranian capital.

A glacial wind blew across the runways. All departing flights had been postponed, for more than an hour, as a security measure. The air-traffic controllers were intermittently on strike, in some places, and so, here, they had been replaced by military personnel.

Mohammad Reza Pahlavi's face was locked into immobility, although he was almost in tears. He was impeccable, as always, in a dark-grey suit, with a finely striped tie and a midnight-blue cashmere overcoat. He stood, straight as a ram-rod, his bearing as haughty as ever.

The Shahbanou, even if she did harbour some vague hope of coming back, was in no doubt that she was about to take part in her last official act in the company of her husband - an act watched and recorded throughout the world, and consigned to history - and so she had taken care over this, her exit from the stage, appearing, with complete elegance, in a beige, lambs-wool coat, trimmed at the neck with fur, a matching hat and snug, patent-leather boots.

As much as care had been taken to keep the event secret, a small group of officials were waiting for the Imperial Couple. There were the President of the Chamber, Djavad Said, who would shortly be shot - mainly because of his presence there, that morning - the Minister to the Imperial Court, Ali Gholi Ardalan, and the principal chiefs of the army. The octogenarian president of the Senate, Mohammad Sadjadi, did not turn up, which helped to save his life, after the triumph of the revolution; and there were no ministers in attendance, and no foreign diplomats.

Prime Minister Bakhtiar did come. He arrived, by helicopter, about an hour after the Imperial Couple - an interminable period, which the Sovereign, longing to get all this over with, had to fill with small-talk, while pretending that his Prime Minister's rudeness was having no adverse effect whatsoever.

Bakhtiar did arrive, however, and the Shah talked with him, for a few minutes, in the Pavilion's reception-room, not forgetting to give him several instructions: "above all, attend to the security of those who have served me and who are still in the country," he said (as he told me later)

Lined up on the steps of the Pavilion, each of his generals stepped forward to kiss his hand. General Badrei, a giant of a man - well over six feet tall - originally from Luristan, who had recently been promoted to become Commander-in-Chief of the army, after leading the Imperial Guard for many years, knelt down with the intention of embracing the Sovereign's knees - a dramatic, tribal gesture of fealty. The Shah bent, extending his right hand to lift him up. He was clutching his spectacles in his left.

"Do not abandon us, Sire!" said Badrei.

388

The Sovereign looked at him, saying nothing, but keeping the general's hand in his, for a moment. Then he passed to the next. Everyone shed tears.

There was no guard of honour, which, it was thought, would have been out of place. In accordance with Muslim tradition, however, a Koran was held up over the couple's heads, as the Shah and Shahbanou climbed into the Imperial Flight, a blue-and-white Boeing-707, which had been given the name "Shahine".

Mohammad Reza Pahlavi invited his Prime Minister on board, wished him, once again, courage and good luck, and then said in a loud voice, "I entrust Iran to you and commend you to God's protection."

Bakhtiar, who, in front of the cameras, a few moments before, had appeared cold and distant, was now visibly moved and bent to kiss the King's hand. When he got back to the Presidency of the Council, however, he announced to the international press, "I've kicked out the Shah!"

The destination was Aswan, in Egypt, but this was only provisional - a staging post. At the end of December, or the beginning of January, the US ambassador, William Sullivan, had conveyed to the Shah an official invitation from his government, to make an, albeit private, visit to the other side of the Atlantic. This was to re-assure him and speed up his preparations for departure. He decided, therefore, to go to the USA, for two months, accompanied only by Aslan Afshar, who was himself a former ambassador to Washington. Protocol had even been applied to the preparation and arrangement of certain matters of business and to the provision of suitable presents for certain people. The Shah, although he had at last realised that the process in train had been orchestrated by Washington, was still sufficiently confident, in his numerous friends and his own powers of persuasion, to believe that he was capable of reversing the current. He wanted to explain to the President, to the Senate, to the National Security Council, in business-circles, and to the CIA, just how important Iran was for the free world, and the USA, in maintaining the regional equilibrium, and how dangerous it would be to allow his country to fall into the hands of radical Islamists.

The American ambassador had assured Mohammad Reza Pahlavi that he would be welcome in Washington, and he believed, or seemed to believe, that the Shah would be. During the last week in January, the Grand Master of Protocol and Ardeshir Zahedi made preparations for the journey, planning all the meetings in secrecy and haste. The aircraft, carrying the Sovereign, would land at Andrews Air-Force Base, not far from Washington. The Shah would stay a few days in the American capital, meet President Carter in the course of a luncheon or a dinner, and other important people, at his convenience. It had been envisaged that he would go on to stay at the house, in Palm Springs, of Walter Annenberg, a billionaire press-baron and former ambassador to London, who was, above all, an old friend. There, he could compose himself in peace and follow up his initiatives.

These arrangements suited the Shah. They constituted a last attempt. Bakhtiar would have to hold out for a few weeks, but that was a chance, which had to be taken. After the Guadeloupe conference, the tone changed, however. To Washington, and to her British and French allies, Mohammad Reza Pahlavi was nothing more than a Head-of-State on his way out. The

Americans were thinking of how to arrange their relations with the future, Islamic regime, and so William Sullivan went to see the Shah again. He could go to the USA, of course, but there was no longer any question of an official meeting with President Carter. His aircraft would have to land at an obscure military base, in Maine, or South Carolina, and at night. Then he would go on to Travis Base, in California, and, from there, by helicopter, to his friend, Annenberg's, estate. Sullivan looked at his watch, and even waved it at the Shah, to indicate that the urgency of his departure was no longer a question of days, but of hours. The Shah resented this deeply and believed that he had been insulted.

That was when the option of a half-way stage in Egypt presented itself, and the hospitality of President Sadat. It was learned that another American friend, the former President, Gerald Ford, was also in Egypt, at that time, and so Mohammad Reza Pahlavi hoped again that he would be able to do something in the way of exploiting his connections.

Anwar Sadat's reaction, to the prospect of the Shah's imminent arrival, was that of a man of honour, a friend and a brother: "never," the President declared, "will Egypt forget the aid which Iran sent to Egypt, during the war of 1973."

In the plane, the Shah took the controls, as was his wont, the Air-Force Colonel, Behzad Moezzi assisting him as co-pilot. It was an amazing feat for a man on the edge of physical and psychological collapse. An hour later, as the aircraft slipped out of Iranian air-space and ploughed on over Saudi-Arabia, the Shah returned to his suite.

"I'm completely done in," he said

"But Sire," Afshar chided, "why did you exert yourself to fly the machine?"

"For reasons of security," was the reply.

He was thinking, no doubt, of Hassan II's unfortunate experience, a few years before. He wanted to have control of the aircraft.

There were three people, in the cabin's Imperial Suite, with the Sovereign - Shahbanou Farah, Aslan Afshar and the doctor, Lucie Pirnia. Mrs Pirnia was the wife of the former head of Teheran University's Faculty of Medicine, Dr Abolghassem, but was herself a general practitioner and paediatrician, who had formerly attended the children of the Imperial Household. Leaving her home and family, with a small suitcase in her hand, she joined the Imperial Couple in exile. She was totally devoted to the Shah.

In the other part of the cabin, were Col. Kioumars Djahanbini, an officer of the Shah's guard, Col. Yazdan Nevissi, the Queen's personal bodyguard, several other bodyguards, who were later sent back to Teheran, two of the Shah's valets, Amir Pourshodja and Mahmoud Eliassi and the palace's chief cook, Ali Kabiri. Kabiri had not received any instructions regarding the meals to be served on board the 'plane, and so, on his own initiative, he had prepared a single Iranian dish, thinking, first and foremost, of the guards. Unfortunately, the airport-services, to which an officer had been dispatched, just before take-off, were only able to provide a few sandwiches, because they were semi-paralysed, and reduced to a minimum, by a strike.

Anyway, lunch was soon over. The King ate almost nothing and sank into silence. Eventually he said, "I'm very tired, and

I don't want to be a nuisance, so I've asked Aslan to keep an eye on things and keep me up to date..."

The trip to Aswan took about three hours. At Aswan International Airport, the Imperial Couple were welcomed, and fittingly received, by President and Mrs Sadat. The Raïs ("leader" or "president", in Arabic) came up the gangway to meet the Shah. The two men shook hands, and then embraced, warmly.

"Be quite sure," Sadat said, "that this country is yours and that we are your people's brethren."

Mohammad Reza Pahlavi was moved to tears.

A guard of honour was drawn up for the Shah; then, a twenty-one gun salute was fired. The Sadats conducted the Imperial Couple to the Oberoi Hotel, situated, in secure isolation, on an island in the Nile. On the way, thousands of people applauded the Shah and the Raïs, along streets hung with Iranian flags and portraits of the Shah. It was a welcome fit for a friendly Head-of-State. After a dinner, taken with the Presidential Couple, a few hours rest, from which the Shah emerged visibly much brighter, and a greatly appreciated excursion, the following day, up the Nile, to Abu Simbel, politics took over once again.

In spite of the Raïs' insistence that the Shah remain in Egypt - he had already suggested to him that he transfer parts of the Iranian Air-Force and Navy, to Egypt, in order to use them as a kind of trump-card, or springboard - the latter persisted in his idea of going on to the USA. There was a lot of telephoning going on between Aswan and America, and several friends were persuaded to take a hand, in this way. The Shah and Gerald Ford met twice - for three hours, on one occasion.

The Imperial Couple had the Iranian ambassador in Cairo, Nayeri, and his wife, to lunch. These two had come to see them as soon as they learned of their arrival.

To have done with the matter, which preoccupied him, the Shah told Aslan Afshar to call the US ambassador at Cairo, and ask him directly, what the position of his government was, and to fix a date, at last. The Grand Master of Protocol did so. The ambassador requested a few hours before replying and called back the following day.

"The government of the United States regrets that it cannot welcome the Shah to American territory," was essentially what he said, effectively banishing all further hope from that quarter.

The Shah had no intention of remaining in Egypt and, thereby, of becoming an encumbrance to his faithful friend, who was anyway about to depart on a state-visit to another country. For one thing, the security-measures, which his presence at Aswan required, were inconvenient for the season's numerous tourists.

It was then, thanks to a call from Ardeshir Zahedi - who had left Teheran, but remained very active - that King Hassan II invited the Imperial Couple to Morocco. This invitation was immediately accepted. On 22nd January, therefore, the Pahlavis were accompanied to Aswan airport, by President and Mrs Sadat, and, after the official ceremony, they set off for Marrakesh.

Arranging the Imperial Couple's stay in Mexico: Ardeshir
Zahedi went, in person, to Mexico and was invited to dinner
by President Lopes Portillo (right) who presented him with
the Mexican Government's written agreement.

(Ardeshir Zahedi Collection)

Part Two

ORDEAL

November 1977 – The White House, Washington DC – a meeting between the Shah and President Carter. Ardeshir Zahedi, who was then the Iranian Ambassador, and to whom Jimmy Carter presented this photograph, is shown to the right of the Sovereign. To the left of the Shah, is shown Abbas Khalatbari, the Iranian Foreign Minister. Sitting next to, and beyond, President Carter, is Zbigniew Kazimierz Brzezinski.

(Ardeshir Zahedi Collection)

Chapter XIII

"The Americans have been trying to bring about my downfall, ever since 1974"

22nd January - 10th June 1979

Mohammad Reza Pahlavi was still the King, but, in Egypt, he abandoned all hope of being able to go to the USA and convince the Americans that they should give up their policy and adopt another. Too many signs had shown, over the years, that their current policy, even though it had been implemented by a Democratic administration, had been conceived and developed long before. American hostility towards him was not just a whim of recent months.

Once he left Iran, the Shah no longer had any cards to play. He no longer had an army to back him up, or the silent majority to appeal to. Both would have stood by him, but he actively discouraged them from doing so, and now he was a king without a kingdom, nor even an objective. While he was in Morocco, he realised it - that his political life was over, that he had no role to play and that the curtain had fallen.

When the Sovereign's Boeing put down, on 22nd January, at Marrakesh airport, King Hassan II was there to welcome him, but there was no guard of honour, no cameras. The local press had even been told to keep quiet about the visit, because it was "strictly private and should proceed without any fuss".

The Imperial Couple were lodged in the Jiran-el-Kabir palace, at an oasis outside Marrakesh, with a wonderful view of the Atlas Mountains - another secure and isolated spot.

Hassan II had agreed to receive the Shah, out of friendship. Certainly, the two men liked each other, but the Malik's (King's) gesture was also a recognition of the fact that Iran had been of considerable assistance to Morocco over the years. All the same, it was provisional hospitality, "for some days". The Moroccan authorities had made it clear to the Shah's entourage that they were not expecting them to stay.

"We do hope," they said, "that His Majesty the Shah's plan, to go to the United States, will be realised according to his wishes."

At first everything was relatively tranquil. After some days at Marrakesh, the Imperial Couple went to Rabat and stayed at another palace belonging to the Sherifian Crown, the Dar-es-Salaam. Mohammad Reza Pahlavi took long walks in the palace gardens, scanned the international press, read several books and began to learn golf, one of the few sports he had never taken up. Hassan II came regularly to see him.

Ardeshir Zahedi, whom Bakhtiar had dismissed from the post of ambassador to Washington, also came to see the Shah and, before long, he would play an important part in shaping the Sovereign's future. Aslan Afshar was constantly at the King's side, frequently accompanying him even when he was out walking and even though he was more often silent and withdrawn than talkative.

The Iranian ambassador to Morocco, Farhad Sepahbodi, was another regular visitor to Dar-es-Salaam, despite knowing that the Cabinet in Teheran would not appreciate this, and that it would cost him dear, if Bakhtiar managed to hang on or, even worse, if the revolution triumphed.

Prof. Safavian, His Majesty's official physician for the last two months, who was spending a sabbatical year in Paris, came to see the Shah and Shahbanou on two occasions. Still, almost no-one knew that Mohammad Reza Pahlavi was dangerously ill. These medical visits were considered to be purely routine, insofar as they were not also a sign of friendship; and so it was that the medical practitioner's famous oath of discretion, concerning the exercise of his profession, was sufficient to ensure that the matter continued to go unnoticed.

To satisfy the urgent requests of the international press, the two Kings prepared themselves for a "photo-shoot" in the palace-gardens. The Shah greeted some of the journalists he recognised, notably Pierre Salinger, but he only gave one interview, and that to the *London Daily Telegraph*, which was one of the few, great, western newspapers to have supported him throughout his ordeal. He did speak also, in private, with an Iranian journalist, who had long been living in France and who was someone he trusted. This was Freidoun Sahebjam. They had a friendly conversation, no account of which was published until much later.

Hassan II urged the Shah to write his memoirs and give his version of events for the sake of posterity, for history; and the Sovereign was enthusiastic about the idea. However, without his usual counsellor, in such matters, Chodja-Ol-Dine, he didn't know how to go about it. The Moroccan King advised him to go to the publishers, Albin Michel, and especially to Henry Bonnier, whom he knew well and who was then the company's literary editor. Bonnier was brought to Rabat and presented to the Shah. A relationship of trust grew up between the two men, and the book, which would be entitled "A Reply To History" was begun.

Requests for audience flooded in, via the Iranian ambassador, or directly to the Grand Master of Protocol, from Iranians living abroad, whose number was now being swelled by those who were fleeing the onrush of the revolution. The Shah would accept none of them. He was tired, he said, and wished to keep his distance. By contrast, numerous friends and allies of the Shahbanou made the journey to see her. The Shah hardly bothered to greet them and took his meals alone, while they were there!

It was at this time that he began an epistolary relationship with Soraya, his former Empress, and the only woman, so some of his close friends say, whom he had ever really loved. After their divorce, they had only met once, in Paris, some ten years before, and, since then, they had ceased writing to each other. Now the letters, from both parties, were entrusted to reliable messengers - three of them, to my knowledge - and I can tell you that Mohammad Reza Pahlavi drew great comfort from them.

Shapour Bakhtiar telephoned him once, very briefly, to ask after his health, as he put it. There was no discussion of the domestic situation in Iran.

The military, meanwhile, were demanding, ever more urgently, the authorisation to restore order, and, when the date of Ayatollah Khomeyni's return to Iran was fixed, these demands became anguished. The Head of the General Staff, Gharabaghi, was silent, however. He was already negotiating with Huyser and with the revolutionary leaders, but the three Commanders-in-Chief, Badrei, of the army, Rabii, of the air-force (another, fine, Kurdish serviceman) and Habibollah, of the navy - as well as General Khosrodad, the commander of the parachute regiment - were expressing their extreme disquiet and their impatience for instructions. The Shah took note of their messages, but he too remained mute. Was this for fear of shedding his compatriots' blood - or because he no longer had the strength to make the least decision?

In fact, at Teheran, these officers, and some others, whom the international press were calling "the army hard-liners" had prepared a "plan for national salvation". Their idea was to strike hard at the radical opposition and set up a military government under General Badrei. This would have been a coup-d'État, since Bakhtiar would thereby have been deposed. The cost, in terms of casualties, would have been high, as it was, much later, in Algeria, when the military intervened to put down the Islamists, but, on balance, the bloodshed would have been far less than that occasioned by the revolution, with its hundreds of thousands of victims.

On the day after Khomeyni's arrival in Teheran - the 1st February - I called General Badrei to tell him how worried I was, about the situation. I was not a party to his plan, but I knew enough about it to guess that something was being prepared. Badrei told me, "everything is ready.
"I'm not afraid of this character and his gang.

"I'm just waiting for a word - for a sign - from His Majesty, because I will not act illegally."

No word, nor even any sign, ever came.

For months, the King had been preventing any manifestation, by those who wished to organise one, either of support for himself, or of opposition to the revolutionary process. He desired, so he said, "to avoid confrontations between Iranians, and any spilling of blood". Perhaps he also feared - though, naturally, he would not have said this - that the size of any demonstrations in his favour, would not have matched that of the opposition's demonstrations.

After 16th January, these forces were liberated and set in motion. Small, semi-secret publications came to light, proclaiming counter-revolutionary ideas. Only one, established weekly, *Khandaniha* - whose editor, Ali Asghar Amirani, was shot, for this reason, when the revolution triumphed - and which had been critical enough of all the governments of the previous twenty years - maintained a counter-revolutionary stance. All the big dailies, on the other hand, passed into the hands of revolutionary committees. The writer and pamphleteer, Mehdi Bahar, published a small work, decrying the fundamentalist threat, which sold thousands of copies, although how it was photocopied and distributed remains a mystery. Small meetings were held "to organise resistance", mobilise forces and set up networks.

One small committee, taking advantage of the prevailing anarchy, occupied the Amjadieh sports-centre, in the middle of a very lively part of the capital, and transformed it into a counter-revolutionary head-quarters. In the course of a few days, three public meetings took place there. The well-established continuum of residents' associations of the capital, a big sporting-club - the TADJ - and another, smaller one - some farming cooperatives on the outskirts of the city, a trade-union and some some small, ad-hoc groups of academics, all lent their support to the initiative. A coordination committee of ten members was created and presided over by the young journalist and Teherani municipal councillor, Mohammad Reza Taghizadeh. It decided to hold a public demonstration, on 25th January, and despatched a delegation to Shapour Bakhtiar. The Prime Minister voiced grave reservations, saying, "you will aggravate divisions, and you won't get 2000 people."

He also told them that they could expect "neither help, nor support," from him Later, he wrote, "they asked me to assist them with this demonstration, but I refused."

He did ask the delegates from the organisation-committee, nevertheless, not to use any slogans in favour of the Shah, and to limit themselves to calling for the defence of the constitution. They accepted. At least, Bakhtiar did not send out messages via National Radio-Television to dissuade people from attending!

On Friday 25th January, twelve columns of demonstrators startled the capital. The main one came from the Amjadieh sports-centre. All converged on Baharestan Square, a symbolic spot, in front of the Houses of Parliament. It was an immense crowd. Even the national press, which was under the control of revolutionary committees, estimated it at between 150 000 and 300 000 people - and that was without a column of about 50 000 workers, from the factories to the west of the capital, who, on the orders of the Prime Minister, were prevented from reaching the Square. There was an impressive display of Iranian flags, covering miles of the city's thoroughfares. If it had been a pro-Khomeyni demonstration, the media would have made no bones about saying that there were half-a-million people there.

In Baharestan Square, the celebrated orator, the Hodjatoleslam Behbahani (who was assassinated on the day after the fall of the imperial regime) spoke, calling upon all present to defend the nation, and Mohammad Reza Taghizadeh read out a resolution to this effect.

At that moment, the demonstration began to get out of hand! One young man cried, "djavad Shah!" ("long live the King!") - a very traditional and familiar slogan - and some other demonstrators took it up. Then it was suddenly a huge clamour, passing in waves throughout the throng, and many wept with the emotion of it all, as the march transformed itself into a popular demonstration in favour of the absent Shah.

When he learned, from some friends, of the size of the crowd, the Prime Minister went up in his helicopter to over-fly the Square. By the beginning of the afternoon, the workers from the west of the capital had succeeded in reaching the Presidency of the Council, and Bakhtiar received a delegation from them; but he only said that he was astonished by the size of the demonstration and invited the delegates to keep calm and disperse to their homes.

The same evening, the organising committee met again, to draw lessons from the event, and agreed to organise another demonstration a fortnight later, in the firm belief that they would be able to assemble as many people, next time, as the Khomeyni-ites had been able to muster, a few days earlier.

On the next day but one, my wife and I were lunching at home with Admiral Ardalan (head of the national armaments industry) and vice-Admiral Deyhimi, the deputy Commander-in-Chief of the navy. General Moin-Zadeh, head of military intelligence, was supposed to be joining us an hour later. We discussed the political situation, the imminent arrival of Khomeyni and the impact of the powerful demonstration, two days before. The telephone rang. It was the Shahbanou. I presented my respects and those of my friends present, and asked for "news of His Majesty". She asked me about the situation in Iran, which I then described in a few words, and especially about the demonstration the previous Friday. She seemed stunned by its dimensions. The foreign press had hardly mentioned it - neither the numbers present, nor the slogans. I beseeched her to speak to the King about it. She thanked me with her usual affability and asked me, in turn, to say hello, from her, to the officers at my table. The latter were also greatly impressed with the amplitude of Friday's gathering and the content of the cries expressed. Were we, we wondered, witnessing a spectacular turning of the tide of popular opinion?

Later, in Mexico, during my first private conversation with the Shah, after his flight, I told him about that demonstration and the shouts of "God save the King!" merging into one vast, continuous shout. He was touched, became pensive and fell silent for a few moments, before pronouncing that terrible admission: "Perhaps, I deceived myself about the feelings of my people towards me," and he looked at me for a long time, with the gaze of bottomless regret.

After much hesitation, the Ayatollah Khomeyni arrived in Teheran on the 1st February 1979. All the published accounts, including those most favourable to him, agree that he was afraid - afraid of the army, of an "accident" and of being arrested - but things went exactly as his sponsors and supporters wished. He was hailed as a victor and the future master of Iran. American officials even took part in the committee for organising the welcome, which will strike many as surreal. Bakhtiar continued to make declarations about the firmness of his democratic convictions, while attempting to gain favour in secret negotiations with Khomeyni's group. According to the memoirs[*] of Mehdi Bazargan, who was openly sympathetic to Bakhtiar, he even proposed, as a token of his goodwill, to go to Morocco to obtain the Shah's abdication; but, without the army behind him, he represented nothing. However, he was more worried about the army than he was about the extreme Left or about their temporary allies, the Islamists - a position reminiscent of that of Kerensky, in revolutionary Russia, long before.

In the aftermath of Khomeyni's arrival, an impressive military procession, through the streets of the capital, was organised - on the initiative of General Ali Neshat, Commander of the Imperial Guard[**] - in order to show off the army's armoured vehicles and fire-power. In many quarters of the city, the populace massed in the streets to applaud the soldiers; in others, some stones were thrown. There were counter-revolutionary demonstrations also in numerous, provincial cities, where pro- and anti-Khomeyni factions confronted one another, sometimes violently.

It only remained to arrange the transfer of power, and, once again, the Americans were foremost among the intermediaries employed for this purpose.

---

[*] *Iranian Revolution In Two Movements*, Teheran 1983.
[**] He who was assassinated shortly after the revolution.

On 5th February, this person - now based in a secondary school near the centre of Teheran - nominated a Prime Minister. His nominee was Mehdi Bazargan, a retired academic, prosperous businessman, former colleague of Mossadegh and a *moderate* Islamist. An Islamic, revolutionary council was set up to take over the country's supreme, governing functions. Various ministers performed ceremonies of allegiance to the new "prime minister", but Bakhtiar still occupied the Presidency of the Council, and some ministers continued to attend at their offices, even though these were now empty of staff.

On 11th February, towards noon, an ad-hoc council of senior army-officers - consisting of twenty-seven generals - proclaimed "the neutrality of the army" and placed all barracks "under the protection of the people". The mastermind of this move was army-General Hossein Fardoust, who had been a friend and companion of the Shah, since the days of their primary education. He was one of Iran's most powerful men, Director of the Imperial Inspectorate and of the Special Bureau for coordinating and controlling the security-services; but he was a shadowy figure, with strange attitudes and morals. He was to be the founder of the "Savama", the security-service of the revolutionary regime, and would, in general, play - though always out of the limelight - an important role in government, after Khomeyni came to power. Five years later, his death was announced, with no other comment. He might have been, as certain, highly-placed people in western intelligence have since told me, a Soviet agent, a mole of long standing - like many others of high rank in the great countries of the West - who was placed in proximity to the Shah, or he could have been a double, or even a triple, agent. According to the same sources, he was not dead, as was announced, but recalled by his controllers to the Soviet Union. This remains a minor mystery in the great sweep of true history, which will be elucidated, one day.

The other organiser of the set-up was the Chief of the General Staff, Gharabaghi. Not only did he take care of the neutralisation of the army, but, instead of preserving the army, by confining officers and men to barracks, he ordered them to disperse.

Witness-statements gathered, about the next decisive hours, are particularly significant. At Echrat Abad, a barracks of the National Police's rapid-reaction unit, were 3000 men trained for urban intervention, and their specialist vehicles, who had been kept in reserve since the very beginning of the unrest. Their commander, General Firouzbakhch, was on the 'phone all day to his superiors trying to obtain orders from them; but the answer was always the same: "do not react, avoid bloodshed."

Towards midday, shots were fired, from the surroundings, towards the barracks, and it appeared that some machine-guns, mounted on the roof of a nearby cinema, the "Moulin Rouge", were aimed directly at Firouzbakhch's men. Naturally, he wanted to do something positive about this.

"If I make a sortie," he told the brass-hats, "I can sort this out, and stop any nonsense round here, in less than an hour."

The brass replied, "get your men under cover!"

At about four-o-clock, the final orders came through: "hoist a white flag and disperse!"

Firouzbakhch could only comply. His men remained disciplined until they were disbanded.

That morning, a similar situation arose at the barracks of The

Guard, where, the approach of attackers having been observed, and General Neshat's order, to remain on site, having been received, a decision was made to resist "to the last cartridge and the last drop of blood". Everyone took up his position. Then the order came through not to resist but to give up and disband, which they did. There, considering that they were the Imperial Guard, was merciless carnage not inevitable?

The airborne division at Baghe-Shah, apart from three cases of indiscipline in the ranks, underwent the same process.

The men of the Special Forces, many of whom were former paratroops, and all of whom were particularly well trained, were based at Mehran. They were surrounded by a mob of several thousands, which had been placed there to shield an attacking force consisting largely of foreigners. The encircled soldiers had received the order, as in other cases, not to react, even though they were threatened with massacre. Of their 480-man strength, 168 were killed. The others were able to get away, some of them still armed. Afterwards they re-formed as a resistance-network, which persisted for some years, until age took its toll.

The capital's police-stations, where the men were very poorly armed, all resisted and would not surrender. A slaughter ensued. No-one knows how many died.

So it was also with the elite units in Teheran - a mighty force, which, with the support of a fraction of the population, could have changed destiny. They too were made to surrender almost without firing a shot. It was, almost entirely, a political defeat, the direct cause of which was the behaviour of the Head of the General Staff. Afterwards, he attempted to justify himself, mainly by blaming Shapour Bakhtiar, who, it is true, had worked to avoid the intervention of the army, and who had disappeared in the process. Perhaps he felt obliged to obey the Shah's instructions, as formulated in his political manifesto. The Americans probably got to him too. I can't think of any other likely explanation.

The assassination of General Badrei, in the course of that decisive afternoon, deprived the army of the chief it might have had. The waste was enormous. It was a terrible blood-letting.

In general, the process of the destruction of the armed forces, begun, as it was, by the Shah's disastrous speech of 6th November ("I have heard the voice of your revolution") is explicable in terms of the command-structure of the army, which was so constituted that it could not act without the agreement, or rather, the expressed order, of its constitutional Commander-in-Chief, the King.

The decision to "neutralise" the army, as taken by Gharabaghi, however, was contrary to Iranian, military regulations and traditions, because, even though the ad hoc council, convened by generals Gharabaghi and Fardoust, was able to propose it, the final decision should have been made by the National Security Council, presided over by the Prime Minister, who became, in fact, the supreme head of the armed forces, after the departure of the Shah. It has not been grasped, even if, as it seems, it has been confirmed, that those, who thus permitted, or actively desired (according to some) the disintegration of the army, were guilty of the gravest crime one can commit, in the eyes of history and of one's country. No more than two or three of them should be permitted to keep their heads.

After the meeting of the ad-hoc council came to an end, an acrimonious exchange occurred between General Badrei, Commander-in-Chief of the army, and Fardoust and Gharabaghi: "things will be intolerable if the army gives way to someone like Khomeyni!" he said to them, before shouting, "I'm going to stop the country plunging into bloody anarchy."

Then he boarded his helicopter, to return to his control-centre, and called his second-in-command, Lieutenant-General Wochmguir, telling him to convene an urgent meeting of the senior officers of the army and make immediate preparations for troop-movements. After the flight, Badrei disembarked and walked towards his offices. As he did so, he was shot in the back by a volley of automatic gunfire. One of his deputies, who was with him - Major General Amine Beyglari, another Kurd, and like Beyglari, a man after the heart of the Commander of the Military Academy - was also mortally wounded.

In the hours which followed, Teheran decided that the two men had been killed by an American, military adviser to the army, but this was just an unverifiable rumour. As for General Wochmguir, he was arrested shortly afterwards, tortured and eventually put to death; but, from prison, he managed to pass a short note, to one of his close friends - the journalist Firouz Modjallali - concerning the circumstances of his superior officer's assassination. I had the privilege of reading this heart-rending scrap of paper, when this mutual friend and I, both found ourselves in exile, in Paris.

The declaration of neutrality, or rather, the neutralisation, of the army was announced every half-hour on national radio, while Bakhtiar, having declaimed in the Senate, that morning, that he would stand and fight, gun in hand - and compared himself to Salvador Allende - left the Presidency, jumped into a helicopter and made off. He was arrested the day after next, kept for some days, under guard, in the same building as Hoveyda and a few other dignitaries, and then released, reaching France, incognito, a few weeks later. He survived an assassination-attempt, at Neuilly, on 18th July 1980, but had his throat cut by the agents of the Islamic Republic, on 6th August 1991, at his house in Suresnes.

On the evening of 11th February, three heavy-transport aircraft, which were never officially identified - but they could have been Syrian, or Libyan - disembarked, at Teheran, several hundred Palestinian irregulars, who had come to put the Imperial regime to death, definitively and by main force. Towards half-past-nine, with looting already well under way, a beardless mullah, unknown the public until then, and presented as Hodjatoleslam Rafsandjani, proclaimed on TV that Khomeyni was now the master of Iran.

The following day, the 12th, found the Shah thinking about the legal status of the Imperial aircraft. Always this astonishing concern for details with him!

"It's not ours," he said, "we'll have to send it back to Teheran."

Some of his suite advised him that this was his personal aeroplane and that he should retain control of it, but he would only snap angrily, "it's an aircraft of the Iranian Air-Force," and everyone present noticed that his habitual use of the phrase, "Imperial Air-Force", had suddenly ceased.

"It has to go back," he pronounced with finality.

414

Then he went personally to thank Colonel Moezzi, who had been his pilot for some time, and all the on-board personnel, before asking Aslan Afshar to give each of them a considerable sum of money in rials - in Iranian money - and not in any foreign currency.

"In this way," he said, "if they are asked, on arrival, where they got this money from, they can say that it belongs to them."

Unfortunately, rials are not easy to exchange in Morocco. Before leaving Iran, Aslan Afshar had drawn the twelve months salary, which was owing to him, from the Department of Protocol's budget, but this was not a very large sum. The others emptied their pockets. Luckily, Djafar Behbahanian, manager of the Imperial Couple's personal fortune, had just arrived in Morocco, bringing with dollars, in small and large denominations. Consequently, the accumulated rials were exchanged for dollars, and Behbahanian went to see Moezzi and his aircrew, giving to each of them, according to his rank, an envelope of a certain size, on behalf of His Majesty.

Then the King told Aslan Afshar to get clearance, from the Moroccans, for a late-night take-off: "if they are asked to explain themselves, in Teheran," the Sovereign said, "they only have to say that they left here, at dead of night, without our permission."

At eight-o-clock, he gave audience to Moezzi, Moezzi's co-pilot, the engineer and the air-stewards, all of whom wept. The Shah thanked each one, with emotion, and bid them all goodbye. Moezzi went down on his knees before the King, took the royal hand in both of his own and said, "Sire, I shall avenge you!"

On their return, they were interrogated, but not troubled. Such are the vagaries of fate that Colonel Moezzi flew, in the same aircraft, the first President of the Islamic Republic, Bani Sadr, to Paris, when the latter was sent into exile. He subsequently rejoined the islamo-marxist opposition to the Teheran-regime.

In the days after the proclamation of the new government, most of the world's states, including, of course, the USA, recognised it officially. In their eyes, Mohammad Reza Pahlavi was now no more than a deposed King, an exile and an embarrassment.

When he had arrived in Morocco, it had already been made clear to him that his stay was only expected to last a few days. Now he was shown the door; but where could he go?

The Imperial Couple were about to experience the same cowardly inhospitality, experienced by Nicholas II and his family, after the last Tsar abdicated, and was refused asylum, not only by his British and Danish cousins, but also by his preferred allies, the French. Now the Shah, who had succoured all exiled sovereigns, albeit with the greatest discretion, could find no-one to take him in.

Mohammad Reza Pahlavi had wished to prolong his visit to Morocco by several weeks, or even more, but King Hassan - from behind a facade of perfect courtesy - was becoming more and more impatient to get rid of him, which the Moroccans did not neglect to let the Shah's entourage know.

Ardeshir Zahedi, supported at first by Aslan Afshar - who was, however, soon obliged to leave by the worsening state (to the point of death) of his mother's health - set his world-wide network of contacts to work, looking for a solution. The Swiss excused themselves. After the Neauphle-le-Château episode, a French refusal was never in doubt and was also very swift in coming. London was approached as well, despite the Shah's opposition - he knew only too well British diplomacy's hostility towards him, and his father before him - and provided the expected negative result. It was known, all the same, that Margaret Thatcher, leader of the Conservative Party, had promised officially that, if she won the forthcoming elections, she would willingly welcome the Iranian Imperial Family, but that was still only a prospect for the future.

The American envoys, Richard Parker - the ambassador to Morocco, who was also a CIA agent - and Lyndon Johnson's former under-secretary of commerce, Don Agger, came to tell the King about Moroccan disquiet, concerning the prolongation of his visit to Morocco, and to repeat Washington's refusal to accept him. They did express interest in finding him a more permanent destination, without, however, proposing anything, which was acceptable to the Shah.

They suggested Paraguay. The Shah refused point-blank. Then they mentioned South Africa, a country which had been friendly to Iran, and which, conveniently, was ready to take him in. The Shah hesitated. He didn't like the idea of going to the country of apartheid - a move which his enemies would not hesitate to use against him. Also, South Africa held unpleasant memories for him, for his father had been deported to that country, by the British, and had died there. Nevertheless, he did not actually say no.

It was then that a man, whom Mohammad Reza Pahlavi considered to be a personal friend, appeared in Morocco. The two men had met discreetly many times over the years, and

417

this man - Count Alexandre de Marenches, head of the French intelligence-services - in his turn, respected and admired the Shah and was also a friend and confidant of Hassan II, who was responsible, on this occasion, for asking the Count to come and see the Sovereign and attempt resolve the situation. The Paris government too encouraged the Count to intervene, fearful that the Sovereign's presence in Morocco might stir up trouble there. The Shah and Shahbanou received the Count together.

"This," the Shahhbanou noted later, "was one of the most tragic interviews of my life."

De Marenches described, in particular, the threats which had been made, against Hassan II and his family, by certain elements, who were, in general, exploiting the implications of his hospitality to the Shah, whereupon the Sovereign's hesitation ceased.

"Both sovereigns honoured me with their confidence," the Count concluded, "and accepted that I was acting in the general interest."

When the Grand Master of Protocol was about to take his leave, the King reflected on their wanderings to date: "in Teheran," he said, "I asked Anthony Parsons, 'what would you do if Khomeyni wanted to go the United Kingdom?' to which he replied at once, 'if he had a valid passport, he could stay for three months and apply, thereupon, for permission to stay longer,' but I am quite sure that the British will not allow me to travel to the United Kingdom."

Indeed, this had already become clear. He then proceeded to an historical analysis of his relations with the West: "from the middle of the 'sixties, when Iran concluded its agreement with Mattei [President of the Italian oil-company, AGIP, whose 'plane exploded in flight and whose policies had been at variance with those of the major oil-companies] I was increasingly mistrusted, by the big players in the industry, because I wanted to dissolve the constraints they were imposing; and the more I succeeded, the worse it got - especially after the adjustment in oil-prices at the beginning of the 'seventies.

"Now," he added, "they are taking their revenge: ever since 1974, the Americans have been trying to bring about my downfall."

At last! Mohammad Reza Pahlavi had acknowledged the principal source of his problems.

On Saturday, 24th March, the American emissaries already knew of the Shah's decision to leave the country, but they were determined to have done with the matter, as soon as possible, and returned once more to the palace to tell him that Hassan II's aircraft would be at his disposal on Friday 30th. Seeing the Sovereign's astonishment, at this bald statement, Don Agger, one of the two American envoys, said, "Majesty, I am authorised only to tell you that the aeroplane will be ready on Friday."

The Shah got up and left the room, without a word.

On the morning of 30th March, the Shah and Shahbanou, Colonel Djahanbini and Dr. Pirnia, accompanied by the Sovereign's two, personal valets, went to Rabat airport, where

Hassan II's 747 awaited them. The initial flight-plan was registered as being to South Africa; but, in the previous two or three days, the efforts of Princess Ashraf, the Shah's twin-sister, of the indefatigable Ardeshir Zahedi - and of David Rockefeller and Henry Kissinger, who, it is alleged, did not want to lose control of Mohammad Reza Pahlavi - had succeeded in pinpointing an unforeseen, alternative, temporary destination, namely, the Bahamas. Agreement had only just been reached. A new flight-plan was registered for the International Airport at Nassau.

Most recently, the Shah had expressed a desire to go and live, if all else failed, in Mexico, where the government had already been approached. A response was awaited. Thus, by going to the Bahamas, he was getting closer to a possible, final destination.

During his stay in Morocco, the King ceased to trust one of those rare foreigners whom he had considered - just like Count de Marenches - as a friend. This was Nelson Rockefeller, the former vice-President of the USA and former Governor of New York. Throughout the last, difficult months, Rockefeller had been an assiduous counsellor to the Shah, who was deeply affected by his disillusionment.

The enforced departure of the experienced diplomat, Aslan Afshar, who had been the Shah's only real confidant for more than a year, had deprived him of the company of a knowledgeable and useful man, whose loyalty was beyond doubt. After this, he felt more alone than ever. Ardeshir Zahedi, moreover, went back the Europe and did not rejoin the Shah until later.

A man of about thirty, slim and elegant - the head of a

discreet, New York, public-relations agency, which bobbed up in the wake of the Chase-Manhattan Bank and the Rockefeller brothers - was awaiting the Imperial Couple on the tarmac at Nassau airport. This was Robert Armao.

Princess Ashraf had chosen him, and his right-hand man, another American, Mark Morse, with the agreement - if not at the suggestion - of David Rockefeller, to be the Imperial Couple's factotums.

At the airport, Armao quickly ushered the little group, of arrivals from Morocco, into a waiting helicopter, which soon deposited them all on Paradise Island - one of the 700 islands and islets, which make up the Bahamian archipelago. There, they were shown to a villa belonging to one, James Crosby - a local businessman - which Armao had rented. It was a mean building, damp and uncomfortable, if agreeably close to the shore, with room for no more than the Imperial Couple and one servant. The couple's other companions were to be lodged in rooms rented from the Ocean Club, for $250 per day, on another island.

The Shah and Shahbanou were firmly requested, by the local authorities, not to leave Paradise Island, not to contact the media and not to receive any political guests. It was, to all intents and purposes, the same as being placed under house-arrest, and life in this place was peculiarly tiresome for the exiles. There was little else to do but read - or pretend to do so. The Shahbanou, and some of their companions, followed the news from Iran, which hardly enhanced their serenity. Executions were becoming commonplace at home. The former Prime Minister, Hoveyda, the ministers and high officials of the former regime, dozens of soldiers, the centenarian Principal of the Koran-School attached to the Sepahsalar Mosque in

Teheran, and many celebrated intellectuals, all went the same way. Everyone was grievously affected and many tears flowed. The Shah often went off on his own, whereupon no-one dared to approach him. The Shahbanou chain-smoked and even the Shah took to smoking a few cigarettes.

The most difficult problem, however, was that of security. The local police were not trained to deal with professional terrorists; and yet the new authorities in Teheran and the Palestinian leader, Yasser Arafat, were constantly uttering threats against the Shah. Some additional policemen were provided; but, since protection was still woefully inadequate, Armao engaged a specialist, American firm, which deployed about thirty, properly-trained men and sophisticated surveillance-equipment for detecting intruders at night.

In spite of all this, the couple experienced a time of real joy, when the Imperial Children arrived from the USA, and, in their presence, seemed to forget their own anxieties and regrets; even though this situation, with its attendant fears of kidnapping, aggravated the security-problem. The atmosphere became more relaxed, and there were games and laughter.

Generally positive was the contribution of the British, French and American tourists, who, seeing the Shah, applauded him and showed him other signs of goodwill. This prompted him to remember the habits of a lifetime and go round, shaking hands and signing autographs.

On the whole, however, the couple's isolation appalled them. They felt abandoned, not only by the world's great leaders, but even by their own countrymen, so that life sometimes became almost unbearably like a hearing-in-camera of agonising monotony. The Shah's health was affected by this and grew worse. Dr. Flandrin, Prof. Jean Bernard's assistant, was alerted, and made a furtive visit to see the patient, but he could do no more than confirm the damage and proffer advice.

There were some rare diversions, as when the Shahbanou gave an interview to *Paris Match* and a poignant account of herself; or when a letter was received, from the local authorities, complaining that one of the couple's dogs had strayed from the house. This letter, which, on top of everything else, might have reduced them to tears, actually made them helpless with mirth. They had passed the point, where such a complaint seemed anything but ridiculous.

Another contrast was provided by an unexpected visit from Sir Dennis Wright, a former British ambassador to Iran. He was a diplomat of the old school and a fervent connoisseur of Iranian culture, but imbued with the imperialist, if not colonialist, prejudices of the nineteenth century. He had little time for Iran's current ambitions and virtually dismissed out-of-hand the Shah's admiration, for the nationalism of de Gaulle, and protests about the conduct of the English-speaking powers. It is said that Sir Dennis was instrumental in persuading Queen Elizabeth II to absent herself from the Persepolis Festival. He loved Iran sincerely, but only as an exotic destination for curious tourists and authentic, or pretended, orientalists. He could not accept that the country had become a modern power.

When the Conservatives won the 1979-elections in Britain, several of the Imperial Family's adherents recalled the position, formerly taken by Mrs Thatcher, and discreetly enquired of London whether the Shah and Shahbanou might now go to live in the United Kngdom. The new Prime Minister was personally in favour of this and said so; but the Foreign Office formally opposed it, and Sir Anthony Parsons, who was still, for a while, the British ambassador to Iran - and who had just been appointed deputy-head of the British Diplomatic Service - was ferociously hostile to the idea. Economic and political considerations were cited; the security-problem was raised; and the future "iron lady" gave in. To close the file, as it were, it was decided to send an emissary to the Shah. The former ambassador was chosen and, with almost comic precautions, despatched to the Bahamas. Thus, Sir Dennis, travelling under the assumed name of Edward Wilson, arrived at the ocean club - in the finest traditions of second-rate spy-thrillers - sporting a huge pair of sun-glasses, so that no-one would recognise him. He then announced his arrival, to the Shah's retinue, in his own name, and the Sovereign agreed to see him forty-eight hours later. The audience took place on 20th May at 6.00 pm.

Sir Dennis explained to the Shah that, things being as they were, Her Majesty's Government could not offer him asylum, adding that he hoped the King would accept, and understand, this position. The Shah evinced no reaction to these remarks, but turned the conversation to other matters, whither Wright, being well-acquainted with the subtleties of Iranian diplomacy, readily followed him; and, for the next hour, they spoke of their memories, of history and of archaeology, before the former ambassador returned to the question at issue.

The Shah's reaction was not at all diplomatic. He accused the West of initiating the Iranian crisis and of nurturing the rise of Islamic fundamentalism. Sir Dennis listened politely and then said again that his minister needed to know that the Shah understood, and accepted, the British position. Mohammad Reza Pahlavi retorted, serenely, and somewhat sarcastically, that he had no choice but to resign himself to, and accept, London's position, but that he understood it not at all. Then he demanded that Sir Dennis formally recognise that he had never requested entry to Britain and that, consequently, the former ambassador's mission was void of any objective.

He was right, of course, and the British emissary admitted it, so that, after more than an hour of discussion, the Shah was able to register a victory of sorts; but the British got what they wanted: there was no more talk of Mohammad Reza Pahlavi's residing in, or even visiting, the United Kingdom.

However, the initiatives of the mighty Rockefeller-machine, and of Rockefeller's agent, Armao - which were now controlling every aspect of the Shah's life - as well as the efforts of Princess Ashraf and, above all, those of Ardeshir Zahedi - who went himself to meet President Lopes Portillo, in Mexico City, and was received, by the President, to sort matters out, over dinner - finally, produced an outcome. President Lopes Portillo, who had formerly been welcomed, with great magnificence, to Teheran, and who thought very well of the Shah, agreed - as did the Mexican government - that the Imperial Couple should come to their country.

"The most painful period of my exile", as the Shah called it, then came to a end; but he said this in Mexico, not knowing what trials still awaited him.

On 10th June 1979, the Shah, the Shahbanou and their companions arrived in Mexico, in a small, rented, private jet.

Chapter XIV

"I really am ill"

10th June - 24th October 1979

C uernavaca is an agreeable, pretty, residential town, about eighty miles from Mexico City. It has been very fashionable, ever since the reign of the Emperor Maximillian.

Three villas had been rented there, by Ardeshir Zahedi - one each for the Shah, the Shahbanou and the entourage. The King's house, called "Of The Roses" - as well as another, which was to be used for notable, invited, and uninvited, guests - was sited, in a cul-de-sac, and would, therefore, be easy to guard. The third, for the accompanying personnel, was not far away.

A few hundred yards off, the Shah's elder sister, Shams, and her husband, Mehrdad Pahlbod, had rented a very charming house, where the octogenarian Tadj ol Molouk (Queen Mother) also lived. She was said to be much disturbed by the events she had witnessed in Iran.

The villa, "Of The Roses" was very pleasant and had a beautiful garden, which the Shah was very fond of. He liked especially the wide, flowery terrace, where he often rested, read or listened to music. After his worrying relapse in the Bahamas, his health quickly improved once he arrived at Cuernavaca. Contrary to what the sensationalist press liked to write, security was very light, or, at least, discreet.

On one occasion, an incident perturbed this tranquillity, when a helicopter flew very close to the villa. The guards, fearing an asssassination-attempt, fired a few warning shots, and the machine moved away. Soon afterwards, it was realised that the over-flight had been a joke, on the part of Prince Reza, coming to pay his parents a visit. According to those present, the Shah did not take this "incident" at all kindly. Prince Reza's joke could, indeed, have turned out very badly.

Whenever the Shah went into town, he always drove his own car and was tailed by an unmarked police-vehicle. Once, he paid a long visit to President Portillo, who welcomed him cordially. Sometimes, he had visitors. Iranians were infrequent - mainly members of his family, including the Imperial Children, whose visits always cheered everyone up. A few of the Shahbanou's friends came too, but they were more discreet than they had been in Morocco.

Among others, he received visits from David Rockefeller, Henry Kissinger and Joseph Reed, Rockefeller's deputy, who would be the US-ambassador to Morocco, under the Reagan administration. Well though one knew of the criticisms, expressed by Kissinger, concerning Iranian policy after 1974, his attitude to the Imperial Couple, since they went into exile, had been correct and he was constantly denouncing, publicly and privately, the cowardice of western diplomats in their dealings with the Shah, who was grateful to him for this.

A visit from the ex-President of the USA, Richard Nixon, gave the Shah special pleasure. They spent 24 hours together, and the Sovereign retained a happy memory of the occasion. The two men liked each other very much. Afterwards, Nixon confided some details of his conversations with the Shah: "He did not weep for himself," Nixon said, "but for the destiny of his country.

"He suffered when his friends were executed and when he contemplated the fate, which the new regime had in store for the people of his country.

"The Shah," added Nixon, "had analysed, in one amazingly clairvoyant survey of the scene, just what the consequences of detachment from the USA would be, and he reproached the Americans, bitterly, for the way in which they detached themselves from him."

Later, the Shah also expressed great satisfaction with the visit, saying, "I believe that we were so content to see one another again, because our relationship was not founded only on a feeling of mutual sympathy, but also on the fact that we had, on many points, the same way of looking at things, especially geopolitical matters.

"No-one appreciated better than he did, the necessity of the West to have a strong, reliable ally in that part of the world."

In the relative quiet re-discovered at Cuernavaca, the Shah got down to writing and editing "A Reply to History", and, several times, Henry Bonnier brought a small team to Mexico, to help him with this. The Shah dictated and recorded what he wanted to say, and Bonnier's researchers did the required work and completed the text. The Shah then revised it, corrected it minutely and often changed it considerably. However, by the middle of September, the book was finished.

Albin Michel received the exclusive rights and the advance sheets for the European editions. The American edition would not be ready until the very last stage of the exile, in Egypt, whereupon a new, French paperback-edition, including the amendments made in Cairo, would also be finished.

From September to the beginning of November, the Farsee text was also being prepared. The Shah initialled the bottom of each page of the manuscript, after making all the necessary changes. His precision, in reading and comparing the two texts, which he wanted to be identical, almost line for line, was highly professional, and often irritatingly meticulous. After all, this was, in a way, his political last-will-and-testament.

The French version came out in December 1979, and the Farsee edition, three weeks later. Despite its caution, and desire to avoid rhetoric and sensationalism, the book was a great success in the shops and started numerous arguments in the press and the audio-visual media.

Having been condemned to death in Iran, where the regime did me the honour of putting a price on my head, I succeeded at last in leaving the country, towards the end of June, and in joining my wife in Paris on 16th July 1979.

Before long, I telephoned from the French capital to announce my arrival to the Imperial Couple, who both expressed their joy on finding that I was safe and sound. The Shah asked me to go to Mexico, to Cuernavaca, to talk with him. I arrived on the night of the 18th September 1979, stayed until the 23rd, and got back to Paris on the 24th.

After a brief meeting with the Shahbanou - who saw me at greater length that afternoon - I was received, a little after ten-o-clock, on the 19th, by the King, who was as punctual as ever, just like his old self. This, our first interview for more than seven months, lasted three hours, and was not interrupted, except for the two occasions when tea was served.

I found the Sovereign perfectly calm and resigned, as regards his personal situation. He was quite unconcerned about this; but he was very worried about the future of Iran.

"I am happy to see you again, at last," he said to me, by way of greeting, "I know that you have suffered much.
"Come - tell me all about it!"

I told him the story of my months in hiding, of the terror and cowardice I had witnessed, and, more to the point, of the magnificent courage of certain friends - some of whom he knew by name, if not personally - and of certain colleagues, who had saved my life at the peril of theirs. Then he asked me asked me how I managed to get out of Iran, and about the Kurdish friends, who had helped me to do this, and whose family he knew - so I recounted the tale of crossing a large part of the country by car, of the atmosphere in this town or that, and the hostility of the population, to the new regime, which was already becoming apparent. I had to tell him too about the terrible memory of various, small towns and villages, in Kurdistan, which had been happy and prosperous such a short time before, but which had been bombarded with napalm, destroyed and emptied, by the guardians of the revolution, following demonstrations against the new order. He listened to me intently and without saying a word.

Then I told him about my sojourn at Sanandaj, the provincial capital of Kurdistan, where I was finally able, after months of anxiety, to get a good sleep, and about my meeting, shortly afterwards, with a leading member of Kurdish society, who received me at his villa, deep in the mountains, and gave me a message of loyalty and support, which he begged me to convey to the King.

"I know him well," the Shah told me, "I received him at Teheran and during my tours of the region.

"He has great influence, which extends well beyond Kurdish lands and into Central Asia, where he has many followers; but he has always remained an Iranian patriot.

"Please tell him that I have not forgotten him!"

Naturally, I did so, as soon as I returned to Paris.

Next, he enquired about feeling in the country, neighbouring Iran, where I had stayed for a while before travelling to Paris; and I described the fear, which the Iranian revolution was arousing there, and also the welcome, which I received.

"That doesn't surprise me," the Shah said simply.

I also reported my interview with the President of this country.

"You asked to see him?" the King wanted to know.

"No, Sire," I said, "after the months of trepidation, which I had just gone through - and despite all the good wishes I was receiving - meeting the President was a pleasure I had not even considered.

"What could I have said to him?

"No, it was he who wished to see me and to ask me to bring

a message to Your Majesty, by word of mouth and without intermediary."

Then I was able to repeat, word for word, what the President had assigned me to say, some of the allusions of which I did not understand. Mohammad Reza Pahlavi heard, and seemed touched. I learned later that this was a message of support, in the event of the Shah's initiating a counter-movement, in Iran, or going back himself, to his country.

"Did he ask you for a reply?" asked the Shah.

I replied in the negative, whereupon the Sovereign said, "I see - that's clear enough - and quite right too."

When I told him that, at the moment of parting, the President had - to my complete amazement - embraced me, he laughed, saying, "yes, it's true, that's a habit of his - one which I don't like much."

After hearing this story, the Shah asked me about Iran's domestic situation. He had received several Iranians, both in Morocco and Mexico, but, apparently, I was the first person he had seen, who, after the revolution, had lived for any length of time, hiding and being pursued, in the country. My view of things had been necessarily somewhat limited - if supplemented by what I had been told later - but there were certain things I had to tell him, and which he had to know, even if they were going to cause him great pain.

For about forty minutes, and frequently unable to control my emotion, I portrayed, in detail, the bloody repression which was raging everywhere, the looting, assassinations by the thousand, the unbearable scenes, which were being shown

on television to terrorise the population, how Hoveyda was put
to death - as some of his companions in misfortune explained
it to me later - the dignity and courage of officers like Rahimi,
Khosrodad and Djahanbani, who cried "God save the King",
just before they were shot, and of this man and that, who were
murdered under torture...

He listened, palefaced, sometimes with lips trembling. He
gripped his chair 'til it shook, but his attention never wavered.
My portrayal was very incomplete, but sufficiently so for me
to say, "it is dreadful, dreadful; and we say that, in leaving, we
intended to prevent bloodshed?
"Where," I added, "are the defenders of human rights now?"

He changed the subject, recalling memories, details. It was
almost noon.

Then he asked me about the resistance. He was more or less
acquainted with the brave efforts of his nephew, Commander
Shafigh, and with the founding of the "Ara" - a resistance-
network linking the army and officers-in-exile, led by Oveyssi's
former deputy, General Moin Zadeh.

Suddenly, he burst out, "how can it be that no-one, no-one
at all, among all those who served their country, has dared to
raise his voice - to say something - to reply in the press, not
even in France?"

I said that, on this point, I was probably not very well
nformed, but that, since July, I personally had written a long
ticle for *Le Figaro*, which published it, then another, for the
ʒ, Parisian morning-daily, *L'Aurore*, and several more for
ʒlications in Beirut, Kuwait and elsewhere, adding, "I also
copies of all these articles to Your Majesty."

"But," he fired back, "I never received any of them."

After lunch, he put he question to the Shahbanou, who said they had been placed on his bedroom mantelpiece. Suddenly, then, I sensed - 'though whether it is true or not, I don't know - that, around the Shah, there was a certain retention of information going on.

"And what of Bakhtiar?" the Sovereign asked me, "no-one talks about anyone else, here."

"He's just launched an appeal, at a press-conference," I replied, "it appears that he's getting a lot of help from somewhere, but I've no idea from whom."

Then, all of a sudden, this strange reaction: "have you read my interview with the *Keyhan*," he asked, referring to the Teherani evening-daily, "on the day after the 28th of Mordad?"

That was the day after the fall of Mossadegh, in August 1953!

"No, Sire," I said, "I was a law-student, in Paris, at that time."

"So you were," he mused, "you're younger than me; but I was saying, in this interview, that some people in the immediate circle of that stubborn old man" - for this was always how he referred to "the old lion", never by name - "betrayed him, and one of those was Bakhtiar."
"I named him," the Shah went on, "he betrayed his leader, because he was a spy in the pay of the British, and I've never said anything different.

"He's a traitor - that's his nature - and betrayal was his way of life then, just as it always will be."

I did not know then about the circumstances of Bakhtiar's arrest, and release, by Khomeyni's henchmen, although rumours were circulating about the matter. Did the Shah know? He hadn't really mentioned it. Anyway, my reaction was quite spontaneous - it was the same, old question - "then why, Sire, did you nominate him as Prime Minister?" and it received the same, old answer.

"He was the only man ambitious enough to accept the post of last Prime Minister of the Empire.

"All the others I approached," continued the Sovereign, "made the same condition - that I should not leave Iran - but you know that this would have been impossible."

Indeed, I knew nothing of the sort, and he too would live to regret abandoning his country; but I was not there to dispute the matter, or to interrogate him. Rather, I was trying to gather his impressions, like assembling the pieces of a jig-saw puzzle, in order to understand the tragedy Iran was experiencing, and, consequently, bear witness to it.

However, Mohammad Reza Pahlavi took up the question again, "it was absolutely essential," he said, "that I go: they all thought - the Americans, the British, the French and even my own counsellors - that, with me gone, everything would fall into place.

"In the end, when it all went to pieces, there would have been no alternative, but to fire on the crowds, which, as you know, I did not wish to do.

"Another mistake I made," he added, "was to place my trust in people who were not worthy of it."

At this point, he mentioned the speech he had given, when the Azhari government was formed, in November the previous year - hardly ten months before, but already it seemed like a century - referring to it as "a criminal act of treason". Then he tackled the guilt of Iranian Radio-Television in conditioning public opinion during 1977 and 1978, and especially the latter six months of 1978. This had become one of his favourite targets.

"And yet," he went on, "although we were warned about the presence, in responsible posts in radio and television, of under-cover, communist agents, the necessary measures were never taken - and then we were surprised to see films on TV caricaturing the monarchy!"

I wanted to know the Shah's opinion of those of his officers, whom some were accusing of treason - such as General Fardoust, who had been his friend in childhood and confidant in maturity, but who was now organising the secret services of the revolutionary regime - or General Gharabaghi; but he would not reply, and I sensed in him a sorrowful embarrassment. However, I could not resist adding that the nomination of Gharabaghi as Head of the General Staff had surprised many, because everyone was expecting the promotion of Oveyssi, who was thought tough and had a good reputation in the army: "I venture to surmise," I said, "that someone dissuaded Your Majesty from nominating him to this post."

Silence!

By then, it was nearly one-o-clock and time for lunch. The Shah said, "we still have a great many issues to raise."

Luncheon was announced.

During the few days, which I spent at Cuernavaca, lunching and dining at their table, I shared the Imperial Family's present, very simple life. Calm and dignified though he was, and eating well, the Shah gave an impression of health, which was illusory. His reading consisted mainly of historical works - at the moment, a biography of Talleyrand - but he had re-assumed the habit of leafing through the international press.

As at all our meals together, there were four of us at this first lunch - the Imperial Couple, Mrs Pirnia, serene and smiling as ever, saying almost nothing, but affectionately attentive to what the King was eating, and myself. The table-talk was very light: at times the King alluded to things I had said to him that morning, but only in a very off-hand manner, as though they were references to events, which had taken place long ago, on another planet. Then, out of the blue, he said directly to me, "if I had made you Prime Minister, you would have been assassinated."

What could he have been thinking of to have lighted suddenly on that observation? The Shahbanou, opportune as always, created a diversion and switched the conversation to something else.

After lunch, which we took on the terrace, and the traditional cup of tea, which everyone drank, the Shah retired, saying, "I'm going to rest for a little and then do some work on my book - which I'd like to talk to you about this evening - go and take a short siesta!"

I went back to the guest-house, and, from there, telephoned Mehrdad Pahlbod about going to see him later in the afternoon. It was with great pleasure that I met again this pacific and thoughtful man. I asked how his wife was - for Princess

Shams was nowhere to be seen - "Her Highness is very well," he said.

I asked also after the Queen Mother. "She's in a state of shock," said Pahlbod.

Then, regarding Bakhtiar, he said, "I don't hold out much hope for anything he might do;" and, curiously, he asked me what "His Majesty" thought of the situation: "is he an optimist or a pessimist?" Pahlbod enquired.

He continued to observe court-protocol, never speaking unless the King asked him a question; and now the King wasn't asking any questions.

At dinner, the King broached the subject he wanted to discuss with me - his book. He told me a little about its contents and about the hard work of Henry Bonnier ("a good man") asking me to read the manuscript carefully - he gave it to me there and then - and give him my frank advice: "sacrifice some sleep," he said, "as I have done, and we shall meet again, tomorrow morning at eleven.

"Thus you will have time," he added, smiling, "what's more, this is the kind of intellectual work you will enjoy."

After dinner, the couple decided to watch a film, and I took my leave.

I read the "Reply To History", during part of the night and the following morning, taking notes as I did so. It was well-planned, firmly constructed and properly documented. I picked up on some small errors relating to dates, names and events, which the French team, not being familiar with the extreme detail of Iranian affairs, had missed. Above all, it was politically very uncontroversial, as I said to the King, that day.

"Sire," I asked, "why did you not display your ideas openly and make your testimony more directly?

"Why not bring in your recollections?

"You know so many things, which you could have referred to, in some degree: why not make some revelations?"

"Indeed," the Shah said, "I only reveal a very small part of what I know; but don't forget that I am a guest of the Mexican government!

"I would not wish, at any price, to make trouble, as they say, for President Portillo: he has plenty of problems to deal with, as it is, without my making waves."

He was not being entirely honest. If he had written a harder-hitting book, in a less restrained tone, he would have made political trouble for himself and compromised the chances of national rehabilitation for his reputation - for his "myth", as one, high, American official put it. However, he knew that his illness was gaining on him and he wished to pass the last months of his life in peace.

That afternoon, after the inevitable "siesta", the Shah and Shahbanou went to a tennis club, where they had become regulars. The Sovereign asked me to join them in the car. On the way, he related briefly, to the Shahbanou, some of my observations on his book. Mehrdad Pahlbod met us there. The King played tennis for nearly two hours - first a singles match and then a doubles, partnered by his brother-in-law. The Shahbanou also played a little. Everyone chattered in a relaxed manner. I was very impressed by the Shah's physical fitness and stamina. Perhaps, I thought, rumours of his illness were, in fact, groundless.

On my third morning at Cuernavaca, the Shah received me, once again, at precisely ten-o-clock. I complimented him on his physical condition. He answered with a smile.

Later, he asked me bluntly, "what are you going to do with yourself now?"

"Earn a living," I replied, "but also bear witness, write, speak and rally the patriots.

"I don't know where this will get us, but I do know, Sire, that I shall not surrender to those people, for as long as I live.

"I shall not hold my tongue: I shall proclaim the truth, in order to preserve the sense of my own honour."

"I know," he said, "but you do have to rally people.

"I have no confidence in Bakhtiar: get to know him, but do not speak to him on my behalf!

"I've spoken at length with Oveyssi and provided him with some funds and other assistance, which he wanted, because only the army can still do anything, and I see Oveyssi as the only person who could even make the attempt.

"He doesn't have a political brain, but he's well acquainted with the army and the gendarmerie, and the officers like him.

"I have ordered him to Paris, to launch an initiative from there."

Subsequently, the conversation wandered on to various topics, memories and reflections.

On Sunday 23rd, Cuernavaca's Chief-of-Police invited the Imperial Couple and their friends to an open-air luncheon at the police-club. At first, the Shah wanted to decline: he was afraid that he no longer had the necessary patience or good humour. Then it occurred to him that a refusal might offend the officials, who were being so amenable, and simply kind, towards the Imperial Family. Besides, they had even been so thoughtful as to arrange for a small, local orchestra to play, during the meal, Iranian songs and melodies, the music for which could not have been easy to find.

These policemen and their wives were not the kind of folk the Shah was used to. He was as charming to them as could be, but his performance was clearly costing him considerable effort. At the end of the repast, he said that he was not feeling well and took his leave. The Shahbanou wanted to go with him, but he opposed this, saying, "they will be disappointed."

Mrs Pirnia went with him. I thought that he must be suffering from a kind of home-sickness, whereby the state of his nerves would not stand any more conversation of a sort which interested him little; but, when I went to see him early the next day to take my leave - for I was departing that evening - he was in bed and received me in his bedroom.

"I understand, Sire," I said, "that, during the lunch yesterday, the talk really tired you out."

"No," he replied, "they're fine people - I had a genuine attack - I really am ill, you know."

I soon had confirmation of this.

The Shah's health continued to deteriorate, and Mark Morse

called Robert Armao, in New York, about it. Armao decided - though perhaps not on his own - that Mohammad Reza Pahlavi should be looked after by American doctors. Accordingly, after consultations with the Rockefeller organisation, and probably with the State Department too - but without, apparently, any authorisation from the Shah or the Shahbanou - Amao asked for Dr. Benjamin Kean, a high-society, New York, general practitioner, to be called to come and see the Shah. Kean had a private practice on Park Avenue and was very popular in trendy circles. He was well known for his love of travel, cigars and women and had been married several times. He arrived in Cuernavaca on the 29th, and examined the Shah, who told him, not without a certain brusqueness, that it was not he who had asked to be seen and that he had every confidence in his French physicians, who had looked after him very well. Dr. Kean asked for a blood-sample, which the Shah refused. Dr. Kean then said angrily, without, however, discovering what medicines had been prescribed for the Sovereign, that the Shah needed much more sophisticated treatment than he had been receiving hitherto; and, with that, he went off back to New York.

While the Park Avenue GP was returning to the USA, Dr. Flandrin, one of the four-man team of French physicians, which was tending the Shah, and in which he had every confidence, arrived in Mexico, at the request of the Shahbanou. Flandrin decided that the patient should go into hospital at once for a thorough examination. The Shah's response to this was quite definite: he was ready to be examined and treated in hospital, but not in the United States.

"After what they have done to me," he said, "I wouldn't go there, if they begged me on bended knee."

Some members of his circle, including, it seems, Ardeshir Zahedi and the Crown Prince Reza, wholeheartedly agreed with this.

At the beginning of October, without going into further detail, the Shah asked me to sound out the French government, in a personal capacity and without any publicity, on the question of whether he could go into hospital, and receive treatment, in France.

Among the people I knew in the upper circles of power in Paris, I immediately thought of Alain Peyrefitte, the Minister of Justice and Keeper of the Seals, whom I had known for several years. After the publication of his book, *When China Awakes*, I had invited him to appear at a series of conferences, at Teheran University, which had been a great success. At that time, he was received by the Shah, who had, of course, read his book, and the Sovereign impressed him, although Peyrefitte found his ambitions "frightening". Our friendly relations continued, after the revolution and my arrival in Paris. He was a reliable man, who could keep a confidence: I could speak to him without beating about the bush. I therefore asked to see him as a matter of urgency, and, forty-eight hours later, he saw me, rather late in the evening, at his office in the Place Vendôme. I explained the situation. He questioned me about the Shah's state of health, and I told him what I knew and of what I had seen - not very much, in fact. We both agreed that the matter had to be kept absolutely quiet. Furthermore, this eternal Gaullist told me yet again that he had never approved of Khomeyni's being welcomed to France. At any rate, he promised to raise the question, of the Shah's possible hospitalisation in France, at the Élysée Palace, and give me an answer as soon as he could.

I could only wait, which I did, for a very long time.

It was in April 1974, during a thorough examination made by Prof. Fehlinger, at Vienna, that the first signs of the malady, which would end the Shah's life - although this did not become public knowledge until October 1979 - were detected. The word, "cancer", was never uttered. Later there was talk of Waldenstrom's disease, but this was never confirmed by the doctors, either. According to a recent enquiry by Austrian physicians, the illness in question could have been Hodgkin's disease, the pathology of which resembles that of cancer in many ways. In her memoirs, the Shahbanou refers to Waldenstrom's disease, which ought to put an end to controversy about the matter.

A renowned medical team had been assigned to attend the Sovereign. It included two, leading, French professors of medicine, Jean Bernard and Paul Milliez, Dr. Georges Flandrin (Bernard's assistant) and Prof. Abbas Safavian, who had formerly been an intern at more than one Paris hospital, was a qualified teacher of medicine and was a former Rector of Teheran's Melli University; but it was Flandrin who supervised the Shah's treatment, on behalf of the French specialists, and monitored the illustrious patient's response, in the absolute secrecy, which was not penetrated until the beginning of October 1979.

In September 1976, while on a private trip to Paris, the Shahbanou was informed of the situation, by the four practitioners - although the Shah was not told about it until two months later - in medical terms, which did not include mention of the word "cancer", but which did not hide the importance, nay, the gravity, of the sickness, which was eating him away.

"How long have I got?" he then asked.

"From six to eight years, if you are well looked after, which you are, Sire," was the reply.

"That," said the Sovereign, "'is enough for me."

Thereafter, the seriousness of his illness would not be mentioned again, in his presence, until the end of September, or the beginning of October, 1979.

It was from the end of 1976 that the Shah quickened the pace of Iran's development projects, began a systematic reform of the Court and the Imperial Protocol - especially the Shahbanou's staff - and initiated a plan of education for the Heir-to-the-Throne.

After that, only six people knew about the Sovereign's medical condition - the four medics already named, the Shahbanou and the old, military doctor, Ayadi; for we know that the secret was very well guarded: neither the chancelleries, nor the secret services, whether American, British, Israeli, or even French - despite their obvious interest in Iranian affairs, especially after the outbreak of disorder - seemed to have any inkling of the matter.

Medical analyses were regularly done, without the use of the Shah's name, in various French laboratories. After the Sovereign's death, none of the doctors, who had looked after him until October 1979 - apart from Dr. Flandrin - let slip the slightest hint of what they knew. On the other hand, the final phase - the American phase - of treatment took place virtually in public. However, without detailed information about the preceding years of the case ('74 - '79) a trustworthy history of the entire process will not be possible, and conjecture concerning the matter will remain.

Did the Shah's illness, and the treatments he received for it, influence his behaviour and his ability to make decisions and govern? In theory, the answer is no; but medical practice does not exclude secondary effects (excessive fatigue, depression, indifference) on the behaviour and the psychological state of the patient, as much from the medications prescribed as from the complaint itself. It has also been established that, during the last months of his reign, the Shah was taking - for perfectly understandable reasons, and always under medical control - more tranquillisers than the "little pills" he usually took to help him sleep. This too could have affected how he behaved.

Nevertheless, everyone who knew Mohammad Reza Pahlavi, in those final years, was quite sure - albeit in retrospect - that he suffered from the rapid enfeeblement, of his previously prodigious memory, and from a certain detachment from contact with everyday life. It is also true, that he tried, in the last two years, to speed up the completion of certain projects and to broach ideas, if not reforms, which were sometimes contradictory, and that this provoked new anomalies, which contributed, in their turn, to the wave of popular discontent, of the last months of his reign, and thus to the exploitation of this unrest, by foreign influences.

On the basis of my own investigations, and of the cross-checking of information from various witnesses, I think I can say that the Shah was suitably cared for until the last week of September 1979, when his treatment was taken over by different doctors, who were always selected under confused circumstances, often contrary to his own wishes and, sometimes, to those of the Shahbanou as well.

Squabbles, between the doctors and the Shah's retinue, broke out all around the patient. Armao arrived from New York, met Dr. Flandrin for the first time and, on learning that he was Prof. Jean Bernard's assistant, contacted New York to tell Kean of this. Kean had not heard of Flandrin, but the global reputation of Jean Bernard was enough to intimate to him what kind of disease the Shah might be suffering from, and what political reasons might have motivated the Shah's refusal to submit to various tests. He then told enough people in Washington and New York, of his suspicions, for the Shah's condition to preoccupy "one of the major newspapers", within a few days. Confidentiality, concerning the medical problems of prominent people, is not a convention, which is respected in the USA. A long-running dispute ensued between, Flandrin, the Imperial Couple's trusted adviser, and Kean, Armao's nominee.

The Shah ordered Flandrin and Pirnia to inspect some Mexican hospitals. They agreed to propose that the Sovereign undergo treatment at a university-hospital, whose cancer-unit was run by a French-trained specialist. Kean, egged on by Armao, opposed this. Flandrin's English was correct but hesitant, while Kean could neither speak French nor understand that Flandrin's English was not perfect. Nevertheless, they did manage to concur on the urgency of hospital-treatment, and an operation on the gall bladder, before going on, perhaps, to tackle the problem of the spleen.

The question, of which hospital to choose, remained. The American contingent would not hear of a Mexican hospital being used. Paris continued stubbornly silent. The patient refused to go to the USA, and Ardeshir Zahedi, when consulted on the matter, strongly supported the Shah in this; but Kean and Armao, ignoring these reservations, initiated the procedures necessary for committing the Shah to a hospital - that connected with Cornell University - in New York.

At first, Jimmy Carter and the State Department looked unfavourably on having the Shah admitted to this, or any American, hospital; but David Rockefeller, Joseph Reed, and numerous, other, influential Americans, were in favour of it and exerted pressure on the White House to this effect. The US-ambassador in Teheran was asked to put the matter to the Iranian government, whereupon Mehdi Bazargan, Khomeyni's Prime Minister, and Ibrahim Yazdi, the Foreign Minister, who was an American national, agreed with Jimmy Carter. They said they were not convinced that the Shah's indisposition was genuine. They were very afraid of him. The State Department then sent its own medical team to examine the patient. The Imperial Couple, overwhelmed and almost crushed, by the operation of this American machinery, allowed things to be steered, or manipulated, by it. Dr. Flandrin's services were dispensed with. While the Shah's health was getting worse by the day, stories about it spread through the international press, whereby the least occurrence, and the slightest rumours, in connection with it, were given coverage. This personal publicity was a new humiliation for Mohammad Reza Pahlavi: there was the Sovereign, wandering in exile, grievously sick and searching for a hospital, which would give him treatment!

Carter had never wanted to refuse the Shah entry in an un-diplomatic manner, and now the pressure exerted by some powerful individuals, and the medical report from the State Department, persuaded him to relent further. Perhaps, also, he was afraid of being accused of responsibility for the death of a great friend of the USA, after having connived at his downfall. Eventually, he authorised a visit, of limited duration, for purposes of medical treatment only. Mohammad Reza Pahlavi, who was in a very bad way, allowed himself to be talked into it, but not without first obtaining assurances, from President Lopes Portillo, that he could return to Mexico afterwards.

On the night of 22nd October, the Shah left Cuernavaca, and the peaceful "Villa of Roses", with its flower-beds, its beautiful terrace and the stream, which flowed at the bottom of the garden - the last place where he had bee able to nurture some illusions of hope - and boarded a chartered jet to fly to the United States of America. He could hardly walk, but sat upright in the aircraft, bearing his pain bravely, as always.

On Washington's orders, it had been decided that the flight would land first at Fort Lauderdale, in Florida, so that the formalities of customs and immigration could be completed, but no-one at the airport had been warned of this. An agricultural inspector wanted to know whether the 'plane was carrying any plants, and to assure himself that it was not about to scatter noxious substances on US-territory. It was warm in the cabin and no-one on board was allowed to leave the machine. They had to wait for more than an hour, while the officials, charged with carrying out the procedures for entering the US, moved towards giving them authorisation for take-off.

The Shah of Iran arrived, at last, at New York's La Guardia airport, in the small hours of the morning, on 23rd October 1979, to experience, at that season, after the heat of Florida, New York's damp chill.

His arrival was supposed to have been kept secret. The passengers were conducted discreetly, from the 'plane, to some waiting cars, which sped off, as arranged, towards Princess Ashraf's residence, on the East Side. A few hundred yards from their destination, however, they received a signal. A pack of press- and TV-reporters and -photographers, from all over the world had massed in front of the house! The party was obliged to change direction and head for the "New York Hospital".

Mohammad Reza Pahlavi was admitted to the NYH under the name of David Newsome, a high official of the State Department responsible for, among other things, the file on Iran. In the few minutes following the Shah's "secret" arrival at the hospital, the media were alerted and, henceforth, formed a permanent camp outside. From the 24th onwards, demonstrations hostile to the Shah were held, with government-authorisation, in front of the building. The sick man's supporters, on the other hand - who tried to assemble there - were forbidden to do so. Even the numerous bouquets, which were delivered to the hospital, were retained and sequestered by the police. Mohammad Reza Pahlavi was to have his operation on 24th October.

On 15th November 1979, Alain Peyrefitte wrote to me, saying, "Alas, the terrifying event, which has occurred since our last meeting, seems to have rendered the question, which you asked me, hypothetical...

"Like you, I am extremely fearful of what might happen now..."

More than six weeks had passed since "our last meeting". Alain Peyrefitte's response was no more than a diplomatic courtesy; but everything, in this concluding episode of the life of Mohammad Reza Pahlavi felt strange and unreal, as though "hypothetical".

Chapter XV

"I am dying, but I would like to die with dignity"

24th October 1979 - 23rd March 1980

Every decision concerning the treatment of his illness was now made without the participation of Mohammad Reza Pahlavi, or the medical team, which had so diligently attended him, and looked after him, for years. Also excluded was the Shahbanou, who, since the beginning, had been associated with every political and moral option chosen.

Dr. Kean and the Armao team controlled the situation from now on. One Dr. Morton Coleman, a famous specialist, was asked to perform the operation, but, with Dr. Flandrin out of the picture, everything had to be started again from scratch. According to the press, kidney-stones were discovered and a spleen enlarged to three times its normal size.

Dr.Coleman agreed to operate. At the same time, he wanted to know for sure whether the patient was suffering from Waldenstrom's disease, or anything like it, and the extent of any such damage. Preparations were made for him to operate on the gall bladder and remove the spleen.

Almost the entire world was following the case, hour by hour, devouring official and unofficial declarations, indiscretions, by all and sundry, journalistic investigations, and vast amounts of pure speculation. The confidentiality of the French, medical team was no more than a distant memory. The grand spectacle was being staged. On the 24th, when Dr. Coleman arrived at the hospital to operate, he was staggered to discover - so he relates - that a team of relief-surgeons had already been lined up. The excision of the spleen was postponed, which, as the specialists said later, was a fatal mistake. Also, a week later, a radiographical check revealed that one stone had not been removed, and that the bile duct was still blocked. The operation had, therefore, been a failure, and, given the state of the patient, it seemed too dangerous to try again.

It was decided instead to continue treatment at a nearby clinic, linked to the hospital by a tunnel. This was the Sloan-Kettering Memorial Hospital. Years before, the Queen Mother had received treatment there, and, as a gesture of thanks to Sloan-Kettering's doctors, the Shah had donated a million dollars to the hospital-fund. Hearing that Mohammad Reza Pahlavi was about to be admitted, some of the medics spoke out against the plan, but came round under the dire threat of revelations to the press. Nevertheless, there was a proviso: the special sessions, during which the stone, and a tumour in the neck, would be irradiated, would have to take place at night - at five-o-clock in the morning, at the latest. This must have been particularly humiliating and exhausting for someone already gravely ill.

For each of the six sessions of treatment, the patient was taken down in the lift and then through the tunnel, in a wheelchair, surrounded by numerous bodyguards, in a terrifying state of high security-alert. Each time, the Shahbanou accompanied

454

her husband and tried, as best she could, to keep his spirits up. Her courage, and her determination to protect the Shah, won the admiration of all, even the couple's enemies.

On 4th November, while the patient's condition - once stabilised - was beginning to improve, Khomeyni's gangsters got together a group of extreme leftists - called, for the occasion, "students" - and occupied the US-embassy in Teheran, taking all the diplomatic personnel hostage. This was the first time in history that a state had taken hostages, and it was to last 444 days.

It became quite clear later that this operation was controlled, at a distance, by Moscow, with the sole objective of eliminating pro-American elements from the regime in Teheran - as, indeed, it rapidly did, during the following weeks - and to bring the Islamic Republic firmly under Soviet influence; but the pretexts presented for it, by Teheran - demands for the extradition of the Shah and, possibly, his family, and the restitution of his fortune - plunged Washington into one of the gravest diplomatic crises in the history of the United States.

This situation provoked a new wave of hatred against the Shah, who, watching television in his hospital-room, could not but see and hear extremely malevolent commentaries, on his reign, from all those self-styled experts, journalists, politicians and academics. What made it particularly depressing for him was that he could not reply. He was physically unable to, let alone politically. The hullabaloo raging all across the world, and especially in the USA, would have drowned his voice; and so he was silent, or almost so.

Nevertheless, he received thousands of letters and cards, not just from Iranians, but also from Americans, expressing sympathy and the admiration people felt for his work, and for the service he had rendered to his country, and wishing him a speedy recovery. Hundreds of bouquets of flowers also came to the hospital. Such was their number that the police were unable to get rid of them all. Then there were the celebrities, who came to visit him, including David Rockefeller, Henry Kissinger, Giovanni Agnelli (the owner of Fiat) and the singer, Frank Sinatra, who publicly slated the administration's attitude to the Shah and invited him to come and live at his house in Palm Springs. Ronald Reagan, then a candidate for the presidency, and whom he had received in Teheran, sent him a kindly message.

By the end of November, the Shah's health had improved sufficiently for him to consider returning to Cuernavaca, and Armao's deputy, Mark Morse, was assigned to preparing the "Villa of the Roses" for the exiles' return; but the Mexican authorities informed Armao that Mohammad Reza Pahlavi was no longer welcome in their country. Apparently, Jimmy Carter was furious. He was impatient to see the back of the Shah, because he believed, or seemed to, that this would help in the liberation of the hostages.

Once again, the Shah was at a loss for a destination. He had intended to move, temporarily, into a house owned by his sister, Ashraf, at Beekman Place in New York, and to convalesce there, before returning to Cuernavaca; but now the Mexicans were refusing to have him back, and, on top of that, the State Department had just informed him, officially, that it would not allow him to stay, even for a short time, in New York.

One of Carter's counsellors was despatched to suggest to the Shah that he should go, without delay, to Lackland Air-

Force Base, in Texas. The base had a well-equipped hospital, he said, was perfectly secure and safe from demonstrations, and there the Shah could wait until some other country could be found to accommodate him.

In despair, Mohammad Reza Pahlavi resigned himself to this proposal and informed the Shahbanou of his decision. Departure was scheduled to take place at night, in order to avoid any incidents.

Accordingly, a little after midnight, in the small hours of the 1st December, the security-team put the Shah into a wheelchair and took him, through the sinister, deserted corridors of the hospital, to the basement, with its dirty, grey walls, and gangways littered with broken furniture and rubbish-bins. In the garage, the wheelchair, surrounded by dozens of FBI-agents, all armed to the teeth, was hoisted into an ambulance, which fled, with sirens bellowing, and accompanied by numerous police-cars, towards the airport.

The Shahbanou, whom the Shah had alerted, shortly before, to their imminent removal, received the same treatment. There were even security-agents with her in the car, which was led, and followed, by police vehicles. The racket woke little Princess Leila, nine-years-old, the Imperial Couple's last child and, so they say, her father's favourite. Her mother had gone, while she was still asleep. Leila tried to follow, looking for her mother, sobbing and weeping. It was a distressing sight.

The two convoys headed for La Guardia, where a military DC9, guarded by a squad, armed with machine-guns, and wearing bullet-proof jackets, awaited them. The couple were bundled unceremoniously into the aircraft, which took off immediately for Texas.

At Lackland Base, in the early morning, there was an impressive turn-out of the security-forces. The Imperial Couple were pushed unceremoniously into an old ambulance, which had internal partitions and was very uncomfortable, and conveyed, at high speed, to the base's psychiatric hospital.

Reza Pahlavi later described the discomfort his parents experienced on this journey: "the King and Queen," he said, "were both seated very awkwardly and being shaken about in an incredible manner, as the vehicle hurtled along unmade roads, bumping their heads repeatedly, first on one side, then on the other.

"Was this any way," Prince Reza asked, "to transport a sick man, who had recently undergone major surgery?"

The couple were put in a room with carefully-sealed, barred and shuttered windows, which admitted no light. The door had no handle on the inside. In the adjoining bed-room, shackles and straitjackets had been placed ready, in case the Pahlavis protested noisily. The American administration had thought of everything!

The couple felt that they had been abducted and imprisoned in order to be handed over, by Carter, to Khomeyni. The Shah, suffering in dignified silence, said nothing at all. The Shahbanou exploded. Her protests were answered with a statement to the effect that this was the most secure place on the base.

Some hours later, the Shahbanou was at last permitted to make a telephone-call. She alerted some American friends, in New York, to what had happened, and described briefly the conditions, under which she and the Shah were being held. At least, someone on the outside now knew where the couple were, which, they felt, made them less vulnerable.

The "American friends" intervened rapidly and effectively. The following day, the Shah and Shahbanou were moved to an, albeit sparsely furnished and small, three-roomed bungalow. The main feature of the living-room was a vinyl sofa. General Acker, the commander at the base, while asking the couple not to show themselves outside the house, invited them to dinner and apologised many times for the quality of their accommodation. He also intimated his disagreement with the government's official policy.

Numerous Iranian pilots had been trained at Lackland and made friends there. Several of the American officers had served in Iran, and remembered the country kindly. As soon as they saw the Shah, therefore, many inhabitants of the base applauded him and saluted him respectfully. They also engaged him in discussion, about aircraft and military matters, and were surprised by his erudition. The Shah, in turn, allowed himself to be photographed and signed autographs. The Shahbanou even played a few tennis-matches. The couple settled down, to some extent, but the tense question remained: where would they go?

After quite a while, the White House sent an envoy, Steve Oxman, to discuss, with the Shah, possible destinations for the couple.

On 7th December, in Paris, the Shah's nephew, Shahryar Shafigh, who had been the captain of a corvette, and a brilliant and popular officer in the Imperial Navy, was shot twice outside the Villa Dupont, where he lived, in a cul-de-sac off the rue Pergolèse, in the 16th arrondissement.

He was preparing to go back to Iran and start a military action against the revolutionary regime, but the regime got news of it, on the grapevine, and sent two assassins to Paris. Having done the deed, they slipped away again, without any difficulty. Teheran officially acknowledged responsibility for the murder. Paris did not turn a hair - the government did not even protest. It was later discovered that the notorious General Fardoust planned the crime and might even have come to France to supervise it.

The Shah was thunderstruck and mourned in silence. He had loved and respected his nephew. Shafigh's mother, the much disparaged Princess Ashraf, faced her bereavement with great dignity: "I have lost a son today," she said to the press, "whom I cherished.

"He was a convinced patriot and a devoted and competent naval officer, who strove with his comrades to ensure that the Iranian flag flew high."

The White House was under pressure to decide what to do about the Shah, a matter about which American public opinion was strongly divided. Some criticised Carter's harbouring a controversial figure, saying that he had thereby provoked the taking hostage of American diplomats in Teheran. Others, including the Republicans and what might be called "America-in-depth", condemned, in no uncertain terms, what they saw as Carter's "weakness", in allowing Iran to fall into the hands of the ayatollahs, and his "apparent" support for an extremist regime, which was being manipulated by Moscow. The invasion of Afghanistan by the Red Army, at the end of that year, was ultimately a reflection of the principal objective of the hostage-taking at Teheran: namely to engage the USA in an endless crisis, which would prevent her from acting in another sphere.

Some American leader-writers went so far as to demand openly that the Shah should give himself up to the Teheran-regime, in exchange for the hostages! Mohammad Reza Pahlavi's reply was not slow in coming: "I've been called many things, in my time," he said," but 'imbecile' is not one of them."

The idea of exchanging the Shah for the American diplomats, imprisoned in Teheran, seems to have been conceived, at that moment, by certain circles, in Washington; but, for the time being, the government's attitude was still that he was an embarrassment and that he would have to leave.

Egypt's parliament passed a motion solemnly repeating an invitation, to the Imperial Couple, to be received fittingly in their country; but the Shah hesitated. He knew what difficulties the Raïs had encountered ever since the conclusion of the Camp David Accords; especially the attacks, made by Arab-radicals, against his person; and he did not wish to add to Sadat's problems, so he put this solution aside, at least, provisionally. South Africa was always a possibility, but the Shah was reluctant about that too. His closest advisers suggested Chile, or Taiwan; but he only pulled face. These three countries were seen in a very bad light, by the Left and by "dominant" opinion, but they would have provided secure locations and good medical facilities, for the months of life which remained to him. Then a most unexpected invitation was made - from Romania! It was unthinkable, of course, and the Shah thanked Ceaucescu, but refused. All the "normal" countries had closed their doors to him - a latter day Nicholas II - and his family, except for a few nations in Central America.

The left-leaning dictator of Panama, Omar Torrijos, was a friend of Fidel Castro, but was also obliged to Carter, who had just signed a treaty withdrawing American troops from the Canal Zone. He was worried, above all, that the hostage-affair might precipitate a Republican victory in the next US-elections, so he made a discreet offer, to the State Department, to receive the exiles. Accordingly, Hamilton Jordan, the White-House Chief-of-Staff, and a close confidant of Carter's, was despatched to see the Panamanian President, who confirmed the invitation.

On Jimmy Carter's orders, Jordan then went to Lackland, with two other high officials, to try to persuade the Shah. The latter's first reaction was negative, but he did say that he was ready to speed up his departure, if it would help to get the hostages released, and that he would think about it.

As he was leaving the room after the audience, Jordan bumped into Princess Ashraf, who had just arrived in Texas to commiserate with her twin-brother, following the assassination of their nephew, Shafigh, three days before. The American held out his hand to the Shah's sister, but she gave him a look of angry contempt and refused to take it.

Having received assurances that he would be able to avail himself, if necessary, of the American military hospital in the Canal Zone, the Shah agreed, in principle, to go to Panama.

Then it was a matter of finding a place to settle, and so, once again, Ardeshir Zahedi was called upon. He had a good relationship with the Panamanian President, who was, however, lacking in any real power. Taking Prince Reza with him, Zahedi then visited several possible sites in Panama. A pleasant and spacious villa, belonging to another friend of Zahedi's - the Panamanian ambassador to Washington, Gabriel Lewis - was chosen. It was a charming holiday-location on

Contadora, an island in the open Pacific Ocean, about forty miles from Panama City - and its international airport. Lewis agreed at once and even proposed to put his small, personal aircraft at the Shah's disposal in case it was needed.

The President invited Zahedi and Prince Reza to dinner. Torrijos, the actual master of the country was also a guest; and the first thing he said to his Iranian table-mates was highly significant: "I don't understand how, or why, your King, with a loyal army of 550 000 men, with his police and so many supporters, came to abandon his country; but assure him, nevertheless, that we shall open the gates wide to receive him."

He did not keep his word, except at the beginning.

Once the decision had been reached - Colonel Djahanbini recalls - he was given the task of accompanying Armao and Jordan to make the necessary, practical arrangements. Then, on 15th December, the Imperial Couple and their small entourage disembarked, not at the international airport, but on an American, military base; and it was from there that they flew, by helicopter to the island of Contadora.

At first, a sojourn on the Pacific coast offered some advantages. Mohammad Reza Pahlavi's health improved somewhat. He took walks, and even played tennis, briefly, on one occasion. He read a great deal, or pretended to read, in order to avoid disturbing anyone.

General Omar Torrijos visited the Imperial Couple several times, and was very obsequious towards the Shah, calling him "Senor Shah", which exasperated the Sovereign, no end. However, when he got wind of the secret negotiations, between

Washington and Teheran, regarding the Shah's fate, his attitude changed. He started presenting property-developers, each one dodgier than the last, in the hope of getting some money out of the situation, and his boorishness did not stop there. He brought flowers for the Shahbanou and tried to get her to come to dinner. General Noriega, already a strong-man in Panama, a CIA-agent and infamous drug-trafficker, soon began to do the same. It was clear that Noriega was going to succeed Torrijos, after the latter died in an accident. In his turn, the General soon obtained the opportunity to end his days in a federal, American penitentiary, where, indeed, he remains incarcerated, today, for trading in narcotics!

All of these unfortunate occurrences were deeply resented by the couple, whose lives on Contadora, became less and less bearable from the beginning of 1980 onwards.

In Washington, Jimmy Carter would have sold his own parents to free the hostages, for achieving this, he knew, would be the best way to secure his re-election, and the campaign for the presidency had already begun.

Two hundred of Noriega's police and soldiers guarded the villa round the clock. Telephone-conversations were recorded and the mail was intercepted, read and photocopied, before being given to its addressees. Before long, letters were simply retained, and, towards the end, the telephone was cut off as well. The Imperial Couple were, once again, prisoners.

Visits were not categorically forbidden. The Imperial children came for a few days. This obliged the couple to maintain appearances, and seem less depressed themselves, in order to avoid demoralising the family. There were also visits from Ashraf, from Ardeshir Zahedi and from a very few journalists.

President Royo, Torrijos' young puppet-Head-of-State, came to pay his respects to the Shah and was impressed by the latter's dignity, cultivation and belief in the future of his country. Torrijos, on the other hand, came often, when he wasn't too drunk, even though the style, reserve and haughty bearing of Mohammad Reza Pahlavi, sick and emaciated as he was, annoyed him. The Shah, however, was obliged to put up with Torrijos, for he was the master of the country, to which adversity had driven him.

To have handed over the Shah, to the regime in Teheran, while he was still on US-territory, might have damaged the USA's image. Jimmy Carter would perhaps have done it, if it could have guaranteed his re-election, despite the prospect of arousing a political storm within the country, where a large proportion of the public were severely critical of the White House', and the State Department's, attitude in this matter; but, as soon as the Shah was no longer on American territory, it became much easier to exchange him for the hostages, and this is what American diplomacy was actively getting down to doing.

Two envoys from Teheran arrived in Panama on 24th December 1979: one was the extremely left-wing, French lawyer, Christian Bourguet, and the other was the Argentine adventurer, Hector Villalon. The top-secret nature of their mission - to negotiate the extradition of the Shah - did not remain so for long, for a protracted wrangle commenced between Washington and Teheran, with Panama in a subordinate capacity. Hamilton Jordan would be the principal, American actor in this drama.

The pressures, which were being exerted against the Shah, became stronger, and he knew, from the beginning of January, that Panama was negotiating his extradition, or, to put it another way, that the Americans were negotiating his surrender. He consulted the eminent, British jurist, Lord Shawcross, formerly a judge at the Nuremberg Trials, who was also president of the Anglo-Iranian Friendship Society, and whom he considered to be a reliable friend. The English lawyer reassured him. If, he said, a legal action should be brought against the Shah - which he himself found inconceivable - he would conduct the defence and defeat it. A few days later, Lord Shawcross telephoned to say, with sincere regret, that, notwithstanding his legal opinion - which still stood - he would not be able to defend the Shah's interests in court "for political reasons, which Your Majesty will be able to guess".

Mohammad Reza Pahlavi had not the least doubt that the London-government was also involved in the negotiations and had dissuaded the distinguished jurist from taking a hand.

Hamilton Jordan kept on plaguing the Shah, suggesting to him that he make an official request for political asylum in Panama, that he abdicate and renounce all rights to the throne; but the Sovereign was violently opposed to these suggestions. He would not demean himself so far as to ask for political asylum and he would never abdicate.

Then it was put to him that, in order to facilitate Washington's efforts to obtain the release of the hostages, he allow himself to be arrested and imprisoned by the Panamanian police. A firm assurance was given that he would be set free immediately afterwards! He was also told of a plot to assassinate him.

His arrest was even announced - in Teheran - and a special cage was constructed there to hold Mohammad Reza Pahlavi, and in which to parade him through the capital.

Chapter XV: *I am dying, but I would like to die with dignity*

Under Jordan's supervision, the negotiations were going well. Noriega's guards forbade the couple to leave the villa. From mid-March, the Shah knew that his arrest was imminent. He decided to leave, whatever the cost.

Then the Shah's health suddenly got worse again, in the form of his continuing spleen-trouble, which should have been sorted out in New York. Dr. Kean intervened, and the Shahbanou consulted Dr. Flandrin. An operation was urgently needed. There were hopes that the well-known Coleman would be the man for the job. Washington then sent, goodness knows why, a leading medic, Prof. Michael de Bakey, who was a specialist in cardio-vascular surgery! The removal of the spleen was considered essential, and a Panamanian hospital was chosen, but for reasons of prestige - so it was said - local practitioners demanded, with the support of their government, to carry out the operation themselves. De Bakey would be allowed, they said, to act as an assistant. The quarrel was brought for resolution before the Shah. He listened to the different points of view, got up, said, "Gentlemen, good day!" and went off, banging the door behind him. Departure was a necessity.

Several friends and allies warned the Imperial Couple that the Shah's arrest and extradition could occur at any time.

Aslan Afshar, a former ambassador to Washington, was in Nice, when he received a telephone-call from a highly-placed, American friend: "tell the King to leave Panama as soon as possible," the caller said, "or he will be prevented from doing so."

Afshar immediately called the Shahbanou, who said - either because she was still confident, or in order to re-assure the Grand Master of Protocol, "Don't worry, His Majesty is not disturbed in the least; he is even taking a walk in the garden, today, with General Torrijos."

This recorded conversation served, at least, to give the Panamanians and the Americans the impression that the Imperial Couple were not aware of the secret negotiations concerning their fate. Perhaps this is why the Shahbanou said what she did. On 19th March, Hamilton Jordan was ordered to Contadora to dissuade the Shah from leaving. He saw de Bakey first, and got a cool reception, being told that the surgeon did "not take political orders".

"I doubt whether anyone could persuade the Shah to have his operation here," de Bakey added.

Jordan then asked him to consider the freeing of the hostages and got an even more scathing reply: "That's your problem, and the President's; my problem is the Shah's health."

De Bakey ended by saying that there seemed to be no prospect of operating in Panama.

In desperation, Jordan went to see Omar Torrijos. He knew, from the CIA, that the Shah was preparing to leave for Egypt, so he told the dictator this and asked him to dissuade the Shah from such a course, but without any of the brutality, which might arouse a reaction in the USA, and damage Jimmy Carter's campaign. The conversation ended without a decision being made.

Jordan then called the White House and was told, by Carter,

in no uncertain terms that the Shah "must on no account be allowed to go to Egypt". Next, he called President Sadat to tell him of his disquiet concerning any possible return, by the Shah, to Egypt - to which the Raïs retorted, "don't you worry about Egypt; just you mind those hostages!"

There was only one possibility left; to try to dissuade the Shah directly, and so he went, with Lloyd Cutler - President Carter's special envoy - and two other diplomats, to see the King. At the Contadora villa, preparations for departure were clearly going on. The Americans recited all their prepared arguments, including the interests of the hostages and the long friendship between Iran and the USA. It was enough to provoke laughter, but the Shah remained serene. They also suggested that, if he abdicated, he could go to the USA for treatment. The Shah remained as impassive as marble, but replied drily, "I shall feel better among friends: I know I'm dying, but I wish to die with dignity."

He called a halt to the conversation at that point.

In Panama City vigorous negotiations were going on about the Shah's arrest, and everything was being done to delay him while agreement was being reached between the three parties, the USA, Iran and Panama. A message arrived from Teheran: "the hostages have been brought together in one group.

"If you now prevent the Shah from reaching Egypt, they will be given up immediately."

Hope rekindled in the Carter-camp.

President and Mrs Sadat had repeated their invitation to the Imperial Couple, the baggage was prepared and the heavy bills paid. It was now a matter of leaving Contadora and traversing the forty-or-so miles to Panama City International Airport, where President Sadat's DC8 was awaiting them, ready for immediate take-off.

During the 22nd and 23rd March, three small aeroplanes, rented to make the hop to the airport, did not appear. In the end, David Rockefeller had a 'plane sent from the USA to get the party off the island. The Imperial Couple, Dr. Lucie Pirnia, Col. Djahanbini, Col. Nevissi and the faithful Amir PourShodja at last managed to take off. Robert Armao and Mark Morse went with them.

Having arrived at the airport - and in spite of his weakened state - the Shah almost ran towards the Egyptian, presidential aircraft, his port-in-a-storm. Television-newsreels, all over the world, preserved the sight.

The DC8 did take off immediately. It was 2.00 pm on Sunday 23rd March 1980. The sojourn in Panama had lasted three months.

Between the moment the Shah and his retinue had arrived at the airport, and the take-off of the DC8, whose engines were already running, a mere 15 minutes had elapsed.

The Shah was still uneasy, however. There was to be a stopover at an American, military base, on the Azores, where a group of Portuguese and American officials would come to greet him. The King rested. He was very tired and running a high temperature. When they reached the Azores, he rose, dressed and hailed the officials politely.

The machine was supposed to refuel and take off again at once, but it remained on the runway. For two hours, the base refused to give authorisation for take-off. In fact, Hamilton Jordan and Omar Torrijos had interceded with the Defense Department in Washington to have the aircraft arrested. If, at this point, the hostages had been assembled, in Teheran, in a secure setting, and presented for exchange, the Americans would have placed the King under restraint, by virtue of an extradition-judgement, by the Panamanian authorities, aggravated by the charge of attempted escape.

In Teheran, however, night had fallen, and the President, Bani-Sadr, had not yet sent the order. He was asleep, and no-one, it seems, dared to wake him. Besides, the documents finalising the operation had not been completely translated, so it was not, after all, possible, with any semblance of decency, to hold the Egyptian, presidential aircraft any longer.

It took off and encountered no further obstacles on its way.

Chapter XVI

"May God protect Iran!"

24th March - 27th Juillet 1980

A s the Egyptian aircraft took off at last from the Azores, Mohammad Reza Pahlavi knew that a decisive point had just been passed: he would, after all, be ending his life with dignity and honour in a friendly country. In this matter, at least - thanks to his own persistence, and that of his friends and of a man of integrity, President Sadat – he had, in the last few moments, triumphed over his enemies. He was comforted, almost happy. The flight passed off without incident. The Shah was suffering physically, but he was at peace.

At Cairo international airport, President and Mrs Sadat were waiting for the Imperial Couple. The Sovereign had not been forewarned of this, and was probably not expecting it. When he was told, his emotion was visible: he got up and was the first to alight from the 'plane. The Rais embraced him as a brother and a friend and as a man of honour and courage.

The Rais' helicopter conveyed the presidential couple and their guests to the Koubbeh palace – a huge, kitsch building, which the Egyptian kings had constructed with a view to reproducing the style of the Palace of Versailles – where the state received its distinguished visitors. In taking the Shah there first, the Rais wanted to show the King that Egypt had not forgotten what Imperial Iran had done for her, had not ceased to pay the Sovereign all due respect and was not treating him as an exile and a fugitive.

After a few minutes, the helicopter resumed its flight and disembarked the two couples at the Ma'adi hospital in Cairo, where the doctors, who would be taking care of the Shah, were already assembling. In response to a call from the Shahbanou, Dr. Georges Flandrin had arrived from Paris – a circumstance, which was highly reassuring for the patient and his wife. Prof. de Bakey, and six other American practitioners, including Dr. Kean, had come from the USA. Three, eminent, Egyptian medics, including the President's son-in-law and personal physician, also formed part of the team.

On the 28th, in an operation lasting an hour and twenty minutes, the removal of the spleen took place. There were no complications. The surgeons did not consider it absolutely necessary to install a drainage-tube, which, anyway, the Shah would have found unacceptable, and so none was fitted. There was no further surgery to the pancreas.

After the success of the operation, in yet another generous gesture, the Rais conferred decorations on de Bakey and all the members of the surgical team. In this way, Egypt expressed her gratitude to them, for having saved the life of a friend.

Routine, pathological analyses, carried out by the Egyptians, demonstrated at once that cancer had spread to the liver, which meant that a fatal outcome could not be long delayed. At an ensuing press-conference, nevertheless, Prof. De Bakey was cautiously optimistic, saying that much was hoped of the chemotherapy, which had been prescribed.

Ten days later, his general condition having greatly improved, and benefiting enormously from his restoration to a life of calm and dignity, Mohammad Reza Pahlavi returned to the Koubbeh palace.

Life at the Koubbeh palace was pretty monotonous. Visits from intimates - from the Shah's children, from his sister, Ashraf, or from Ardeshir Zahedi – were rare. There were several encounters between the Imperial Couple and the Sadats, when the Shah and the Rais discussed international and Middle-Eastern politics, sometimes without others present; but mainly the Sovereign read and took walks in the gardens. He ate well enough, enjoyed "siestas", played cards now and again in the evening, and, having dined at about eight-o-clock, usually watched a film and went to bed early.

On the 25th of April, some very strange news disturbed this humdrum routine and gave rise to much discussion and some sarcasm. Having failed to secure the release of the hostages, in an exchange for the Shah, Carter's government – which would stop at nothing to secure his re-election – decided to mount a spectacular, military operation. This was to be a fiasco, so complete that it would have been comical, if it had not resulted in loss of life.

'Planes and helicopters set off towards Iran from an aircraft-carrier, which was patrolling the Persian Gulf, and converged on a place in the Great Central Desert, not far from the oasis of Tabass. Huge amounts of information had been provided by the world's most sophisticated intelligence-services, but, apparently, no-one had noticed that the small, military airfield, chosen as the point-of-incursion, was – because it had been closed and abandoned years before – completely covered in sand. Besides this, it was hundreds of miles from Teheran, where the hostages were being held. Why, one wonders, was this airfield chosen as the operational base?

Several enquiries into the affair were later held, but no-one ever managed to answer this question. Three helicopters became bogged down in the sand, and another crashed into an aeroplane and exploded, killing eight. The survivors of the operation were told to return with all haste, before the unusual hullabaloo attracted first, the local peasants, then the guardians of the revolution and then the TV-cameras of the global mass-media. Nevertheless, America was humiliated and made to look ridiculous.

Towards the end of April, there was a sudden alert concerning the state of the Shah's health: he was having stomach-pains, nausea, vomiting and fever. His retinue were alarmed. Preliminary examinations indicated an infection. Prof. De Bakey and his team, Dr. Coleman (the acknowledged specialist, who had been sidelined in New York and was called in, this time, by Princess Ashraf) and several others, arrived in Cairo to complement the Egyptian medics. The Shahbanou summoned Georges Flandrin once again. The doctors discussed the patient and disagreed, as did the Shah's immediate circle, on all points. The question of the patient's condition became a battlefield. Ardeshir Zahedi tried to arbitrate and calm everyone down.

The medical team went to see the Shah, who was, as ever,

impeccably dressed, calm, and smiling. He joked with the physicians. Then there was a lull, during which the patient felt better. After another examination, the chemotherapeutic dosage was modified, and the team broke up.

As soon as I heard that the Sovereign was getting better, and would be able to receive me, I called the Koubbeh palace and asked to meet him. This request was warmly welcomed, and I was asked for the number of my flight, and time of arrival, so that I could be met at the airport.

So it was that, on Thursday 8th May 1980, I landed at Cairo, and representatives of the Egyptian government took me to the Koubbeh palace, where I arrived shortly after 9.00 pm. The Shah was coming out of the dining-room, on his way to watch a film, when I presented my respects. His first question was surprising, and almost touching: "have you had dinner?" he enquired, " you ought to be hungry!" and he gave orders for me to be served a meal.

Then he said, "I shall see you for a good while tomorrow morning: we shall walk in the park every morning, from half-past-eleven until lunch-time.
"That way, we can talk in peace."

Very early, on the day-after-next, the Shahbanou was going to Jordan, to take a few days rest, and so, before joining her husband in the projection-room, she received me for some time. She was resigned and brave, but visibly fatigued: "you cannot begin to imagine what we have had to put up with," she said to me.

The following day, a Friday, was fine and quite warm. I chatted with various people in the corridors, before greeting the Shah, as he was emerging from his apartments. As we were going down the great staircase leading to the park, he asked me for news of me and mine, and I said I was worried about his health. He replied that his surgery had, "so it seemed", been successful, adding very tranquilly, "one hopes for the same success from the chemotherapy, in which case I may have a respite.

"If not, I might live three months, or six.

"Well, more like three, actually, but, whatever it might be, it is all in the hands of God and I consign myself to Him."

When we arrived in the park, we walked in silence, and I felt pained, and profoundly saddened, to see him so weak and shrunken. I had to make an effort to turn towards him and say casually, "Sire, it seems to me that you have lost rather a lot of hair."

"That's true," he replied, "but," and here he smiled, glancing at my bald pate, "I've still got more than you!

"I have become very thin, and I'm trying to get back into shape by taking some physical exercise, but it's not easy."

I told him then that I had recently started editing a book of memoirs on my personal and professional career, including the revolution, my departure from Iran and my meetings with His Majesty at Cuernavaca – perhaps this meeting also. The book was eventually published, by Albin Michel, under the title of "Iran, Two Broken Dreams."

"You're right," he said, "one must bear witness - tell the truth – we have been so infamously slandered."

He told me about his final months in the USA and Panama, and about various recent events, including memories of a personal nature. He also asked me about what was happening in Paris, among the Iranian community, the resistance groups and the state of feeling in the country. I explained that opponents of the revolutionary regime were very keen to know whether he would support their action, and, especially, what his attitude was to the army, which continued to express its loyalty to him. At this point, he interrupted me quite forcefully.

"But what do people expect from me, at the moment?" he burst out, "what do they want – what do you want?"

"Sire," I replied, "for myself, nothing whatever."

"I know that you," he rejoined, "you want nothing from me – it's the Iranian people – the people I've done so much for, and who have renounced me – what can they still want from me now?"

These were the complaints of bitterness, heard so many times before.

"Sire," I said, " the people watched you leave, abandoning the soil of the motherland, and reflected that loyalty is a reciprocal matter."

"Yes," he sighed, "perhaps you're right: Iran should not have been abandoned; she should have been fought for – but I didn't want to shed the blood of my own people, nor could I have imagined for a moment what those characters were capable of doing.

"Are they really human beings or foul beasts?"

"Sire," I asked, "why, in the final months, did you ban demonstrations, which were in your favour and against the revolutionaries, while the revolutionaries were allowed to demonstrate freely, to loot, burn, destroy and murder?

"The counter-revolutionaries and patriots," I continued, "were prevented, forbidden, to demonstrate and express themselves: Your Majesty was obliged to leave, so that tens of thousands of people could be kept from going out into the streets and crying 'God save the King!' and, a fortnight later, it would have been half-a-million.

"Don't you remember," I persisted, " that evening, when Baheri, Ghassem Motamedi and others, including me, were going to stay in the palace until you agreed not to leave the country?

"On the following morning, several hundred people were already converging on Ayatollah Khonsari's house with the intention of joining us.

"I beg your pardon, Sire," I concluded, "but you chased us out of the palace, and we had to turn all those others back."

"I didn't chase you away," he replied, "I merely asked you to leave; but what's done is done."

There followed a very long silence.

"I dedicated my life to Iran," he said, at last, "is it not true that, in 1945, when we were occupied by the three, greatest foreign armies in the world, I managed to keep the country together and maintain most of her territorial integrity, even if I did have to hive off Azerbaijan, and part of Kurdistan, and leave them to the Russians?

"I re-built the army, so that it became the honour and glory of Iran; so that, in recent years, Iran was the guarantor of her own security, that of the Gulf-region and that of the West's oil-supply.

"My 'White Revolution', which I was obliged to carry out, because no-one else could be bothered to do it, was a positive initiative, which gave the Iranian people a better standard of living than my adversaries themselves had ever known.

"Was not our agrarian reform a necessary measure?

"Who arranged that, then, without any bloodshed whatsoever?

"And what about the emancipation of Iranian women, and the participation of workers in firms' profits?

"What about the 'armies of knowledge and hygiene' and the tremendous growth of the Iranian economy – does all that count for nothing?

"Has the Iranian people been fair?

"And what about the West?

"I was the pillar of peace in the Middle East, playing a leading role in bringing Egyptians and Israelis to Camp David, where they concluded the treaty.

"Sadat, of course, but Carter and Begin also, telephoned me, on the day the treaty was signed, to express their appreciation for my work.

"I raised the price of petrol, and they're making me pay for it now; but I also proposed aid to developing countries, so that, all together, we could save this poor, old world from its folly and organise a more equitable distribution of its wealth.

"And, now that I am no longer there, have you heard that the price of petrol has fallen?

"In my reign, Iran lived in peace with all her neighbours, Iranians were respected by everyone, everywhere, and no country in the world, except the communist ones, required our people to obtain entry-visas; but just look at her now!"

He was speaking not so much to me as for the historical record. Again, there was a long silence.

"Do you know," the Shah resumed, "that, in a quarter of a century, the per capita income of Iran grew from $160 to $2 450?

"Of course, you *do* know, because you're an economist and were involved in the process of development.

"Do you know," he asked again, " that the IMF, and the best, specialised, American institutes, predicted, in 1977, that, by the end of the century, Iran's economic level was going to be higher than that of Spain – not the Spain of that time, but the Spain of today!?

"All of that was possible; everything was possible – there was nothing we could not dream of.

"We had the resources, the skilled people and a stable government.

"The resources, indeed, will remain, more or less – at least as long as they are defended from the kind of pillage we often see in other countries – but the skilled manpower is now being forced to flee, and Iran is ruled by a bloody anarchy.

"Was this not the end foreseen by those who favoured, planned and even organised this kind of retrograde revolution?

"In just a few years – maybe only five or six – Iran would have been the world's principal producer of fertiliser, and its national oil-company would have been one of the world's top-ten.

"Our steel-production too was expanding at an astonishing rate.

"It was all of this, which our enemies abroad wished to halt and destroy."

He stopped speaking, and a further, long silence intervened. I could see that he did not want a reply, but was relishing the opportunity to speak. However, we walked on, for a while, without saying anything, through the extensive gardens of the Koubbeh palace, the Shah showing no sign of fatigue, until, suddenly, he smiled broadly and asked, "do you know that, some years ago, the British ambassador (was it Parsons then, or someone else?) told me – hardly bothering to avoid being patronising – of his surprise that American students were coming to our beloved university at Shiraz to study medicine?"

I had been Rector at Shiraz from 1968 to 1971.

"He said he was amazed," the Sovereign went on, "that Arab princes were coming for treatment to the university's Namazi and Khalili hospitals, and I felt distinctly that this annoyed him.

"He didn't like the idea that people should come to Iran except to visit Persepolis or the mosques.

"But Iran was becoming the leading light of the Middle East, on every level; and people like him were becoming less and less tolerant of the fact that Iran was becoming such a model.

"They knew that Iranians were capable of making extraordinary efforts, and this irked them: one western newspaper, and not one of the least, even reproached me for aiming to increase the consumption of meat in Iran; but why should a Frenchman eat fourteen stone of meat a year – and an American, more than twenty – and an Iranian not?

"This could only mean that I was a megalomaniac!"

"In 1973," the Shah continued, "we succeeded in putting a stop, irrevocably, to sixty years of foreign exploitation of Iranian oil-resources.

"The stubborn, old man," he reflected, referring, as always, to Mossadegh, by means of this epithet, "could have done it twenty-five years earlier, with all the trumps he held, if he had been less egotistical and more clear-sighted.

"However, in 1974, Iran at last took over the management of the entire oil-industry, including the refineries at Abadan and so on, when the new oil-law was decisively voted through; and I am quite convinced that it was from this moment that some very powerful, international interests identified, within Iran, the collusive elements, which they could use to encompass my downfall.

"Unfortunately, these ambitious, or unhappy, people allowed their hatred or bitterness to be manipulated.

"We should have been more watchful."

For a long time, he fell silent again. Then, amazingly, he alluded to something, which I had thought quite insignificant and had completely forgotten: "It must have been three or four years ago," the Shah began again, "during one of your professional visits to the USA, that Mr -" - and here he named a CIA-asset, who was regarded as a sort of visionary, in the intelligence-field, and whom he had frequently received in Iran – "came to see you in Salt Lake City and put his personal jet at your disposal so that you and your wife could go to his estate in Los Angeles, for the weekend.

"This was at exactly the time, when you were first spoken of as my potential Prime Minister.

"He told you that he wanted to get to know you better and introduce you to other prominent Americans – to evaluate you, as they say.

"You politely declined the offer, which few politicians, Iranian or otherwise, would have done, and which I appreciated very much: it told me that you were not prepared to go behind my back; but how many others could I say that of?"

I was touched, if surprised, by this sincere, but belated and, as things turned out, useless observation. The man in question – one of America's biggest businessmen and a benefactor, and member of the board, of several universities – was reckoned as highly influential both within the CIA and in politics generally.

"Quite a few, Sire," I replied, "well, I think so anyway."

"You really think so?" he asked.

"Perhaps I'm wrong," I said, "but I sincerely believe it."

"Of all those who gravitated towards America," the Shah rejoined, "the worst ones, perhaps, were those who were attracted to the IMF, as you well know; the people, some of them brilliant men, who were happy to play the servant.
"I was always opposed to their leader's becoming a minister."

"He had other, equally important, functions," I argued.

"But he shouldn't have become a minister," insisted the Sovereign.

Now the tone of his monologue changed, becoming derisive. He noticed this himself, as he ran over his principal points again and returned to the question of American policy.

"For me, you see, the real reasons, the underlying reasons – the reasons of state, if you like – for the American attitude, are still incomprehensible.
"Iran was working, producing and constructing; she was a good customer, as well as being an important and vital force for peace and stability in the Gulf-region.
"I just can't see how these positive factors could have become negative in their view – and to such an extent that our strength should have become a reason for deposing me.
"It's true that the Democrats never liked me, and that some of them, led, at the beginning by Humphrey, and by others later, looked upon Iranian, military power, and upon my unashamed

regional and global ambitions, with a jaundiced eye."

He consulted his watch with a habitual, perfunctory movement. Our private talk was nearly over.

"Sire," I said, "let me say once more that Your Majesty made a grave mistake in leaving Iran, and that I have never regretted so much my inability to persuade you to remain."

"I'm sorry too," he replied, "more than you will believe, and I have to take responsibility for it; but the pressures I was under – not just from abroad, you understand, but also from my entourage - got stronger and stronger until they became irresistible.

"It's true that Sadat and Hussein [of Jordan] told me, in no uncertain terms, to stay and tidy up the mess; so too did the Chinese, in their way, and for different motives, no doubt.

"It's true that, within the country, there were a great many like you, who tried to dissuade me from leaving – all those officers, for example, who were so dear to me – but I didn't want any bloodshed, so I couldn't give the order to shoot.

"I was horrified at the thought of a fratricidal, civil war.

"Sadly, seeing what has happened, I am in no doubt that the relatively few casualties of a restoration of order, whose families we would have looked after in the traditional manner, would have been a drop in the ocean compared to the numbers of those, who have fallen victim to the massacre, which is still going on.

"Thousands of innocents murdered, lootings, rapes ... how can anyone commit such crimes in the name of God?

"How can the hundreds of thousands of people, who have fled the country, ever be persuaded to return?"

Suddenly, with almost uncontrolled anger, "and where are

the defenders of democracy and human rights now?" he raged, "there is nothing there but evil and destruction."

Colonel Nevissi, who had been following us, a few paces behind, for more than an-hour-and-a-half, then came up to us and, after a discreet gesture of respect, announced that lunch would be served very shortly.

"We shall continue this conversation," said the Shah.

After lunch, and a long nap, the Sovereign, who was about to play cards for an hour, said to me, teasingly, "I'm not going to invite you, because I know you don't play, although I do wonder why this might be.

"However, if it wouldn't bore you, do please come and watch."

This I did. Afterwards, he withdrew "to do a bit of reading", so he said. I thought he looked rather lost: he had nothing to do; he had no illusions about his health - was no longer worried about his security – he was treading water, waiting.

After dinner that evening, there was the inevitable film-show, attended by a small group, consisting, besides myself, of the Imperial Couple, Mrs Pirnia and Dariouch Panah-Izadi, a renowned consulting-engineer, living in exile at Paris, who had come to Cairo to greet the Shah, but was not staying at the palace. We watched a police-detective production, set in Athens and starring Omar Sharif.

"We've already seen it a thousand times," the Shah said, "but, since we have nothing else to do..."

On the following day, very early in the morning, I accompanied the Shahbanou to the airport. When I returned to the palace, I was intrigued to discover that the Shah was at a meeting with, so I was told, some Americans. Just after eleven-o-clock, the visitors left, Mohammad Reza Pahlavi emerged from the room, where he had received them, and he and I went down into the park.

He said: "let's go on with our conversation: I do hope you will not forget what I have said to you here and at Cuernavaca.

"You will have to decide, of course, what can, or cannot, suitably be published, and choose the right time for publication: I'm depending on you."

I was able to tell him frankly that I completely understood his concern. He added, to satisfy my curiosity, I assume, "those people, you saw leaving just now, are lawyers and bankers.

"Things being as they are, we have to sort out some private problems for the future."

Then we talked about the activities of the Iranian opposition abroad. The Shah knew that I was not a member of any of the groups, but that I knew about almost every one of them, and he liked to keep abreast of all their aims and intentions. He was careful not to get involved directly, as much for reasons of health as from a desire to avoid causing political embarrassment to his friend Sadat, but he could not avoid becoming the focus of numerous requests and pressures from every quarter and knew that these would continue as long as he lived.

His position was clear: he would not abdicate, either in favour of his son and legitimate heir or, indeed, at all. It appeared that the Americans were continually asking him "to clarify the situation", but he was his country's legitimate

Sovereign and, after his demise, his son would do his duty. The "pseudo-referendum", which was held in Iran on the 30th and 31st of March, was "null and void".

Neither would he acknowledge any other referendum – even one, which was properly organised – on the political future of Iran, whose constitution, which had to be respected, provided the procedures to be followed. The present Iranian regime was not legitimate, but the result of overthrow by violence. It was no more than a *de facto* administration. Sovereignty lay with the Iranian people, which might, if need be, express its will within the constitutional framework. He bitterly regretted having left Iran, having pronounced the disastrous discourse of 6th November 1978 and having prevented the armed forces from restoring order and legality.

His resentment towards all those, who had betrayed him, and towards the world-leaders, whose cowardice had so discomfited him, was very great, but, ever since then, he had kept his distance from them. He knew that his end was nigh and he could only resign himself to it. He was glad that he would be able to pass away with dignity, thinking of nothing but history and the judgement of his compatriots and of succeeding generations.

"It's quite natural," he said, "that a Sovereign in exile should be little regarded: it's quite simple: he has nothing to offer.
"I was powerful, when the people of Iran were happy; but now they are unhappy, and there's nothing I can do for them."

All the same, the visionary in him – the fine connoisseur of history – retained great optimism concerning the long-term future of Iran.

"That bloody and absurd regime," he told me, "is the puppet of foreign interests.

"It might last – perhaps for years – thanks to terror, and terrorism, and the weakness of the West.

"An enfeebled Iran, swaying like a reed, suits so many interests; but, inevitably, as so often in previous centuries, my country will be re-born and will be strong and well-respected once again, standing like an oak, recovering the habit ordained by destiny and its rightful grandeur.

"This contemptible regime is, so to speak, a graft, which will not take: the eternal Iran will reject it, because it is incompatible with our past, our culture and our traditions.

"It has stolen the soul of the Iranian people, for the moment, but our chequered history has seen it all before."

"Another revolution will unavoidably put things right one day; and when it does, Iran will dazzle the world once again."

"It is from a return to the deep sources of our culture and civilised values that we may expect our salvation, of which, at the right moment, one man will doubtless become the symbol and standard-bearer."

After this rousing speech, he said no more for several minutes, until, as though thinking aloud, he murmured, referring to the heir-to-the-throne, "will it be Reza?" and fell silent again.

"He would have to be strong enough to rally everyone around him," he said at last, "Iran has no use for the merely decorative."

The Shah looked at me for a long time, but he might not have been seeing me. He seemed absent. Finally, although we had not received the customary signal, "it's time for luncheon," he said.

That was the end of the interview. On the following day, I returned to Paris.

Mohammad Reza Pahlavi was yet to enjoy a brief period of peace and quiet, but his condition would soon deteriorate rapidly, and, from now on, his family, and doctor, knew that his days were numbered.

I was due to make another visit to Cairo, from 2nd to 4th June 1980, in the company of General Bahram Ariana, who had been Head of the General Staff until the end of the 'sixties. The General was a fine patriot, whose integrity was a by-word and who was universally respected. He had been living for some years in Paris, a city, which he loved, having received much of his education there, and having also served as a military attaché to its Iranian embassy. He led a modest and simple life, working on small publications about Iranian history, visiting museums and reading.

Seeing that the various groups opposing the Teheran-regime were becoming embroiled in useless squabbling – most notably between Shapour Bakhtiar and General Oveyssi – many Iranians had tried to persuade Ariana to make a last-ditch attempt to unify them. Some French, American, Egyptian and Turkish, senior officers, acting in their personal capacities, had also urged him to do this. Now the Egyptian government had invited him to Cairo to discuss the matter, and he asked me to go with him. I accepted at once, mainly because of his probity and idealism. The Egyptian general staff had made detailed arrangements for the trip.

On 4th June, we telephoned the Koubbeh palace to ask if we

might come and greet the Shah. His staff did not know that we were in Cairo, but the Shahbanou immediately invited us to attend her, that day, at the beginning of the afternoon. The Shah's health had deteriorated suddenly, she told us, and he was in no condition to accord us an audience. When we met her, however, and in spite of her natural anxiety, she appeared full of confidence and spent an hour with us, discussing the situation in Iran and asking after the fortunes of various people. At about half-past-six that evening, she telephoned us, saying that the Shah wanted to see us, but only for a few minutes.

At the Koubbeh palace, whither we repaired with all haste, we were taken straight to the Shah's apartment. He was in bed with pneumonia and a temperature of 104. His face impressed me: it was calm, but with the tranquillity of total resignation. I knew that he was now at death's door and was no longer struggling to overcome his sorrows, which, I guessed, were indeed terrible. He told us that he had been informed, by Sadat, of our presence in the city. We stood, one on either side of his bed. The Shahbanou sat a little further away.

The General, who had not seen the Shah for some years, was deeply moved. He explained to him briefly how very numerous were the Iranians who remained loyal to their patriotic ideals.

"I want to tell you ..." the Shah began and then interrupted himself, "no, I'm very tired and have great difficulty in speaking."

"Perhaps, Sire," General Ariana asked, "you would prefer that, instead of leaving early tomorrow, at four-o-clock, we take the next 'plane, and come to speak with you in the morning?"

"No," the Sovereign replied, "I know that you are working

492

for Iran and I don't feel I have the right to delay you, be it only for a few hours.

"Iran is on the way to dissolution, sinking bit-by-bit, and every hour is precious: go, and may God aid and protect you!

"May God protect Iran!"

I was never to see the Shah again.

As usual, the Shahbanou alerted Dr. Flandrin, who opined that it was necessary to operate on the Shah's pancreas. Prof. De Bakey had, it appears, withdrawn from the medical team (at any rate, he was not available) so, with the agreement of Prof. Safavian, Flandrin called Dr. Pierre Louis Fagniez, who consented to lead the team jointly with him.

However, it seems that Princess Ashraf trusted only the Americans, and she brought in Dr. Coleman and his team. Once again, the French and Egyptians, on one side, and the Americans, on the other, disagreed about the course to be taken, and the quarrels among the medics were augmented by periodically hot-tempered ones, within the family. In the end, the Shahbanou and President Sadat – who had been asked to give his view – decided to put their confidence in Dr. Flandrin; and, on 30th June, surgery was performed, by the French and Egyptian team.

There were problems, but the operation was a success: the remains of the pancreas were removed. Nevertheless, according to some, this should have been done months before. Moreover, remission was brief. The patient's suffering soon began again, and grew worse, and his condition went downhill with every passing day. The Shah continued to despatch details of his final revision of the American edition of "A Reply To History", but his speech became less and les audible. He was put into an intensive care-unit, where he was tended by Dr. Flandrin and Egyptian physicians. Dr. Kean and Prof. De Bakey could not be contacted.

All the witnesses agree that the Shah suffered dreadfully and lost a great deal of blood, but that he remained lucid and never complained. Rather, he consoled others and even joked from time to time. During the last days of his life, he often expressed a desire to be buried, in Iran, beside the officers and men, who had been martyred by the revolutionaries. Naturally, this cannot happen until after Iran has been freed; but it was possible to guess, from certain hints he dropped, exactly where he imagined, and we shall one day see, his final resting-place.

His detachment, from what was going on around him, became complete; and he ceased to speak, when he could speak at all, of anything but Iran. There was no hatred, resentment or bitterness any more.

Three days before his death, he confided as follows, to his last Grand Master of Protocol: "I did everything in my power for the greatness of my country and the welfare of my people, wishing to lead them towards a pre-eminent civilisation, which, alas, is now in danger of never coming about."

He was afraid, more than anything, that centrifugal forces would appear, which, ultimately, would bring about the disintegration of Iran: "the Iranian revolution," he said, "did not arise from deprivation, as some pretend, because Iranians were quite capable of comparing their country's condition, and their own standard of living, with the way these things were fifty, or even ten, years before.

"Indeed, the agitation took place, very largely, among the more affluent, who were manipulated into taking a course, which would prove suicidal for them."

"In order to hear him," Aslan Afshar notes, "I had to put my ear almost to his lips, so feeble had his voice become."

"I wait upon Fate, never ceasing to pray for Iran, and for my people," whispered the Shah, "I think only of their suffering," and these were the last words the King ever uttered.

Dr. Flandrin said later, "he spoke only of his country, at that time, which I greatly admired in him."

After the 25th July, as a result of a virulent, new infection and a bout of fever, the Shah entered a state of shock. A very imminent conclusion was then inevitable. It was only a matter of hours. The Imperial Couple's children were in Alexandria, and the eldest, Reza, was called on the night of 25th/26th. Understanding the situation, he became deathly pale and told his sister, Farahnaz, that the Shah was dying. She broke into sobs. They set out at once with their two children.

On 26th, the medical team resigned itself to letting nature take its course and to halting all positive therapies, as serving no useful purpose. To this, the family agreed and the patient fell into a coma. This day, the 26th, was the anniversary of the death of the Shah's father.

The Shahbanou, Princess Ashraf, the couple's four children, Dr. Pirnia, Ardeshir Zahedi, Aslan Afshar, Mark Morse and Amir Pourshodja remained continuously at the hospital.

On Sunday 27th, early in the morning, the Shah took several audible breaths and gave a great sigh. That was the end.

ᴴis body was then disencumbered of the paraphernalia of medical assistance. Dr. Pirnia took off his wedding-ring and gave it back to his wife. An Egyptian physician closed his eyes.

Icarus had fallen.

At ten-o-clock, that morning, death was officially pronounced and the corpse was transferred to the mortuary.

Controversy arose at once, in the Iranian media, and elsewhere, over whether the Shah had left a political will. I am in a position to respond to this question. In 1976, in his office, the Sovereign called together several important people. Present were Prime Minister Hoveyda, the Presidents of the two Chambers, Mohammad Baheri - then acting Minister to the Imperial Court (Alam being very ill and receiving medical treatment abroad) - Azhari, who was Head of the General Staff, Moinian (Head of the Imperial Cabinet) and Djamchid Amouzegar, the Secretary General of Rastakhiz.

"No-one lives for ever," the Shah told them, if not in these exact words, "life and death are subject to Divine Will.

"My duty is to look ahead and ensure the continuity of the state and the security and integrity of the nation.

"When I am gone, the Constitution must be observed in everything, whether it be under the rule of my heir, he having reached the required age [of twenty years] or under the regency of the Shahbanou, governing through a council, in which you will take part.

"If this procedure, which I hereby enjoin you to sustain and assure, should fail – if it goes astray through the intervention of some grave occurrence – it will be up to the army, the Head of the General Staff and the three Commanders-in-Chief, to take matters in hand and to rescue the motherland, at whatever cost.

"I have had these orders, which are my will, drafted, with several copies, and each of you, including the secretary of Rastakhiz [the sole, political party] will receive one of these."

What became of this document? The Prime Minister's copy was handed, literally, by him, to Prof. Hadi Hedayati, the Minister of State delegated to assist the Prime Minister, and he deposited it, in a sealed envelope, in the Presidency's secret vault. The Imperial Cabinet's copy is now kept in a foreign country. The army's copy ended up in the hands of General Gharabaghi, who worked, with General Huyser, to prevent any action by the armed forces, and who had, therefore, no desire to publish it. The same might be said for Bakhtiar, when he became Prime Minister: he might have learned of the document; but we cannot be sure of this. The copy given to Mohammad Baheri has been rescued, after a fashion.

Under the circumstances, in which the Imperial regime foundered, and which fulfilled exactly the last of the hypotheses mentioned by the Shah, no-one had any wish to evoke this text. This applied to the Shahbanou, who probably knew about it, and who was counting on Bakhtiar, and to Bakhtiar himself, who preferred to see the revolution triumph, rather than precipitate a military coup, as all the relevant documents confirm. It applied also to the Head of the General Staff. As for the first party to the injunction, the Shah, he had abandoned the reins of government.

A baffling state of affairs!

EPILOGUE

29th July 1980 – Cairo – The Shah's Funeral. Behind the
Shahbanou and President Sadat, are ranged the Imperial Family,
almost in its entirety.
To the extreme right, Ardeshir Zahedi.

(Ardeshir Zahedi Collection)

Cairo, 29th July 1980

That 29th July, in the suffocating heat of the Egyptian capital, the funeral-rites of Mohammad Reza Pahlavi, who had wanted a simple ceremony, assumed grandiose proportions.

"In recognition of all he achieved," President Sadat declared, "we now bid him farewell with the same honours and the same respect, with which we welcomed him on his arrival here.

"Egypt will never forget the aid, which Iran brought to her, during the war against Israel, of 1973."

A few days before, knowing that the Shah's end was near, Aslan Afshar had come to pay him a final visit. Afshar would be responsible too for the funeral-arrangements, all of which he made in collaboration with Teymour, his Egyptian opposite-number. In this, Ardeshir Zahedi rendered him valuable assistance - especially by dealing effectively, in his somewhat abrupt manner, with the tiffs and mood-swings of the entourage – but also by making the numerous 'phone-calls necessary for resolving matters of diplomacy.

As soon as she learned of the death of Mohammad Reza Pahlavi, the Empress Soraya let it be known that she wished to take part in the funeral-ceremony, and, in the course of several, long telephone-conversations, Ardeshir Zahedi took enormous pains to dissuade her, explaining, on the strength of the friendship and mutual respect, which had always existed between them, that her presence would raise too many difficulties, both within the family and in terms of official protocol. Soraya, who had sent a last letter to the Shah, just before his death, gave in and contented herself with contributing a sumptuous wreath.

The tomb, in the great El-Rifai mosque, had been made ready. This was the same resting-place, in which the mortal remains of Reza Shah had been deposited, during the Second World War, before they were taken back to Iran.

The coffin, lying on a gun-carriage and covered with the Iranian, national flag, was drawn to the mosque by two horses. Three officers in dress-uniform marched in front, each carrying, on a cushion, one of the Shah's decorations. These symbolised the insignias, of the highest grades, of almost all the prominent orders of all the countries of the world, which the late Sovereign had received during the course of his long reign; but why three?

This ceremonial detail had created a delicate problem, which divided the entourage. The Shah's loyal valet for thirty years, Pourshodja, had packed all his master's decorations, in a confused mass, in a large suitcase, which he had trundled around everywhere. Some family-members thought that, in accordance with the protocol of normal times, all the Shah's decorations, each on a cushion, should be carried before the

502

cortege, but Aslan Afshar was decidedly opposed to this. For one thing, there were not enough Iranian officers to carry them. Besides, he argued, why should they exhibit, and honour, decorations given by countries, whose attitude towards the deceased had been ignoble? It was not really possible to make a suitable selection. Ardeshir Zahedi agreed, and, eventually, the Grand Master of Protocol prevailed. Three decorations were chosen, two of which - the insignias of the Grand Master of the Zolfaghar military order – were Iranian, the other being Egyptian. This seemed only fitting.

Behind the coffin, walked the Imperial Family almost in its entirety, including the Shahbanou, the couple's four children and, of course, President Sadat, in his capacity as an honorary brother of the departed, and his wife, Jihane.

Many Iranians had wished to go to Cairo to pay their last respects to the Sovereign, but the interval – less than forty-eight hours – was too brief, and some no longer had valid travel-documents. Thus, General Bahram Ariana, the oldest, living holder of the highest rank in the Imperial Army, let the Imperial Family know that he would like to come to Cairo to represent the army at the funeral. He wished to attend, in uniform, wearing all his civil and military decorations. Zahedi and Afshar were not consulted about the response, which was sent to the General, telling him that his presence would not be welcome. I have not been able to discover who was responsible for this.

Richard Nixon, the former President of the United States, was there: "I think," he announced, "that the way our government has behaved in this situation marks one of American history's black pages."

No other internationally recognised figure, crowned head or ex-sovereign, attended, except for King Constantine of Greece, who was a friend of the family and owed the deceased much.

Only four ambassadors, represented their nations. These were the legates of the USA, the German Federal Republic, Israel and France. Britain and Morocco sent diplomats of lesser rank. King Hussein of Jordan sent a wreath, as did several other Heads-of –State.

Three million Egyptians followed the great procession.

On the evening of 27th July, the world's major newspapers filled their front pages with the story of the last Shah's death. Notable was the favourable change in editorial attitudes, towards the former ruler, following widespread recognition of the tragedy, which had occurred in Iran, and of the revolution's repercussions further afield. The story of the Shah's decease was the premier item on the evening news of France's three TV-channels, the principal one of which ran a lengthy biography, covering the period, from the glory of the celebrations at Persepolis, to the horrors of the revolution, and showing, most strikingly, the tears the Sovereign shed when he left the country, on 16th January 1979. Shapour Bakhtiar, his last Prime Minister, appeared on the second channel, making unjust accusations against the historic figure, who had just passed away, which were highly unbecoming from one, who had agreed to serve under the Shah in such a capacity. I appeared on Channel-3.

Chapter XVI: *May God protect Iran!*

Numerous messages of condolence and sympathy were sent to Mohammad Reza Pahlavi's family. In that of President Valéry Giscard d'Estaing, the writer succeeded in omitting to mention, either the Shah's name, his position or even his memory!

The White House treated the matter offhandedly, without reference to the ties between the deceased and the United States or the role played by Iran in what was still being called "the free world". The communiqué merely recalled that "he ruled Iran for the exceptionally long time of 38 years, which history would register as a period of profound change". It concluded by saying that "his death marked the end of an era for Iran".

Henry Kissinger sent a message. His attitude to the Shah had been extremely ambivalent during the last years of the reign – as the Sovereign finally admitted, implicitly, in the English version of "A Reply to History" – but became exemplary once the Shah was in exile. His message read, "he was a good friend of the United States, who supported us through every crisis, but he died forsaken by all, except by Sadat."

Another, former, American Secretary-of-State, James McCloy, said, "we conducted ourselves towards him in an unworthy fashion."

Some of the world's leaders dared, in private, to express themselves suitably, including King Baudouin and Queen Fabiola of Belgium, the Prince of Monaco, the Count of Paris and others.

To all these messages and tributes, Aslan Afshar, re-discovering his function as Master of Protocol to the late Shah, addressed proper replies, signed by the Shahbanou.

In Iran, news of the death of the Sovereign aroused no response, but this was an expected blow. For all Iranians, however, the event did mark the end of an era, the end of a way of life and the end of a legend. Many Iranians, whether unfailingly loyal to the King or wearied by 18 months of the revolutionary experience, which had put their country to fire and the sword, and who had become disillusioned with it, discreetly mourned the Shah's death. Others appeared indifferent. Some groups, which the regime sent into the streets to dance and sing, were obliged to desist, amidst the silent anger and disapproval of the majority.

Some days later, Ali Akbar Hachemi Rafsanjani, future President of the Republic and already the regime's strong-man, declared, "the Americans killed the Shah."

The wife of Bani Sadr (the regime's first President) averred, "the people of Iran are saddened by the loss of the times, which are gone, and even miss the Shah."

Mohammad Reza Pahlavi's mortal remains are entombed at Cairo to this day.

APPENDIX

WHAT BECAME OF THEM?

The Imperial Family

Princess Shahnaz, daughter of the Shah and Princess Fawzieh of Egypt, born 27th October 1940 at Teheran, married, for the first time, to Ardeshir Zahedi, then divorced and re-married, now lives in the USA.

Shahbanou Farah: recently published her memoirs and often gives interviews, recalling times past, to weekly magazines. Divides her time between her Parisian and American residences. Of the Imperial Couple's four children, Prince Reza (b. 31.10.60) Princess Farahnaz (b. 12.3.63) and Prince Ali Reza (b. 28.4.66) live in the USA. The youngest, Leila (b. 1970) the Shah's favourite, they say, died tragically in London on 10.6.01.

The Queen Mother (Tadj-ol-Molouk) died, Los Angeles, 10.3.82 from a painful illness. She had never been able to accept the death of her son.

507

Of the Shah's two sisters, the elder, Princess Shams, died, USA, 29.2.96. Her husband, Mehrdad Pahlbod, long-serving, former Minister of Culture, is still alive. Mohammad Reza Pahlavi's twin-sister, Princess Ashraf, lives in France.

Of the Shah's half-brothers, only the eldest Gholam Reza (b. 1923) is still alive. The others, Abdolreza, Ahmad-Reza and Mahmoud-Reza, as well as the Shah's half-sister, died in exile after the revolution. The youngest, Hamid-Reza, was sundered from the family, remained in Iran and died in Teheran's Evrni prison. The revolutionaries employed him as a gardener.

Of the Shah's nephews and nieces, Prince Ali-Patrick, son of the Shah's only brother, Ali Reza, who died in a 'plane-crash (26.10.54) lives and works in France. The others, with the exception of Shahryar Shafigh, whose fortunes are mentioned in this book, all live abroad.

The Shahbanou's mother, Farideh Diba, and her uncle, Mohammad Ali Ghotbi, died abroad. The latter's first son, Reza, mentioned several times in this book, lives in the USA. The two, successive wives of Mohammad Ali Ghotbi, Louise, Reza's mother, and Elahe, both live in Europe, as does Ghotbi's youngest son, the child of the second marriage.

The Shah's Immediate Entourage During His Exile

Mrs. Lucie Pirnia, loyal and devoted physician, throughout the exile, now lives in the USA.

Col. Yazdan Nevissi and Col. Kioumars Djahambini, who, throughout the exile, took turns, round the clock, keeping watch over the security of the Imperial family, have, since the Shah's demise, lived and worked in the USA, as have the Shah's two personal valets, Ali Pourshodja and Mahmoud Eliassi.

Politicians and Non-Governmental Prominenti

On 12th February 1979, Amir Abbas Hoveyda stayed on alone, under house-arrest at the villa in Lavizan, even though his guards had fled. His telephone being in working order, he kept in touch with his family, but, although he had many friends who might have helped him, he called no-one else. He could have sought asylum at a foreign embassy, but he did not. As we have seen, he was hoping to receive a trial, relishing the prospect of defending himself with parley and pen. He could have made some very embarrassing revelations.

On 12th February, he called the Presidency of the Council, on the number, which had been his own for thirteen years. To all appearances, he then spoke with Mehdi Bazargan, who was a protégé of his, and was asked to remain where he was. Some hours later, Darioush Forouhar – Minister of Labour under the new regime – came in person, riding discreetly in an unremarkable ambulance, to look for him.

Thus, Hoveyda was re-arrested and conveyed to the Alavi High School, where Rouhollah Khomeyni had chosen to reside and to keep his most important prisoners. There, Hoveyda was kept in a room apart, in complete isolation. He was interrogated, but, so it seems, not too badly treated.

On 15th March 1979, he was transferred to Teheran's central prison, the Qasr, where the conditions of his confinement were frightful. He was wearing a hood, when he was brought before judges, of whom he wrote that one was a traitorous General, very highly placed in the Imperial Army, and another was a far-Left, French barrister. It has not been possible to confirm their identities.

That part of his defence, which was made public, was

widely reproduced in the international press. He was accused of having "declared war on God". In reply, he asserted, "I have never 'declared war on God' – however I might be thought to have done that – seeing that I am a believer and have made a pilgrimage to Mecca; but, if you are convinced of my guilt, how could it be otherwise?

"Do what you must!

"However, we have all lived here under the same laws and the same system of government.

"All our laws have been promulgated by Parliament and so have been approved by all."

Following certain discourteous commentaries in some western newspapers, the question then arose concerning which laws Hoveyda should be judged by, and the trial was suspended.

On 5th April, the Revolutionary Council adopted "revolutionary, Islamic," penal provisions, having retrospective effect.

On 7th, Hoveyda appeared again before the "tribunal", which was presided over, so he wrote, by that American national of Iranian extraction, Ibrahim Yazdi, whose voice he thought he recognised, and for whom he recalled certain, inconvenient facts. After a televised interview with Christine Ockrent, which he was obliged to give in his prison-cell, he realised that his fate was sealed and that this publicity was designed only to prepare international, public opinion for news of his death. He decided, therefore, to take the offensive; but his speech was at once curtailed, and the trial, which had hardly begun again, was once more halted. Hoveyda was then taken, blindfold, but with his hands free, into a corridor, and shot, in the back of the neck, with a revolver. Some days later, one

Hadi Ghaffari, notoriously an adherent of a local criminal gang, and subsequently awarded the title "Hodjatoleslam", claimed responsibility for the deed.

Djamchid Amouzegar, Djafar Charif Emami and General Gholam Azhari, Hoveyda's successors at the head of the Cabinet, fled the country voluntarily before the departure of the Imperial Couple.

Sharif Emami died in New York in 1997, having used his power-of-attorney, for the Pahlavi Foundation, over which he presided until almost the end of the regime, to authorise the transfer of its assets – most notably, a Manhattan sky-scraper, which is often said to have been part of the Shah's personal fortune – to the new regime.

General Azhari died in 2002, also in the USA.

Djamchid Amouzegar, now in his eighties, worked for a private company in Washington, before retiring there.

The fate of Bakhtiar, whom the Shah called "the last Prime Minister of the Empire", has aroused some controversy.

In the hours after his disappearance from the Presidency of the Council, on 11th February 1979, at about the middle of the day, Teheran radio announced, first, that he had been assassinated, and then that he had committed suicide. On the following day, it was announced that he had been arrested and was being held in the same building as Hoveyda and several other military and civilian prisoners. This turned out to be true.

An official spokesman said, "Bakhtiar will be interrogated: if he is found guilty, he will be punished; if not, he will be freed."

Le Monde, whose agents had good communications, at that time, with the leaders of the revolution, claimed to have it from "a reliable source" that "the former head of government is in a secure place and in contact with Mehdi Bazargan."

After that, silence fell, concerning the circumstances and fortunes of the former Prime Minister.

During the summer of 1979, Bakhtiar turned up in Paris, having spent several days, so it appears, at Chambéry. Later, he accounted for this, in writing, saying only that he had left the capital from Teheran International Airport, having "slightly changed my looks, with a small beard and a pair of dark glasses, and bearing a foreign passport".

Shortly thereafter, his appearance in Paris created a furore in Teheran. Several of the regime's main figures accused Mehdi Bazargan, his Foreign Minister, Karim Sandjabi, and the Ayatollah Behechti of having secretly set Bakhtiar free and of facilitating his clandestine flight abroad. If this is true, as seems likely, and as has been written by numerous authors, it could not have been done without the assent of Khomeyni. If so, it might have represented some kind of recognition of the fact that it was Bakhtiar who had presented Khomeyni with "the keys to the city".

Bakhtiar has never denied this nor, despite the controversy about it, ever allowed himself to discuss, or even mention, the matter. In Paris, Bakhtiar started a campaign against the Islamic regime, which action received support, initially, from quite a few expatriate Iranians, including some members of the Imperial family, despite the Shah's aversion to Bakhtiar. Principally, however, it was sustained by generous donations from the regime in Iraq, so that the Iran-Iraq war (1980 to 1988) on top of the former Prime Minister's ambiguous position, was fatal to him, politically.

Having escaped a first assassination-attempt, on 18th July 1980, at Neuilly-sur-Seine, where he lived, Bakhtiar had his throat cut – a characteristic method – at Suresnes, in the suburbs of Paris, on 6th August 1991, and the assassins' trial categorically established the Iranian regime's responsibility for this, although it left many worrying elements of the affair in shadow. Bakhtiar had called a halt to all his political activity, several months before, and was preparing to leave France. Apparently, Teheran had felt aggrieved by his ingratitude. It has often been said that the Paris operation was facilitated for "politico-commercial" reasons.

Among the other civilians in the former regime, who are mentioned in this book, Prof. Mohammad Baheri now lives in the USA, after a long spell in France, and Dr. Darioush Shirvani lives in Germany, where he has worked as a gynaecologist for more than twenty years.

After making his famous speech, in the Iranian Parliament, attacking the Bakhtiar Cabinet, Shirvani, his parliamentary immunity notwithstanding, was designated, by the Prime Minister, for arrest by the Savak; but he got wind of this and managed to escape from his house a few minutes before the officers arrived, reaching Europe with his family.

Rector Parviz Amouzegar, witness of an important episode related here, now lives in France, heading a prominent university-faculty in Paris.

Prof. Abbas Safavian, the Shah's personal physician, has lived in Paris since the collapse of the Imperial regime. He has taught, at the College of Faculties of Medicine, for many years, and practices also, as a physician, in the public health-service. He has recently been elected to the National Academy of Medicine.

Chodja-Ol-Dine Chafa, the Sovereign's cultural adviser, has lived in France, since the revolution, dedicating himself entirely to the study of Iranian, and Islamic, history and publishing monumental, authoritative works on these subjects.

Prof. Gholam Hossein Sadighi died, in Teheran, on 29th April 1991. Since the revolution, he had been subjected to somewhat blatant surveillance, his visitors, of whom he had few to begin with, often being openly examined by the police. Despite opposition from the authorities, the people of Teheran accorded him a sumptuous funeral.

Mozaffar Baghai, was, at first, not disquieted. No-one knew about his meetings with the Shah or his abortive attempt to form a government. At one point, he even received permission to leave the country. However, in 1986, following his publication of a pamphlet, which was strongly critical of the regime, he was arrested and tortured to death in prison.

Ayatollah Sayed Kazem Shariat-Madari had sent a message to the Shah, by a secure route, shortly before the fall of the Imperial regime: "this is no time for concessions," it read, "any concession, from now on, will be seen as a sign of weakness and may prove fatal.

"Faced with the current sedition, one must be firm, and react vigorously.

"Let the King have the army arrest me – at least that would show that he still has power – for, if Khomeyni reaches his goal, he will drown Iran in blood and fire."

This prophetic counsel was ignored, even though it came from a man with whom one could still negotiate, and might have reached a settlement, right up to the middle of the autumn of 1978. Shariat-Madari's authority would be progressively undermined and supplanted by that of Rouhollah Khomeyni. At the time of the regime's collapse, a group of the latter's followers, including some who came to power with Mehdi Bazargan, went to Qom to ask the prelate to retreat to Tabriz, his home-town, where he would have been safe: but Shariat-Madari refused to go, even when, shortly afterwards, Qom fell under the dominion of Khomeyni's people.

"I know I'm in danger," he told the delegation, "but destiny cannot be changed: the will of God be done!"

He tried, nevertheless, to influence the course of events as much as he could: on 24th February, he lent his support to the formation of a political party, the Muslim Republican Party, to which many academics, and other intellectuals, and numerous business-people and National Front activists rapidly rallied, the National Front having failed to create even a modest party-structure, in spite of the immense prestige of the name and record of the late Mohammad Mossadegh, whom it pretended to represent. On 30th July 1979, Shariat-Madari issued a fatwa – a kind of imprecatory ordinance – which damned the stance of the regime and the bloody oppression it had loosed across the country, and called upon the clergy to retreat from political life. On the 18th October, in a second fatwa he took up the defence of "intellectual liberty and artistic integrity".

He was put under surveillance, at his home, in 1982. Then he was imprisoned, tortured and exhibited on television. He was refused the right to be seen by any doctor other than one appointed by his gaolers. His death was announced at the beginning of April 1986 and demonstrations of grief, in his memory, were sternly suppressed. Thus, he paid the price of his moderation, patriotism and anti-communism. The Soviets and their agents, who were then highly influential in Iran, had never forgotten, and never pardoned, the role he played in the Azerbaijan affair.

The torment suffered by Ayatollah Shariat-Madari recalls the agonies endured, in Hungary and elsewhere, by Cardinal Mindezenti, and so many other men of faith, at the hands of the communists.

Ardeshir Zahedi, who had been the Shah's brother-in-law, and was always close to him, was formerly the head of the Iranian diplomatic service (1966 – 1973) having been ambassador to London (1962 – 1966) to Washington (1959 – 1962) and, from

1973, ambassador to Washington, for a second time.

It was thanks to his personal intervention that the Imperial Couple were able to stay in Morocco, and then in Mexico. He also arranged their accommodation in Panama, on the island of Contadora, and was beside the Sovereign during the last days, in Cairo. Zahedi lives today in Switzerland and holds an important position in a section of the Iranian diaspora.

Amir Aslan Afshar, last Grand Master of Protocol to the Imperial Court, a career-diplomat, formerly ambassador to Bonn, to Vienna and to Washington, was the Shah's closest counsellor, colleague and confidant during the last months of the reign and the early exile, in Cairo and Morocco, returning to be with the Sovereign during the last days. With Ardeshir Zahedi's help, and in collaboration with the Egyptian department of protocol, he organised Mohammad Reza Pahlavi's funeral at Cairo. He now lives in the South of France, where he plays a prominent role in the life of the important Iranian community, which has established itself in those parts.

The Fate of Certain Soldiers

General Gholam Ali Oveyssi, Commander-in-Chief of the Imperial Army, whose candidacy to lead a "government of authority" was turned down, owing mainly to American pressure, was asked to leave Iran at the time Shapour Bakhtiar took power.

From the summer of 1979, he organised an opposition-movement to the new regime, urged on by numerous army-officers, who had fled the country, and many who had remained, and was supported in this by the Shah; but his action was unsuccessful. He was killed, along with his brother, on the 8th February 1984, in the Passy quarter of Paris, by agents from Teheran.

General Bahram Ariana, former Chief of the General Staff during the 60's, who lived for a long time in Paris, also attempted a military venture against the new regime. He received much encouragement for this, at first, and established a base in Turkey; but he was gradually abandoned thereafter. He died in Paris on the 21st June 1985, at the age of 83.

General Abbas Gharabaghi, the Shah's last Chief of the General Staff, who was General Huyser's main accomplice and, thus, one of the principal architects of the neutralisation of the armed forces. He left Iran without inconvenience and died in Paris a few years later.

At least 1200 officers of the Imperial Army were put to death by the revolutionary authorities, often without so much as a pretence at due process. Thousands more were dismissed from the service, many of whom were obliged to leave the country.

Of the last three heads of the Savak, the irreproachable last two, General Hassan Pakravan and General Nasser Moghaddam, were executed on 11th April 1979. The latter's highly controversial predecessor, General Nematollah Nassiri, suffered the same fate on 16th February 1979, after being atrociously tortured and exhibited on television, when he nevertheless succeeded in pronouncing, albeit almost inaudibly, a declaration of loyalty to the Sovereign.

On 12th February 1979, General Gharani, former Head of the Second Bureau of the General Staff, who had been sacked from this office following some dubious affair, some years before, and who was appointed Chief of the General Staff by Khomeyni and Bazargan, proclaimed a pardon and guarantee of security, for all general and superior officers, and invited them to report to General Staff Headquarters. This proclamation, which was read again and again on the radio, was officially approved by Ayatollah Taleghani, who was then Khomeyni's second in command, and in it, Gharani gave his word of honour as a soldier that respondents to this amnesty would be treated with respect and allowed to go unhindered, after presenting themselves to the high command.

Numerous officers took the bait and believed the word of their old comrade. They were all arrested, on the spot, and delivered to torture and execution. A few days later, Gharani was killed by a burst of machine-gun fire, as he was leaving his house. The Teheran rumour-mill attributed this to a thirst for vengeance among counter-revolutionary, junior officers; but those responsible were never caught or identified, in spite of the revolutionary authorities' efforts in that direction.

Among the first, official victims of torture, were General Mehdi Rahimi and General Manoutchehr Khosrodad, who are often mentioned in this book, as well as General Nadji, the military Governor of Isphahan.

Parts of the interrogation of these officers were shown on television, Ibrahim Yazdi acting as master of ceremonies. After his interrogation, general Rahimi managed to get his hands freed, by demanding to sign his statement, where it lay with his death-warrant appended, and struck Yazdi two enormous blows to the head. Frothing with rage, the admonished Yazdi ordered the hand, which had "sacrilegiously" struck him, to be cut from Rahimi's wrist. This was done there and then, before the General was put to death. Both Mehdi Rahimi, however, and General Khosrodad found the strength to cry "God save the King!" in the faces of their executioners. Nadji prayed to God to pardon his murderers. Nassiri's bloodied body was barely alive, so they stretched him out and shot him as he lay on the floor.

These atrocities, like many others, took place on the roof of Khomeyni's residence! On the following day, the capital's newspapers reported that Khomeyni had gone up, to the place of torture, "to offer a prayer for the dispensation of divine grace". The rumour spread in the city that Khomeyni performed his ritual ablutions using the blood of his torture-victims. Perhaps he did. Those who know the man can believe it.

So many other cases to relate ...

Index

Chahrestani Djavad, Mayor of Teheran, 323, 324
Channel-3, French TV-channel, 504
Chapour I, dam, 41
Charif Emami Djafar, Prime Minister, 160, 162, 163, 164, 165, 166, 167, 169, 170, 171, 172, 173, 175, 176, 177, 189, 195, 202, 205, 211, 223, 231, 254, 286, 289, 290, 305, 314, 322, 327, 511
Charles-Roux François, Ambassadeur de France, 9, 382
Chase-Manhattan Bank, 421
Chile, 461
China, 38, 183, 444
Chopin, 67
Christians, 296
Churchill Winston, 54
Church Frank, Democrat Senator, 59
CIA, 55, 77, 233, 239, 390, 417, 464, 468, 484
City of the roses, 36
Coleman Morton, Dr, surgeon, 453, 454, 467, 493
Committees-of-support for the Ayatollah (Khomeyni), 241
Communism, 12, 14, 99
Communists, 138, 166, 186, 205, 210, 214, 329, 356, 379, 515
Communist agents, 437, 515
Constantine, King of Greece, 32, 37, 131, 504
Constitutional Revolution, 122
Count of Paris, 505
Croesus, King of Lydia, 21
Crosby James, 421
Cutler Lloyd, President Carter's special envoy, 469
Cyrus-the-Great, dam, 41

Cyrus-the-Great, hotel, 24, 39, 41, 46, 184, 186
Cyrus Scroll, 21
Cyrus the Great, 16, 19, 21, 22, 23, 33, 50, 258, 267
Czechoslovakia, 87

D

"Dr. Behechti", self-proclaimed Ayatollah, 319, 320, 343, 512
Danechi Hodjatoleslam, 363
Danechvar Hossein, Ardeshir Zahedi's right-hand man, 342
Dar-es-Salaam, palace in Rabat, 400, 401
Darius-the-Great, hotel, 24, 39
Darius the Great, King, 20, 32, 34, 36
Dashti Ali, great writer, 153
Debré Michel, 244
Delay Raoul, French ambassador to Teheran, 238
Democratic Party (USA), 59, 60, 116, 141, 289, 328, 485
Denmark, 30, 35
Deyhimi, Admiral, 102, 262, 263, 264, 375, 407
Diba Farideh, Shahbanou's mother, 212, 213, 219, 377, 508
Djafarian, Lieutenant General, military governor of the province of Khouzistan, 321
Djahanbani Nader, Officer, 434
Djahanbini Kiourmars, Colonel, Shah's personal body-guard, 9, 102, 263, 386, 392, 419, 463, 470, 508
Dochan Tapeh, air-base, 291
Doctor-Eghbal Hospital, 184, 187
Dowlatshahi Janine, palace librarian, 385

twin-sister, 32, 420, 421, 425, 451, 456, 460, 462, 464, 475, 476, 493, 495, 508

Pahlavi Fahranaz, Shah's eldest daughter, 377, 495, 507

Pahlavi Foundation, 117, 156, 160, 177, 248, 285, 322, 350, 511

Pahlavi Gholam Reza, eldest Shah's half-brother, 508

Pahlavi Hamid-Reza, youngest half-brother of the Shah, 508

Pahlavi Leila, Imperial Couple's last child, 377, 457, 507

Pahlavi Mahmoud-Reza, half-brother of the Shah, 508

Pahlavi National Library, 46

Pahlavi Reza, Crown Prince, eldest of the imperial couple's children, 10, 151, 261, 428, 444, 446, 458, 462, 463, 490, 495, 507

Pahlavi Reza, Mohammad Reza's father, 41, 94, 220, 235, 294, 349

Pahlavi Shahnaz, Princess, 260, 507

Pahlavi Shams, Princess, Shah's elder sister, 148, 427, 439, 508

Pahlavi Tadj-ol-Molouk, Queen Mother, 138, 147, 150, 151, 427, 439, 454, 507

Pahlbod Mehrdad, Shah's brother-in-law, husband of Princess Shams, 148, 149, 150, 182, 258, 427, 438, 439, 440, 508

Pakistan, 30, 45, 108, 125, 222, 307

Pakravan Hassan, General, 107, 113, 206, 323, 517

Panah-Izadi Dariouch, renowned consulting-engineer, 487

Panama, 461, 462, 463, 464, 465, 466, 467, 468, 469, 470, 479, 516

Paraguay, 417

Paris Match, 423

Parker Richard, CIA agent, 417

Parsons Anthony, British Ambassador, 10, 181, 243, 311, 312, 336, 354, 365, 418, 423, 483

Pax persica, 21

PDG (local branch of the Anglo-Iranian Oil Company), 364

Pedrazzani Jean-Michel, Shahbanou's biographer, 8, 10, 376

Persepolis, 19, 24, 26, 28, 30, 31, 32, 34, 36, 39, 45, 46, 47, 179, 267, 423, 504

Peyrefitte Alain, French Minister of Justice, 444, 451

Philip, Duke of Edinburgh, 30, 35

Philippines, 32

Piettre André, French economist, 19

Pirasteh Mehdi, former ambassador to Baghdad and later to Brussels, 323, 324

Pirnia Lucie, Imperial Family-doctor, 159, 314, 315, 386, 392, 419, 438, 442, 448, 470, 487, 495, 496, 508

PLO, 345

Podgorny, USSR President, 30, 37

Poland, 30, 77, 87

Pol Pot, 14

Pompidou Georges, 31

Poniatowski Michel, 301, 356

Porthault, 28

Portillo Lopes, Mexican President, 282, 396, 425, 428, 440, 450

Potel et Chabot, 35, 47

Pourshodja Amir, Shah valet, 392, 470, 495, 502, 508

CONTENTS